THE RIGHT TO STRIKE:
FROM THE TRADE DISPUTES ACT 1906
TO A TRADE UNION FREEDOM BILL 2006

Front cover collage: CreativityJones

TUC Mayday march photo by Stefano Cagnoni (reportdigital.co.uk)

Thanks to RMT for a picture of the original Taff Vale cheque.

Thanks to the National Working Class Movement Library

for the copy of the banquet invitation.

THE RIGHT TO STRIKE: FROM THE TRADE DISPUTES ACT 1906 TO A TRADE UNION FREEDOM BILL 2006

EDITED BY K D EWING

THE INSTITUTE OF EMPLOYMENT RIGHTS
LIVERPOOL

Institute of Employment Rights
The People's Centre, 50 - 54 Mount Pleasant, Liverpool L3 5SD
0151 702 6925
office@ier.org.uk, www.ier.org.uk

First published 2006

ISBN 0 9551795 4 8
ISBN 978 0 9551795 4 9

British Library Cataloguing in Publication data
A catalogue record for this book is available from the British Library

Designed by the Institute of Employment Rights
Typeset by CreativityJones
Printed by Gemini Press Limited, West Sussex

Contents

Foreword viii

Preface ix

List of Contributors xi

List of Sponsors xii

Part 1 Introduction xvii

Chapter One: **From the Trade Disputes Act to a Trade Union Freedom Bill** 1
K D EWING and CAROLYN JONES

Part 2 Legal Origins of the Trade Disputes Act 9

Chapter Two: **Taff Vale and the Trade Disputes Act 1906** 11
GRAEME LOCKWOOD

Chapter Three: **The Belfast Butchers: *Quinn v Leathem* after a Hundred Years** 31
JOHN McILROY

Part 3 The Trade Disputes Act 1906 69

Chapter Four: **The Trade Disputes Act of 1906** 71
JOHN SAVILLE

Chapter Five: **The South Shields Case - Subverting the Trade Disputes Act 1906?** 101
K D EWING

Chapter Six: **The Scottish Case – *Crofter Hand Woven Harris Tweed v Veitch*** 129
DOUGLAS BRODIE

Part 4 The 1906 Act: Parliament, Employers and Judges 147

Chapter Seven: **The 1906 Act: The First Fifty Years – Industrial Relations, Picketing and the Employers' Challenge** 149
DAVE LYDDON and PAUL SMITH

Chapter Eight: **The 1906 Act: the Second Fifty Years -From *Thomson v Deakin* in 1952 to *P v NASUWT* in 2003** 175
BOB SIMPSON

Chapter Nine: **Judicial Mystification of the Law: *Rookes v Barnard* and the Return to Judicial Intervention** 195
ROGER WELCH

Part 5 – Towards a Trade Union Freedom Act? 219

Chapter Ten: **European Laws: Help or Hindrance?** 221
BRIAN BERCUSSON

Chapter Eleven: **British Trade Union Rights Today and the Trade Union Freedom Bill** 247
JOHN HENDY and GREGOR GALL

Chapter Twelve: **The Economic Case for the Trade Union Freedom Bill** 279
SIMON DEAKIN and FRANK WILKINSON

Appendices

Appendix 1 The Trades Dispute Bill 1906 (The Labour Bill) 295

Appendix 2 The Trade Disputes Bill 1906 (The Government Bill) 297

Appendix 3 The Trade Disputes Act 1906 299

Appendix 4 Early Day Motion 1170 and signatures 301

Latest IER publications 305

Foreword

The law in Britain on trade disputes is today more restrictive on trade unions than it was 100 years ago after the passing of the Trade Disputes Act 1906. There is now growing pressure for change. New legislation is long overdue.

This is the background to the publication of this book and explains why it is of special importance. It is scholarly in content but also very practical in its advocacy.

Trade union rights are human rights. A state that fails to uphold these rights – at least to good international standards – is not a fully democratic society. In Britain we have fallen behind good international standards. The time for change is now.

The special significance of this book is that it argues the case for new legislation, both informatively and persuasively. A number of outstanding scholars, lawyers and active trade unionists collaborated in the discussion and preparation of the contents of the book.

The various chapters demonstrate that the struggle for trade union rights has a long history. The unions emerged from total illegality less than 200 years ago. Stage by stage they established certain limited rights, only to see some of them taken away either by statute or by decisions of the courts. The struggle never ceases and there is no final and assured victory.

There is, nevertheless, plenty in this history of struggle to provide confidence that progress can and will be made. The campaign for the 1906 Act was one of the most successful in British history. Its roots were in the trade union movement. It won support not only amongst working class people but among others in the electorate who were persuaded that trade unionists were suffering an injustice. The successful campaign was a testimony to democratic action and to the potentiality of Parliamentary power. It was a major influence in the establishment of the Labour Party and its early electoral growth.

There have been a number of occasions since 1945 when Parliament, in response to campaigns by trade unionists and the votes of the electorate, swept away restrictions imposed by statute or decisions of the courts. The first was under the Labour government of 1945 when the Trade Disputes and Trade Union Act 1927, carried by a Conservative majority after the general Strike of 1926, was totally repealed. A second example was provided by the Labour government of 1974, when it repealed restrictive legislation introduced by the preceding Conservative government and replaced it with legislation to restore the previous rights of unions and to extend new rights to working people in the Employment Protection Act 1975.

A new piece of legislation is now required and this book charts the way forward.

J E Mortimer

Preface

On 21 December 1906, the Trade Disputes Act 1906 received the Royal Assent. On the eve of its final stages in the House of Lords a 'complimentary banquet' was held by the TUC, the GFTU and the Labour Party, ostensibly to honour David Shackleton MP for his 'tact, judgement and ability' in piloting the Trade Disputes Bill through the House of Commons. A number of speeches were made at the banquet, with the toast to Shackleton being proposed by Keir Hardie. All the speakers emphasised the injustice of the *Taff Vale* decision of 1900, its importance in generating a determination in the ranks of the Labour movement to have the decision reversed, and the unity demonstrated by Labour in Parliament to see that determination realised.

In his response to Hardie's warm words, David Shackleton reinforced the sense that 'the *Taff Vale* decision' was a 'serious blow' undermining the 'usefulness' of trade unions 'for the future'. For his part, the veteran Charles Fenwick MP concluded that the Trade Disputes Act was evidence that 'out of evil sometimes did come good'. However, that 'good' came only after a sustained and dramatic political struggle, both in Parliament and in the country, with the historian of the miners' union noting not only that *Taff Vale* was the 'making of the Labour Representation Committee', but that 'the complete reversal of the *Taff Vale* judgment was made a test question for candidates' at the 1906 General Election (R Page Arnot, *The Miners* (1949), p 347).

This book tells the story of the Trade Disputes Act 1906, in celebration of its centenary. It was one of the most important pieces of labour legislation ever passed by a British Parliament. As such, it provided very simple legal protection for the right to strike for sixty-five years, and left a legacy which is found on the statute book to this day. The substance of the current law is, however, far removed from the position established in 1906, and is the subject of the proposed amendments in the Trade Union Freedom Bill, designed to address some of the worst injustices of the Thatcher bequest. There are many lessons to be learned from the campaign for the 1906 Act in the campaign for the Trade Union Freedom Act.

Many people have been involved in this project since it was launched by Jim Mortimers's lecture on *The Trade Disputes Act 1906*, held in the House of Commons on 8 December 2004. I would like to pay a warm tribute to Jim, not only for kindly agreeing to provide the Foreword, but also for his unequivocal support for the Institute and the work that we do. I would also like to thank the participants in our consultative conference in May 2006, and the contributors to this volume for their commitment and for producing such fine papers. A special thanks to Dave Lyddon who was unable to attend the conference because of illness, but who has been an important source of advice and guidance throughout.

Finally, I would like to thank the sponsors of this project for their generous financial contributions. These reveal a deep interest not only in labour history, but also the need for labour law reform. I would also like to thank my colleagues in the Institute: the Executive Committee for supporting this project; John Hendy QC for his work on the Trade Union Freedom Bill and for his unfailing commitment to the cause of trade union rights; Geoff Shears, for a similar commitment combined in his case with an unerring ability to keep us on the financial straight and narrow; and above all Carolyn Jones and Phelim Mac Cafferty, without the dedication of whom there would be no Institute of Employment Rights.

KDE
21.12.06

List of Contributors

Brian Bercusson is Professor of European Law at Kings College London and is a member of the Executive Committee of the IER.

Douglas Brodie is Reader in the School of Law at the University of Edinburgh.

Simon Deakin is Assistant Director at The Centre for Business Research, Cambridge University.

K D Ewing is Professor of Public Law at Kings College London and President of the Institute of Employment Rights.

Gregor Gall is Head of the Centre for Research in Employment Studies at the University of Hertforshire.

John Hendy, QC is Head of Old Square Chambers, Chairman of IER, Joint National Secretary of the United Campaign for the Repeal of Anti Union Laws and a Vice-President of International Centre for Trade Union Rights.

Carolyn Jones is the Director of the Institute of Employment Rights.

Graeme Lockwood is a Lecturer in Business Law and Employee Relations at the Department of Management, King's College London.

Dave Lyddon is a senior lecturer in the Centre for Industrial Relations, Keele University and joint editor of the journal *Historical Studies in Industrial Relations.*

John McIlroy is Professor of Industrial Relations at Keele University.

Jim Mortimer is a former General Secretary of the Labour Party and former Chair of ACAS. He is a Vice President of the Institute of Employment Rights.

John Saville is Professor Emeritus of Economics and Social History at the University of Hull. He is the author of many books and editor of several others, including the first ten volumes of the Dictionary of Labour Biography (1972-2000).

Bob Simpson is a member of the Law Department at the London School of Economics, specialising in Labour Law, particularly trade unions and industrial disputes.

Paul Smith is Senior Lecturer in the Human Resource Management and Industrial Relations Department at Keele University.

Roger Welch is Principal Lecturer in Law at the University of Portsmouth.

Dr Frank Wilkinson is Emeritus Reader, University of Cambridge and Visiting Professor, Birkbeck College, University of London.

List of Sponsors

Trade Unions and Organisations

Amicus: Head Office

Amicus: London United Craft Branch

Amicus: Cambridgeshire Medical Branch

Amicus: Eastern Regional Council

ASLEF: Waterloo/Nine Elms Branch

ATL: The Education Union

CWU: Head Office

CWU: Darlington Branch

CWU: Eastern No. 4 Branch

CWU: Essex Amalgamated Branch

CWU: S W No 1 Branch

CWU: Gtr Manchester Amalagamated

CWU: Gary Heather

CYWU: Community & Youth Workers Union. Dave Proctor

FBU: Head Office

FBU: Region 6 East Midlands

FBU: London Region. Joe McVeigh

FBU: Dean Mills

GMB: Head Office

GMB: Scotland

GMB: Southern Region

GMB: Barking B10 Branch

NGH: National Group on Homeworking

napo: The Trade Union and Professional Association for Family Court and Probation Staff. Head Office

NASUWT: National Association of School Masters Union of Women Teachers

National Assembly of Women
NUJ: Head Office
NUJ: John Foster
NUT: Leeds
NUT: Retired. Frank Scholfield
PCS: Head Office
PCS: Retired Members. Geoff Orton
POA: Head Office
POA: Lancaster Farms Branch
Preston Trade Union Education
Reclaim Our Rights (Scotland)
RMT: Scottish Regional Council
RMT: Basingstoke Branch
RMT: Blackpool and Fylde Coast Branch
RMT: Bristol Rail Branch
RMT: Croydon 3 Branch
RMT: Central and North Mersey Branch
RMT: Darlington No. 1 Branch
RMT: Deptford Branch
RMT: East Kent Branch
RMT: Eastleigh Workshops Branch
RMT: Glasgow & District Engineering Branch
RMT: Glasgow No. 5 Branch
RMT: Glasgow Shipping Branch
RMT: Grantham Branch
RMT: Great Northern Branch
RMT: Holyhead Shipping Branch
RMT: Humber Shipping Branch
RMT: Kings Cross Branch

RMT: Picadilly and District West Branch

RMT: St Pancras Branch

RMT: Stratford No. 1 Branch

RMT: Swindon Rail Branch

RMT: Transport for London No. 1 Branch

RMT: Wakefield and Healey Mills Branch

RMT: Wirral Branch

Scottish Low Pay Unit

TGWU: Head Office

TGWU: London, South East, and East Anglia Region

TGWU: Grampian and North Isles District

TGWU: Branch 1/128

TGWU: Landrover Branch 5/909

TGWU/BASSA

TGWU: Devro Ltd, Bellshill Branch

The Left Field Glastonbury. Geoff Martin

TSSA: Network Rail Yorkshire Branch

UCATT: Terry Clarke

UCU: University College Union, Head Office

UCU: Brooklands College Branch

UNISON: Head Office

UNISON: Blaenau Gwent County Council

UNISON: Brighton and Hove

UNISON: City of London

UNISON: Haringey

UNISON: Liverpool City Branch

UNISON: NW Gas Branch

UNISON: Rochdale

UNISON: SE Electricity Branch

UNISON: Tameside

UNISON: United Utilities

UNISON: York City

Unity: Unity the Union, Head Office

URTU: United Road Transport Union, Head Office

TUC Regions and Trades Councils

South East Region TUC

South West Region TUC

Chelmsford Trades Union Council

Greater Manchester Association of Trade Union Councils

Havering Trades Union Council

Ipswich and District Trades Union Council

Kingston & District Trades Union Council

Merseyside Trades Union Council

Sefton Trades Union Council

Southampton Trades Council

Watford and District Trades Council

Wirral Trades Union Council

Individuals and Lawyers

Geoffery Goodman

Cllr Gordon Nardell

Jim Mortimer

Rashad Suffee

Morrish & Co. Solicitors

O H Parsons & Partners Solicitors

Old Square Chambers.

Rowley Ashworth Solicitors

Thompson Solicitors

Part I

Introduction

Chapter One

From the Trade Disputes Act to the Trade Union Freedom Bill[1]

K D Ewing and Carolyn Jones

It is questionable whether in the history of recent politics an instance is to be found which more conclusively proves the advantage of concentration upon a well-defined object than does that of the Trade Disputes Bill.[2]

2006 is the centenary of three overlapping events – the Liberal landslide government, a great reforming administration; the emergence of the Labour Party from the embryo of the Labour Representation Committee; and the enactment of the Trade Disputes Act, vindicating the importance of trade union political action. Described as Labour's Magna Carta, the Trade Disputes Act 1906 was a seminal measure designed to keep the courts out of industrial relations. Seen by Keir Hardie as the latest in a number of milestones 'on the rough and thorny path' along 'the journey from serfdom to freedom',[3] it survived on the statute book for 65 years. Yet although the Trade Disputes Act ('the final and definite legalising of the right of combination')[4] was repealed by Ted Heath's Industrial Relations Act 1971, the substance of the 1906 settlement was re-instated by the Wilson and Callaghan governments between 1974 and 1976, before being gradually dismantled by the Thatcher and Major governments in the 1980s and 1990s. Indeed, despite a different regulatory environment, some of its core provisions survive to this day, albeit in a heavily qualified form.

The 1906 Act in Outline

The Trade Disputes Act 1906 was passed in order to reverse decisions of the courts, most notably the famous *Taff Vale Railway* case where the House of Lords decided that a trade union could be held liable for the losses suffered by an employer in a strike. In that case liability was assessed at £23,000.[5] On top of that, the union also had to pay another £19,000 in legal fees. Today that amount of money would be equal to £2,430,000. The other significant decision which the Act addressed is *Quinn v Leathem,*[6] in which the House of Lords famously established liability in tort where trade unions used industrial action to put pressure on an employer, in the process apparently contradicting the decision in *Allen v Flood* [7] only three years earlier. Both of these cases are considered in some detail by Graeme Lockwood and John McIlroy in chapters 2 and 3 respectively.

In providing an anchor for the freedom to strike, the 1906 Act was a model of simplicity and precision, as was pointed out by Jim Mortimer in a lecture delivered in the House of Commons in December 2004.[8] It gave the unions and their officials an immunity from known liabilities for organising industrial action, where the action was done 'in contemplation or furtherance of a trade dispute', a phrase that was lifted from an Act of 1875 and one that remains an aspect of today's law. The 1906 Act gave legal protection for the right to picket, with no restriction as to place or numbers, and gave solid protection for trade union funds. The story behind the enactment of the 1906 Act is told in chapter 4 by John Saville who considers the implications of the great increase in the number of Labour MPs in 1906 and examines the politics which led to the enactment of the 1906 Act in a form which met the approval of the contemporary trade union movement.

The 1906 Act was a long way in advance of where we are today. As Jim Mortimer also pointed out, it 'was both a landmark and an achievement in the history of British trade unionism', the outcome of 'one of the most successful campaigns ever generated from within the trade union movement'.[9] It was not long, however, before attempts were made to restrict its scope in the courts, with the first legal challenge taking place within a year of its enactment. The story of that case – the *South Shields* case as it was known at the time – is told in chapter 5. That case ended up in the House of Lords, reported as *Conway v Wade.*[10] Chapter

6 by Douglas Brodie is concerned with an examination of the second House of Lords case following the enactment of the 1906 Act. This is the Scottish decision in *Crofter Hand Woven Harris Tweed v Veitch*,[11] in which the union won what may be seen as a Pyrrhic victory. In that case it was held that the trade dispute immunity did not apply, though it was also held that the action of the defenders was not tortuous.

Judicial Attacks

Although the 1906 Act 'compares very favourably with what exists today',[12] it never provided a very secure basis for the freedom to strike. As trade unions grew in strength at different periods in the twentieth century, so employer resistance grew, as shown by Dave Lyddon and Paul Smith in chapter 7. Employers were never reconciled to the Act, and used both parliamentary and judicial means to restrict its scope, with considerable success. Lyddon and Smith consider in some detail the much neglected and the much under-estimated Trade Disputes and Trade Unions Act 1927, which included important restraints on picketing for which employers had long lobbied. Judicial resistance to trade unionism grew more intense in the second half of the twentieth century, with a number of landmark decisions extending the boundaries of common law liability. These included *Rookes v Barnard*,[13] *J&T Stratford & Son v Lindley*,[14] and *Torquay Hotel Co Ltd v Cousins*.[15] The re-introduction of the immunities in 1974 following the brief interlude of the Industrial Relations Act 1971 saw a new phase of judicial restraint based on a narrow interpretation of the critical words of the statute giving immunity for 'acts done in contemplation or furtherance of a trade dispute'.

These latter developments are fully addressed by Bob Simpson in chapter 8 (which examines the operation of the 1906 Act since the 1950s), and by Roger Welch in chapter 9. The latter emphasises how attacks on trade unions were made easier as a result of the form in which the 1906 Act was drafted, allowing judges to paint trade unions as privileged bodies in the eyes of the law because they had been given an immunity from existing legal liability. Judges did not stop to question this simplistic reasoning. Trade unions had immunities from common law liabilities that had been applied to deal with trade unions and which in practice applied only to trade unions. How many people, other than trade unionists engaged in an industrial dispute, found themselves as defendants in legal proceedings for conspiracy to injure, or for inducing breach of a contract of employment? The short answer is very few, if any, until more recent times. Welch also reveals a continuity of approach and attitude on the part of the common law to trade unions, with deep roots in the 19th century. Since 1900, the courts have had two concerns, which run like an unbroken thread through the relationship between trade unions and the courts for the entire 20th century.

The first concern of the courts throughout this period was the closed shop, with a number of famous disputes being concerned with the anxiety of trade unionists where work was being done by non – members. Industrial action to enforce the closed shop was clearly protected by the 1906 Act, and a closed shop dispute fell within the statutory definition of a trade dispute. But the courts wriggled by saying first that such disputes were not genuine trade disputes with the result that the immunity did not apply, or that they involved the commission of unlawful acts for which there was no immunity. The second concern of the courts was with secondary and sympathy action. It is true that in the early cases the House of Lords reluctantly acknowledged that some forms of secondary action were protected by the immunity, as being action in furtherance of a trade dispute. But this was to be short-lived, as the courts found ways of shutting down secondary action as well, even where the secondary action was directed to securing trade union recognition. Here too, the courts interpreted the immunity narrowly and invented other new heads of legal liability to control secondary action.

Lessons from the 1906 Act

It is true that the 1906 Act was revised and strengthened in 1974 and 1976 in the light of these judicial attacks, when a Labour government attempted to restore the freedom that a Liberal government had tried to create in 1906. But that too failed, as union after union found itself on the wrong side of attacks from the Court of Appeal in particular, in clear breach of Parliament's intention. The unions included the broadcasting union, the print unions, the ISTC, the ITF, and the NUJ.[16] The main thrust of this attack was secondary action, though other action was also caught, including industrial action aimed at the apartheid regime in South Africa, and industrial action organised by the TUC to protest against the Tory government's labour law restrictions.[17] In these cases the Court of Appeal was at its most inventive in diminishing the freedom to strike as a mere immunity, and in creating new qualifications which had to be met before the immunity could apply. It is also true that several of these important decisions were undone on appeal by the House of Lords, which delivered a series of powerful judgments restoring the immunities to where they had been intended by Parliament.[18]

But by then it was too late and the damage had been done. A Conservative government was in power pledged to clip the wings of the unions and to rewrite the immunities. Given the previous form of the

House of Lords on the trade union question, there is no reason to believe that they would have been so liberal had Labour and not the Conservatives won the election in 1979. The unfolding nature of that legislation is also dealt with by Bob Simpson in chapter 8. As Simpson points out, little has been done since 1997 by the incoming Labour government to address the harsh features of the anti-trade union laws gradually introduced since 1980. Yet as John Hendy and Gregor Gall remind us (chapter 11 below), recent events at places as different as Gate Gourmet and Friction Dynamics remind us of the importance of this freedom as an essential weapon of trade unionism. Recent events also remind us that it is a weapon that trade unions are prepared to use sparingly and responsibly. The changing global economy makes its existence and possible use all the more important than in the past as workers and their unions must now confront huge trans-national corporations of a kind never contemplated in 1906.

But as we celebrate the centenary of the great Liberal landslide, the election of a corps of MPs under the Labour Party banner, and the Trade Disputes Act 1906, we should also acknowledge the limitations of that great statute. It was hobbled from birth by casting the freedom to strike in the form of an immunity rather than a right, and by creating an immunity from known liabilities, failing to anticipate the possibility that new liabilities would arise in the future. Parliament seriously under-estimated the power of the judiciary which danced to a different tune, and which eventually produced a script that Parliament itself adopted during the Thatcher years. That script has been adopted by the Blair government. One of the key lessons of the 1906 Act is that trade unions should not be treated as second class citizens by the legal system. Employers large and small, public and private, all have rights. These rights are the source of great power. Trade unions should also have rights which empower them and their members. These rights should be clear and unequivocal, and they should properly equip trade unions as autonomous bodies to act within the boundaries of international labour standards to protect the interests of their members. That means a right to organise, a right to bargain and a right to strike in a new legal settlement for British trade unions to deal with the sharp practices of globalisation.

Conclusion

A possible agenda for the future of the right to strike in British law is considered in chapters 10, 11 and 12. In chapter 11, Brian Bercusson considers the litigation on the right to strike taking place in the European Court of Justice at the time of writing, and its implications for domestic law. Here Bercusson also draws important comparisons between the Trade Disputes Act and the forms of legal protection for the right to strike in other European countries, drawing attention also to the many international treaties which address the position. This is followed in chapter 11 by the consideration by John Hendy and Gregor Gall for a Trade Union Freedom Bill, an initiative which now has the support of the TUC. Rooted in controversial industrial disputes, chapter 11 examines the case for such an initiative and explains the content of the proposed Trade Union Freedom Bill. The case for the Bill is picked up in the last chapter by Simon Deakin and Frank Wilkinson where an argument based on considerations of legality under international law and social justice is complemented by an economic argument in favour of removing the legal chains that continue to bind organised labour, in the tenth year of a Labour government.

Notes

1 This is an expanded version of an article which first appeared in *Federation News*, September 2006.

2 J Keir Hardie, Chairman's Report, Labour Party Annual Report 1907, p 38.

3 TUC Report 1907, p 62 (Report of the speeches at the celebration banquet on 19 December 1906 – see cover of this volume).

4 W Stewart, *J Keir Hardie* (1922), p 227.

5 *Taff Vale Railway Co Ltd v Amalgamated Society of Railway Servants* [1901] AC 426 (Graeme Lockwood, ch 2 below).

6 [1901] AC 495 (John McIlroy, ch 3 below).

7 [1898] AC 1.

8 Jim Mortimer, *The Trade Disputes Act 1906* (Institute of Employment Rights, 2004), p 5.

9 *Ibid.*

10 [1909] AC 506.

11 [1942] AC 435 (Douglas Brodie, ch 6 below).

12 Jim Mortimer, above, p 5.

13 [1964] AC 1129 (Bob Simpson, ch 8 below; Roger Welch, ch 9 below).

14 [1965] AC 269 (Bob Simpson, ch 8 below; Roger Welch, ch 9 below).

15 [1969] 2 Ch 106 (Bob Simpson, ch 8 below; Roger Welch, ch 9 below).

16 See *BBC v Hearn* [1977] ICR 686; *Duport Steels Ltd v Sirs* [1980] ICR 161; *Star Sea Transport Corporation of Monrovia v Slater* [1978] IRLR 507; *Express Newspapers Ltd v McShane* [1979] ICR 210.

17 In addition to the cases already cited, see *Express Newspapers Ltd v Keys* [1980] IRLR 247.

18 *Express Newspapers Ltd v McShane* [1980] ICR 42; *Duport Steels Ltd v Sirs,* above.

Part 2

Legal Origins of the Trade Disputes Act

Chapter Two

Taff Vale and the Trade Disputes Act 1906

Graeme Lockwood

Introduction

IN order to appreciate the development and nature of contemporary trade union law, it is necessary to have a basic understanding of its history.[1] The British industrial relations system has traditionally been characterised by minimal legal regulation and, as far as possible, the minimal involvement of the State. As such, the system was labelled voluntarist or abstentionist.[2] Otto Kahn-Freund wrote in 1954:

> *There is, perhaps, no major country in the world in which the law has played a less significant role in the shaping of industrial relations than in Great Britain and in which today the law and the legal profession have less to do with labour relations.*[3]

However, whilst abstentionism meant that the State refrained from legislating in the arena of industrial relations, it did not equate to complete withdrawal of the law.[4] First, the State intervened to ensure basic standards of health and safety in the workplace.[5] Second, there was State involvement in the establishment of statutory immunities to protect trade unions from the hostility of the common law (as illustrated in the decision of the House of Lords in *Taff Vale Railway Company v*

Amalgamated Society of Railway Servants).[6] The Trade Disputes Act 1906 gave trade unions a blanket immunity by prohibiting legal actions in tort against them; and for persons acting 'in contemplation or furtherance of a trade dispute', it provided immunities from liability for the torts of simple conspiracy, inducing a breach of employment contract and interference with the trade, business or employment of some other person, as well as apparently confirming their right to picket peacefully.[7] Aside from such limited intervention, governments actively refrained from legislating to affect the workplace. Regulation of the workplace was instead left to trade unions and employers, to develop their own norms and their own sanctions. Kahn-Freund characterised the limited role of the law as collective *laissez-faire*, observing that 'it is in connection with trade disputes that the retreat of the law from the scene of industrial relations can be most clearly seen'.[8]

This chapter will look at the background to the Taff Vale strike, the legal action that ensued, and the political consequences of the House of Lords decision that a trade union could be held liable for the actions of its officials and for the losses suffered by an employer as a result of industrial action. The decision was of considerable concern to trade unionists, who realised that an award of damages in such circumstances against a trade union could easily ruin it. Members of Parliament were put under pressure from the trade union movement to clarify the law and introduce changes to protect unions from this threat. It was remarked:

> *The very existence of trade unions is at the mercy of political action. Political action could render trade unionism powerless, or it could make it all-powerful. Political action could solve the labour problem forever, or it could make the labourer a slave in name and fact. Political action could give us all that we shout for from the trade union platform or it could damn our movement for years to come.*[9]

The Taff Vale dispute turned out to be one of the most notorious strikes in British industrial relations history and has resulted in coverage in many academic works from both a sociological and historical perspective.[10] It has been observed that 'the change caused by the decision of the House of Lords in the *Taff Vale* case in July 1901, had more far-reaching effects for trade unionism than any other which the courts had ever been called upon to decide'.[11] Its reverberations came to dominate the political landscape for the next 100 years. The interest in this case grew out of the fact that it established that a trade union, although not a body corporate, was nevertheless responsible for the tortious acts of its officials and members.

The Taff Vale Railway Company

In the 1830s, the Dowlais ironworks in Merthyr Tydfil were the largest in the world. Josiah Guest, who owned the ironworks, realised that it would be an advantage to link his ironworks with Cardiff docks. Guest entered into a joint venture with Anthony Hill, owner of another ironworks near Merthyr Tydfil, to form the Taff Vale Railway Company. The Taff Vale railway was completed in 1841, making it possible to transport goods from Merthyr Tydfil to Cardiff in less than an hour. Subsequently, branches of the railway were built to link the mining valleys with the Welsh ports and England's fast growing industrial towns and cities. The railway network reduced transport costs to such an extent that it became profitable to export Welsh coal to many countries overseas. For much of the nineteenth century, the Taff Vale Railway Company was amongst the most profitable railway companies in Britain.[12] It was also regarded as a good employer, providing above-average wages and welfare benefits. However, the positive industrial relations environment changed during the late 1880s, culminating in a seminal legal dispute.[13]

Attitude of the Company to Trade Unions

Between 1810 and 1875, all trade unions were expanding at an unprecedented rate amid boom conditions. From 1867, trade unionists had learned to use Parliament and public opinion to create a more favourable legal framework for their activities. The Criminal Law Amendment Act 1871 removed liability for criminal conspiracy, where the conspiracy consisted of doing an act that was not in itself illegal. The Conspiracy and Protection of Property Act 1875 changed the law, making it no longer a criminal offence to withdraw labour from one's employer. However, trade unionism had by its very success again become unpopular among propertied and professional classes as well as the business world.[14] It was contended by some observers that trade unions were accumulating significant strength, and it was believed that militant unions could, through their collective strength, have an adverse impact on labour costs, introduce restrictive practices, impose inflexible pay arrangements and engage in costly strikes, disrupting economic performance. Two people who held such opinions became involved in the management of the Taff Vale Railway Company, namely Mr Ammon Beasley and Mr RLG Vassall respectively. Beasley, who was appointed as general manager, held the belief that trade unions had too great an influence and he sought to ostracise them from any involvement in negotiations on conditions of service. The Amalgamated Society of Railway Servants (ASRS), the most successful railway trade union, was regarded by Beasley as the 'enemy' of the railway industry to whom employers should not surrender.

Vassall, who from 1895 onwards held the office of Chairman, was also vehemently anti-trade union and of the view that it would be unwise for the company to recognise the ASRS, since he believed trade unions were 'a very pernicious body as regards railway companies'.[15] It is particularly striking how this type of discourse is echoed in the subsequent rhetoric of the New Right and particularly Hayek.[16] At the vanguard of this New Right thinking, Hayek regarded trade unions as a coercive restraint upon the market place. He stated:

> *The legalised powers of the unions have become the biggest obstacle to raising the living standards of the working class as a whole. It is this group, by its collective action and group pressure, which is noxious.*[17]

Prior to the Beasley and Vassall era of management, industrial relations at the Taff Vale Railway Company had been cordial and only commenced on a downward spiral from this juncture. One cannot help but detect a sense from the historical documentation that the management of the company actually welcomed the confrontation with the trade union movement. During the period 1898-1900, the railway industry was becoming well known for increased unionisation and this was resented by some employers. The management of the Taff Vale Railway Company viewed a confrontation with the ASRS as a chance to defend managerial prerogative, to take a firm stand against increasing unionisation and an opportunity to curb union power. The management was convinced that with careful planning any action taken by the ASRS could be defeated.

Deteriorating Working Conditions

The coal strikes of 1893 to 1898 had a detrimental impact on the financial position of the company. As soon as the 1893 coal strike commenced, the company suspended its guaranteed 60 hour week, introduced in 1890. The reduction in working hours and lay-offs meant this was an arduous time for the South Wales railway workers. Whilst the coal strike was of short duration, the restriction on working hours was not; the workforce were annoyed by Mr Beasley's refusal to resurrect the guaranteed working week until much later.[18] The discontent was compounded further when Mr Beasley refused to convene the Standing Committee of the workforce (the joint representative body of all grades of employee). He asserted that this decision was justified because the committee was a 'sham', as it consisted of delegates and representatives of the ASRS, which he refused to recognise. A series of mass meetings of the railway employees were held in Cardiff between September and December 1893, when considerable anger was expressed at the labour management methods being adopted by the company. Beasley responded by claiming that 'the whole staff was combined in an endeavour to frustrate his management'.[19] The workforce countered that this was as a 'most unwarrantable accusation'. It seems that the daggers of confrontation were drawn.

Discontent surfaced again amongst the workforce with the decision by the company in May 1895 to dismiss more than 200 employees, whilst many other workers were being required to work longer than the 60-hour working week. The workforce expressed their concern to the company and the directors decided to give way, agreeing to reinstate the dismissed men.[20] However, only three months later, discontent raised its ugly head again, as there began a five weeks' strike of the company's fitters in response to the unilateral introduction by management of new piecework rates that had not been negotiated with the Amalgamated Society of Engineers, of which most of the men concerned were members. The demands of the workforce for improved terms and conditions fell upon deaf ears. Beasley's hostile management style, cost-cutting measures and stricter approach to industrial relations were designed to improve the financial position of the company. But although the policies had a degree of success in a financial context, they were a disaster in terms of industrial relations, alienating the majority of a previously largely cooperative and compliant workforce.

Role of the ASRS

Against this background of industrial discontent in the Taff Vale Railway Company, the ASRS were leading a campaign for improved pay and conditions for the railway workers of South Wales. The movement was directed, by Richard Bell a national official of the ASRS, and the Executive Committee of the union. He told the railway workers that if they were to win they must be 'men of sound calibre, men with backbone, not jellyfish'. However, it was a local official and activist, James Holmes, who was prominent in encouraging the railway workers of South Wales to get organised and through collective strength secure better wages. A Joint Committee of all grades employed on the Barry, Rhymney, Taff Vale and Cardiff Railways was duly elected on 1 October 1899. At the end of the month, Bell gave his permission for the submission of pay demands to all four of the railway companies. Each of the general managers received a letter on 16 November 1899 containing proposals for improved rates of pay for the principal grades. The only replies received to this letter for increased pay were simple acknowledgments from the Rhymney and Cardiff railways. The Taff Vale and Barry railways sent no reply.[21]

Dispute on the South Wales Railway

The Executive Council of the ASRS considered the situation in South Wales at its meeting in December 1899 and instructed the General Secretary to offer to submit the questions in dispute to arbitration. If the companies failed to reply within six days, a ballot on the question of strike action would be held. As the four companies replied at the end of the year with acknowledgements only, a mass meeting of 1,800 men was held at Park Hall, Cardiff, on 14 January 1900, at which it was decided, with only two dissentients, that unless the companies agreed to meet representatives of their employees within seven days, notices would be handed in. As on the first occasion, the companies replied with acknowledgments only; there was no offer to meet deputations or to resort to arbitration.[22] Local official and activist James Holmes realised that this would have been the most opportunistic time to have taken strike action. However, Richard Bell was inclined to avoid confrontation with the employers and, in so doing, took a less conflictual and more accommodating stance than that being advocated by his fellow union brethren. Bell resolved that the companies should be given a little extra time, 'seven to ten days', to reconsider their position.

When Bell made the directors of the Barry and Rhymney railway companies aware of the growing discontent amongst the men, they agreed to meet the union. As a result of these discussions, wage increases of up to four shillings a week were granted to signalmen and some other grades employed on the Cardiff, Barry and Rhymney railways. The Taff Vale Railway Company also met deputations of signalmen, brakesmen and guards on 9 February 1900, and small concessions were made to some of the guards and signalmen. But more substantial demands for increases of two shillings a week and the eight-hour day were refused. Thus, the situation reached was that on three of the railways concessions had been made; the demands of the Taff Vale men, however, remained unmet. In response to these developments, a mass meeting of the men employed on the Taff Vale, Cardiff, Barry and Rhymney railways was organised, and it was decided that if at least 90 per cent of the employees on the four lines voted by ballot in favour of strike action by 19 March 1900, strike notices would be handed in. However, the momentum for united industrial action had been lost since large numbers of workers on other railways had received increases in their pay. The outcome of this was that when the result of the ballot was announced by Mr Bell on 22 March, the percentage favouring a strike fell to between 72 and 81 – below the 90 per cent minimum agreed to 11 days earlier. The EC passed a resolution criticising the result of the ballot, which it said reflected 'no credit on those affected'.[23]

Dispute at Taff Vale Railway Company

Under the leadership of James Holmes, the Joint Committee of the men reflected on the effects of Richard Bell's decision not to take industrial action and instead continue negotiations. They considered it to have been a mistake not to take collective industrial action earlier when over 90 per cent of the men had been willing to strike. They were determined that when discontent erupted again they would manage the situation themselves and realised the importance of local activists organising and mobilising the rank and file. James Holmes, a charismatic leader, had encouraged large numbers of the men into the union, and had played a pivotal role in earlier successes to improve the pay and conditions of South Wales railwaymen. Holmes was keen to take industrial action against the Taff Vale Railway Company in order to teach the autocratic Beasley a lesson. Local activists believed that the cautious approach of Bell had let the Taff Vale Railway Company off the hook. Holmes and the Joint Committee planned to campaign vigorously to nurture support for collective action when the next opportunity presented itself.

It was not long before this opportunity arose. Industrial relations problems emerged again within the Taff Vale Railway Company when there was an allegation of unfair treatment against a long serving employee. What *prima facie* was a trivial problem became a catalyst for discontent. Signalman Ewington was informed by his station-master that he would have to move to another signal box 16 miles from his home. The company stated that this constituted a promotion since the signal box to which he was to be moved was larger, qualifying him for an increase in pay. However, Ewington did not wish to transfer, for a variety of personal circumstances. First, he calculated that he would in fact be financially worse off, because he would have to give up two secretarial jobs he was doing in his spare time, which brought him more money than he would have received by the increase in pay from the Taff Vale Railway Company. Second, his wife was ill, which made caring for his ten children, all under 17 years of age, extremely difficult. Given these circumstances, Ewington wanted to stay where he was. However, the view of the Taff Vale Railway Company was that it was not a question of what Ewington wanted, but that he was required to move to the other signal box.[24]

The Dispute Erupts

Shortly after this decision to move him was made, Ewington fell ill, suffering from rheumatic fever. When he was fit to return to work, he was informed that both his old post and the new one had been filled. Ewington was then offered the post of sick relief signalman covering 17 boxes in the Aberdare valley. He did not consider this alternative post suitable and asked to be reinstated to his original job. The company refused this request. Members of the Joint Committee, being familiar with earlier cases of victimisation, were convinced that the stance adopted by the company towards Ewington was motivated by his union involvement. As a leading member of the ASRS in the area, he had been involved in communications with Beasley over increased pay demands. The belief amongst his fellow workers was that an injustice was being done. Ewington was seen by the company as someone they considered responsible for causing disturbances and agitation amongst his fellow workmen. Ewington was not being moved for reasons of promotion, but was being deliberately victimised for being a trade union activist. The general feeling amongst the local union activists was that 'here is a man who has put forward the union case and has acted for us and now he is suffering and we will stand by him.'[25] The company took the view that Ewington had brought his problems on himself, particularly by refusing even to give the job of relief signalman a trial for a month.

The Union Demand

The actions of management were presented as uncaring and unjust, the Ewington case adding to the sense of discontent amongst the men. Together with the disquiet over unsatisfied wage demands, it helped to ignite a volatile situation. James Holmes was ready to make the most of the feelings of unrest and secured the backing of the men to demand from management recognition of the union, increased pay, and shorter working hours. On 29 July 1900, the campaign to secure better wages and shorter hours was mounted. At a large public meeting held in Pontypridd a resolution in favour of demanding increases in pay for brakesmen, shunters and guards was enthusiastically carried. The meeting also resolved that strike notices would be handed in if Ewington was not reinstated in his old position by 6 August 1900. Holmes was determined to lead with conviction and take the men with him. In a highly charged speech, he said that if the men had any grit they would not allow the company to defeat them again. 'It was not a matter of intelligence but courage'. However, there was legal danger if the men acted impetuously, before strike notices expired. In a letter to the *South Wales Daily News* a week later, Holmes advised the men to delay handing in notices until 13 August 1900, so that they would all take action together.[26]

The workforce was keen to act, and knew that Holmes regarded this as the most 'effective time' to assert their claims. But the action was badly organised and it resulted in disjointed and legally dangerous action. The majority of the signalmen, brakesmen and guards handed their notices in on 5 August 1900, and these would be due to expire 14 days later. However, this constituted less than a third of those employed by the company as a whole, and 400 more notices were handed in a week later, but since these were not due to expire until 26 August 1900 there could be no simultaneous withdrawal of labour without a breach of contract. Holmes had failed to exercise sufficient control over the movement and to impress on the Joint Committee with sufficient forcefulness the necessity of the men acting together and keeping on the right side of the law. The lack of organisation and control annoyed Richard Bell. He was angry that Holmes had failed to follow established union procedures for obtaining prior EC permission for the handing in of notices, and his failure to keep the movement within legal bounds. Given the willingness of the employers to resort to the law and the growing hostility of the common law towards trade unions, Bell could foresee that this errant organisation on Holmes' part could be a real danger to the union at some future time. As events unfolded, Bell's concerns were well-founded.

A Failed Peace Bid

Despite the issuing of strike notices, peace might still have been possible if Beasley had been prepared to discuss the outstanding differences with Holmes. However, management obstinacy meant the chances of a negotiated settlement of the dispute were remote. Beasley steadfastly refused to allow Holmes even to accompany an all-grade deputation of the workforce: Beasley stated:

> *I am prepared to see any reasonable number of the company's servants and give full and careful consideration . . . but I regret I cannot receive officially or unofficially any person not in the company's service.*[27]

As little progress seemed to be being made with the company, Holmes made two more attempts for peace. First, he suggested that the demand for improved pay and conditions should be submitted to an arbitrator acceptable to both Beasley and himself. Beasley spurned this offer on the ground that it would undermine management prerogative. Second, Holmes offered an olive branch by not insisting on his accompanying a delegation of the men, on the condition that Beasley would agree to meet one representing all grades. However, this effort for peace failed because the grades delegation interviewed by Beasley insisted on having Holmes or Taylor (another ASRS official) with them before they would negotiate further.[28] Beasley's resolve to repel any union involvement in collective bargaining was intense. He firmly believed that granting recognition to the ASRS and giving into the pay demands could only shift the balance of power in favour of labour at the expense of capital.[29]

Since 22 March 1900, neither Richard Bell nor the EC had played any part in the South Wales railwaymen's movement. But when a strike appeared imminent, Bell travelled to Cardiff on 17 August 1900, with the support of Mr CT Ritchie, President of the Board of Trade, and tried to secure an interview with Mr Vassall, the company chairman. But Vassall refused even to meet Bell.[30] Returning to London, having made no headway, Bell called a special meeting of the EC for Sunday, 19 August, at 10.00 am. The committee deliberated for six and a half hours, finally passing by seven votes to five the following resolution:

> *The Executive have just decided, after hearing the evidence of the deputation from the Taff Vale Railwaymen, and seeing the correspondence relating to the dispute, that they cannot but conclude:*
>
> 1 That the conduct of the men in taking action prior to obtaining the consent of the Committee was most condemnatory.
> 2 That by the removal of signalman Ewington the management of the Company have acted arbitrarily and have incited the men to their present act.
> 3 Having regard to both sides of the issue we, as the Administrators of the Society, decide that every effort be made by the General Secretary and others we may appoint to bring the dispute to a speedy termination.
> 4 We have, after careful consideration hereby decided to support the men financially.

While the EC was convened in London, James Holmes was holding a rally of the workforce at a large meeting at Pontypridd. He told those about to engage in picketing duties that they should not exceed the limits of the law, though 'there were many ways of persuading men'. In support of a resolution that the men should stop work as one body at midnight, almost every hand in the building was raised. The men had determined to strike, irrespective of whether the union's executive decided to give them financial support.

The Taff Vale Strike

At midnight between 19 and 20 August 1900, 1,227 men went out from the employment of the Taff Vale Railway Company. 564 of them had not given notice, and a further 400 had given inadequate notice. During normal operation, the company gained 70 per cent of its revenue from coal, but in the first three days of the strike no mineral trains ran and even on the last day of the strike, 31 August 1900, only a quarter of the number of the mineral trains normally run were in service, despite the importation into the district of a large body of substitute labour to fill some of the places left vacant by the withdrawal of 98 per cent of the labour force. It has been remarked that 'the strike was undoubtedly the most complete yet organised on any railway in Britain'.[31] The transportation of coal was severely disrupted by the picketing that took place. This had a particularly damaging impact on the financial position of the Taff Vale Railway Company, since 70 per cent of its income was derived from moving coal.

Strikebreaking and Picketing

Richard Bell wrote to Ammon Beasley, supporting the action of the employees in stopping work, and stating that all further negotiations were to be conducted through him. Bell was however, anxious to resolve the matter and went directly to Cardiff with the support of the EC to try and obtain a settlement of the dispute as soon as possible. But Beasley was determined to stand firm against trade union demands, and he refused to sit down and negotiate. Beasley had resolved that if he was not able to run his railway with the old labour force, he would raise a substitute one, if necessary recruiting men from all parts of the country. This approach angered the rank and file membership even further, and resulted in a minority of people committing occasional acts of violence and intimidation. The majority of new recruits were persuaded not to work, and many of those who avoided pickets or who remained unconvinced by their arguments, were found incapable of performing the tasks assigned to them, and had to be returned to their homes. Bell and Holmes had warned the strikers that their picketing was to be conducted 'without any violence of any description and within the boundaries of the law[32].

There were however, accusations that the strikers were adopting intimidatory practices, and threatening vengeance on all those who did not comply with their demands. There were also several occasions when substitute labour was subject to violence.[33] Bell published and circulated a pamphlet, known as the 'Blackleg circular', which was regarded as intimidatory to the replacement labour.[34] The circular stated:

STRIKE ON THE TAFF VALE RAILWAY

Men's Headquarters, Coburn St., Cathays.

There has been a strike on the TVRC since Monday last. The management are using every means to decoy men here whom they employ for the purpose of blacklegging the men on strike. Drivers, firemen, brakemen, and signal men are all out. Are you willing to be known as a blackleg? If you accept employment on the Taff Vale that is what you will be known by. On arriving at Cardiff call at the above address, where you can get information and assistance.

(signed) RICHARD BELL
General Secretary

These events were portrayed in a manner highly prejudicial and damaging to the union case, which was unfortunate, as on the whole picketing was peaceful and the strikers restrained in their actions. Beasley was convinced that the agitation was being whipped up by union 'radicals and militants' who should have no involvement in the affairs of the company.

Pressure for a Settlement

The respective actors' positions were becoming ever-more entrenched. The dispute was escalating into a bitter war of attrition between Beasley and the rank and file. Beasley's patience evaporated as he became dissatisfied with developments and decided to consult the company's solicitors. This was done with a view to gaining an injunction to restrain both Bell and Holmes, as well as the union from 'watching and besetting' the company's premises, the Great Western Railway station at Cardiff, and the non-strikers' residences. However, he was advised that since the introduction of the Trade Union Acts 1871 and 1876 it had been assumed that such an action could not be entertained against a trade union in its registered name. Beasley was confident of a positive outcome to any legal action, being convinced that the acts of violence committed by some of the men (and the words of a circular issued under Bell's name that referred to 'blacklegs') would influence legal opinion to decide in his favour. *In J Lyons & Sons v Wilkins*, Byrne J[35] had ruled that picketing which took the form of 'watching and besetting' was illegal, and that to call a man a 'blackleg' was a form of intimidation not permitted by the law.[36]

Richard Bell made strenuous effort to resolve the dispute and to obtain a return to work on conditions that would avoid loss of face for both sides. He became particularly concerned to resolve matters because the company had commenced legal action against some of the men who had broken their contracts. A significant obstacle was, however, the refusal of both Vassall and Beasley to negotiate. They regarded the dispute as a titanic battle they were determined to win. Subsequently, the Board of Trade became involved, and through their representative, Mr Hopwood, sought to mediate in the dispute. This attempt to find a settlement was bolstered by the publication of two letters in *The Times*.[37] One was from James Inskip, former Chairman of the Taff Vale Railway Company, who wrote that it was lamentable that the directors had not taken the one step (negotiation with Bell) that would have averted a daily loss of hundreds of pounds. The other letter was written by Sir W T Lewis, one of the most influential industrialists in Cardiff, who advocated the establishment of a Conciliation Board for the railways of South Wales. Following the appearance of these letters, the Taff Vale directors were under pressure to make some concessions, and on the following day they published their terms for a settlement. They agreed to the question of Signalman Ewington being referred to the Board of Trade for arbitration; they undertook to re-employ as many as possible of the strikers immediately and all of them within two months; the claims of the men would be considered with deputations of the various grades; and the legal proceedings taken against the men would be abandoned.

Failure to Resolve the Dispute

The barrier to resolving the dispute that caused the continuation of the strike until the end of the month was the question of the substitute labour. The company was reluctant to dispose of the replacement workers quickly by the payment of compensation; the men's committee would not accept the proposal that some of the substitute workers would continue to be employed on the railway for two months after the strike was over, as this would have meant unemployment for employees of the company. It was at this point that Sir W T Lewis intervened again, an intervention made possible by the fact that the Vice-Chairman of the Taff Vale Railway Company, Mr Russell Rea, disagreed with the rest of the Board in that he was more favourable to the union. In informal conversations between Bell, Holmes, Rea, and Lewis, the differences between the two parties were narrowed.[38] Late at night on 30 August 1900, a settlement was reached. The company agreed to take back all the strikers within one month; to accept the Board of Trade's arbitration on Ewington; to guarantee the men's pension rights; and to stop all legal proceedings against the strikers. A Conciliation Board was to be set up for the South Wales railways 'if possible' by 31October 1900, and the claims of the men could then be placed before it.[39] The strike was brought to an end, and normal services were in operation by 1 September 1900.

The Legal Action

No Conciliation Board materialised and on 6 November 1900, the directors reneged on their promise following a meeting with Beasley. Beasley was adamant that the company could not 'depute the management of the staff to any outside body'.[40] The company also failed to fulfil its promise to dismiss the substitute workers.[41] Instead, the Taff Vale Railway Company decided to bring legal action against the union and some of its officials, claiming an injunction to restrain them, their servants and agents from watching or besetting the premises of the plaintiffs for the purpose of persuading persons from working for the company and from procuring persons who had entered into contracts with them to break these contracts. On 30 August 1900, two applications were made to Farwell J in the High Court, one from the Taff Vale Railway Company seeking an injunction against Bell and Holmes and the Society; and the other, on the defendants' behalf, that the name of the Society should be struck out of the action on the ground that it was neither a corporation nor an individual and could not be sued in a quasi-corporate or other capacity. On 5 September 1900, Farwell J granted an interim injunction against Bell and Holmes restraining them from all forms of picketing in the dispute except 'merely to obtain or communicate information' to non-strikers. The judge stated that Richard Bell had 'put his name to a most improper circular', which was a 'distinct threat' to the substitute labour.[42] He also dismissed with costs the motion to strike-out the name of the defendant society, declaring that a union could be sued in its registered name.

The question in this case turned on the Trade Union Acts 1871 - 1876, which relieved the trade unions from the penalties under which they laboured at common law as illegal conspiracies. Did these Acts 'incorporate' the unions so as to allow them to sue and be sued as legal persons?[43] Farwell J stated:

> *Has the legislature authorised the creation of numerous bodies of men, capable of owning great wealth and acting by agents, with absolutely no responsibility for the wrongs they may do to other persons by the use of that wealth and the employment of those agents? I do not think so ... It would require very clear and express words of enactment to induce me to hold that the Legislature had in fact legalised the existence of such irresponsible bodies with such wide capacity for evil.*[44]

The *Taff Vale* decision portrayed trade unions as the most iniquitous combination against the public interest and the social well-being of society. Thus, trade unions were viewed as influential and powerful organisations whose activities needed to be subject to legal control by the courts. The judgment of Farwell J caused grave concern among trade unionists as they realised the dangers of the decision for the trade union movement, making them susceptible to significant damages. It resulted in hampering trade unions in their work for fear of the consequences of too active participation in trade disputes. The Society, with the support of the TUC, therefore appealed to the Court of Appeal where the injunction was discharged and the Society's name ordered to be struck out. The Master of the Rolls declared that he 'could find nothing in the Trade Union Acts' that stated that 'a trade union was liable to be sued in its registered name'.

In the House of Lords

The company made a further appeal to the House of Lords. On 22 July 1901, the five Law Lords found unanimously in favour of the company, and restored the decision of Farwell J. The decision was certainly surprising, for 20 years after the passage of the Trade Union Acts it was universally assumed, first, that a trade union, not a body corporate, though an organisation recognised by the law for certain purposes, could neither sue nor be sued; second, that as a strike was legal in itself, so the methods necessarily employed by the strikers were also legal, provided they led to no breach of the peace. The House of Lords declared that a registered union itself, as distinct from its officials, could be liable in tort for damages, thereby destroying the main advantage to unions of their legal status of unincorporated associations, with the result that many trade unions could be made liable to pay heavy damages and costs. The pronouncements of Farwell J and the House of Lords seemed to have had scant regard for the wording of the Trade Union Acts.[45] The legal decisions were shaped by a particular ideology towards the activities of trade unions. Farwell J considered it settled that trade disputes were evils to be discouraged, and regarded the ASRS to be acting with maliciousness for the sake of gain. The judgments of Mr Justice Farwell and the House of Lords would afford interesting reading to those who believed that justice was being impartially administered in English courts during this period. The *Taff Vale* judgment struck a blow at the heart of the trade union movement.[46] It placed such legal hazards in the path of would-be strikers that discontent was often bottled up until the law was revised by the Trade Disputes Act 1906.[47] The fear felt by the unions can be seen in the fact that, in spite of rises in the cost of living, the number of strikes declined sharply between 1900 and 1906 when the

Taff Vale judgment was reversed.

When the terms of a settlement of the strike were being negotiated between Mr Hopwood of the Board of Trade and Mr Vassall, the Taff Vale Railway Company chairman, the latter agreed, in a letter written on 28 August 1900, that 'all legal proceedings' would be discontinued once the strike ended. This promise was repeated in the final terms of settlement with the men on 30 August 1900. On the following day, the union's solicitors wrote to the company's solicitors stating that it was understood that all legal proceedings against 'your client's servants or their representatives (Trade Union or otherwise)' were to be withdrawn. The exemption was the question of the injunction on which the union wanted 'a friendly fight'. On 1 September 1900, the company's solicitors replied that the company had agreed to withdraw all pending summonses, but they made no mention, either way, of summonses against the union.[48] Although Richard Bell feared that the company would apply for damages, it looked at first as if they had decided against any such application. The Lords' judgment, which declared that a union could be sued, was delivered on 21 July 1901, but it was not until 13 December of that year that a claim for damages against the ASRS was lodged by the company. The company put in a claim for damages amounting to £24,626, and the hearing of the case in the King's Bench Division of the High Court lasted from 3 – 19 December 1902. The Taff Vale Railway Company agreed to accept the sum of £23, 000 in settlement of all claims. The ASRS, in fact paid damages and legal costs totalling £42,000.

Conclusion

The management of the Taff Vale Railway Company believed that they had struck a devastating blow against the power of organised labour. The chairman of the company, Mr Vassell, remarked that 'the importance of the judgment could not be exaggerated'.[49] During a strike it would be possible to carry on with business so long as an alternative suitable workforce could be found who would now be free of 'intimidation' from the unions. If the unions could be held to have acted in an unlawful way they would have to pay losses to the company from their funds. This meant their power to promote and engineer strikes would be extinguished. The trade union movement characterised the decision in the *Taff Vale* case as 'the unjust judgment of unjust judges', and as 'a pernicious example of judge-made law'. Historically, an important function of the common law has been to oil the wheels of commerce and enterprise. The common law makes no attempt to recognise the legitimacy of the strike as a feature of workplace relations.[50]

The *Taff Vale* judgment of 1901 placed considerable legal restrictions in the path of would-be strikers. It meant that strikes were legal, but almost all forms of picketing, necessary to make the strike effective, were not. A union could be sued for damages caused by a strike. Some even asserted that the idea of the right to have a trade union was now to be seen as an illusion. Trade unionists were determined to get the law amended and mobilised political activity to that end. The *Taff Vale* judgment was the catalyst that bolstered support for independent labour representation. The crux of the significance of the *Taff Vale* judgment was that it constrained by legal decision the ability of trade unions to engage in industrial action, in order to advance and protect the interests of their members. The *Taff Vale* judgment demonstrated to trade unionists the need for their voices to be heard directly in Parliament. It has been remarked that 'the *Taff Vale* decision did more to secure independent labour representation than anything else between 1900 and 1906 to attract trade union support for the Labour Representation Committee [LRC] as the forerunner of the Labour Party'.[51] Thus since the trade unions could not campaign against the *Taff Vale* judgment by the use of industrial action, they engaged in the political process. Large numbers of trade unions affiliated to the LRC and lobbied Parliament for a change in the law.

The vociferous campaigning led eventually to the Trade Disputes Act 1906, which is considered fully below by John Saville. The 1906 Act significantly strengthened the position of trade unions, giving them greater confidence to organise and exercise a collective power which went some way to counteract the overweening power of the employer at the workplace. For the last 25 years however, these achievements have been reversed. Between 1980 and 1993 Conservative administrations introduced legislative provisions that sought to restrict and control the activities of trade unions in the sphere of industrial action. The current Labour government has reaffirmed its commitment to retain the essential features of the trade union reforms of the 1980s, rejecting suggestions that the law regulating industrial action should be significantly relaxed. The Government considers that trade union activities in this domain should be the subject of some regulation to provide necessary protections and proper standards of accountability. On this point, the Labour government has remarked:

> *Unions are extremely important organisations that regulate, or strongly influence, the employment relationship between many millions of people and their employers. This sets them apart from other voluntary organisations.*[52]

The trade union movement must once again mobilise politically to change Conservative anti-trade union laws to at least regain the freedoms enjoyed from 1906.

My thanks to Geoff Revell for comments on an earlier draft and Taylor Francis Publishing for permission to use extracts from P Bagwell, *The Railwaymen* (1963)

Notes

1 Lord Wedderburn, *Employment Rights in Britain and Europe: Selected Papers in Labour Law* (1991), p 201.
2 R Lewis and B Simpson, *Striking a Balance?* (1981), pp 7-8.
3 H Clegg and A Flanders, *The System of Industrial Relations in Great Britain (1975)*, p 44.
4 R Taylor, *The Trade Union Question in British Politics: Government and Unions since 1945* (1993), p 147.
5 H Clegg, *The Changing System of Industrial Relations in Great Britain* (1979) p 290.
6 *Taff Vale Railway Company v. Amalgamated Society of Railway Servants* [1901] AC 426 HL; [1901] 1KB 170 (CA).
7 Lord Wedderburn, above, p 201.
8 P Davies and M Freedland, *Kahn-Freund's Labour and the Law* (1983), p 260.
9 From a leading article in the *Railway Review*, 25th November 1898.
10 See J Saville, 'Trade Unions and Free Labour, the Background to the Taff Vale Decision', A Briggs and J Saville (eds), *Essays in Labour History* (1960), p 337; P Bagwell, *The Railwaymen* (1963); and C Harvey, and J Press, 'Management and the Taff Vale Strike' (2000) 42 *Business History* 63.
11 H Pelling, *A History of British Trade Unionism*, (11th ed, 2004), p 113.
12 C Harvey and J Press, above, p 64.
13 D Barrie, *The Taff Vale Dispute* (2002), p 1.
14 S and B Webb, *Industrial Democracy* (1920), p 597.
15 G Revell, *The Story of the Taff Vale Railway Strike* (2006), p 1.
16 F Hayek, *The Constitution of Liberty* (1960), p 144.
17 F Hayek, *1980s Unemployment and the Unions* (2nd ed, 1984), p 15.
18 P Bagwell, above, p 209.
19 *Ibid.*
20 *Ibid*
21 G Revell, above, p 2.
22 *Ibid.*
23 *Ibid*, p 3.
24 *Ibid*, p 2.
25 P Bagwell, above, p 213.
26 G Revell, above, p 5.
27 P Bagwell, above, p 214.
28 G Revell, above, p 6.
29 C Harvey and J Press, above, p 72.
30 P Bagwell, above, p 215.
31 *Ibid*, p 216.
32 G Revell, above, p 6.
33 P Bagwell, above, p 219.
34 J G Steffee, 'The Taff Vale Case' (1903) 37 *American Law Review* 25.

35 *J Lyons & Sons v Wilkins* [1899] 1 Ch 255.
36 J Saville, 'The Trade Disputes Act 1906' (1996) 1 Historical Studies in Industrial Relations 1.
37 P Bagwell, above, p 221.
38 *South Wales Argus*, 30 August 1900.
39 *The Times*, 1 September 1900.
40 G Revell, above, p 10.
41 *Railway News*, 16 February, 1901.
42 G Revell, above, p 11.
43 M Barlow, 'The Taff Vale Railway Case' (1901) 11 *The Economic Journal* 447.
44 *Taff Vale Railway Company v Amalgamated Society of Railway Servants* [1901] AC 426.
45 M Barlow, above, p 448.
46 R Lewis, 'The Historical Development of Labour Law' (1976) 14 *British Journal of Industrial Relations* p 4.
47 H Clegg, above, p 591.
48 P Bagwell, above, p 223.
49 *Ibid*, p 224.
50 K Ewing, 'Rights and Immunities in British Labour Law' (1989) 10 *Comparative Labor Law Journal* p 34.
51 J Mortimer, *The Formation of the Labour Party* (Socialist History Occasional Papers Series, 2000).
52 Department of Trade and Industry, Review of the Employment Relations Act 1999: Government Response to Public Consultation (2003), p 68.

Chapter Three

The Belfast Butchers: *Quinn v Leathem* after a Hundred Years

John McIlroy

TRADITIONAL accounts of the events which provoked the Trade Disputes Act 1906 centred on an offensive by capital and the judges in response to the threat of the militant 'new unionism' which emerged after 1889. Answering public opinion and the mood of employers, the courts demolished key aspects of the legal settlement of the 1870s. In the *Magnificent Journey* – 'Forward March of Labour' historiography, case after case delivered blow after blow to the labour movement, climaxing in the summer of 1901 when *Quinn v Leathem* was decided weeks after *Taff Vale*. The working-class response was immediate and effective, culminating in the development of a new and enduring legal compromise and the establishment of the Labour Party in 1906.

The probing approach of contemporary historians, alert to detail, difference and divisions, which, without neglecting class conflict, is sensitive to chance and contingency, unveils a more complex picture of what remains a major working-class advance. Dissolving before recomposing unified narratives, recognising both the significance of class and its fissures, illuminating human agency, acknowledging both the general and the particular, such an approach emphasises that each legal case possessed its own initiation and its own unique features. Each arrived in court impelled by individual decisions taken by a variety of protagonists typically more conscious of their own predicament than national dramas, decisions in which accidents of circumstance played a part. Each left the courtroom after judgment by lawyers whose conclusions, inflected by ideology and class, influenced history in ways they had not intended.

That *Quinn v Leathem* was an Irish case is rarely expanded upon. Nor is the fact that its trade union protagonist, the Belfast Journeymen Butchers, was, in comparison with many other unions involved in the pre-1906 litigation – the Railway Servants, the Builders, the Boilermakers and the Miners – a tiny, fragile organisation whose members might be perceived as ambiguous in class terms. They were scarcely emblematic of working-class militancy; indeed, they were marginal to a local proletariat divided, more than anywhere else in the United Kingdom, by politics and religion, whose distinctive collectivism centred on the shipyards, linen textiles and engineering. It is rarely remarked that while the Journeymen Butchers was a new union, its methods had more in common with the craft unionism of earlier decades than the stereotypical 'new unionism' of the 1890s. Or that Henry Leathem's law-suit was, at least on the face of it, contingent on the unusual obduracy of these unlikely militants who rejected a union shop in favour of complete control of entry to Leathem's workforce. Or that wider support for the butchers required organisation and persistence and remained less than spontaneous or overwhelming.[1]

The problematic issue of an employers' offensive against the unions in the 1890s has received sophisticated attention.[2] The role of the courts also merits further scrutiny.[3] The anti-union creativity of the judges is undeniable and the leading role of the Lord Chancellor of England, Hardinge Stanley Giffard, first Earl of Halsbury and a Tory to his fingertips, requires emphasis. But conflict ran through the judiciary just as it fractured capital, labour and the legislature. The judicial offensive must be set within a political, ideological and legal struggle *between* the judges, a contest over opposed conceptions of collectivism and the policy that the State should apply to trade unionism.

Here again the accidental and contingent, as well as the role of human agency in influencing the precise ways in which the facts and the problems were constructed, interpreted and pronounced upon in crucial cases, in *Allen v Flood* on the one hand and *Quinn v Leathem* on the other, were important. The attitudinal differences between the judges and the decision which the majority reached in *Allen* qualifies notions of ideological homogeneity and a unified judicial offensive: the former Lord Chancellor, Farrer Herschell, a Liberal from a family of Jewish immigrants from Poland, embodies the opposition to its co-ordination. But for Herschell's death and Halsbury's determination, things may have turned out differently. Moreover, as subsequent events would demonstrate, if some judges believed that they were lubricating and legitimising an employers' offensive, they were mistaking the intentions of most employers. And, as the ineffective attempts to overrule *Taff Vale* and *Quinn* from 1902 to 1904 demonstrated, were it not for the fortuitous Liberal landslide in the general election of 1906 a different legal settlement might have endured. Were it not for the extraordinary decision of the new Prime Minister, Sir Henry Campbell-Bannerman, to support the trade unions' bill and the pragmatic decision of the Unionist leader Lord Lansdowne to accept it in the second chamber, the detail of the 1906 settlement might have been a little less palatable. To echo Eric Hobsbawm, to achieve proper understanding of the complexity of these events we need to employ the microscope before we reach for the telescope.[4]

Beginnings: A Butchers' Union and Henry Leathem

The six-year saga of *Quinn* began in 1895 in Lisburn, County Antrim, a small town of 12,000 inhabitants, the vast majority of them Protestant. Only eight miles from Belfast, Lisburn had its own identity, sustained by its own industry and commerce based on linen manufacture. The plaintiff, Henry Leathem, was a prosperous beef butcher born in County Antrim in 1840. He had been in business on his own account since the mid-1870s and owned shops in Bridge Street and Bow Street. A widower who lived with his unmarried niece, Leathem aspired 'to give honest value to all classes alike and content myself with Small Profit',[5] proudly advertising his rump steak and mutton chops at 9d and best boiling and stewing meat at 6d a pound.

The meat trade in the north-east of Ireland was traditionally dominated by small, independent retailers who bought and slaughtered local produce, while some like Leathem, a skilled flesher, also sold meat on to other butchers. The last quarter of the 19th century brought increased consumption, competition, intervention and insecurity. Across the United Kingdom, the number of butchers grew from 95,563 in 1881 to 128,000 by 1901. Co-operative stores were appearing, while the advent of steamships and refrigeration saw American meat arriving in Belfast via Liverpool. Local authorities used the Public Health Acts to inspect and crack down on private slaughterhouses and diseased cattle, and license municipal abattoirs. A feeling developed among some butchers of 'the small-scale trader as being locked in a struggle for his very existence'.[6] Belfast and its environs experienced additional disturbance: butchering was an occupation in which Catholics had traditionally predominated but Protestants were moving into the trade in substantial numbers.[7]

The background was the explosive growth of Belfast as an industrial centre. Its population increased from 174,000 in 1870 to almost 350,000 by 1901. It was an increasingly Protestant – although more than a quarter of its population was Catholic – and, in reaction to successive Home-Rule crises, an increasingly Conservative city. Protestant-dominated skilled labour markets and occupational segregation were combined with growing residential segregation and even the small Catholic *petit-bourgeoisie* was excluded from urban government.[8] The labour movement was cautious and fragile. Its solidarities constrained by denominationalism and the ever present danger of sectarianism, it articulated a minimalist labour politics which in practice privileged Conservatism and Unionism. Formed in 1881, the Belfast Trades' Council was, by the mid-1890s, a vital local parliament and organising centre, providing this distinctive labour movement with identity and coherence. By 1895, its seventy-seven affiliated unions enrolled almost 19,000 members. The council embraced not only the established Irish craft unions in linen and flax, and the admittedly under-represented British craft unions in shipbuilding and engineering, but also the British-based new unions of dockers, gasworkers and general labourers, as well as a baffling variety of local societies, of hodsmen, plasterers, paviors, brush-makers and municipal employees together with news agents' assistants, booksellers, hairdressers, chimney sweeps and butchers.[9]

Like their industry, the butchers' societies, a neglected aspect of 'new unionism', were small-scale and localised. In Britain, the Newcastle and Gateshead Butchers' Association was established in 1891 with 90 members, the Oldham Butchers in 1892 with 137 members, and the Journeymen Butchers' Apprentices and Assistants' Association of Blackburn in 1900 with 31 members. They remained outside the Journeymen Butchers' Federation of Great Britain formed the same year but embracing fewer than 200 members. In Ireland there were butchers' unions in Cork and Dublin and a small society in Belfast.[10]

The defendants in *Quinn* were the leading officials and activists of the Belfast Journeymen Butchers and Assistants' Association, a shadowy and almost forgotten organisation. John Craig, the president, John Davey, the secretary, Joseph Quinn, the treasurer, and two longstanding members from Lisburn, Henry Dornan and Robert Shaw sought to develop their association, which was established in 1891 and enrolled with the Registrar of Friendly Societies and Belfast Trades' Council, an indispensable helpmate for new and inexperienced organisations, in 1893, the year of another Home-Rule crisis and sectarian disturbances, along traditional craft-union lines.[11] They attempted to control entry into the trade, enforce apprenticeship and safeguard quality and skill. An indenture I discovered was agreed for a period of three years between Mary Davey, a Catholic flesher, on behalf of her grandson, the 14 year old Patrick Shearer, and the union activist, Hiram Morgan – at least two members of the union were employers. The agreement required Morgan to 'teach, instruct or cause to be instructed with due Correction' the young Shearer in the 'Art' of butchery.[12] As early as 1894 the butchers refused to admit a Mr Firth to membership on the grounds of his lack of competency, although when he appealed they were prepared to find a beast for him to kill as a test of his proficiency.[13] The butchers paid benefits to unemployed members and determined that members would neither work with non-union labour nor handle meat from non-union establishments. Their first recorded dispute with the Belfast firm H and A Close occurred in spring 1894 and their success in projecting a craft ethos was reflected in unfounded rumours that they had closed their books to new recruits.[14]

In reality, the Journeymen Butchers with around 100 members was a 'young' and 'weak' society.[15] But it possessed a spirit of aggression. The union had members in Lisburn and in early 1895 its leaders made overtures to Leathem's employees. In what follows, it must be remembered that the version of events which appears in the law reports consists of Leathem's own self-interested account of developments. Believing on the basis of earlier case law that there was no case to answer, or accepting that Leathem's story was largely accurate, or worried by the impression they might make on the jury, the butchers did not go into the witness box or call evidence at Belfast Assizes in July 1896. Professor Heuston suggests the last of these explanations.[16] However, the union's counsel, Thomas O'Shaughnessy, QC, poured scorn on Leathem's tale and derided the use which his adversary, Sergeant Dodd, made of it:

> *... his courageous client, that man of iron, that village Hampden had gone to the Society with his men, and asked them to admit them as members and said he would pay the fees for them. Nothing so bombastic or ridiculous he scarcely ever listened to.*[17]

Ridiculous or not, Leathem's facts became the facts and the linchpin of the case. But the facts as found by the jurors who, the assize judge observed, would draw their own conclusions from the butchers' silence, and accepted by the higher courts, are not binding on the historian and we can find alternative accounts of the causes of the dispute. A later chronicler commented: 'Leathem refused to dismiss men who had been expelled for not paying union dues.'[18] This version of events, which posits a pre-history to Leathem's story and contextualises the butchers' behaviour went unrehearsed in the courts. Moreover, it is unsupported by corroboration or citation.[19]

There is, nonetheless, some contemporary evidence for a different origin to the dispute and one which provides some explanation for the butchers' intransigence. The able Belfast representative of the Amalgamated Society of Carpenters and Joiners, the socialist Unionist William Walker, furnished an alternative pre-history when he informed the 1900 British Trade Union Congress in Huddersfield that the conflict was precipitated by Leathem's discharge of union members.[20] But Walker, who would prove a good friend to the butchers, was also an interested party although his explanation might go some way to explaining the 'angry feeling'[21] which characterised the confrontation between Leathem and the butchers which took place at John Magill's Ulster Hotel, Market Square, Lisburn, in July 1895.

Their opponents saw the association's fortunes in the ascendant: 'some of the highest and best men in the business had gone down before it'.[22] On his own evidence, and it remains surprising that it was not directly contested by the union participants if it was false, Leathem was willing to join them. His story begins, not with the discharge or disbarring of union members, but with his own generous response to attempts to recruit his employees:

> *I said that I came on behalf of my men, and was ready to pay all fines, debts and demands against them; and I asked to have them admitted to the society. The defendant Shaw got up and objected to their being allowed to work on, and to their admission, and said that my men should be put out of my employment, and could not be admitted, and should walk the streets for twelve months. I said it was a hard case to make a man walk the streets with nine small children and I would not submit to it ... Craig was in the chair; I was sitting beside him. He said there were some others there that would suit me as well. He picked some out and said they could work for me. I said they were not suitable for my business, and I would keep the men I had. They said I had to take them. I said I would not put out my men. Craig then spoke, and told me my meat would be stopped in Andrew Munce's if I would not comply with their wishes.*[23]

Whether Leathem's memory was good or bad, whether he dispensed with relevant earlier history, his account, uncomplicated by earlier conflicts about expulsions or dismissals, came to constitute the substance of the case and tilted it against the butchers. As the orthodox version, it would be repeated and repeated. Leathem won the fight over the facts. He seized the high ground as a caring employer who would not tolerate the vividly expressed victimisation of his servants, but a flexible master who was willing to face the changing world and meet the union half way. The butchers were applying Rule 11 of their society's constitution, a rule which made it their fraternal responsibility to assist members to secure employment before non-members. Moreover, it was claimed by their counsel in cross-examination at the Assizes that one of their objections to Leathem's existing staff was that they had not served a proper apprenticeship. There was antipathy to hackers and sawyers who substituted for trained meat-cutters. More conjecturally, the butchers' insistence on trade unionism *in extremis* was conditioned by a past history of problems over union membership. The prudence of hindsight suggests that they were over-reaching themselves and might better have consolidated their progress by accepting Leathem's offer.

However, they believed with some justification that they held high cards. Leathem sold around £1,000 of meat annually to the Belfast butcher, Andrew Munce, whose employees were members of the society. Initially Munce refused to bow to pressure. His son wrote to the butchers in language which would have warmed the hearts of many judges infused with the ideology of individual rights: 'he could not interfere to bring pressure to bear on Mr Leathem to employ none but society men by refusing to purchase meat from him, as that would be outside his province and interfering with the liberty of another man.'[24] The Munces loved liberty; but they loved their livelihood more. When the society, having taken the precaution of gaining the support of the more experienced leadership of the trades' council, moved to instruct its members to cease work the moment Leathem's beef reached Belfast, Munce telegrammed Leathem: 'Unless you arrange with the society you need not send any beef this week, as men are ordered to quit work'.[25] As Lord Brampton bleakly recorded: 'On and from that day Munce took no more meat from Leathem, to his substantial loss'.[26]

The Journeymen Butchers pressed home their advantage. Three of Leathem's assistants, Edward Dickey, Henry McDonald and Edward Rice, now enter the narrative as union members – 'were somehow or other induced to join the society'[27] – and went on strike. Dickey was provided with a new job in the shop of the Lisburn society member, Henry Dornan, while the others were paid their 15s weekly wages by the association. Davey circulated a blacklist of non-union shops which included Leathem's. In consequence, at least one Lisburn employer, John McBride, ceased to deal with him. In the face of these developments and his bruising personal encounter with the butchers' leaders, it is fair to assume that Leathem saw only one way out. Forced to sell off his prime beef steak at the reduced price of 5d a pound, he consulted a solicitor.

In the received rendering at least, here was no aggressive anti-trade unionist on the model of Ammon Beasley, the manager of the Taff Vale Railway Company[28]. Leathem's back was to the wall. In the estimation of his advocates, he was fighting to stave off ruin. His opponents calculated that he was 'attempting to wreck this little trade union of butchers' assistants because they had combined together to protect their own interests'[29]. Yet despite the assistance which the trades' council gave the butchers, their methods found critics within its ranks. Alexander Taylor, an experienced leader of the Irish Linenlappers' Union and a former secretary of the trades' council, remarked: 'Sorry would he be to injure the butchers' case; but he could not conceal the fact that he believed the butchers acted with great indiscretion at the time they did, and naturally endangered their own case by what they then did'.[30]

There was another dimension to the affair on which the law reports and newspaper coverage of the case were understandably silent. Leathem, an adherent of the Church of Ireland, was the worshipful master of Loyal Orange Lodge 557, Lisburn.[31] The solicitor who advised him on legal proceedings – Leathem, as was not uncommon at the time, could read but not write – George Wilkins, was chairman of the Lisburn Unionist Association and chairman of Lisburn Urban Council. Two of Leathem's fellow butchers who sustained him in the conflict, William Davis, another prominent Orangeman, and David Hastings, who in response to the action against Leathem changed his stance and refused to employ union labour, also served on the council. Leathem enjoyed the support of the *petit bourgeois* establishment of Lisburn.[32] In contrast, several of the leaders of the Journeymen Butchers came from the small enclaves of Catholic working-class Belfast – although the union seems to have embraced Catholics and Protestants as members and supporters – and their solicitor, Joseph Donnelly, is remembered as a Catholic Nationalist.[33]

Craig, the butchers' president, lived on Norfolk Street, which connected the Catholic Falls Road with the Protestant Shankill. It is impossible to state categorically that he was a Catholic – he died before the 1901 census and his name is typically Protestant – but his wife and nephew were. Davey, the union secretary, was a Catholic who lived in

Cullingtree Road near the old Cattle Pound. Quinn, the treasurer, lived in Durham Street, another predominantly Catholic area. Among the Lisburn activists, Henry Dornan was also a Catholic. The threat such a group presented to the interests of a Lisburn Orangeman would scarcely have endeared them, even in those less polarised days, to the town's Protestant elite.[34] On the evidence available, it is impossible to do more than register these points.

The Advocates and the Judges

Religious and political differences were reflected only minimally in the two parties' legal representation. O'Shaughnessy, who, as we have seen, led for the butchers in the Irish courts, was a Catholic and future Recorder of Dublin but he was assisted by the Protestant Unionist supporter of Sir Edward Carson, J H Campbell, QC, subsequently Lord Chancellor of Ireland, who, however, became chairman of the Free State Senate in 1922. Leathem, in turn, was championed by Sergeant Dodd, another fixture of the Irish courts, subsequently National Liberal MP for Tyrone North, supported by John Gordon, subsequently Liberal Unionist MP for South Derry and Attorney-General of Ireland, and James Chambers, the future Unionist MP for Belfast South. The trade union team during the House of Lords' hearing consisted of the Protestant Home Ruler, Edmund Vesey Knox, National Liberal MP for Derry, 1895–98, seconded by the Catholic, William Martin McGrath. Leathem, in status terms at least, had the superior services of Richard Haldane, KC, who had argued the union's case in *Taff Vale*. Haldane, then Liberal MP for East Lothian and a future Labour Lord Chancellor, was seconded by a barrister born in his constituency, Francis Wall.[35]

These advocates affirm that the late-Victorian bar was an intensely political profession and this was certainly true of the judiciary.[36] Table 1, which lists the judges who heard the case, illustrates this. There is some controversy regarding who sat in the House of Lords. Paterson states that there were six peers and that Lord Davey, the former Liberal MP and Solicitor General who had been in the majority in *Allen v Flood*, was not invited to sit by Halsbury. Heuston refers to a panel of seven which includes Davey. But Davey delivered no speech, not even the terse concurrence contributed by Lord Robertson. The only part he took was in reading the opinions of the three absent law lords in August – he did not hear the case in May–June 1901 for whatever reason. The table therefore includes the six who gave speeches, making a total of fifteen judges in all.[37]

We must not overlook the important body which stood at the base of the pyramid, the special jury, which, despite O'Shaughnessy's efforts, found for Leathem at Belfast Assizes. In the Irish Appeal Court Sir Peter O'Brien, who, despite his Catholicism, was not immune to complaints from Nationalists about juries packed with Unionists, affirmed his personal faith in 'the constitutional tribunal – and there could be no better of its kind – a jury of the citizens of Belfast'.[38] This assessment was questionable: the property qualification for such jurors, as O'Brien knew, excluded the majority of Belfast workers and the vast majority of Belfast Catholics. In the debates on the 1906 Trade Disputes Bill, the Solicitor-General remarked, a trifle more accurately, 'every dispute between employers and workmen requires justification before a tribunal either of employers or of men drawn from the employing class.'[39] G R Askwith, the Board of Trade chief conciliator, who had rather more direct experience of the conflicts of capital and labour than Sir Peter, remarked, pertinently to the issues to be decided in *Quinn*, that he had never encountered a single case of a strike where the jury decided that the purpose of industrial action was to benefit trade unionists rather than to inflict damage on the employer.[40] *Quinn* would prove no exception.

Table 1 demonstrates the background of the judges who delivered opinions as the case moved up the judicial pyramid from July 1896 to June 1901. The information generally accords with Duman's conclusions about the professional middle-class spine of the Victorian judiciary, although there is a strong dash of land ownership and an element of social mobility from the *petit-bourgeoisie*, while the aristocracy is represented by Edward Macnaghten. The table attests to judicial maturity: nine of the 15 were born before the year of Victoria's accession. The overall average age was 66 years while for the law lords it was 72, ancient in terms of the life expectancy of the majority of the population.[41]The table confirms the Irish dimension. Of the fifteen judges who heard *Quinn*, eleven were Irish or from an Irish background. In the House of Lords, Halsbury, who came from an Irish Protestant family, and Macnaghten, sat with two Scots and only two Englishmen.

The table evokes the limited ecumenism of the Irish establishment – two of the nine judges in the Irish courts had been educated by the Jesuits, although their careers, particularly that of Sir Peter O'Brien who worked with Carson against the Nationalists, suggest we should not confuse religion with nationalism, still less with radicalism. It illustrates the extent to which judges were, had been and would be members of the Ascendancy and political activists. Once again it raises questions about the separation of powers, the independence of the judiciary, and the nature of the judicial process. Ten of the 15 judges had been elected MPs or held political office earlier in their lives. Of the 15, six were Conservatives while Sir Peter O'Brien served in Conservative administrations, and three were Liberals. In addition, Andrews was a Liberal Unionist and Shand was identified with the Liberals. Only three, Brampton, William O'Brien, and Lindley had no known history of significant political activism. These were conservative judges, their hostile mindset towards effective trade unionism underlined by the stereotypical 'non-political' judge Lindley's commitment to employer prerogative and antipathy to industrial action.[42] *Quinn v Leathem* turned on policy-making rather than legislative interpretation. In the absence of a radical lead from the legislature, conservative values might be expected to produce conservative judgments. The lead was in the other direction.

Halsbury, on the Woolsack and in the Cabinet throughout the progress of *Quinn v Leathem*, cast a long shadow over the case. A self-righteous and militant Conservative, active in both the political second chamber and Britain's final court of appeal, he stood high in the counsels of his party and government. The antagonism to effective trade unionism which permeated his judgments was registered in his opposition to the 1906 legislation. He observed of its key provisions, ' ... was there ever such a thing heard of in a civilised country?'[43] In the legal controversies of the time Halsbury, a supporter of the Liberty and Property Defence League, forcefully pursued his belief that employers had a prerogative to employ 'their' labour as they wished and that to impose 'undue' impediment on this 'right' was actionable. He appointed judges on political grounds, applied political considerations in selecting panels to hear appeals, and utilised his authority as Lord Chancellor to influence key decisions.[44]

This was taken to extraordinary lengths. In *Allen v Flood*, Halsbury supported the reasoning of Lindley in the Court of Appeal, finding the union official liable for civil conspiracy and malicious interference with trade. He unsuccessfully canvassed his colleagues to support the decision in the Lords. He reneged on assurances he had given to the leading Liberal, Herschell, about the case which had been argued before the Law Lords in December 1895. Halsbury availed himself of the latter's absence to carry a motion for re-argument in March 1897, resurrecting without consultation the obsolete practice of summoning the lower court judges to advise the Law Lords. Despite the backing of six out of the eight judges, Halsbury was thwarted by a six–three vote of the Law Lords, a significant reverse which would prove relevant to *Quinn v Leathem*.[45]

When the Irish case reached the Lords in 1901, Halsbury found himself in more favourable circumstances. Of his three strongest opponents in *Allen v Flood*, Herschell had died the previous year. Davey, as we have seen, was either not invited to sit or declined the invitation to do so. His

Table 1. The Judges in *Quinn v Leathem*

Judge	Social Origin	Education	Age
Belfast Assizes, July 1896			
Fitzgibbon, Gerald, LJ (1837–1909)	b. Dublin, father barrister, Master in Chancery	Private; Trinity College, Dublin	59
Divisional Court of Queen's Bench, 19, 20 April, 22 November 1898			
O'Brien, Sir Peter, Lord Chief Justice, Ireland (1842–1920)	b. Ballynacklen, County Clare, land-owning family, son of Whig MP	Clongowes Wood, Trinity College, Dublin	56
Palles, Christopher, Chief Baron (1831–1920)	b. Dublin, legal family	Clongowes Wood, Trinity College, Dublin	67
Andrews, William Drennan, Judge (1832–1924)	b. County Down, linen employers	Royal Belfast Academy, Trinity College, Dublin	66
O'Brien, William, Judge (1832–1899)	b. County Cork	Middleton School	66
Irish Court of Appeal, 17–19, 23 January, 2 May 1899			
Gibson, Edward, Lord Ashbourne, Lord Chancellor of Ireland (1837–1913)	b. Dublin, Tipperary, landowning family	Private; Trinity College, Dublin	62
Porter, Sir Andrew Marshall, Master of Rolls, Ireland (1837–1919)	b. Belfast	Royal Belfast Academy; Queen's College, Belfast	62
Holmes, Hugh, Lord Justice of Appeal (1840–1916)	b. Dungannon, Co. Tyrone, landowning family	Royal School, Dungannon; Trinity College, Dublin	59
Walker, Sir Samuel, Lord Justice of Appeal (1832–1911)	b. Finea, Co. West Meath, landowning family	Arlington House School, Kings County; Trinity College, Dublin	67

Politics	**Religion**	**Other Offices**
Belfast Assizes, July 1896		
Conservative	Church of Ireland; also Freemason	Solicitor- General, Ireland
Divisional Court of Queen's Bench, 19, 20 April, 22 November 1898		
Whig Unionist, Conservative	Catholic	Unsuccessful Parliamentary candidate; Solicitor-General, Attorney-General, Ireland; Lord Chancellor, Ireland.
Liberal	Catholic	Attorney-General, Ireland
Liberal-Unionist	Church of Ireland	
Liberal		
Irish Court of Appeal, 17–19, 23 January, 2 May 1899		
Conservative	Church of Ireland	Conservative MP; adviser to Conservative leadership
Liberal	Presbyterian	Liberal MP; Attorney-General, Solicitor-General, Ireland
Conservative	Church of Ireland	Conservative MP; Attorney-General, Solicitor-General, Ireland
Liberal	Church of Ireland	Liberal MP; Attorney-General, Soliticor-General, Lord Chancellor, Ireland

Table 1. The Judges in *Quinn v Leathem*

Judge	Social Origin	Education	Age
House of Lords, 14, 17, 20 May, 11, 13, June 1901			
Earl of Halsbury, Lord Chancellor (1823–1921)	b. London, Irish family, father barrister	Private; Merton College, Oxford	78
Lord Macnaghten (1830–1913)	b. London, family Co. Antrim landowners	Dr Gowan School, Sunderland; Trinity College, Cambridge	71
Lord Shand (1828–1904)	b. Aberdeen, merchant family, step-father solicitor	University of Glasgow, University of Edinburgh	73
Henry Hawkins, Lord Brampton (1817–1907)	b.Hitchin, Herts, son of solicitor	Bedford School	84
Lord Robertson (1845–1909)	b. Forteviot, Perthshire, son of clergyman	Royal High School, Edinburgh; Edinburgh University	56
Lord Lindley (1828–1921)	b. Chiswick, London, father professor, University College, London	University College School; University College, London	73

Politics	Religion	Other Offices
House of Lords, 14, 17, 20 May, 11, 13, June 1901		
Conservative	Church of England	Conservative MP; Solicitor-General
Conservative Unionist	Church of Ireland	Conservative MP
Whig, later identified with Liberals	Church of Scotland	
	Became Catholic 1898	
Conservative	Scottish Episcopalian	Conservative MP; Solicitor- General, Scotland
	Church of England	

Sources: F. E. Ball, The Judges in Ireland, 1221–1921, vol. 2 (1926) republished Routledge, 1993; Oxford Dictionary of National Biography; Who Was Who.

fellow former Liberal MP, Lord James of Hereford, an experienced arbitrator conversant with trade unionism and a close friend of Sir Charles Dilke, a strong influence on the 1906 Act, was similarly either not invited, or declined to sit. The 'non-political' but hawkish Lord Lindley and one of Halsbury's recent appointments, the 84-year old Lord Brampton, 'probably the worst judge on the English bench in the nineteenth century: capricious, unfair and deceitful',[46] who had supported the Lord Chancellor in *Allen v Flood*, sat with the three Conservatives and the solitary Liberal, Lord Shand.[47] Beyond a keen belief in the rights of property and the maintenance of the Union, Halsbury had little in common with Henry Leathem, and still less with the Belfast butchers, yet his preoccupations would influence their future lives.

How the Law Stood

Quinn was a landmark in the judicial development of the law of tort: it consolidated civil conspiracy in order to compensate employers for the removal of criminal conspiracy from industrial relations in 1875; it also maintained the possibility of another new tort, intentional and unjustified interference with 'the right to trade'. In discussing *Quinn*, three cases – *Mogul Steamship Co. Ltd v McGregor Gow & Co.*,[48] *Temperton v Russell*,[49] and *Allen v Flood*[50] – are essential reference points.

In *Mogul*, the defendants were members of a combination of shipowners which sought to monopolise the China tea trade by offering shippers a range of benefits and detriments not to use the ships of competing non-members of the consortium. Shippers were offered rebates which were forfeited if non-association steamers were used, competitors' rates were undercut, and agents were threatened with loss of business if they dealt with competitors. The House of Lords, with a strong bench which included Halsbury, unanimously held that the plaintiffs, who had been refused admission to the cartel and lost business in consequence, had no cause for action. Interference with trade was lawful in the absence of intimidation, molestation or breach of contract, so long as its purpose was prosecuting commercial interests, not malicious injury of competitors or interference without just cause or excuse. As Lord Hannen put it: '... a different case would have arisen if the evidence had shown that the object of the defendants was a malicious one, namely to injure the plaintiffs whether they, the defendants, should be benefited or not'.[51] As Halsbury remarked:

> *It is impossible to suggest any malicious intention to injure rival traders, except in the sense that in proportion as one withdraws trade that other people might get, you, to that extent, injure a person's trade*

when you appropriate the trade to yourself. If such an injury, and the motive for its infliction … can be truly asserted to be a malicious motive within the meaning of the law that prohibits malicious injury to other people, all competition must be malicious and consequently unlawful …[52]

To ground liability some motive beyond commercial benefit – a personal grudge, political antipathy, xenophobia – must be demonstrated. This reasoning appeared to benefit trade unions seeking to prevent competition in the labour market and to achieve monopoly control of labour. It strengthened *dicta* in earlier trade union cases in which the courts recognised: 'Where the object is to benefit oneself it can seldom, perhaps it can never, be effected without some consequent loss or injury to someone else'.[53] *Mogul* was invoked in at least one case involving labour relations.[54] More problematic in relation to the laying to rest of criminal, and many believed all, conspiracy in relation to unions in the Conspiracy and Protection of Property Act 1875, however, was the view of some of the judges in *Mogul* that what was lawful on the part of an individual could become unlawful when perpetrated by a combination.[55]

As judicial restiveness at the settlement of the 1870s developed in the face of trade union resurgence from the late 1880s, it became apparent that there were limits to the courts' acceptance in 1892 of *Mogul's* animating principle that judges were not the best regulators of economic competition. Lord Hannen's 'different case' came before the Court of Appeal in the shape of *Temperton v Russell*. The decision confirmed the reality of civil conspiracy and the willingness of the judges to broaden the decision in *Lumley v Gye*,[56] a case which had demarcated the tort of inducement to breach of contract. Unable to pressurise Temperton, a supplier of a construction company with which they were in dispute, to boycott the firm, a committee of building unions in Hull persuaded one of his customers to break an existing contract and refuse to deal further with him. The court held the trade unionists liable not only for interference with existing contracts, sufficient in itself to ground liability, but, apparently extending *Lumley v Gye*, for conspiracy to interfere with the creation of future contracts – even though the defendants' conduct would have been lawful if perpetrated by an individual. The argument of Lord Esher seemed to be that even though there was no intention, separate from pursuit of trade union interests, to maliciously injure Temperton, combination to injure him by interfering with his right to freely conduct his business was itself malicious and unlawful. The firmest articulation of conspiracy to injure came from Lopes LJ: 'A combination to induce others not to deal with a particular individual, if done with the intent of injuring him, is an actionable wrong'.[57]

By the time *Quinn v Leathem* commenced its lengthy passage through the courts in 1896, this position had received sustenance from the Court of Appeal's decision in *Allen*. However, the reversal of that decision by the Law Lords in December 1897 raised doubts about the Hull case and may well have encouraged the successive appeals on the part of the Belfast butchers. On the face of it, there was a clear affinity between the two cases. In *Allen*, members of the United Society of Boilermakers discussed action against a group of shipwrights who were also employed by the Glengall Iron Company at Millwall but who had allegedly undertaken boilermakers' work for Mills and Knight at Rotherhithe. Thomas Allen, London district officer of the union, told management that the boilermakers would strike unless the shipwrights were removed, observing in *Quinn*-style language that 'they would not be allowed to work anywhere in London river.' They were discharged and sued Allen for interference with trade by maliciously inducing the company to dismiss the shipwrights.[58]

In what we have seen was a 6–3 majority verdict, the House of Lords assumed that on the facts there was no combination and therefore no conspiracy. Acting on his own initiative with no specific authority from the union leadership, Allen had simply informed the managers of the situation; he had not threatened them. Furthermore, no breach of contract was involved as the shipwrights were employed on a day-to-day basis and it was not wrongful to interfere with expectation of future trade relations. The majority declined to follow Halsbury's quest for the holy grail of an all-encompassing right of the individual to utilise his capital or labour as he wished, free of all interference – a quest Halsbury had temporarily forsaken in *Mogul*. No right to protection from malicious interference with employment relations subsisted. Allen had violated no legal right of the shipwrights to pursue their trade unmolested, and used no unlawful means in procuring their discharge. The case fell within the *Mogul* principles. Forceful pursuit of business or trade union interests was legitimate and could not be rendered unlawful by labelling, without precise legal definition and explanation, inevitable injury of the interests of competitors as 'malicious'.

For some of the judges, bad motive was irrelevant where pursuit of business interests was at stake: '... the existence of a bad motive in the case of an act which is not itself illegal will not convert that act into a civil wrong'.[59] If motive *was* relevant then no malicious motive could be discovered on these facts: ruthless competition between craft workers was analogous to cut-throat competition between entrepreneurs and should be treated analogously. Lord Shand concluded that the object was to benefit the boilermakers in their trade and the inescapable presence of the intrinsic element of injury or punishment did not detract from the legitimacy of their objects, still less render their actions malicious in any legal sense.[60] Lord Herschell criticised the tendency of jurors to interpret prosecution of self-interest as activated by malevolent rather than market motives:

> *I can think of no greater danger to the community than that a jury should be at liberty to impose the penalty of paying damages for acts which are otherwise lawful, because they chose, without any legal definition of the term, to say that they are malicious. No one would know what his rights were.*[61]

The case was notable for the intransigence of Halsbury, who insisted that the decision transgressed the traditional principles of the common law, and the defiant dignity of Herschell. He replied that he required no lessons in liberty from the Lord Chancellor and that freedom of action was at hazard when the courts restricted its principles because they found particular circumstances distasteful. Such circumstances would recur and the problem that Herschell put his finger on was exacerbated by the judges' refusal to spell out precise examples and codify principles beyond deciding on the facts facing them.[62] The determination not to absorb specifics into general principles when judging trade-union behaviour was signalled by Lord Macnaghten who supported the majority but acknowledged the limits of *Allen*. There could in other circumstances be civil liability for conspiracy, conduct by two might be actionable where the conduct of an individual was protected: '... the decision in this case can have no bearing on any case which involves the element of oppressive combination, the vice of which seems to me to depend on factors which are conspicuously absent in this case.'[63] He would discover such factors in *Quinn*.

The Case in the Courts

In *Allen* the majority of the Law Lords had been prepared to overturn the verdict of the jury, the decisions of the lower courts, and the 6–2 advice of the judges summoned by Halsbury to counsel them, by insisting on the application of similar criteria to both capital and labour and by taking craft unionism at its, perhaps sanitised, face value. In *Quinn* the jury, charged by the assize judge with deciding the issue, likewise found for the plaintiff. They held that the defendants had exceeded trade union purposes, of which it may be plausibly assumed the jurors possessed a restricted conception. The butchers had wrongfully and maliciously conspired to induce Leathem's customers or servants to refuse to deal with him and published blacklists with the intent and the effect of injuring him in his business. £200 damages were awarded against the butchers and an additional £50 against Davey, Dornan and Shaw who were held responsible for the blacklists. The Queen's Bench Divisional Court refused a motion to set aside the verdict with only a single dissentient, the Chief Baron Palles, and the decision was unanimously affirmed with costs in the Court of Appeal and the House of Lords.[64]

The majority view in *Allen* was replaced by representations of trade unionism as a vehicle of class war whose objectives and methods – the obstruction, even destruction, of business and the oppression of wage earners – were anything but legitimate. There was no room for analogy or assimilation to competition between capitalists here. In the lower courts the judges perceived the Irish events in terms of class and deplored 'the passions, the interests, the ignorance and error of a class, prone to dangerous means, conscious of political power, arrogant from past concession and confident in further aggression'.[65] As representatives of that class, the Belfast butchers were implicated in 'the intolerable scourge of boycotting ... great and galling oppression ... vengeance and an attempt to coerce and intimidate ... terrorism ... vengeance pure and simple ... their real operative motive was the punishment, injury and harm of Leathem.'[66] The Law Lords were more restrained. But they, too, saw Craig, Quinn and their confederates as 'wreaking their vengeance on Leathem's servants', inflicting 'acts of wanton aggression', and perpetrating 'organised and ruinous oppression'.[67]

The Irish courts remained unimpressed by O'Shaughnessy's attempts to normalise the episode and assimilate the butchers to the conventional desire of trade unions in Belfast and Dublin, not to speak of 'the greatest trade society in the world ... the profession to which he (counsel) belonged', to achieve a closed shop.[68] The Bench would have none of it. In the judicial narrative, what happened in County Antrim in 1895 is a morality tale, insulated from quotidian conflicts between capital and labour, quarantined from natural trade-union activity. The Belfast butchers appear as an alien intrusion bent on nothing less than Leathem's destruction: 'For no fault of his own, save that he would not obey the behest of a number of strangers who had no interest in him or his business, he has been ruined.'[69] McGibbon LJ, a Freemason, set the political tone at the Assizes: ' ... if it was in any other part of Ireland that would be what was called boycotting'.[70] It is difficult not to discern in

Quinn's far from judicious discourse of 'terrorism', 'boycotting' and 'vengeance' the shadow of the violence of recent Irish history. It is primarily freighted by ideological objections to militant trade unionism and genuine revulsion at the butchers' methods.

In important aspects the courts' version of what happened in *Quinn* – taken word for word from Leathem – differs little from the facts in *Allen*, at least the facts which were questioned in the Lords only by Halsbury and the shipwrights. In *Allen* as well as *Quinn*, trade unionists acted to control what they considered to be their job territory. In both cases dismissed workers could have 'walked the streets' or never again 'worked anywhere in London river' as a consequence of trade union demands, although that would probably be contingent on the state of the labour market. But there were also important differences of detail and depiction which permitted of emphasis and amplification. The English tradesman, Allen, was portrayed, after some argument between the judges, as little more than a postman communicating the boilermakers' resolve to quit work unless the shipwrights were removed. In the drama at Magill's Hotel, Lisburn, re-enacted through Leathem's memories, the belligerent butchers – 'unscrupulous enemies ... activated by malevolence ... the bearers of hatred, spite and ill will'[71] – are the flesh and blood engineers of Leathem's tragedy. The shipwrights, in contrast, are shadowy figures. Compared with William Flood, the butchers' intended victim Robert Dickie and his nine children – one judge generously increased his progeny to ten – are palpably real.

Leathem's conciliatory offer to concede ground and to enrol his servants in the Journeymen Butchers was central to this differentiation. The plaintiff in *Mogul*, too, had been refused admission to a combination and by analogy it could be urged that it was in the interests – it was certainly in the rules – of the butchers' union to give preference to unemployed members over those joining to keep their jobs. But *Mogul* dealt with discord between reified capitalist personalities, *Quinn* with a struggle between an articulate small businessman and real fleshers with bloody aprons and sharp cleavers. This is not to deny that the butchers' intractability towards Leathem's compromise was questionable. The emotive power of their peremptory rejection, in comparison with Allen's similar but diluted act of petty inhumanity, provided the basis for Halsbury's legally evasive assertion, embedded in the other judgments, that civilised jurisprudence demanded a remedy and that, comparing *Quinn* with *Allen* and *Mogul*, every case turned on its facts.[72]

The distinguishing of *Mogul* was unconvincing. The use of 'attractions and allurements' in that case, even if they destroyed a business, were not for Lord Brampton compatible with 'active interference in the right of every trader to carry on his business in his own manner' in *Quinn*.[73] Lord Lindley similarly asserted without argument that no infringement of rights had occurred in *Mogul*.[74] As the butchers' 'sheet anchor', *Allen* attracted greater attention. It was assailed in the lower courts for 'going very much too far' and for 'its disastrous character as affecting the liberties and property of at the least a very important class of the community'.[75] Even the sole dissentient in the Divisional Court claimed extravagantly that he was 'coerced' by *Allen*; that decision left him impotent to protect Leathem from 'the tyranny of a trade union'.[76] The judgments in the Divisional Court and the Court of Appeal are replete with deference to the minority view of Halsbury, termed, in keeping with the reputation for obsequiousness of the Irish judges, 'the supreme guardian of the law', whose 'masterly exposition of the law' enjoyed the allegiance of 'the vast preponderance of judicial opinion'.[77] *Allen*, it was claimed, had done no more than 'settled the law for the present as to a single defendant'.[78]

Such sentiments received the cordial commendation of Halsbury, although in another guise he was a powerful advocate of *stare decisis*. In relation to *Allen* he observed:

> *... every judgment must be read as applicable to the particular facts proved ... the generality of the expressions which may be found there are not intended to be expositions of the whole law, but governed and qualified by the particular facts of the case ... a case is only authority for what it actually decides. I entirely deny that it can be quoted for a proposition that may seem to follow logically from it.*[79]

Thus fortified, the Law Lords went on to decide, in the words of Lindley: 'The facts of this case are entirely different from those which the House had to consider in *Allen v Flood*.'[80] In *Allen v Flood* there were no threats and no conspiracy; simply a passing over of information by an individual in pursuit of legitimate trade interests with no overriding and contaminating intention to injure. The obvious irony was that Halsbury had not himself accepted the 'facts' of *Allen*; yet he now invoked them to reverse his earlier defeat.[81]

In *Quinn*, Lord Robertson simply concurred in the judgment of Holmes LJ in the Appeal Court that there was a conspiracy to injure, while Halsbury was terse. He relied on the judgments of Brampton, a poor civil lawyer, and Lindley whose reasoning has been subjected to fundamental critique, for the insertion into the law of the tort of conspiracy to injure through violation of his cherished right of freedom of property. If the courts could discern a motive to occasion harm in combination with others, the use of unlawful means to achieve that object was not necessary. The principle that behaviour lawful on the part of an individual acting on his own account became unlawful when an individual acted in concert with others with intent to inflict harm now carried the day.[82] Crucially, the fact that trade unionists were presumed to act in furtherance of the perceived interests of their members provided no lawful justification for interference with an individual's freedom to dispose of his capital or labour as he wished by inducing employees or customers of the latter to break their contracts, or, expanding on *Lumley v Gye*, not to deal with him.

Essentially, *Quinn v Leathem* adopted the position of Lord Esher in the Court of Appeal which informed the views of the minority in *Allen*: if persuasion to disrupt contractual relations embodied intent to injure, the persuasion was malicious and the malice rendered unlawful what otherwise would be lawful. However, the judgments were uneven and at times confusing. Lord Macnaghten's earlier desertion of conservatism in *Allen* was revealed as temporary: for him the case was covered by *Temperton* and involved the two torts of conspiracy to injure and unjustified interference with contractual relations which were largely assumed rather than argued and specified. There was no written contract between Leathem and Munce and none of Munce's workers suffered inducement, indeed the only inducement to breach which pertained appeared to be the resignation of one of Leathem's assistants.

Lord Shand, like Macnaghten a member of the majority in *Allen*, also changed his position. He asserted in an unimpressive opinion that Allen intended to promote the boilermakers' interests while Quinn's purpose was to injure Leathem's business. Brampton based himself on broad grounds: liability lay for conspiracy and for 'invasion of the civil rights of another person'. For Lindley there was a right to earn one's living in one's own way and to deal with those who are willing to deal with you. This applied equally to capital and labour. But no such right, he claimed without persuasive explanation, had been infringed in *Mogul*. Leathem, in contrast, had been intimidated and coerced, the phrases went undefined, by the butchers. While they could probably be assumed to have acted in what they conceived as the interests of their members, they had also acted maliciously with intent to injure. That was the overriding object. Lindley concluded that collective action may coerce where individual action may not. What was involved was malicious conspiracy and malicious inducement of customers and employees not to deal with Leathem. The majority stated that the 1875 Act's prohibition of criminal conspiracy was irrelevant while Macnaghten believed that there was no trade dispute and Lindley felt that it did not matter.

Quinn confirmed the existence of a tort of conspiracy. But as Shand and Lindley stated that the butchers' behaviour might have been actionable if perpetrated by an individual, it also kept alive the issue of a tort of interference with freedom of trade, business or employment.[83] The comfort that trade unionists had extracted from *Mogul* and *Allen* evaporated. Despite Lindley's protestations, what went for capital did not go for labour. Before the Lords, Quinn's counsel had insisted:

> *... the law is settled by the Mogul case ... whether the effect or intention be to injure another, it is lawful to do these things in order to secure a monopoly, or benefit oneself... To promote the interests of a trade union is as legitimate as to struggle for the monopoly of a particular business.*[84]

Despite the harshness of its execution, the purpose of the butchers, as the purpose in *Mogul* or in *Allen*, was to secure a monopoly by interfering with the liberties of competitors who might injure the butchers or the shipping cartel by undercutting or the boilermakers by taking their work. The conclusion that, unlike the boilermakers or the shipping cartel, whose activities likewise threatened to provoke loss of profits and/or employment, the butchers harboured a defining malicious intention or acted from bad motive extraneous to the prosecution of trade purposes, was imputed, unargued and unproven. In *Quinn*, there was no proper attempt to analyse intention, confront and weigh mixed motives or formulate distinctions between predominant and subordinate motives as occurred in later case law. There was no express endeavour to disentangle foreign, malicious motive from the pursuit of economic and organisational self-interest, registered legitimate in *Mogul* and accepted in *Allen* – still less to explicitly discuss social policy.[85]

What dominated the judgments was the rhetoric of individual rights stemming from revulsion at rough justice sanitized and tolerated in earlier cases. Whether we attribute the course of events to ideological or class bias,[86] *Quinn* affirmed, as the contemporary constitutional analyst A V Dicey noted,[87] the legislative role performed by the judiciary, although he failed to emphasise the unsuitability for that role of men not only with their background and interests but with their methods. It is unfortunate that the working-class response did not embrace reform of the judiciary as well as reform of their decisions.

Quinn, the Labour Movement and the Trade Disputes Act 1906

Who paid for the butchers' appeals? What was the extent of trade union support for their case? What was the response to the Lords' decision? We know little about the earlier progress of the case. The trades' council minutes for 30 August 1895 record that 'the Butchers' Society' had requested that a deputation from the council attend their meeting that evening. Thereafter the written record is silent until February 1899 when the union asked the trades' council to help raise a fund to defray the expenses of the case then awaiting judgment in the Court of Appeal. Advised by Joseph Donnelly, they were already contemplating an appeal to the Lords in the event of a reverse.[88]

Leathem's supporters saluted his determination in confronting 'the almost inexhaustible resources of trade unionism'.[89] The reality was somewhat different. The trades' council's leaders' first reflex was to look towards Dublin and the Irish Trades Union Congress, to which they were affiliated, for financial sustenance. The 1899 Irish Congress agreed to circulate an appeal for funds. But by the following spring, the butchers were complaining that the Irish TUC's Parliamentary Committee had not carried out this instruction.[90] By the time the appeal to the Lords was lodged on 25 April 1900 there were conflicting reports. The butchers themselves were unhappy. Their representatives had visited affiliates of the trades council 'and had met with a very poor reception which was very disheartening on their part, considering it was a test case of the rights of Trade Unions in this city'.[91] They emphasised 'the difficult position' they were in and 'hoped that even now something would be done on their behalf'.[92] Yet at this stage it was reported that £187 had been granted by local societies.[93]

William Walker, the trades' council secretary, a respected leader of Belfast labour, took a hand. He travelled with the butchers' representatives to Dublin and Cork, addressing 37 meetings 'from every one of which they received great encouragement'.[94] Donations were soon arriving from the South but the 1900 Irish Congress produced conflict over the issue. Walker, who was often critical of the Irish Congress, and his supporters from the North took the Parliamentary Committee to task and it was suggested that support for its inaction by Belfast delegates was inimical to the butchers' cause. A problem seems to have been the reluctance of trade unionists to hand over funds until the appeal had been lodged. But the appeal could not be lodged until the butchers paid Leathem's costs into court. Two prominent trades' council activists, the cautious Alexander Taylor of the Irish Linenlappers and Alexander Bowman of the Flaxdressers, a Liberal and the founder secretary of the trades' council, were members of the Irish Parliamentary Committee and they strongly defended its actions. Bowman, its chairman, stated, that the Parliamentary Committee had understandably hushed up the matter because '... it was not right to publish to the world that they had appealed to 50,000 organised workers, in Ireland, without their receiving one penny in support of a weak society'.[95] Some delegates, while insisting that they backed the butchers, maintained their criticism of their methods.[96]

In addition to participating in the Irish Congress from its inception in 1894, delegates from the Belfast Trades' Council had attended the Congresses of the British TUC. This stopped with the exclusion of trades' council delegates and the suspension of special arrangements for Irish representation in 1895, although Irish delegates were sometimes included in the delegations of their British unions. There was some feeling in Belfast that the British TUC was relatively uninterested in Irish problems. This was certainly true of the TUC Parliamentary Committee: it believed that the Irish Congress was divisive and should be dissolved.[97] Nonetheless, attention in Belfast now turned towards London. It was suggested that the butchers should affiliate to the British TUC and send representatives to the 1900 Congress to be held in Huddersfield, in order to gain assistance for their cause. Throughout the affair they had become increasingly dependent on more experienced and articulate advocates, and they were accompanied to Yorkshire by a trades council delegation.[98]

The butchers' visit was prefaced by a letter to the secretary of the TUC Parliamentary Committee, the ailing former Liberal MP and vice-president of the Miners' Federation of Great Britain, Sam Woods, requesting the committee's help in raising funds.[99] But the butchers received short shrift from the Lib-Lab establishment in London. When the letter was read to the committee on 29 August, William Davis, the general secretary of the Amalgamated Brassworkers, a powerful voice in the TUC and a resolute opponent of socialism, moved 'That seeing there are so many appeals in hand the Parliamentary Committee cannot entertain the matter.'[100] Seconded by Robert Knight, the recently retired general secretary of the Boilermakers and another conservative Lib-Lab, Davis's motion was carried, with no opposition minuted. Before the summer of 1900 the leaders of the British TUC knew little about the case and were prepared to do less about it.

There is no record of the butchers' union affiliating to the TUC, but a thousand copies of an appeal for funds were printed and distributed to the delegates at Huddersfield. The Belfast Trades Council representatives were granted speaking rights which they used effectively. Both

Walker and Edward McInnes, the Belfast-based organiser of the British general union, the National Amalgamated Union of Labour, appealed for assistance and funds for the case.[101] The report is a little confusing. After Walker gave details of what was recorded as 'a quarrel at Belfast', for which the blame was placed entirely on Leathem 'who dismissed all his union hands and engaged all non-unionists', McInnes moved support for the appeal to the Lords requiring that 'the Parliamentary Committee be instructed ... to take such action as will give effect to the resolution'.[102] Walker's motion was seconded by the organiser of the Gasworkers and General Labourers, the socialist Scot and Irish nationalist, Pete Curran, who was himself no stranger to litigation. It was carried unanimously. But matters were re-opened by the Bristol miners' leader, the Lib-Lab William Whitefield, who 'argued that the Irish trade unionists ought to bear their own responsibilities'.[103] It was only 'on a division' that the issue was finally referred to the Parliamentary Committee. In October an appeal for funds for *Taff Vale*, *Quinn* and striking Liverpool dockers was circulated and in April 1901 the Committee sent the Belfast Trades Council a far from generous £75 towards the Lords appeal.[104]

Admittedly the British leaders had a lot to occupy them and the butchers' case was overshadowed by *Taff Vale*. But three years earlier the much smaller Dublin Trades Council had collected £150 for the locked out Belfast engineers, while in 1899–1900 the TUC Parliamentary Committee had proposed a levy on members and had collected £740 in support of an abortive appeal of *Lyons v Wilkins* to the House of Lords. Their record on what they called 'the Irish case' was less than remarkable.[105] Further efforts by Walker, who had met Woods in London in February 1901, to extract further support met with mixed success.[106] As late as March, the butchers were seeking a loan from the Railway Servants, similarly ensnared in *Taff Vale*, to cover the costs of the case. Nonetheless, despite conflicting reports of the sums collected, Walker felt able to announce in April 1901 that 'they had now paid over to the solicitor the total amount necessary to prosecute their appeal to the House of Lords. (Hear, Hear.) He hoped it would be as satisfactory there as it had in the past.'[107]

If this was a reference to trade unionists' continuing faith in *Allen* – talismanic short-hand notes of that case were passed by the Boilermakers to the butchers – they were not slow in learning the lessons of the Lords' decision. That October Belfast Trades' Council established a committee to examine the impact on trade union activities of the cases since *Temperton*. Delegates reflected on:

The practical uselessness of expending large sums of money in contesting erratic and technical judicial interpretation … the council were therefore of the opinion that the money thus spent could be more usefully expended on the advancement of direct labour representation in Parliament and that this was the only solution to labour inequalities.[108]

But far from enjoying sympathy, as *Quinn* was applied in other cases and as a four-year debate over reform of the law unfolded, the Belfast butchers endured disregard or criticism from almost all sides. The Lords' decision provoked no great comment in the British press, although it was greeted with approbation in Belfast by both the Unionist and Nationalist newspapers. There was a brief report on *Quinn* at the 1902 TUC. The case scarcely figured thereafter in the deliberations of Congress or the chronicles of the TUC's legislative endeavours: the banner of reform was emblazoned *Taff Vale* and it was *Taff Vale* that was remembered.[109]

Quinn was an embarrassment and a weapon in the hands of opponents of legislative reform who brandished it to muddy and divert discussion of legal principles and social policy. In the 1902 House of Commons debate, Liberal lawyers such as Haldane (who – it is to be recalled – represented Leathem in the House of Lords) were at pains to admit the complaints of Conservative MPs: 'No one in the course of this debate has defended the proceedings of the trade union in the case of *Quinn v Leathem* and nobody has assailed the result arrived at by the judges in that particular case.'[110] It was, he claimed, the confusion of the law that required address. Sir Robert Reid, who, as Lord Loreburn, would steer the 1906 Act onto the statute book, described the conduct of the butchers as 'abominable … Nobody defends that …'[111] He was only concerned at the wider implications of civil conspiracy. Fastidiousness was not general on the Liberal benches. In an ironic endorsement of the social fears of the Irish judges, John Burns suggested to the Nationalist leader, John Redmond, that his support for the TUC Bill would reap its own reward: it would secure protection for boycotting landlords in rural Ireland.[112]

For the Conservatives, however, *Quinn* demonstrated the necessity of the new torts. Invocation of what might have happened on the streets of Lisburn, suitably extended, attained new heights as Sir Edward Carson recited at Westminster the parable of his fellow Orangeman, Henry Leathem:

'I will pay their fines to the union. I will let them become trade unionists so that my men may be working exactly within the new rules.' And

the men for the trade union said, 'No, that is not enough for us. They must be punished. They must walk the streets with their families and children for twelve months before they are allowed to be employed anywhere, and if necessary they must starve' ... I would like to know what will be the remedy after this Bill becomes law for a case which I call not merely a case of tyranny, but a case which is a disgrace to any Christian community.[113]

The architect of *Quinn* remained unrepentant. In the face of the final Bill which set his efforts at naught, Halsbury reflected: 'Language fails me ... Anything more outrageously unjust, anything more tyrannical I can hardly conceive ... This is a Bill for the purpose of legalising tyranny.'[114] It was left to the Liberal MP, Clem Edwards, an advocate and organiser of the 'new unionism', to try to get at the broader issues of inducement to breach of contract, secondary action and conspiracy:

... he could not differentiate the Mogul case from that of "Quinn v Leathem" because in the Mogul case a great body of shipowners combined to compel shippers to accept their terms. The very essence of the whole case was boycotting. What the unions were asking was that the law as laid down for other members of the community should be the law as applied to the trade unions.[115]

Reflections

Like wars and revolutions, trade disputes and strikes rarely assume the form desired or sometimes depicted by their protagonists and partisans and at least some of their chroniclers. Trade union activists are infrequently knights in shining armour or the tyrants deplored by Carson and Halsbury. It is not surprising that, when we examine *Quinn* closely, the armour and the iconography of 1906 and its antecedents appear a little tarnished. The episode suggests the diversity and deficiencies of the labour movement in Britain and Ireland a hundred years ago and the difficulties it faced. Manichean narratives of the events preceding the Trade Disputes Act require recasting. But we should not take revisionism too far so that the significant realities of class struggle dissolve into disconnected episodes and tales of sound and fury signifying very little.

The Belfast butchers attempted, however imperfectly, to impose an element of control and security on the vicissitudes of the labour market and organised to improve the condition of those it exploited. The solidarity that the local labour movement demonstrated was, in the end, impressive. Although there was criticism on the part of some activists, the majority closed ranks and guided and sustained those they recognised as members of their class, whose interests, whatever their differences, they ultimately shared. The Belfast working class was the real protagonist of this story. More broadly, despite something less than enthusiasm for the butchers' methods in some quarters, the combined impact of trade-union activity in a multitude of very different situations facilitated political change. Out of fragmentation and adversity, came unity and progress. Workers were protected from the impact of judicial legislation, the 1906 Act was passed, and the Labour Party was formed. Historians need to acknowledge difference, division and particularity but also their transcendence.

Belfast Trades' Council had subscribed to the Labour Electoral Association as early as the 1880s, and in 1897 six of its representatives had won council seats, albeit on carefully moderated demands which eschewed socialism, nationalism and the Catholic wards.[116] In 1902, the Trades' Council affiliated to the Labour Representation Committee and they were followed in 1906 by the Journeymen Butchers.[117] O'Shaughnessy, the butchers' QC, had prophesied that Leathem's assault on the union would prove 'vain and futile as the society would rise again'.[118] Its subsequent fortunes hardly evoked the Phoenix, but membership did increase from 115 in 1904 to a still tiny 173 four years later.[119] It survived another 30 years before being absorbed by the British-based Transport and General Workers' Union in 1937.[120] In contrast to the relative silence that greeted the butchers' defeat, Leathem's triumphant supporters celebrated his 'indomitable pluck and perseverance' in confounding a Goliath.[121] Leathem's costs had been paid, but it seems that he was unable to extract anything from Quinn and his fellow butchers: Lisburn businessmen floated a fund to raise the £1,000 they claimed he was out of pocket.[122] His name, coupled with that of his antagonist, was preserved for posterity in the law books and in the lecture halls where students sometimes believed that it was Leathem, the Lisburn Orangeman, who was the militant Belfast butcher.

The butchers' staunchest supporter, William Walker, emerged as the animating force of the Belfast Labour Representation Committee, stood unsuccessfully for Parliament and was elected to the executive of the Labour Party, becoming vice-chairman in 1911. But Walker's attempts to reconcile Presbyterianism, Ulster Unionism and socialism fell apart. In 1912, the year of the expulsion of Catholics, nationalists and socialists from the shipyards, he quit the labour movement and became a

National Insurance inspector. His career exemplified the tensions between sectarianism and unity in the extreme conditions of the north-east of Ireland – the context of the trade unionism *in extremis* of *Quinn* – and the triumph of the former.[123]

The Trade Disputes Act in s. 1 and the second limb of s. 3 respectively, sought to immunize trade unionists against the impact of *Quinn* in relation to civil conspiracy and interference with the freedom of capital or labour. Restoring, in the fanciful words of Lord Loreburn, the law as it had existed between the Norman Conquest and 1901, the Act endured for most of the 20th century. The struggle to achieve it, with all its imperfections, retains a relevance for contemporary trade unionists facing the challenges of an unregulated labour market in a new, neo-liberal century. For they graphically affirm the long-term futility of attempts to suppress trade unionism, the dynamism of history, and the enduring ability of political forces to effect fundamental legal and social change.

Thanks to Andrew Boyd, Boyd Black, Keith Ewing, Alan Campbell, Carolyn Jones, Tony Kerr, Dave Lyddon, Emmet O'Connor and Paul Smith for their help.

Notes

1 The case receives very brief attention in most historical work on trade unionism: see, for example, H A Clegg, A Fox and A F Thompson, *A History of British Trade Unions since 1889, vol. 1, 1889–1910* (1964), pp 309–10; W H Fraser, *A History of British Trade Unionism, 1700–1998* (1999), p 100. There is only a sentence in H Pelling, *A History of British Trade Unions* (5th edn,1992), p 111, and A J Reid, *United We Stand: A History of Britain's Trade Unions* (2004), pp 259–60. Moreover, comment is terse in discussions of the 1906 Act: see, for example, K D Brown, 'Trade Unions and the Law', in C Wrigley (ed), *A History of British Industrial Relations, 1875–1914* (1982), pp 121–22. See also A Boyd, *The Rise of the Irish Trade Unions* (2nd ed, 1985), p 71; J W Boyle, *The Irish Labor Movement in the Nineteenth Century* (1988), pp 99, 225–6.

2 See, for example, Clegg *et al*, above, pp 326–63; A Fox, *History and Heritage: The Social Origins of the British Industrial Relations System* (1985), pp 174–279.

3 But see the powerful overview, M J Klarman, 'The Judges versus the Unions: The Development of Labour Law, 1867–1913' (1989) 75 *Virginia Law Review* 1487 , and D Brodie, *A History of British Labour Law, 1867–1945* (2003), pp 27–117.

4 J McIlroy, 'Founding Fathers' (2005) 70 *Labour History Review* 234.

5 *Lisburn Standard*, 28 March 1896. Census of Ireland, 1901, Census Enumerators' Books, Public Record Office of Northern Ireland (PRONI). I am grateful to Heather Stanley and Marc Croft for providing me with copies. For Lisburn, see J Bardon, *A History of Ulster* (2001), p 398.

6 R Perren, *The Meat Trade in Britain, 1840–1914* (1978), p 155. This paragraph draws on Perren, J B Jefferys, *Retail Trading in Britain, 1850–1950* (1954), pp 181–91, and *Belfast News-Letter*, 1 August 1896.

7 A C Hepburn, *A Past Apart: Studies in the History of Catholic Belfast, 1850–1950* (1996), pp 77, 224; B Black, 'Re-Assessing Irish Industrial Relations and Labour History: The North-East of Ireland up to 1921' (2002) 14 *Historical Studies in Industrial Relations* 57 (Table 5). The 1901 census demonstrates that there were women butchers in a male, but often family, profession.

8 See J C Beckett *et al., Belfast: The Making of the City, 1800–1914* (1983); A C Hepburn, 'Work, Class and Religion in Belfast, 1871–1911' (1983) 10 *Irish Economic History* 33; H Patterson, *Class Conflict and Sectarianism: The Protestant Working Class and the Belfast Labour Movement, 1868–1920* (1980); A Morgan, *Labour and Partition: The Belfast Working Class, 1905–1923* (1991), pp 3–23.

9 J D Clarkson, *Labor and Nationalism in Ireland* (1925); Boyle, above, pp 157–188, 224–232; Morgan, above, pp 3–23; E O'Connor, *A Labour History of Ireland, 1824–1960* (1993); Black, above; P G Collins, *Belfast Trades Council, 1881–1921* (Unpublished PhD, University of Ulster, 1988).

10 *Reports of the Registrar of Friendly Societies*, 1891–1908, Part C, Trade Unions.

11 This and succeeding paragraphs draw on *Leathem v Craig* [1896] 2 IR 667; *Quinn v Leathem* [1901] AC 495; *Belfast News-Letter*, and *Irish Times*, 24 July 1896; *Lisburn Standard*, 25 July, 10 August 1896. So far as I can discern, nothing of substance has been written about trade unionism among butchers in Britain or Ireland. For America, see D Brody, *The Butcher Workmen: A Study of Unionization* (1964).

12 PRONI, T/3291

13 British Library of Economic and Political Science, London School of Economics, Origins and Development of the Labour Party at Local Level: Minutes of Belfast Trades Council [hereafter BTC], 16 May, 8 June 1894.

14 BTC Minutes 25 April, 16 May, 8 June, 16 July 1894.

15 BTC Minutes 29 July 1900. No papers of the union from this period can be traced and no returns were made to the Registrar of Friendly Societies. This may suggest a certain secrecy but in 1897, for example, only 33 of the 91 Irish unions registered, which represented a small proportion of Irish members, filed returns. *Report of the Chief Registrar of Friendly Societies*, 1897, Trade Unions, Part C, p 28.

16 [1896] 2 IR 667, at p 671. Quinn's Catholic name and his consorting with Protestants, Heuston reflects, would not have commended him to a jury of Presbyterian merchants. As we shall see, the hazard is plausible, although Quinn was also a Protestant name. The jurors may also have subscribed to competing Protestant creeds and the stratagem, whatever its rationale, proved unsuccessful: R F Heuston, 'Judicial Prosopography' (1986) 102 *Law Quarterly Review* 109.

17 *Lisburn Standard*, 25 July 1896. The reference is presumably to John Hampden who brought the test case on ship money to contest Charles I's oppressive taxation policy.

18 Collins, above, p 102. It should be noted that this account confuses the Belfast Journeymen Butchers with a later organisation, the Northern Ireland Operative Butchers, while Leathem's customer becomes 'Munro' rather than Munce: *ibid*.

19 The only references are to Clegg *et al.* above, which does not support this interpretation.

20 TUC Annual Report 1900, p 58. The references in the law reports to Leathem's men being required to pay 'fines' and 'debts' might also be taken to suggest past dealings with the union.

21 [1901] AC 495, at p 516.

22 *Lisburn Standard*, 25 July 1896.

23 [1901] AC 495, at pp 516–17.

24 *Ibid*.

25 *Ibid*. It is difficult to follow the Trades Council's early involvement in the affair as its papers from late 1895 to early 1897 are missing.

26 [1901] AC 495, at p 518.

27 *Ibid*, the language distilling Brampton's conception of union recruitment; *Lisburn Standard*, 25 July 1896.

28 See Chapter 1 above.

29 *Belfast News-Letter*, 24 July 1896.

30 BTC Minutes, 29 June 1900.

31 *Lisburn Standard*, 21 May, 16 July 1898, 18 July 1901. For a portrait of a Lisburn Orange Lodge in the nineteenth century, see R Dudley Edwards, *The Faithful Tribe: An Intimate Portrait of the Loyal Institutions* (1999), pp 206–27.

32 *Lisburn Herald*, 18 January 1896, 19 January, 20 July, 31 August 1901; *Lisburn Standard*, 20 July 1901.

33 Andrew Boyd to author, 24 August, 3 September 2005.

34 PRONI, 1901 Census of Ireland. The reference to 'Norfolk Street, *Falls Road*' (*Belfast News-Letter*, 24 July 1896, my emphasis) may be relevant in Craig's case. Davey's successor as the union secretary, William Conlon, was almost certainly a Catholic. Many Catholics worked at the Belfast abattoir which was in 'the Markets', then as now an exclusively Catholic area. Cf E Jones, *A Social History of Belfast* (1960), pp 190–99.

35 McGrath was part of the trade union team throughout the case and Michael McInerney, a Liberal QC, joined it in the Irish Court of Appeal. This paragraph is based on F E Ball, *The Judges in Ireland 1221–1921, vol. 2* (1993); *DNB; Who Was Who*; and M Stenton and S Lees, *Who's Who of British Members of Parliament, vol. 2, 1886–1918* (1978).

36 D Duman, *The English and Colonial Bars in the Nineteenth Century* (1983), pp 169–98.

37 A A Paterson, 'Judges: A Political Elite?' (1974) 1 *British Journal of Law and Society* 122; Heuston, 'Judicial Prosopography', above,, p 93; *Quinn v Leathem* [1901] AC 495, at pp 512, 532. R Stevens, *Law and Politics: The House of Lords as a Judicial Body, 1800–1976* (1979), p 93, follows Paterson in stating Davey was not invited to sit. To add to the confusion, Heuston subsequently states that there were seventeen judges whereas even including Davey gives a total of sixteen (*ibid*, p 108). It is clear from the (1901) *Law Times Reports* 289 and the (1901) *Times Law Reports* 749 that Davey did not sit.

38 2 IR 667, at p 726.

39 HC Deb, 25 April 1906, col 1493 (Sir W Robson).

40 Report of the Royal Commission on Trades Disputes and Trade Combinations (Chair: Lord Dunedin), Cd 2825, 1906. Evidence, Qq 613, 625-6, 629.

41 D Duman, *The Judicial Bench in England*, 1727–1875 (1982). Macnaghten was the third signatory after Sir Edward Carson and Lord Birkenhead of the Ulster Covenant in 1912: Stevens, above, p 110.

42 Apart from Lindley's judgments in *Quinn* and *Allen v Flood* in the Appeal Court, see *Lyons v Wilkins* [1896] 1 Ch 811; [1899] 1 Ch 255 and his opinion of the 1906 Bill in *The Times*, 10 December 1906.

43 HL Debs, 4 December 1906, col 705.

44 See R F V Heuston, *Lives of the Lord Chancellors, 1885–1940* (1964), ch 5; Stevens, above. pp 84–5.

45 Heuston, *Lives*, above, pp 118–22. However, Heuston, 'Judicial

Prosopography', above pp 91–2, saw two points in Halsbury's favour: none of the Law Lords had tried a case at first instance in England and there were evidential issues; fundamentally, *Allen* was an extremely important case.

46 Heuston, *Lives*, above p 58.

47 Nonetheless, it is difficult in the light of the alternatives available, to see how a different panel would have provided a decision in the union's favour: see Heuston, 'Judicial Prosopography', above, pp 110–12.

48 [1892] AC 25.

49 [1893] 1 QB 715.

50 [1898] AC 1. On the economic torts see Lord Wedderburn, *The Worker and the Law* (3rd ed,1986), pp 29–33; H Collins, K D Ewing and A McColgan, *Labour Law: Text and Materials* (2nd ed, 2005), pp 869 - 80; Brodie, above, pp 28–38; Klarman, above.

51 [1892] AC 25, at p 59.

52 [1892] AC 25, at p 37.

53 *Connor v Kent* [1891] 2 QB 545, at p 563.

54 *Jenkinson v Neild* (1892) 8 TLR 549.

55 [1892] AC 25, at p 50 (Morris) and p 51 (Hannen).

56 [1853] 2 E & B 216.

57 [1893] 1 QB 715, at p 731. And see R Brown, 'The Temperton v Russell Case (1893): The Beginning of the Legal Offensive Against the Unions' (1971) 23 *Bulletin of Economic Research* 50.

58 [1898] AC 1, at p 71.

59 *Ibid*, at p 92 (Lord Watson).

60 *Ibid*, at p 164.

61 *Ibid*, at p 118.

62 *Ibid*, at p 90 (Lord Halsbury), pp 142, 143 (Lord Herschell).

63 *Ibid*, at p 153. See also pp 168–9 (Lord Shand) and p 170 (Lord Davey).

64 *Quinn v Leathem* [1901] AC 495, pp 495–502. Leathem sought to recover £500. The Appeal Court removed the additional £50 damages initially awarded as the blacklisting was part of the conspiracy: *ibid*, p 502.

65 *Leathem v Craig* [1899] 2 IR 667, at para 701 (O'Brien J). Craig died before the House of Lords appeal was brought and Quinn became the sole appellant.

66 *Leathem v Craig* [1899] 2 IR 667, at paras 680 (Andrews J), 727, 729, 730 (Sir P O'Brien).

67 *Quinn v Leathem* [1901] AC 495, at paragraphs 511, 512 (Lord Macnaghten), 528, 531 (Brampton). The term 'boycotting' was employed by none of the Law Lords although they referred to 'black lists'. 'Boycotting' referred to the ostracism by tenants of Lord Erne's agent, Sir Charles Boycott, and had been coined as recently as the Irish Land League wars of the 1880s – see C Townshend, *Political Violence in Ireland: Government and Resistance since 1848* (1983).

68 *Belfast News-Letter*, 24 July 1896.

69 *Leathem v Craig* [1899] 2 IR 667, at para 775 (Lord Porter).

70 *Belfast News-Letter*, 24 July 1896.
71 *Quinn v Leathem* [1901] AC 495, at p 531 (Lord Brampton).
72 *Ibid*, at p 506.
73 *Ibid*, at p 527 (Lord Brampton).
74 *Ibid*, at p 539.
75 *Leathem v Craig* [1899] 2 IR 667, at paras 675–76 (Andrews J).
76 *Ibid*, at para 701 (Palles CB).
77 *Ibid*, at para 687 (O'Brien J).
78 *Ibid*, at para 689 (O'Brien J) and see the comments of Lord Porter at p 758.
79 [1901] AC 495, at p 506.
80 *Ibid*, at p 536.
81 *Allen v Flood* [1898] AC 1, at p 507.
82 [1901] AC 495, at p 511 (Lord Macnaghten). However, Lord Shand at p 513 and Lord Lindley at p 537 assumed that the butchers' behaviour would have been unlawful if perpetrated by an individual. For criticism of the reasoning behind Lord Lindley's elaboration of the individual's right to earn a living unimpeded, see W N Hohfeld, *Fundamental Legal Conceptions as Applied to Judicial Reasoning* (2001 ed), pp 16–17.
83 For the persistence of the idea through the century, see H Carty, 'Unlawful Interference with Trade' [1983] 3 *Legal Studies* 193.
84 [1901] AC 495, at p 503.
85 In this *Quinn* may be unfavourably compared with *Crofter Hand-Woven Harris Tweed Co Ltd v Veitch* [1942] AC 435, see chapter 5 below.
86 See the illuminating discussion in Klarman, above, pp 1574–90.
87 A V D[icey] (18**) 18 *Law Quarterly Review* 5.
88 BTC Minutes, 30 August 1895, Executive Committee, 10 February 1899. See n 21 above.
89 *Lisburn Herald*, 17 August 1901.
90 BTC Minutes, EC, 12 May 1899, 24 March 1900.
91 *Ibid*.
92 *Ibid*.
93 BTC Minutes, 21 April 1900.
94 BTC Minutes, 19 May 1900.
95 BTC Minutes, 29 June, 27 July 1900.
96 *Ibid*.
97 Boyle, above, pp 146–7, 150–2, 227–8.
98 BTC Minutes, EC, 20, 30 July 1900.
99 TUC Parliamentary Committee, Minutes, 29 August 1900.
100 *Ibid*.
101 BTC Minutes, 3 August 1900; TUC Annual Report, 1900, p 58. The report refers to 'Mr McGuiness' but the speaker was almost certainly Walker's supporter, Edward McInnes.
102 TUC Annual Report 1900, p 58.
103 *Ibid*.
104 TUC Parliamentary Committee, Minutes, 17 October 1900, 29 April 1901;

BTC Minutes 16 November 1900, 3 April 1901.

105 Boyle, above, p 168; TUC Annual Report 1900, p 54; TUC Annual Report 1902, p 50.

106 BTC Minutes, EC, 28 February 1901.

107 BTC Minutes, 14 March, 3 April 1901; Boyle, above p 276, cites a report that by July 1900 the Trades Council had collected £3,000 for *Quinn*, which seems implausible.

108 BTC Minutes, 1 August, 21 September, 19 October 1901.

109 *Giblan v National Amalgamated Labourers' Union of Great Britain and Ireland* [1903] 2 KB 600. See *The Times, Manchester Guardian, Irish Times, Belfast News-Letter*, 6 August 1901. TUC Annual Report 1901, pp 49–50, 48–9, 60–5; TUC Annual Report 1906, pp 53–63; TUC Annual Report 1907, pp 50–61.

110 HC Deb, 14 May 1902, col 320.

111 *Ibid*, cols 308, 314, 316. But see also the comments on *Quinn* of the Attorney-General, Sir J Walton, HC Deb, 19 March 1906, col. 1298, and the Solicitor-General, Sir W Robson, HC Deb, 25 April 1906, col. 1493. Parallels might be drawn between the difficulties which the Sawgrinders, perpetrators of the 'Sheffield outrages' of 1866, proffered to the constitution of a responsible Liberal discourse of reform prior to 1871 and the albeit smaller problems that the butchers represented in 1906. See the comments in J McIlroy, 'Financial Malpractice in British Trade Unions, 1800–1930: The Background to and Consequences of *Hornby v Close*' (1998) 6 *Historical Studies in Industrial Relations* 41; and more generally, M. Curthoys, *Government, Labour and the Law in Mid-Victorian Britain: The Trade Union Legislation of the 1870s* (2004).

112 Brown, above, p 130. Burns's legal opinion was at best controversial.

113 HC Deb, 28 March 1906, col 1324.

114 HL Deb, 4 December 1906, cols 707, 709.

115 HC Deb, 25 April 1906, col. 1516.

116 Boyle, above, pp 157–70.

117 Labour History Archive and Study Centre, Manchester, Labour Party General Correspondence, LP/GC/4/11, LP/GC/5/30–1, LP/GC/11/96–121, LP/GC/13/97.

118 *Lisburn Standard*, 25 July 1896.

119 Collins, above, Appendix 4, p 325.

120 Emmet O'Connor to author, 10 August 2005; Andrew Boyd to author, 24 August 2005. Cf J Eaton and C Gill, *The Trade Union Directory* (1981), p 67: in Ireland the British-based union is known as the Amalgamated Transport and General Workers' Union to distinguish it from the Irish Transport and General Workers' Union.

121 *Lisburn Herald*, 17, 31 August 1901.

122 *Ibid*.

123 See Morgan, above, pp 60–90.

Part 3

The Trade Disputes Act 1906

Chapter Four

The Trade Disputes Act of 1906

John Saville

THE legal position of trade unions had been significantly clarified by the Acts of 1871 and 1875,[1] and during the succeeding two decades this legislation was not seriously challenged through the courts. It was the new unionism of the later 1880s, and especially the events which followed the London dock strike of the late summer of 1889, that began to effect critical changes in public opinion (that is, middle- and upper-class opinion); and there followed militant counter-offensives by the employers of labour, on the ground and in the courts.[2]

The London dock strike in its early days had evoked considerable sympathy from the general public, but whatever degree of passive acceptance had come from the propertied groups in society, it was already beginning to waste away during the last days of the strike. *The Times*, as always in these years, provided an accurate reflection of upper-class opinion, and, as early as Christmas Eve 1889, in a markedly violent leading article, the employers were exhorted to take the lead in organizing anti-union labour forces in their own industry, and, not for the first time, the police were vigorously criticised for their passivity in the face of mass picketing by striking workers. During the months which followed the end of the strike, with 'new unionist' explosions continuing round the country,[3] the opposition to the organisation and practices of the unskilled and semi-skilled began to harden. Anti-union attitudes had never been absent from the consciousness of the middle class, or their betters in the higher propertied groups, but the intensity of hostility had varied over time. During the 1890s the antagonism became pronounced. *The Economist*, a soberly edited journal, was convinced that the rank and file of the new unions were being led away from their real interests by professional agitators. A contributor to the *Quarterly Review* in April 1891 described the leaders of the new unionism as 'our national mafia'.[4]

New unionism had brought about a different phase in industrial relations. The unions which had established themselves, or consolidated their position, during the third quarter of the nineteenth century were largely of skilled workers, or those who could exploit some quasi-monopoly place in the labour process. The new unionists, by contrast, were in trades which always had either a surplus of available labour, or labour which could be recruited from other parts of the economy. As the Webbs noted in *Industrial Democracy*, strikes in well-organised trades would always end with the same labour force going back into work.[5] This was not the situation in the casual or semi-skilled trades, where the problem of outside labour was a continuous threat to those on strike, and it was the employers' use of what quickly became known as 'free', that is, non-union labour, that made the decade after 1889 so different from those that had gone before. Blackleg labour was not, of course, a new feature of industrial relations; what was new was the organisation from the side of the workers in trades which hitherto had never or rarely unionised themselves, and the vigorous action by the employers to counter what was for most an unfamiliar situation. The latter had no experience in conciliation procedures; their reaction was rather to destroy these new, upstart organisations, than to attempt any measure of agreement.

The economic situation worsened in the early years of the 1890s, and one by one the strikes organised by the new unions, especially along the waterfronts, were crushingly defeated. The last major confrontation was a seven-week strike in the Hull docks in April–May 1893. Hull had become the best-organised port in the UK, and the unity of the waterfront workers was broken only by the importation of several thousand labourers under extensive military and police protection. Two gunboats stood off in the Humber; there was a great deal of violence and some, not wholly unsuccessful, attempts at large-scale arson. It was a battleground between the striking labourers and most of the local property owners, backed by the full coercive powers of the state.[6]

The new phenomenon of this decade was the professionalisation of strike-breaking. The shipowners brought together about seven-eighths of British tonnage to form the Shipping Federation in September 1890.

An offensive immediately began against the dockers' and seamen's unions. The Federation set up registry offices in each port and introduced its own ticket of employment, which bound the holder to work alongside union and non-union labour alike. The first general manager of the Federation was George Laws, a tough implacable enemy of trade-unionism in all its forms.[7] The introduction of 'free' labour into the docks was the forerunner to the establishment in May 1893 of the National Free Labour Association, whose general secretary was William Collinson, the 'Apostle of Free Labour' – the title of his 1913 autobiography.

What we have in the decade of the 1890s is the convergence of judge-made law and the vigorous assertion of hostility towards trade unions that was displayed in the literary and journalistic organs of opinion. In 1894 Sir Frederick Pollock[8] had restated the law relating to combinations of workmen in a memorandum that was attached to the Final Report of the Royal Commission on Labour.[9] It was a survey that assumed that the legislation of the 1870s remained the basis for legal judgments. Trade unions were not criminal conspiracies, strikes were legal, and peaceful picketing was specifically provided for in section 7 of the Conspiracy and Protection of Property Act 1875. It was this clause that first brought about new interpretations from the bench. In 1880, Cave J had ruled that the act of intimidation within the meaning of section 7 must involve threatened or actual violence; and in two cases in 1891 the Queen's Bench Division had underwritten that judgment. In one of these cases, however, that of *Curran v Treleaven*,[10] the lower court had pronounced judgment in terms that were to become common in later years. The Recorder of Plymouth ruled that there had been intimidation within the meaning of the 1875 Act, which was capable not of benefiting the workmen, but of injuring the employer. *The Times* summed up the implications of this decision in non-technical language that the greater part of its readership would understand: 'It decides in effect that every strike organised for the purpose of crushing free labour – that is to say, the majority of the strikes undertaken by New Unionism – is illegal, and can be made the subject of criminal proceedings.'[11] As already noted, the decision in the lower court in *Curran v Treleaven* was overruled by the Court of Appeal, but these were the arguments that, from the middle of the decade, the courts were to find increasingly acceptable. It was not, however, a linear process and there were to be contradictory judgments, or judgments that were not pronounced upon by the House of Lords.[12] By the end of the century the conflicting state of the law relating to the unions was widely acknowledged. As Asquith said from the opposition front bench in the House of Commons in 1902, the law on the unions was 'in an unsatisfactory, confused, and I think I might almost say, chaotic state'.[13] The law by this time, however, while certainly chaotic, was being largely interpreted by the judiciary in terms that were hostile and wholly unsympathetic to the particular and general positions of the trade unions. The 1900 *Taff Vale* decision of Farwell J, then denied by the Court of Appeal but upheld by the House of Lords, now placed all unions in danger of being sued in their corporate capacity for tortious acts committed on their behalf.[14] A fortnight after the *Taff Vale* decision, the Law Lords delivered their judgment in *Quinn v Leathem*.[15] The effect of their decision was that a strike or boycott, or threat of strike or boycott, could be held in certain circumstances as a conspiracy, and union funds, as a result of the *Taff Vale* judgment, were available for damages. The position of the unions was now exceedingly hazardous.[16]

Between 1901 and the Liberal election victory of January 1906 the labour movement in its various parts made sustained efforts to remedy these legal disabilities. The Labour Representation Committee (LRC) had been formed in 1900 with only partial affiliations from the trade unions.[17] It was the series of adverse legal judgments that began to alter the attitude of unions towards the issue of parliamentary action. The end of the Boer War in May 1902 helped also to focus attention upon the now serious legal position of the unions, and the membership of the LRC, around 350,000 in the summer of 1900, had increased to 847,315 by February 1903; from this time the LRC began to occupy an increasingly important position within the general politics of the movement. It was, however, the Parliamentary Committee of the Trades Union Congress (TUC), obscured at times by the emergence of the LRC, that was the central organiser of what became victory for the unions by the end of the first year of the new Liberal government of 1906. The history of the Parliamentary Committee's unremitting efforts to effect change was set out in some detail in the committee's reports to the annual conferences of the TUC in 1906 and 1907.[18]

The Parliamentary Committee had been for many years a conservative Lib–Lab organisation, run by a paid secretary and ten elected members from affiliated unions. Its many inadequacies were set out in the first edition of the Webbs' *The History of Trade Unionism*.[19] At the time of the 1893 waterfront strike at Hull, when the coercive forces of the state were being extensively used against the strike, the Parliamentary Committee refused to support fund raising:

> *While the Committee deeply sympathise with the men on strike yet having regard to the fact that the policy of the Parliamentary Com-*

mittee has always been one of strict neutrality in Labour disputes the Committee are of the opinion that they would be forming a dangerous precedent if they were to depart from that policy in this case by issuing an appeal for funds.[20]

These attitudes were soon to change. There were new political forces inside the TUC at its annual conferences; the flow of adverse legal decisions against the unions were alarming even the established skilled unions; and there were the renewed links with Sir Charles Dilke and others of the more radical Liberal parliamentarians.[21]

The Law Lords' decision in the *Taff Vale* appeal was made on 22 July 1901; the Parliamentary Committee called its first conference on 3 December 1901, and among those present, in addition to Dilke, were the three leading Liberal lawyers on the opposition front bench: Asquith, Haldane and Robert Reid. It was decided at this conference that new legislation should be brought forward. The Parliamentary Committee then sought an interview with the Conservative administration and there was a meeting at the Foreign Office on 6 February 1902. Charles Dilke was an additional member of the trade-union delegation. On 14 May there took place a House of Commons debate which was to be an important landmark in the development of the campaign of the coming years. There had already been a series of meetings between Labour representatives and radically-minded Liberals, and on 10 April the Parliamentary Committee had persuaded Campbell-Bannerman, the Liberal leader, to agree to a joint debate. It was opened by Wentworth Beaumont, the MP for Hexham, and seconded by Richard Bell, the railwaymen's leader. They spoke to the motion: 'That legislation is necessary to prevent workmen being placed by judge-made law in a position inferior to that intended by Parliament in 1875.'[22] The debate on the floor of the Commons was accompanied by a large-scale attendance of trade-unionists in the lobbies of the House, including the full committees of the TUC, the General Federation of Trade Unions and the Miners' Federation, as well as contingents from textile and other unions and trades councils. Haldane and Asquith spoke for the Liberal opposition benches, both asking for an enquiry into the laws of conspiracy and picketing. Campbell-Bannerman ended the debate by accusing the government of being indifferent to the sentiment in the country over these important issues, and the motion was defeated only by a majority of 29 (174 voting for and 203 against), the Irish bloc abstaining. It was a result which greatly heartened the Parliamentary Committee.

At the end of this year, 1902, a conference of the Parliamentary Committee, the General Federation and the LRC met to consider details of a proposed bill on picketing. The bill was altered 'on the advice of a high legal authority';[23] David Shackleton,[24] a Lancashire textile union organiser, elected unopposed for Clitheroe in August 1902, took over responsibility for the bill from Richard Bell, and it was first introduced on 8 May 1903. It was defeated by only 30 votes, but in the same debate an amendment was carried for the appointment of a Royal Commission to inquire into the law relating to trade unions. In the summer of 1903, however, the combined groups representing labour agreed to boycott the Royal Commission on the grounds that they were not represented, Sidney Webb not being accepted as their recognised spokesman.[25]

The Parliamentary Committee arranged for what had become known as the 'Congress Bill' to be introduced in the House of Commons in the sessions of 1904 and 1905. On both occasions there was a majority on the second reading in favour of the bill, but further passage through the procedures of the House was obstructed. During these two years, however, the political situation had begun to change in quite striking ways: domestic politics had now swung sharply against the Conservative government; by-elections were being lost from the early months of 1904; and the party was becoming increasingly divided over the protectionist question, which Joseph Chamberlain was now proclaiming with ever-increasing vigour. He resigned from the Cabinet in September 1903 and proceeded on a 'raging' tariff agitation, with disastrous consequences for the internal unity of the Conservative Party.[26]

The Liberal Party had been having its own internal problems and had not yet recovered from the major disagreements over the Boer War; but first the Education Act and then the tariff question began to bring the different groups within the party into a more settled state. There were still personal as well as political differences. Certain of the Liberal Imperialists among the top leadership of the party became increasingly concerned, given the observable weaknesses of the Tory administration, at the prospect of a Liberal government led by Campbell-Bannerman. In September 1905, Asquith, Grey and Haldane agreed on a compact in which none of them would take office unless Campbell-Bannerman went to the Lords and accepted Asquith as leader of the House of Commons and Chancellor of the Exchequer; Grey would be Foreign Secretary and Haldane Lord Chancellor.[27] Had the agreement been held to, and had Campbell-Bannerman accepted these demands of his senior colleagues, cabinet-making would have been difficult and he himself would have had a much weaker direction of the affairs of government.

Rumours of these kinds of problems were beginning to be current within Westminster, and Balfour, the Conservative Prime Minister, resigned on 4 December 1905 without dissolving Parliament. It was a tactic to encourage divisions within the Liberal ranks. Balfour estimated that if the Liberals took office there would be much disagreement over the allocation of ministries, while if they went immediately into an election the divisions within the leadership would also have an opportunity to come into the public domain. Both the Tories and the Asquith group had miscalculated. Campbell-Bannerman was now, after his long years in opposition, much tougher and more radical than was often appreciated. He was almost alone in not succumbing to Balfour's charm, although his own political acumen was probably masked, at least to some degree, by his lack of skills in public speaking. He was, commented Ensor, 'probably the least fluent speaker who has ever come to lead the House of Commons'.[28] Campbell-Bannerman did not, however, go into a general election after Balfour's resignation, and was clear and firm in his ministerial appointments. Grey was offered the Foreign Office and refused unless the terms of the compact were agreed; but Asquith immediately accepted the Exchequer, breaking the agreement with his colleagues on the grounds that the compact had been worked out on the assumption that a general election had already been held, whereas what was wanted now was unity during the election campaign. Grey then changed his mind, and Haldane reluctantly accepted the War Office. Sir Robert Reid (Lord Loreburn), one of Campbell-Bannerman's most reliable allies, became Lord Chancellor.

Campbell-Bannerman's first speech in the election campaign, and his first public statement as Prime Minister, was made in the Albert Hall on 21 December 1905. Free trade would remain and 'Chinese slavery' would be ended.[29] There would be no great changes in foreign or imperial policies. On domestic matters, he promised that the law relating to trade unions would be reformed, and that the Poor Law, workmen's compensation and the rating system would be amended. But his speech in general was not that of a political leader centrally concerned with wide-ranging social change. The election campaign which followed exhibited the same features, and the programme which most Liberal candidates put before their electorates was a version of old-fashioned Gladstonianism, holding, above all, no truck with protectionism, and claiming a return to the 'Hungry Forties'. In the constituencies in which the LRC had candidates, and in the mining regions and the industrial cities of the North, the issues were more focused. The LRC produced an election manifesto as a guide to their candidates. It read:

TO THE ELECTORS

This election is to decide whether or not Labour is to be fairly represented in Parliament.

The House of Commons is supposed to be the people's House, and yet the people are not there.

Landlords, employers, lawyers, brewers, and financiers are there in force. Why not Labour?

The Trade Unions ask the same liberty as capital enjoys. They are refused.

The aged poor are neglected.

The slums remain; overcrowding continues, whilst the land goes to waste.

Shopkeepers and traders are overburdened with rates and taxation, whilst the increasing land values, which should relieve the ratepayers, go to people who have not earned them.

Wars are fought to make the rich richer, and underfed school children are still neglected.

Chinese Labour is defended because it enriches the mine owners ...

As discussed below, the Parliamentary Committee of the TUC issued an election programme that was much more specific in terms of trade-union demands than this LRC document.

The final results of the election astonished everyone. It was no surprise that the Conservatives and Unionists had been defeated, but the scale of that defeat was quite unexpected. The first result came on Friday 12 January, with a Liberal gain at Ipswich, and the next day showed ten Liberal victories in Lancashire, all of which had been Unionist in 1900. The avalanche had begun, with the final result giving 430 seats to the Liberals and Labour members, out of a Commons of 640. The Irish obtained their expected 83 seats, and, of the 51 LRC candidates, 29 were elected. Altogether there were some 53 MPs who could be reckoned Labour in allegiance, although their politics varied quite widely. The miners, with 14 seats, were the largest group outside the LRC.[30]

This appearance of Labour as an independent group in the House of Commons was recognised as the beginning of a new era in the history of British politics. Balfour wrote to Lord Knollys on 17 January 1906:

If you had asked me when we last met whether I should much mind permanently leaving politics, I should have answered in the negative. But I am so profoundly interested in what is now *going on that I should return a very different answer today. We have here to do with something much more important than the swing of the pendulum or all the squabbles about Free Trade and Fiscal Reform. We are face to face (no doubt in milder form) with the Socialist difficulties which loom so large on the Continent. Unless I am greatly mistaken, the Election of 1905 inaugurates a new era.*[31]

Soon after the first election results had been announced, Campbell-Bannerman decided to publish the report of the Royal Commission on Trade Disputes and Trade Combinations.[32] Three out of the five-man commission signed a majority report (two lawyers and Sidney Webb) which favoured a modest compromise to redress, at least in part, the decisions in the *Taff Vale* case and *Quinn v Leathem*. Strikes should be legalised, as should the act of persuading to strike, unless there was an inducement to break a contract. The legal judgments on picketing were to be made more flexible, and there were suggestions for the protection of union funds, with benefit funds to be separated from general trade-union funds and declared immune from liability. It was on the general lines of this majority report that the law officers of the government, closely supported by the two leading lawyers in the administration – Asquith and Haldane – introduced the government's Trade Disputes Bill on 28 March 1906. Sir John Walton, the Attorney-General, was in charge. This was, constitutionally, the first reading. The details of the government's bill had not yet been published, and the debate was in the nature of a curtain-raiser for the second reading, which took place a month later. A long preliminary debate of the kind which is summarised below is no longer parliamentary practice.[33]

Walton began by emphasizing the disarray of the current law relating to trade unions – 'Recent legal decisions have seriously disturbed preconceived notions'[34] – and he then proceeded to summarise the history of trade-union legislation in the 19th century. He acknowledged the limitations of the Acts of 1871 and 1875, their main aim being to remove 'the ban of the common law and the stigma of illegality' from the activities of the unions.[35] Criminal liability was now limited to actions which were criminal if committed by individuals. But there was complete silence in regard to the civil law, and the amalgamation of the systems of judicature as they existed under the common law and the Court of Equity in 1881 made the unions, under new regulations of 1883, liable under a representative action previously only known in the Court of Chancery. It was not until 1892 that a series of legal decisions had begun to alter significantly the position of the unions. There was now, said Walton, a serious situation, the consequences of which he underlined. He noted again that the law of 1875 had 'left that law, in so far as it is a department of civil jurisprudence, entirely untouched'; 'I doubt', he continued, 'whether in our time the serene judicial atmosphere has ever been so much disturbed as it has been by different theories with regard to the law of conspiracy.'[36] To illustrate the confusion, he quoted the late Lord Herschell in *Allen v Flood* [37] and the contrary decision in *Quinn v Leathem*. It was upon Lord Herschell's opinions that the government's bill was based, and Walton now proposed that the principle established in 1875 in respect of the criminal law should be applied to the civil law. On the question of picketing, which Walton preferred to call 'the right of peaceful persuasion',[38] he proposed to revive the Molestation of Workmen Act 1859. It was sometimes argued that this law had been repealed by the Act of 1875, and although Walton did not accept this view, he proposed to make matters certain by incorporating it in his present bill.

Walton then turned to what he acknowledged was the most difficult part of the new bill. This concerned the revision of the law of agency as an alternative to the complete legal immunity which the Parliamentary Committee had proposed in their bill in March 1905. At the time, Asquith had argued that the dangers of *Taff Vale* would almost completely disappear, provided that the law of agency could be limited in ways which would protect the trade unions and their funds.[39] Walton acknowledged that the unions had been subject to considerable 'mischief, and that they had been victims of an interpretation that was wholly inapplicable to bodies like themselves. Agency had been implied from conduct, 'not attributable to any express authorisation',[40] and he proposed to make this kind of decision impossible in the future. There should be a code of conduct within each union which would provide safety for the union and its funds:

> *First the constitution of the committee which shall conduct these operations and by whom alone the acts may be committed for which the union is responsible. In the second place, they have the power of limiting the authority of the agents whom they may appoint; and in the third place, they have the right of repudiation in regard to acts of which they disapprove.*[41]

At this point, Walton went on to consider what he described as the alternative method, 'the royal road out of the difficulty ... why not say no action whatever shall be brought?'[42] This was not, in Walton's opinion, a serious substitute for his own propositions. Complete immunity for the unions would inevitably encourage claims from other bodies, but, more important, to remove trade unions from the law would be to create for them a special privilege within a democratic society:

> *Do not let us create a privilege for the proletariat, and give a sort of benefit of clergy to trade unions analogous to the benefit of clergy which was formerly enjoyed and which created an immunity against actions in favour of certain sections of the population.*

Moreover, Walton continued, by removing the unions and their agents from legal actions, would this not be denying a sense of responsibility? The agents of unions:

> *are often swayed by passion, by excitement, and by natural feeling. Is it right that their agents should move about with the consciousness that whatever they do, the property of the union will not have to bear any loss? Is that feeling likely to produce caution, prudence, self-restraint, and regard for the rights and feelings of others?*[43]

To buttress his arguments, Walton then quoted, at some length, statements from the railwaymen's leader, Richard Bell, and the much respected miners' leader, Tommy Burt, who had represented Morpeth since 1874. Both argued that the unions should remain responsible in law for their actions.[44]

It was acknowledged by Walton that the unions' principal concern was probably the hostility that judges and juries had been exhibiting towards them for the past decade and a half, and he accepted their fears. But public opinion, he suggested, does not stand still, and, in respect of the unions, could be expected to change over time. The real argument must relate to the wording of the present bill and whether, in the way that it was framed, any case before the courts in the future would and could be determined on the basis of fact. The government's bill, it was hoped, would ensure that no unjust claim could be lodged against the unions.

David Shackleton, who was organizing the response on behalf of the Labour Party, then made the first statement in reply. He acknowledged that the Attorney-General had attempted to deal fairly with their concerns, but immediately made it clear that it was the total immunity question that remained central for the Labour members. He first reminded the Attorney-General that during the election campaign Walton himself had replied positively to all the questions framed by the Parliamentary Committee,[45] but his main argument was that what the unions wanted was an equality with the employers, and this was not being offered by the bill. Shackleton was a moderate, and his insistence on this question of equality offers an illuminating insight into the politics of Lib–Labourism in the early years of the twentieth century:

> *The Government must prove most conclusively that the employer could be made responsible for injuring the success of the workmen just as he could make the union responsible for injuring his success in a trade dispute. Unless the Government could put the employer and the workpeople on equal terms, they as Labour representatives would not be satisfied, because they held that it was a most dangerous principle to leave the workers absolutely at the employer's mercy in the questions of damages which arose ... The employer ought to be prepared to go into these labour wars when they occurred, and take the same risk as the trade unionists did.*[46]

Shackleton denied the government argument that the bill as presently framed could be expected to discourage legal actions over its interpretation, and he expected the contrary. He reminded the House that labour organisations had repudiated the Royal Commission which had just reported. They had challenged its composition and had refused to give evidence before its members. Shackleton's most telling point, which came towards the end of his speech and which no doubt the Liberal Whips took full note of, was that he believed that the government should leave the controversial matters in the bill to the judgement of the House of Commons. As a result of the general election there was, he argued, a mandate for a Labour trade-union bill, and MPs would be able to judge the reaction of the House when that bill was introduced two days later, on 30 March. The whole question, he said in conclusion, was a much more serious matter than simply one of party politics, inasmuch as it was a question which affected the great mass of the workers of the country.

Sir Edward Carson, the first Tory speaker in the debate, recognised that without having seen the actual terms of the bill he could not make definitive statements, but, from the Attorney-General's introduction to the debate, he felt that it was 'going to set up class privileges' as relating to the law of conspiracy in civil matters.[47] He noted that if the present bill was accepted, cases such as those dealt with in *Quinn v Leathem* would no longer have a remedy. On the issue of picketing, Carson remarked that the idea of peaceful persuasion was a matter of absolute hypocrisy: 'Peaceful persuasion is no use to a trade union.'[48] While the Conservative opposition would not object to the words that were to be used, there would remain the problem of the prevention of a nuisance within the common law, or the ways in which peaceful persuasion might cloak intimidation of those not connected with a trade union. During his speech, Carson referred both to Asquith – on the law of agency –and to Haldane who was on record as denying the right to complete immunity. It was a lively and intelligent speech which covered all the main points of potential dissension within the Liberal–Labour groups. Carson was followed by William Brace, who commented that, whatever the faults in the present bill, it was a matter of gratification to himself and the Labour members that it was not being introduced by the party to which Carson belonged. They were only asking, Brace insisted, for equality before the law with the employers; and this argument ran through the speeches on the first day of the debate. Most of the Labour members who spoke also noted that they were not only arguing for equality with the employers in legal terms, but for a return to the situation which had existed for the thirty years before *Taff Vale*. This was a political point that was commonly used both within Westminster and outside in the country.

Two days later the Labour group introduced their own bill, entitled 'Trades Unions and Trade Disputes Bill' (see Appendix 1).[49] The second reading was moved by Walter Hudson of the Railway Servants, who had won the ballot for a private members' bill, and it was an interesting introduction by a trade-unionist who was not a lawyer. Hudson performed competently. He disclaimed legal expertise, but insisted that he could speak authoritatively, 'knowing what the representatives of trade unions wanted, as representatives of the organised workers and as representatives coming from the trade organisations of the country'.[50] Hudson's main arguments were concentrated on the third clause of his bill:

> *An action shall not be brought against a trade union, or other association aforesaid, for the recovery of damages sustained by any person or persons by reason of the action of a member or members of such trade union or other associations aforesaid.*

This was the crucial clause on which the attention of the Labour group was concentrated. After quoting it, Hudson went on to comment on the Attorney-General's exposition of the law of conspiracy in his opening speech two days earlier, in which he had said that it constituted one of those spaces on the juridical map to which the wary and prudent litigant gave as wide a berth as possible because it was a region of judge-made law. The law of agency, Hudson emphasised, was a continuation of judge-made law, and the unions had no wish to escape from one set of legal difficulties, such as they had experienced in recent years, to a new and unknown path subject to the legal subtleties of the courts. Why could they not return to their original position, by which he meant the *status quo ante* before the judicial activism of the later 1890s and early 1900s?

Hudson brought to his defence the ageing positivist Frederic Harrison, from whom he quoted at length:[51]

> *I drafted the Minority Report of the Royal Commission of 1869 which led to the Act of 1871. When it was passing through Parliament I was consulted as to its being regarded as a just settlement. In the Taff Vale case Lord Macnaughten cited the Minority Report, referring to me by name. I think he entirely misunderstood both me and the Report in claiming any of us as admitting the liability of trade unions to an action of tort. Whilst in 1901 all the Lords held that a registered trade union was liable to an action in tort, Lord Lindley and Lord Macnaughten laid it down that any trade union was so liable, whether registered or not, and the Lord Chancellor seemed to agree. Those learned Lords may so declare their opinion, but they have not the slightest right to claim our Minority Report as admitting such doctrine ... Lord Macnaughten quotes me as approving the liability of a trade unionist for his own wrongdoing, and infers that this admission includes the same liability of the union as a whole. I neither said nor accept anything of the kind ... Lord Macnaghten quoted the words of the Minority Report as accepting the liability of every person 'in respect of any damage occasioned through the Act or default of the person so sued'. Nothing of the kind 'was intended' either by myself or colleagues on the Commission, nor by the Government when they passed the Act of 1871. Nothing of the kind was possible, even if it had been intended. The words of the Royal Commission Report said, 'All questions of crime apart, the objects at which they (the unions) aim, the rights which they claim, and the liabilities which they incur are, for the most part, it seems to us, such as courts of law should neither enforce, nor modify, nor annul. They should rest entirely on consent.'*

Hudson returned to the legal position of the unions down to the *Taff Vale* case. From 1871, he noted, it was not possible to sue a trade union collectively in tort under the existing rules of common law. It was only in 1883, following the Judicature Acts of 1881, that the judges issued new rules of procedure (General Order No. 16 of 1883, Rule 9) whereby the representative action had been introduced; but until 1901 no trade union had been subject to damages. And what they were now asking was a return to the 1871 immunity which they had enjoyed for thirty years. This was not any specially created privilege, but an equality before the law, and it was this matter of right that he was asking the House to accede to.

F E Smith, the future Lord Birkenhead, was the first speaker for the Conservative and Unionist opposition. He made the usual criticisms of the bill that came from his side of the House, but also underlined the embarrassment that would be caused to certain members of the government if the principles of the present bill passed unchanged. He emphasised the obvious point that if the government were going to leave the House to decide the matter, everyone knew that the approach of the Labour group would be accepted. But this would undoubtedly conflict with the stated principles of a number of the leading members of the government – had not the Attorney-General spoken of creating a privilege for the proletariat? Furthermore, the Chancellor of the Exchequer had said it was wrong. The occupants of the government benches would be voting for the Bill:

> *against their deliberately formed and twice repeated convictions because they dared not face a mutiny which they could not quell – an example which, whether it proved more favourable to their advancement at the polls, would not tend to raise the standard of public morality either in the country or in this House.*[52]

There was no doubt about the majority sentiment in the House of Commons in favour of the unions and, equally, no doubt that the senior Liberal lawyers in the government were strongly against the complete immunity that was being asked for. Almost all those who spoke after F E Smith were in favour of the principles of the bill, but the debate was electrified by the intervention of the Prime Minister. He began by saying that he only wanted to say a few words on the matter before them; that he had been in the House in the 1870s and had followed the debates at that time with great interest:

I never have been, and I do not profess to be now very intimately acquainted with the technicalities of the question, or with the legal points involved in it. The great object then was, and still is, to place the two rival powers of capital and labour on an equality, so that the fight between them, so far as fight was necessary, should at least be a fair one ... The Bills which were passed between 1870 and 1880 had a most beneficent effect. They gave life and strength to the trade unions, very much to the alarm of a great body of opinion in the country, which had contracted a habit of looking upon those associations with dread and suspicion. That prejudice still lurks in some quarters; but the great mass of opinion in the country recognise fully now the beneficent nature of the trade union organisations, and recognise also the great services that those organisations have done in the prevention of conflict and in the promotion of harmony between labour and capital.[53]

Campbell-Bannerman then moved to a consideration of the law of agency which, as it was interpreted by the courts, undoubtedly defeated the intention of Parliament. To make his point, he quoted the views of Sir Godfrey Lushington who, as a leading civil servant, was much involved in the legislation of the 1870s and who had recently denied that Parliament had intended judicial interference of the kind represented by *Taff Vale*. The Prime Minister continued:

Now here we have, as I say, an authoritative opinion from almost the highest authority, and the corollary of this is that the state of things which we seek to amend to-day has been produced by Judge-made law, directly counter to the intended law of Parliament. Meritorious though the Judge-made law may be, or the reverse, it has never been sanctioned; on the contrary, it has been expressly disavowed by Parliament. That makes it all the more unfair to taunt the unions who have been deprived of their legal rights by this action of the Judges with seeking a privilege when they come to this House in search of a remedy.[54]

In the closing remarks to this short but remarkable intervention, Campbell-Bannerman played down the differences between the government's bill and the one at present before the House, and, while not arguing in an absolutist way that the Labour bill was to be preferred, he suggested that this second reading should be passed and the points of difference argued out at the committee stage. It was clear that Campbell-Bannerman was against his own government's bill on the grounds that 'the method of restricting agency leaves pitfalls and loopholes from which there is great danger of producing and multiplying litigation'.[55]

The Tory speaker who followed the Prime Minister said that he had heard the speech with 'blank amazement': 'It was incredible,' he continued, 'that the right hon. Gentleman should on Friday ask the House to vote for this Bill when his Attorney-General had on Wednesday put forward, in solemn argument, reasons for adopting another course.'[56] Here Campbell-Bannerman intervened to say that he hoped the question would be left to the judgement of the House, and he was further supported by an intervention from the Attorney-General. These replies, however, did not meet the question. It was an extraordinary turnabout. There had been rumours of dissent within the Cabinet before the Attorney-General brought his bill into the Commons, but there cannot be many examples in any Parliament where the Prime Minister proffers a complete repudiation of one of his senior ministers within forty-eight hours. It emerged that, on the evening after the Attorney-General's speech in the House on 28 March, Labour members had met the TUC Parliamentary Committee to consider what all regarded as the unsatisfactory character of the government's bill. It was decided to go ahead with their own bill on the following day, and Shackleton was deputed to meet Campbell-Bannerman as soon as possible. They met on the same evening and Shackleton had been given an assurance that the Prime Minister would support the Labour bill: hence Campbell-Bannerman's remarkable intervention.

Some senior members of the Cabinet were against the award of 'privilege' to the trade unions, but the majority backed the unions, and certainly large numbers of Liberal MPs were under electoral obligation to support the changes in law that were being demanded. The progress of an amended government bill was now taken for granted, and the second reading was introduced on 25 April 1906 by the Solicitor-General, Sir W Robson (see Appendix 2). He explained that the Attorney-General was indisposed with voice trouble; a very convenient malady, of course, since it would no doubt have been embarrassing to have confronted the opposition benches with the emendations that had been forced upon him. The Solicitor-General made a clever speech. He began by noting that the government's bill contained four main clauses: these related to conspiracy; picketing; the law of trade interference, 'apart altogether from the law of conspiracy – a very important point which happened to be omitted altogether from the [Labour] Bill';[57] and the matter of the trade unions as corporate bodies liable to have actions brought against them. There was, he said, little difference between the two sides of the House on the first three clauses – not a wholly accurate statement, as is discussed below – but he insisted that the central problem to be resolved was that of the fourth clause. 'It turns', he argued, 'upon the question as to whether or not trade unions are to be treated as corporate bodies to the extent ... of having actions brought against them.'[58]

The Solicitor-General then proceeded to instruct the House upon the consequences which would follow if trade unions were to be incorporated. His central argument was that this would not only allow the unions to be sued, but would also confer upon them the privilege of being able to sue. Obviously there must be an equality of liability and privilege. On the assumption that there was a general contract between a trade union and its members – the Solicitor-General protected himself in this matter by admitting that there was not a single legal proposition he could offer which was not assailed by some legal doubt – it took the form of an agreement such that, in the event of a strike, there should be no return to work without the consent of a majority, expressed through its legally elected executive. This did not exist under the 1871 Act because it was the express intention at that time that unions should not be treated as incorporated bodies. But if they were now to be incorporated, the union could enforce the contract with its members not only for damages for its breach, but also by way of an injunction in restraint of breach. Under incorporation, therefore, a trade union would be able to recover damages from any employer who employed union labour during a strike. In order to avoid these kind of problems, the framers of the 1871 Act had given the unions only a modified legal status, and deliberately refused to put them under either the liabilities or the privileges of incorporation. Lord Morley had expressed the legal situation during the debate in the House of Lords in 1871: 'The objects of trade unions were mostly such as Courts of Law should neither enforce, modify, nor annul, but such as should rest on consent.'[59] The Solicitor-General went on to remind the House of the moderate record which the trade unions enjoyed in Britain: 'The record of England in respect of industrial disorder is marvellous.'[60] It was, of course, understandable that there were some who continued to regard the unions as cruel and evil organisations, and these would be both in the courts and among those who served on juries. The moderation of the trade unions in Britain was not an uncommon theme in the debates of this year and it was an argument not seriously challenged from the opposition benches.

The Solicitor-General then commented on the *Taff Vale* case and the law of conspiracy, in the context of the argument that industrial conflict should not be made the subject of litigation. Conspiracy as a criminal offence in relation to industrial disputes was supposed to have been removed by the Act of 1875; but it had since been decided that the Act removed the criminal character of the offence of conspiracy, but left it in all respects subject to civil actions. The most recent, and the most important, case was *Quinn v Leathem*, whose judgment 'practically cuts at the very root of all right of combination'. Lord Lindley was quoted:

> *A threat to call men out, given by a trade union officially to an employer of men belonging to the union and willing to work with him, is a form of coercion, intimidation, molestation, or annoyance to them and to him very difficult to resist. And to say the least, requiring justification.*

'What justification is possible under the existing law?' asked the Solicitor-General.[61] And he insisted that the right of combination in any substantial sense no longer existed. At this point in his speech his words illustrate well the political ideas and understanding of the greater part of the Liberal Party in these years. They represented what was probably the high-water mark of sympathy for the trade-union movement during the whole of the 20th century. The Solicitor-General said that he regarded the present position of the unions, following the series of adverse legal decisions:

> *as a most serious condition of things, not merely from the point of view of trade unions, but from the far wider point of view of the community. One of the most essential things to the well-being of this country is the condition of the industrial classes. Trade unions are an essential safeguard against this country's being turned into the paradise of the sweater. It is the greatest mistake in the world to suppose that a matter affecting the vital interests of the industrial classes is not an intensely national question. We cannot injure them without injuring ourselves, for we are all members one of another.*[62]

He ended his speech with a brief discussion of clause 4 of the bill he was introducing. This included the introduction into union rules of a specially appointed committee, which would have complete jurisdiction during the period of a strike; but it was a condition that was removed during the passage of the bill through the House. As the Solicitor-General acknowledged in his final remarks, all these matters, and notably this last suggestion, were to be put to the House for their full debate and discussion, and he promised that the government would listen carefully to those most concerned with these matters.

The debate which continued on the Second Reading brought no new arguments into the discussion. Shackleton emphasised once again that 'the position they were taking up was that of absolute immunity from financial responsibility in those cases'.[63] Clement Edwards,[64] whose consistent support of the unions was to be characteristic of his whole period in the Commons, provided a useful survey of the legal background to the bill, while Balfour taunted the government with its rapid change of approach over the crucial clauses. The House now agreed that the bill should proceed. Through the summer months and into the autumn the committee stage saw lengthy debates on the wording of the different clauses. Apart from the final version of section 4, which gave the unions the immunity they were insisting on above all other considerations, the most important amendment was that proposed by Sir Charles Dilke to section 3, which was concerned with the tort of inducing breach of contract. The amendment had been agreed between the Attorney-General and Dilke before the latter moved it on the floor of the House, and it was because of this prior acceptance that Dilke did not proffer a defence of his proposed change in the debate. This was his own explanation, although there might have been other reasons, for the legal consequences which would follow if the amendment was accepted were of quite major significance. Dilke's amendment added significantly to the immunity in *Allen v Flood*,[65] and it overruled the judgment in the 1905 *Glamorgan Coal Co v South Wales Miners' Federation*, which had confirmed tortious liability for inducing breach of contract.[66] The final wording of section 3 would now read:

> *An act done by a person in contemplation or furtherance of a trade dispute shall not be actionable on the ground only that it induces some other person to break a contract of employment or that it is an interference with the trade, business, or employment of some other person, or with the right of some other person to dispose of his capital or his labour as he wills.*

The Conservative opposition was fully aware of what was involved in the Dilke amendment, and, again, the arguments were used that it was contrary to the main report of the recent Royal Commission, and that the Attorney-General himself had originally expressed a contrary opinion. Sir Frederick Banbury moved an amendment which would have added, after 'induces', the words 'other than maliciously'. But the government would not accept this, and the amendment was voted down. The debate then continued on Dilke's amendment. Lord Robert Cecil,

Carson and Shackleton were among those who spoke, and, as with all the votes registered in these long debates on the Trade Disputes Bill, the Liberal majorities were overwhelming.[67]

The third reading of the bill was passed without a division; various amendments by the Lords were rejected by the government and the new Act received the Royal Assent on 21 December 1906. There had been three contentious bills during the first year of the Liberal government: concerning education, plural voting and trade disputes. The first two were butchered by the Lords, but the Labour measure went through untouched, a victory which came from what was considered to be a realistic assessment of party politics and public opinion. Both traditional parties were now acutely aware of the shifting possibilities of the working-class vote, and their assessments of the politics of the future shaped their attitudes towards the Trade Disputes Act.

There were five sections in the 1906 Act. The first had not been seriously disputed; it added to the 1875 Act's provision against criminal conspiracy by eliminating the tort of civil conspiracy in trade disputes: *Quinn v Leathem* was thereby overruled. Section 2 amended the definition of watching and besetting, and peaceful persuasion was once more accepted in the law relating to strikes. This section, while a major advance over recent decisions in the courts, notably *J C Lyons & Sons v Wilkins*,[68] was not wholly to the wishes of the TUC Parliamentary Committee, or to its subcommittee concerned with the day-to-day details of the bill's progress through Parliament. Sir Charles Dilke, on behalf of the committee, wished to move an amendment by which, after the word 'working' at the end of section 2 (1), would be added 'and such attending shall not be held to be a nuisance'. The effect of the amendment would have been greatly to strengthen the clause, but it was not accepted by the Attorney-General, and a deal was struck between the TUC subcommittee and the law officers. In return for the complete acceptance of section 4, concerning immunity, the Labour members agreed not to divide the House on this amendment, 'as they were not prepared to take the responsibility of wrecking the Bill'.[69] Section 3 has been discussed above, whereby the tort of inducing a breach of contract of employment, so far as a trade dispute was concerned, was now denied. Section 4 provided for complete immunity in tort for trade unions – a first in the history of labour law. The decision in *Taff Vale* was thereby rejected, and unions could neither be sued directly nor by a representative action. Section 5 provided definitions, the most important of which was that of 'trade dispute' in 5(3), the first time that this had been given a statutory definition: 'the expression 'trade dispute' means any dispute between employers and workmen, or between workmen and workmen, which is connected with the employment or non-employment or the terms of the employment, or with the conditions of labour, of any person'. In later decades, much was to hinge upon this definition.[70]

The passing of the Trade Disputes Act of 1906 was a landmark in the history of labour law, and its acceptance by the Parliament of 1906 was the result of an unusual conjuncture of events and politics. The emergence of the TUC Parliamentary Committee as a dynamic negotiating factor in the three years before the 1906 general election was unexpected, given its history, yet, without the stubborn campaigning of the committee, the issue would not have become as important as it did. Among other consequences, it meant that large numbers of Liberal MPs came into the House of Commons already pledged to support the demands of the TUC's own Trade Disputes Bill. The unexpected size of the Labour group in the new House – including the LRC members – was immediately recognised as a new factor in domestic politics, although it is likely that, had Asquith and not Campbell-Bannerman been Prime Minister, the unions would not have achieved the complete immunity that section 4 was thought to give them. But, with the Liberal government standing firm on its agreement with the TUC Parliamentary Committee, the Tories also found no difficulty in appreciating the politics involved. The House of Lords would, without compunction, mutilate the Liberal Party's Education Bill and most of the other legislation that was sent to them, but the Trade Disputes Bill was different. Here is the TUC Parliamentary Committee's summary of the approach of the Conservative leader of the House of Lords:

> *On the 4th December, 1906, the Lord Chancellor moved the second reading of the Trade Disputes Bill in the House of Lords. On this occasion a most remarkable statement was made by Lord Lansdowne, testifying to the power of organised labour. He said that he desired to lay before their lordships one or two considerations, not of a technical character, which he thought their lordships would do well to bear in mind whilst listening to subsequent speakers. Everyone had listened with the greatest interest to the history which the noble and learned lord had given of the legislation as it affected these associations of workmen. He could not help thinking that, whatever their opinion might be of this Bill, they had to admit that the voice of the electors had been heard in regard to it. Many extravagant proposals had been put forward upon the ground of an alleged mandate given by the constituencies to his Majesty's Government. He regarded those claims, as a rule, with the utmost*

suspicion; but he thought if they could claim a mandate for anything they had the right to claim one for dealing with this question. If their lordships were to refer this Bill back to the country what would be the result? Could they have any doubt as to the answer which the constituencies would give? They should find the demand for a similar Bill renewed with greater intensity, and in a form embittered by the suggestion that the House of Lords was in conflict with the general desire of the working classes.[71]

To many lawyers and judges, both at the time of the passing of the 1906 Act and later, the immunity that had now been granted to trade anions was outside the general trend of jurisprudence in Britain. A V Dicey, in the second edition of his well-known survey of nineteenth-century law and public opinion, believed the 1906 Act to be the deplorable victory of the collectivism that was now rampant; Holdsworth characterised it as an 'enormous injustice'.[72] When Henry Slesser published his four lectures on the law relating to trade unions in 1921 he ended by emphasizing in his final paragraph that the present legal position of the trade unions was 'anomalous'; and in the foreword to Slesser's book Lord Justice Atkin wrote of the 'remarkable fact':

that in a country where the rule of law has been predominant it has been considered advisable to make immune from civil liability for tortious acts the vast associations of capital and labour styled Trade Unions, equipped as they are with huge resources in money and men and possessing elaborate organisations conducted with consummate abilities, renders it highly important to know the conditions of such immunity and the legal relations of Trade Unions both to their members and to the community at large.[73]

A year earlier, in 1920, the Webbs had published their last revised edition of *The History of Trade Unionism*. In one of the chapters reviewing developments in the trade-union world in the previous three decades they referred to the 'extraordinary and unlimited immunity' provided by the 1906 Act. The Webbs were by no means certain that the provisions of the Act were all entirely in the interest 'of the Movement',[74] and in a footnote they wrote: 'Trade Unionists would be well advised not to presume too far on this apparently absolute immunity from legal proceedings. It must not be imagined that either the ingenuity of the lawyers or the prejudice of the judges has been exhausted.'[75] But while the prescience of the Webbs was to be fulfilled in the long run, for over half a century after the 1906 Act there were no fundamental changes in labour law or in the judicial decisions that were delivered in labour cases. The aftermath of the General Strike of 1926 was only a limited exception with the passing of the Trade Disputes and Trade Unions Act 1927. No doubt it was the weakness of the trade-union movement in Britain from 1926 to 1939 that was responsible for the absence of legal challenges to the unions, just as it was the new political situation after 1945 that also influenced their general position in society. During the 1950s, as Griffith commented, 'recourse to the courts was almost unknown as a means of resolving industrial disputes or challenging industrial practices'.[76]

The political situation in Britain, however, was changing. The Tories had come back to power in 1951 and were to remain in office for thirteen years. Virtually full employment was affecting, in many ways, the relations between managers and their workforce, and the publication in 1958 of *A Giant's Strength* by the Inns of Court Conservative and Unionist Society was one indication of the legal problems and possible changes that were now being seriously discussed. The position of the unions began to be challenged in the 1960s, with *Rookes v Barnard*[77] as a major landmark in what was to become an increasingly judicial activism in respect of the legal position established by the 1906 Act. When the Conservatives came to power in 1979 for what was to be the longest period in office of any political party during the twentieth century, legislative changes were introduced which steadily constrained and confined the industrial power of the unions. The Trade Disputes Act of 1906 itself came after a decade of Tory government, and the possibilities of political change in the closing years of the twentieth century offer interesting comparisons – similarities as well as differences – with the mood of the victorious party and their allies over which Campbell-Bannerman presided on the government benches in 1906.[78]

This chapter was first published in 1 *Historical Studies in Industrial Relations* 11 (1996). It is reproduced with the permission of John Saville and *Historical Studies in Industrial Relations*.

Notes

1 The Criminal Law Amendment Act 1871, the Trade Union Act 1871, and the Conspiracy and Protection of Property Act 1875, for which see Lord Wedderburn, *The Worker and the Law* (3rd edn,1986), esp chs 1 and 7. General histories of labour law before the judgments and legislative changes after 1960 include H H Slesser, *The Law Relating to Trade Unions* (1921); R Y Hedges and A Winterbotham, *The Legal History of Trade Unionism* (1930); A L Haslam, *The Law Relating to Trade Combinations* (1931); N A Citrine, *Trade Union Law* (1950; 2nd edn, 1960); H Vester and A H Gardner, *Trade Union Law and Practice* (1958). There is a broad survey in R Lewis, 'The Historical Development of Labour Law' (1976) 14 *British Journal of Industrial Relations* 1.

2 J Saville, 'Trade Unions and Free Labour: The Background to the Taff Vale Decision', in A Briggs and J Saville (eds), *Essays in Labour History* (1960), pp 317–50. S and B Webb, *Industrial Democracy* (1897), included an appendix 'The Legal Position of Collective Bargaining' (pp 853–62), which surveyed the position to November 1897. In the 1902 edition, a new introduction described the changes in the law down to the decisions of the Law Lords in *Quinn v Leathem* [1901] AC 495 and the *Taff Vale* case [1901] AC 426; see pp xxi–xxxvi.

3 H A Clegg, A Fox and A F Thompson, *A History of British Trade Unions since 1889, Vol I: 1889–1910* (1964), ch 2; E J Hobsbawm, *Labouring Men* (1964), chs 10 and 11.

4 *Quarterly Review*, April 1891, p 507; and for examples of the attitude of *The Economist*, see 'Strikes and Poor Relief', 22 March 1890, and 'The Cause of the Epidemic of Strikes', 12 July 1890.

5 S and B Webb, above, p 719, n 1. The Webbs gave as examples cotton-spinners and coalminers in well-organised districts.

6 The Hull strike was in all the national papers as well as the local and regional papers of Yorkshire during April–May 1893. There is a short account in Saville, 'Trade Unions and Free Labour', pp 328–30.

7 George Laws' testimony before the *Royal Commission on Labour, Minutes of Evidence*, Group B, vol 1 (C 6708), Qq. 4918–5471, exhibits his ideas on trade-unionism in all their crudity. See especially his long reply in Q 4954. L H Powell, *The Shipping Federation: A History of the First Sixty Years, 1890–1950* (1950), the official history, is a colourless account of little use to the historian.

8 Sir Frederick Pollock, third baronet (1845–1937), one of the great English jurists of the past two centuries. There is a percipient entry in *Dictionary of National Biography, 1931–1940* (1949), pp 710–13.

9 *Royal Commission on Labour, Fifth and Final Report*, Pt. 1, C 7421, 1894, pp 157–62.

10 [1891] 2 QB 545.

11 *The Times*, 12 January 1891.

12 *Temperton v Russell* [1893] 1 QB 715, was an early example of a decision hostile to the unions that was not taken to the House of Lords.

13 HC Debs, 14 May 1902, col 328.

14 *Taff Vale Railway Company v Amalgamated Society of Railway Servants* [1901] AC 426. The judgment of the Law Lords was that although the Amalgamated Society of Railway Servants was not a corporate body, the union could be sued in a corporate capacity for damages alleged to have been caused by the actions of its officers. It was also held that an injunction could be issued restraining the union not only from criminal acts, but also from other acts deemed unlawful.

15 1901] AC 495.

16 The general position of the unions after *Taff Vale* and *Quinn v Leathem* is described in detail in Clegg *et al*, above, ch. 8. What is often missed in the discussion of the Taff Vale case is that other unions began to be mulcted for damages in cases brought against them. The Webbs estimated that around £200,000 was lost in damages and expenses after the Law Lords' decision: S and B Webb, *The History of Trade Unionism* (1920), p 602.

17 F Bealey and H Pelling, *Labour and Politics 1900–1906* (1958), is subtitled *A History of the Labour Representation Committee.*

18 TUC Annual Report 1906, pp 53–63, and 1907, pp 50–61. These reports by the TUC Parliamentary Committee are a largely unused source, but they remain the best summary that exists of the organised campaign initiated and pursued by the committee.

19 S and B Webb, *The History of Trade Unionism* (1894), pp 470–4. 'The whole organisation', the Webbs wrote, 'is so absurdly inadequate to the task, that the committee can hardly be blamed for giving up any attempt to keep pace with the work. The members leave their provincial headquarters fifteen or twenty times a year to spend a few hours in the little offices at 19, Buckingham Street, Strand, in deliberating upon such business as their Secretary brings before them. Preoccupied with the affairs of their societies, and unversed in general politics, they either confine their attention to the interests of their own trades, or look upon the fortnightly trip to London as a pleasant recreation from hard official duties' (p 472).

20 TUC Parliamentary Committee, *Minutes*, 3 May 1893, quoted in Clegg *et al*, above, p 266. There is a great deal of information on the TUC Parliamentary Committee scattered through the pages of R M Martin, *TUC: The Growth of a Pressure Group, 1868–1976* (1980).

21 D Nicolls, *The Lost Prime Minister: A Life of Sir Charles Dilke* (1995), pp 284–8, 298–301. While the TUC Parliamentary Committee exhibited a steady increase in its political activity from 1901 until the Act of 1906 was on the statute book, there were notable differences of opinion as to tactics and strategy throughout these years. Dilke and his radical colleagues in the Liberal Party exercised considerable influence in stiffening the resolve of the members of the Parliamentary Committee, although the committee continued to have its own independent mind, as the text which follows will show.

22 HC Debs, 14 May 1902, cols 277–339; and for a more extended discussion of the initiatives of the Parliamentary Committee in this first phase, Bealey and Pelling, above, pp 90–5.

23 TUC Annual Report 1906, p 55. The 'high legal authority' was not identi-

fied.

24 For details of David Shackleton, see J M Bellamy and J Saville (eds), *Dictionary of Labour Biography, Vol. 2* (1974), pp 335–9. He was to prove a hardworking and very efficient parliamentarian and became the driving force within the TUC Parliamentary Committee.

25 It is always interesting to observe historians chronicling their own interpretation of events and personalities. N. McCord, 'Taff Vale Revisited' (1993) 78 *History* 253, at p 245, refers to the 'distinguished engineer and coal owner Sir William Lewis' who negotiated the final settlement on the ground in the Taff Vale dispute. The same Sir William Lewis, 'a leading South Wales employer' (*ibid*, p 254), was appointed a member of the Royal Commission on Trade Disputes and Trade Combinations in 1903. Clegg *et al*, above, p 231, refers to 'Lewis's extreme hostility to trade unionism'; and W R Cornish and G de N Clark, *Law and Society in England, 1750–1950* (1989), now a standard text, have a footnote which reads: 'The [Royal] Commission consisted of two conventional lawyers (Viscount Dunedin, chairman, and Arthur Cohen, KC), an industrial arch-foe (Sir William Lewis), a fair-minded civil servant (Sir Godfrey Lushington) and Sidney Webb' (p 335, n 80).

26 For general historical surveys, see E Halévy, *Imperialism and the Rise of Labour* (1929), pt 3, ch 1; R C K Ensor, *England, 1870–1914* (1936), ch 11.

27 Details of the compact are to be found in most histories of these years. E Halévy, *The Rule of Democracy, 1905–1914* (2nd edn, 1961), pp 3–8, has an excellent brief account, and see p 5 n 1 for a useful bibliographical guide to the formation of the first Campbell-Bannerman Cabinet. See also J A Spender, *The Life of the Right Hon. Sir Henry Campbell-Bannerman GCB, Vol 2* (1923), ch 28; B E C Dugdale, *Arthur James Balfour* (1936), vol 1, ch 19 and vol 2, ch 2; J Harris and C Hazlehurst, 'Campbell-Bannerman as Prime Minister', (1970) 55 *History* 360.

28 Ensor, above, p 384.

29 For a general account, see A Briggs, 'The Political Scene', in S Nowell-Smith (ed), *Edwardian England, 1901–1914* (1964), esp pp 59ff. The issue of 'Chinese slavery' became important from 1903; it referred to the extensive use of Chinese labourers on the Rand in South Africa, and is discussed in all the histories of the period. As an example: W S Adams, *Edwardian Heritage: A Study in British History 1901–1906* (1949), pp 98ff.

30 Keir Hardie, Will Crooks, Arthur Henderson and David Shackleton were among the sitting MPs returned with increased majorities. Most of the members of the TUC Parliamentary Committee were now in the Commons. Labour and trade-union members returned for the first time included G NBarnes, C W Bowerman, J R Clynes, Fred Jowett, Ramsay MacDonald, G H Roberts, Philip Snowden and Will Thorne. For a notably perceptive biography of the last named, still unfortunately not translated: F Bédarida, Will Thorne: *La Voie Anglaise du Socialisme* (1987).

31 Quoted in Dugdale, *Balfour*, vol 2, p 21. The campaign for the general election began in late December 1905, but the results were not announced

until mid-January 1906; hence the reference at times to the 1905 election and at others to 1906.

32 Report of the Royal Commission on Trade Disputes and Trade Combinations, Cd 2825, 1906. The report was delayed first by Balfour and then by Campbell-Bannerman, on both occasions because it was thought its findings would 'confuse' the election issues.

33 I am much obliged to Professor John Griffith for explaining the procedures of the House of Commons in these matters. It would seem probable that the Liberal government introduced the long preliminary discussion and debate in order to make clear the distinction between its own bill and that of the Labour group two days later, on 30 March 1906. There was a Standing Order of 1902 which restricted debate before the second reading, but the latest (1989) edition of Erskine May consulted still uses the words: 'usually this is not the proper time for any lengthened debate upon its merits': C Boulton (ed), *Erskine May's Treatise on the Law, Privileges, Proceedings and Usage of Parliament* (21st edn, 1989), pp 462–3.

34 HC Debs, 28 March 1906, col 1295.

35 *Ibid*, col 1296.

36 *Ibid*, col 1298.

37 [1898] AC 1; and see note 65 below.

38 HC Debs, 28 March 1906, col 1301.

39 HC Debs, 10 March 1905, col 1097.

40 HC Debs, 28 March 1906, col 1303.

41 *Ibid*, col 1305.

42 *Ibid*, col 1306.

43 *Ibid*, col 1307.

44 *Ibid*, cols 1307–8. The views of both Bell and Burt are examples of the differences within the TUC Parliamentary Committee, and the trade-union movement in general, referred to in note 21 above.

45 *Ibid*, cols 1312–13. At the general election Walton had been opposed by a Labour candidate in the Leeds South constituency. Alf Mattison was the Labour agent and had photographed one of Walton's election posters: 'Vote for Walton and the Trade Disputes Bill'. Keir Hardie made a further challenge to Walton in the debate two days later: HC Debs, 30 March 1906, cols 47–8. Both Shackleton and Keir Hardie made the point that, at the time of the election, there was only one Trade Disputes Bill – that introduced by the Labour group on behalf of the TUC Parliamentary Committee in the 1904 and 1905 sessions. In the 28 March debate Walton denied any blanket support for the bill's clauses.

46 HC Debs, 28 March 1906, col 1314.

47 *Ibid*, col 1321.

48 *Ibid*, col 1325.

49 HC Debs, 30 March 1906, cols 21ff.

50 *Ibid*, col 22.

51 *Ibid*, cols 24–5. The exact source of this quotation was not given. Frederic Harrison died in 1923 at the age of 92. There is an interesting account of

the English positivists and the Labour movement in R Harrison, *Before the Socialists: Studies in Labour and Politics, 1861–1881* (1965), ch 6.

52 HC Debs, 30 March 1906, col 33.

53 *Ibid*, cols 51–2.

54 *Ibid*, col 53.

55 *Ibid*, col 54.

56 *Ibid*.

57 *Ibid*, 25 April 1906, col 1482.

58 *Ibid*, cols 1483–4.

59 *Ibid*, col 1489.

60 *Ibid*.

61 *Ibid*, col 1493.

62 *Ibid*, col 1494.

63 *Ibid*, col 1506.

64 Allen Clement Edwards (1859–1938) was an important personality in these years on the radical wing of the Liberal Party. Self-educated, he became a barrister in 1899, and had been deeply involved in the organisation of new unionism from 1889. From this time he was consistently supportive of the unions' causes. He entered Parliament in January 1906 for Denbigh Boroughs as a member of the Liberal Party, and was an active member of the group which collaborated with the TUC Parliamentary Committee: *Dictionary of Labour Biography, Vol 3* (1976), pp 69–78.

65 Wedderburn, above, pp 24 and 586, suggests that only Dilke really understood the critical importance of the amendment and, moreover, that it was introduced late on a Friday afternoon at a time of 'confused' debate. As the text above notes, Dilke had previously given notice of his amendment and it was accepted by the Attorney-General. It would be unlikely that Dilke did not discuss his amendment with the TUC subcommittee which was organizing the case for the bill before he submitted it. This does not gainsay Wedderburn's point that it was Dilke who really appreciated what his amendment involved, or that it may not have been moved had Dilke not been involved. Dilke is on record to the effect that he found his Labour colleagues 'too easily satisfied': S L Gwynn and G M Tuckwell, *The Life of the Rt. Hon. Sir Charles Dilke, Bart, M P*, 2 vols (1917), app 2 to ch 52. Dilke's amendment was carried by 255 to 30. *Allen v Flood* held that malice alone was not sufficient to render otherwise lawful conduct actionable. Lord Halsbury counter-attacked with the judgment in *Quinn v Leathem*. In *Allen v Flood*, 'Lord Herschel said that there was a 'chasm' between doing an act that 'violated a legal right' and an interference where 'no legal right was violated'': Wedderburn, above, p 612.

66 [1905] AC 239.

67 The debate on Dilke's amendment is in HC Debs, 3 August 1906, cols 1677–92.

68 [1896] 1 Ch 811; [1899] 1 Ch. 255. This most celebrated of all picketing cases was not taken to the House of Lords, for reasons which are not wholly clear. For a brief historical background to the legal judgments, see Saville,

'Trade Unions and Free Labour', above, pp 346–8.

69 The agreement between the TUC subcommittee and the Attorney-General was summarised in TUC Annual Report 1907, p 52. A labour lawyer has noted the unfortunate consequences that have followed the rejection of Dilke's amendment of 'nuisance': R Kidner, 'Lessons in Trade Union Law Reform: The Origins and Passage of the Trade Disputes Act 1906' [1982] 2 *Legal Studies* 50.

70 J W Orth, *Combination and Conspiracy: A Legal History of Trade Unionism, 1721–1906* (Oxford: 1991), pp 151–2.

71 TUC Annual Report 1907, p 55. Lansdowne ended his speech in the Lords with a statement of what he really felt about the bill before them: 'If, however, we allow it to pass this House we have at any rate the right to say we disclaim all responsibility for its provisions, and to express our hope that the common sense of employers and employed may prevent any untoward consequences from attending the reign of licence which the recklessness of His Majesty's Government is about to inaugurate': HC Debs, 4 December 1906, col 704.

72 By collectivism, Dicey meant 'the combination of socialistic and democratic legislation [which] threatens the gravest danger to the country': A V Dicey, *Lectures on the Relation between Law and Public Opinion in England during the Nineteenth Century* (2nd edn, 1914), p xc. Holdsworth's full sentence reads: 'The fact that it was possible in 1906 to pass a statute which perpetrated the enormous injustice of freeing trade unions of masters or men from liability for torts is, I think, due primarily to the prevalent *laissez faire* doctrines, which induced Parliament, at the end of the eighteenth and the beginning of the nineteenth centuries, to refuse to set up any legal machinery for the equitable adjustment of industrial disputes': W Holdsworth, *A History of English Law, Vol 11* (1938), p 500.

73 Slesser, above, p vii.

74 S and B Webb, *History* (1920 ed)), above, p 607.

75 *Ibid*, p 606 n 3.

76 J A G Griffith, *Judicial Politics since 1920: A Chronicle* (1993), p 94.

77 [1964] AC 1129; for an examination of its importance, see Wedderburn, above, pp 38–47.

78 Griffith, above, ch. 6; J Moher, *Trade Unions and the Law: The Politics of Change* (Institute of Employment Rights, 1995).

Chapter Five

The South Shields Case - Subverting the Trade Disputes Act 1906?

K D Ewing

THE Labour movement was to discover within a year of enactment that its new 'charter' did not extend quite as far as it had thought, the Act failing in its first test before the courts.[1] The decision of the House of Lords in *Conway v Wade* [2] in fact appeared to mark a retreat by the judges, in the sense that the conduct complained of was similar to the conduct in *Allen v Flood*,[3] which had been found just over 10 years earlier not to yield any liability. In that case, an official of the Boilermakers' Society had warned the Glengall Iron Company at Regent Dock, Millwall that there would be a strike unless a number of shipwrights were dismissed in the course of an inter-union dispute (the other union being the Shipwrights' Provident Union). According to Lord James of Hereford in a speech concurring with the majority of a divided House of Lords, it was not unlawful for a union official to inform an employer of an intention by employees to stop work.[4] Yet in *Conway v Wade* such conduct was now found not only to be unlawful, but also to be uncovered by the new protections enacted in 1906. *Conway v Wade* was thus seen, at least initially, to 'set aside all protection that was formerly supposed to exist under *Allen v Flood* and render useless the 3rd section of the 1906 Act unless the men are actually on strike'.[5]

It is remarkable, nevertheless, that there was no major campaign to reverse the Lords' decision, and no proposal to amend the Act in its aftermath. The union paid the plaintiff's damages and costs, a burden duly relieved by TUC affiliates (with the giant MFGB contributing about a third, though not without protest).[6] There were possibly many reasons for this rather mute response, but principally it is to be explained by an apparent belief on the part of the trade unions that a fundamentally sound piece of legislation had been subverted by the legal process. Civil cases in 1907 were still heard by middle class juries, and it is to a reform of the jury system that trade unionists directed their attention, nursing a grievance that the jury in *Conway v Wade* had been perverse. In any event, the explosion in the number of strikes in the period immediately after the decision revealed that the latter was at worst only a mild irritation, which could not by experience be said to be a serious restraint on trade union freedom. Moreover, in three important cases (involving different unions) immediately before and immediately after the First World War, the Court of Appeal moved some way successfully to distance itself from the Lords' decision, which was isolated to its own facts (as determined by the jury). But the failure to attend to the substance of the judgment, along with aspects of the legal process that produced it, was to return to haunt the Movement some 55 years later,[7] in a case with striking similarities to *Conway v Wade*.

The Dispute in South Shields

Conway was a boiler-scaler in South Shields dismissed in late 1907 by a company referred to in the Law Reports as Readhead, almost certainly the ship-building company which is said to have built over 600 vessels between 1872 and 1984. The founder of the firm, John Readhead had died in 1894, the business now being run by his sons, and becoming a limited company only in 1909, with one of the sons assuming the role of chairman and managing director.[8] At the time of *Conway v Wade*, the company was run by James Readhead, who was a prominent local citizen, being chairman of the South Shields Gas Company, the president of many local charities, and the occupant of Westoe Hall, South Shields. Created a baronet in 1922, he also betrayed Conservative sympathies in his membership of the Carlton Club and the Constitutional Club respectively. There was no evidence, however, that the company was anti-union, at least at the time of this episode, though there is a so far uncorroborated claim by J N Bell (the General Secretary of the National Amalgamated Union of Labour - the union involved in the case) that the company was in some way involved behind the scenes.[9] The company survived many financial crises during the 20th century, but was bought by British Shipbuilders in 1977 when the industry was nationalised. The yard was closed in 1984.

The National Amalgamated Union of Labour

The union involved in the dispute that ended in the House of Lords was the National Amalgamated Union of Labour (NAUL). Formed in 1889 as the Tyneside and General Labourers' Union, the NAUL was one of the three unions which later amalgamated in 1924 to form the National Union of General and Municipal Workers (now the GMB). The union was based in Newcastle, and it is said to have been strongest on the Tyne, though it also had a presence in other major centres (such as Liverpool, Belfast and Glasgow). In terms of its recruitment, the main concentration of membership appears to have been 'in the shipbuilding, ship-repairing and engineering industries',[10] though it also had members in a wide range of other industries (notably chemicals and cement, food and drink, and local authority maintenance). At its peak in 1920, the union had 170,000 members, though by the time of amalgamation this had fallen to 53,000, no doubt as a result of the slump in the early 1920s. In 1907, when the litigation started, the union had 22,411 members, and an annual income of £16,647. In terms of the government and administration of the union, it has been said by Clegg to have been 'the nearest approach to simple democracy amongst the general unions'.[11] Thus, 'having grown up in the shipyards and engineering shops it had imitated much of the terminology of the craft unions. Its organisers were called official delegates, and its constitution was intended to give working members absolute power over them'. This was said in turn to explain the suspicion of its executive committee towards powerful officers of other unions.[12]

The litigation in the South Shields case took place between 1907 and 1909, a period of extreme difficulty for the union in the North East. The quarterly and annual reports give details of the full extent of that difficulty which began to be noticed in the last quarter of 1907, coinciding with the events in *Conway v Wade*. Although the General Secretary could report at the end of 1907 that the year had been a 'fairly satisfactory one' for the union, a fall in membership in the September and December quarters of that year was 'a significant commentary on the decline in the amount of employment available'.[13] Membership on the Tyne was in decline, being hit hardest in Mid-Tyne and Shields, and problems were beginning to be reported by Owen Wade in his quarterly reports to the union. In the third quarter of 1907, it was reported that 'work in the shipyards during the quarter was only moderate, and the same applies to the ship-repairing industry',[14] while in the final quarter of 1907 Wade was to report that matters were 'very bad' with 'nothing but empty docks and the prospects for the incoming year . . . anything but bright'.[15] The problems facing the union and its members were to escalate following the announcement of both engineering and shipbuilding employers that they planned to impose pay cuts because of the adverse economic conditions. By the end of 1908, the General Secretary was to report that the previous year had been 'exceptionally bad' for the union, with income having declined as a result of a fall in membership of about 25% at a time when spending on lock out benefit had risen sharply.[16] In March 1908, a special levy had to be imposed on the members to help pay for benefits to colleagues laid off in three big disputes in the North East, the union 'having to pay on account of other people's troubles'.[17]

The Dispute at Readhead's

Conway, it seems, had been a member of the union intermittently for 18 years. In 1900, he had been fined by the No 173 (South Shields) branch for breach of the rules, but never paid the 10 shilling fine, despite having been told about the penalty by a shop steward. Under the rules of the union, unpaid fines were treated in the same way as unpaid contributions, so that non-payment could lead to expulsion from the union. In this case no attempt was made to enforce payment of the fine, and Conway left the union in 1905. He re-joined two years later, and became a member of another branch (the No 52 branch). On 23 September 1907, Conway secured employment with Readhead and shortly after beginning his employment, he was interviewed by Wade in his capacity as a full time delegate of the union. Wade raised no objection to Conway's employment, unaware of the unpaid fine, at a time when arrears of contributions appear to have been a significant problem to which Wade regularly referred in his quarterly reports.[18] On 30 September 1907, however, a shop steward of Branch 173 told Wade - 'at the request of the union men and on their account' - that unless Conway was 'stopped', the men would 'come out'. On the following day, Wade was told by the treasurer of Branch 173 that he had been deputed by the men to inform him of the outstanding fine. On the following day, Wade had a meeting with a foreman, who had previously been approached by the afore-mentioned shop steward about the matter.

In what was to be a major complication of the position,[19] the rules of the union provided that disputes between members and branches were to be decided by district committees, and that 'under no circumstances' were district delegates (such as Wade) 'to take part in a movement initiated by members or a strike which has not first been sanctioned by the executive council' in accordance with the rules of the union. Nevertheless, Wade advised the foreman that there was a problem about 'money matters' between Conway and the union, and that he had better 'stop' Conway in order to avoid trouble. Conway was summoned by the foreman and told to put things straight with the union. Conway then saw Wade twice, and 'remonstrated' with him but declined to pay the fine. Consequently he had to leave his job at Readhead's and was unable to get work anywhere at Smith's Dock in South Shields. His claim for £50 represented about seven and a half month' wages, as he had been taken on as a charge-hand at a rate of 33 shillings a week. According to Lord Shaw of Dunfermline in the House of Lords, the union accepted 'no responsibility whatever' for Wade's conduct.[20] The hapless Wade, who appeared simply to be the cipher of the men's discontent was branded by the House of Lords as a 'mischief – maker', an 'outsider', and a 'mere intermeddler'[21], condemned in the Court of Appeal for contemplating 'with complacent indifference the result that [Conway] would have to choose between starvation and the workhouse'.[22]

The Legal Proceedings

At some point, Mr Conway consulted Hannay, Hannay and Stuart, a firm of solicitors still practising in South Shields, now under the name of Hannay and Hannay. A letter from the firm to the union complaining about the action of Mr Wade towards J Conway was considered by the Executive Council of the NAUL on 12 October 1907. It was agreed at that meeting, that the Executive Council could accept no responsibility in the matter,[23] and at a subsequent meeting on 1 November 1907, a letter from the union's own solicitor was read 'stating there was no claim against the union'.[24] At this point, however, the union was on notice that legal proceedings had commenced in the Durham County Court, with Conway seeking £50 in damages for having:

> *unlawfully and maliciously, by threats and other coercive acts directed towards the plaintiff and to his employers, procured the dismissal of the plaintiff and prevented, and continued to prevent, his employment, and, in the alternative, that the defendant, acting as district delegate of the union, but without authority, unlawfully, and for the sole purpose of punishing the plaintiff for non payment of a fine, molested the plaintiff and, by threats directed to his employers, procured the plaintiff's dismissal from service, and had threatened to prevent, and had in fact prevented, the plaintiff from obtaining services elsewhere, whereby the*

plaintiff had suffered injury and loss.[25]

The County Court's Decision and the Union's Response

Owen Wade disputed the allegations against him and argued that even if he had done these things, his conduct was protected by the 1906 Act. The jury sitting in South Shields disagreed, and on 14 November 1907 found that:

- there was no trade dispute, existing or contemplated 'by the men';
- Wade did not act as a result of a trade dispute being communicated to him by the men;
- Wade made a threat to the employer and that this prevented or was intended to prevent Conway from retaining employment;
- the threat was made in order to compel Wade to pay the fine and to punish him for not having done so;
- Wade's actions were not done only to warn the employer that the union men would leave as a result of their being unwilling to work with Conway;
- Wade's actions were not done as a result of the men objecting to work with Conway; and that
- what Wade did was more than act on behalf of the men employed at Readhead's.

On the basis of these findings, the county court judge found for Conway and refused a request from Wade for a new trial on the ground that the decision of the jury was perverse. Perhaps unsurprisingly, the findings attracted a furious response from J N Bell, who reported to his Executive Council on the following day (15 November 1907) that the case had been decided 'without regard to the evidence or the amendment of the law as contained in the Trade Disputes Act 1906'. According to the minutes, Bell 'went into the whole matter and showed that [Wade] had simply done the duty which it was expected was covered by the law', yet despite the 'plain facts, the Judge had summed up without regard to the Trade Disputes Act, and a middle class jury had as usual over-ridden an Act of Parliament and given a perverse verdict'.26

The matter was revisited in greater detail some five days later, the General Secretary having had the opportunity to consult with the union's solicitor, from whom a report was read to the Executive Council. A representative of the solicitor also attended to answer questions from the Committee. The union was advised that the verdict of the jury was 'a travesty of justice', which 'took no account of the evidence' and 'ignored' the 1906 Act which was 'specially drafted to protect the officials of a Trade Union when performing the functions of their office, and the will of the members'. It was also acknowledged that the case was important 'as being the first of its kind since the passing of the Act, and for that reason ought to be fought out in another Court'. Concern was expressed that if the verdict was accepted, 'it would mean that the Act of 1906 was valueless to the Trade Unions of the country, as it would be impossible for the officials to carry on the duty of their office without liability to actions at law, at every turn, at the whim of an unscrupulous employer or workman'. As a result, counsel 'strongly advised' an appeal to 'a Court free from middle-class prejudice', a view shared by the union's solicitor. The perception was thus that the union official would have a better chance of a fair hearing in the High Court without a jury than in the county court with a jury. After a general discussion of the matter, it was unanimously resolved as follows:

> *That after hearing the written report and opinion of our legal advisers in this matter, this Executive Council in the interests of our members (sic) welfare and the Union, hereby advises Mr Wade to appeal against the verdict, and agree to support him in doing so. Further, we instruct our legal advisers to take the necessary steps to Appeal in the Divisional Court on our behalf, and leave them with the discretionary power to employ leading Counsel or otherwise as they may deem best.*

Owen Wade was thus fully supported by the union, and it was further agreed that the general office should 'forward any sums necessary to our solicitors for carrying forward the appeal'.27

From the County Court to the House of Lords

A Divisional Court of Channell and Sutton JJ refused to disturb the decision of the county court on the ground that it did 'substantial justice' and showed no evidence of perversity. The decision was considered by the Executive Council on 8 May 1908, the Committee being briefed again by their solicitor. Explaining 'the position at great length', he pointed out that 'counsel and solicitors were agreed that the case should be taken to the Court of Appeal because if the present judgment were to stand it would make a portion of the Trades Union (sic) Act of 1906 inoperative and useless, besides making it most difficult for any Trade Union Official to perform the work of the members and the Union by whom he was employed'. The Executive accepted this advice, but concluded that 'in so important a case to Trade Unions of the country, an appeal for some financial assistance should be made to carry the case to a higher court, because it was hardly fair to expect this Union to carry the whole burden'.[28] This was to be done through the Parliamentary Committee of the TUC, which – although sympathetic - declared itself unable to render any assistance until the case reached the House of Lords.[29] In the meantime, however, the Court of Appeal decided in favour of Wade on 30 July 1908, a decision greeted with some satisfaction by the Executive Council of the union on the following day, especially as it carried with it costs in the Court of Appeal, the Divisional Court and the county court. Although some doubt appears to have been expressed about whether the money would be recovered, the union was also advised that 'there was little chance of the other side making a further appeal to the House of Lords as the judgment was unanimous'. Nevertheless, the minutes record that on the recommendation of the General Secretary, 'it was agreed that our local members be asked to restrain their jubilation at the satisfactory termination of the trials'.[30]

This was wise advice, for any jubilation would be short-lived. By the time Bell addressed the TUC Annual Congress on 11 September 1908 at the request of the TUC Parliamentary Committee,[31] there was now uncertainty about an appeal, with Conway having been given until 22 October to decide whether or not to proceed. Bell reported to Congress that in October 1907, members of his union in South Shields had decided to strike, and instructed one of their officials to inform the employer of their decision. The employer had removed the man against whom objection had been taken, and he chose not to pursue reinstatement, although this option had been open to him. Bell explained the course of the litigation, which had already cost the union 'something like £500', costs which the union were unlikely to recover.[32] Concerned that the matter might yet end up in the House of Lords, Bell raised the question of financial support under Standing Order 11 which provided that

> *In the event of a legal point arising, which in the opinion of the Parliamentary Committee [of the TUC] (after consultation with counsel) should be tested in the House of Lords in the general interest of Trade Unionism, the Committee shall be empowered to levy the affiliated societies pro rata to provide the necessary expenses. Any society failing to pay the levy shall be reported to Congress.*

Conway did of course pursue the matter to the Lords, where the union incurred costs of £456.12.6d.33 In 1910, the Parliamentary Committee reported that a levy on the affiliates was 'responded to in the most ready manner, and that the National Union of Labour (sic) has been reimbursed the whole of the costs involved in defending its interests in the appeal to the House of Lords'.34

A Judicial Challenge to the Trade Disputes Act

Of the four courts involved in *Conway v Wade*, it was thus only the Court of Appeal that decided for the defendant, though it did not do so willingly. The Master of the Rolls, Sir Herbert Cozens – Hardy, set the scene by claiming that the 'main purpose' of the 1906 Act was 'to put trade unions in a peculiar and preferential position and to treat trade disputes differently from all other disputes'. Although there was some discussion by him of the various liabilities to which the 1906 Act was addressed, there was no consideration of the question whether the appellant's conduct was tortious; and if not, whether it needed the protection of the 1906 Act; or if so, whether the 1906 Act would provide the necessary protection. The case turned wholly on whether there was a trade dispute for the purposes of section 3, the assumption being that there would be no liability if Owen Wade's action was in contemplation or furtherance of a trade dispute. In addressing this question, the Master of the Rolls thought it 'impossible to doubt' that there was an existing trade dispute, in furtherance of which the threats were made, namely 'a dispute between some members of the union and the plaintiff arising out of the non-payment of the fine'. With impeccable logic, there was ground for holding that the threat was in contemplation of another dispute, namely 'a dispute between the employers and the union men if the plaintiff continued to work'. So far as the Master of the Rolls was concerned, it made no difference for the purposes of the Act that the defendant had not the authority of the union to call out the men, and that there may have been motives of jealousy prompting [his] action'.[35]

The Attack in the Court of Appeal

The second judgment delivered in the Court of Appeal was something of a feast of self-indulgence, for which the Master of the Rolls' opening remarks were but a modest *aperitif.* Farwell LJ had full bodied views about trade unions, having given the High Court judgment (against the union) in the *Taff Vale* case, a decision he acknowledged in *Conway v Wade* as being one with which it was 'common knowledge' trade unions were 'dissatisfied'. In so holding in the *Taff Vale* case, Sir George Farwell did not mince his words, taking the view that trade unions were 'irresponsible bodies with such wide capacity for evil'. Sir George was to earn his spurs as an uncompromising opponent of trade unionism, popping up again in the *Osborne* judgment only a few months after the Court of Appeal decision in *Conway v Wade*, to denounce the arrangements for trade union support of the Labour Party as 'utterly unconstitutional'.[36] In *Conway v Wade*, however, he expressed himself in even more intemperate terms, with Sir Frederick Pollock writing with some understatement in the *Law Quarterly Review* that the judgment of Sir George Farwell 'contains, we think, the most vigorous denunciation of an Act of Parliament which has been reported in modern times'. Sir Frederick pointed out that Sir George had 'roundly declared that it was an Act not for preventing but for promoting strife, and cursed it in the name of Bacon's Abridgement, Blackstone, and the Book of Proverbs', before adding in a sniffily superior way that 'we only wish he had quoted Bowen LJ instead of Bacon, a book of no authority' (unlike the Book of Proverbs, it seems).[37]

Lord Justice Farwell was certainly vigorous in his criticism, in a polemic that occupied more than five pages of the Law Report. It started with 'the struggle for individual freedom', which began before Magna Carta, and was 'enunciated by one of its provisions'. It moved on to the time of Charles II, since when 'every man has been free to dispose of his capital or his labour in any lawful manner that he chose'.[38] It culminated in 1906, until when this 'right of freedom to dispose of capital or labour has always been enforced by the courts'. But not any more, now that trade unions had 'the unrestricted capacity for injuring other people by the use of that capacity which they had not, a privilege possessed by no other person or corporation in the realm'. The 1906 Act was 'in entire contradiction of those doctrines of personal freedom and equality before the law which have hitherto been its main aim and object'.[39] Not only that. The Act challenged the principle settled for centuries that 'disputes are evils to be discouraged, and that a barrator, ie, one who for maliciousness or for the sake of gain raises discord between neighbours, is guilty of an offence at common law'. But not any more, the intention of the 1906 Act being to encourage trade disputes whether trade unions were concerned in them or not, the 'aim and object' of the Act being 'the stirring up of strife', a practice as wicked in 1908 as when King Solomon denounced those who 'soweth discord among brethren'.[40]

A Miscarriage of Justice

In light of the foregoing, counsel for the respondent argued that it was therefore necessary to place a limit on the statutory language, to prevent some of its more outlandish consequences. But although wedded to Dicey-esque notions of the rule of law,[41] Sir George was bound by a more fundamental rule of law, namely the rule of parliamentary sovereignty. It proved to be impossible to restrict the scope of the Act, as there was 'no ambiguity' on which the courts could gnaw, leaving Sir George to lament that:

It was possible for the courts in former years to defend individual liberty against the aggression of kings and barons, because the defence rested on the law which they administered; it is not possible for the Courts to do so when the Legislature alters the law as to destroy liberty, for they can only administer the law. The Legislature cannot make evil good, but it can make it not actionable.[42]

Farwell LJ was thus unable to agree with the Divisional Court, commenting that it was 'clear on the plaintiff's own evidence that the defendant's act was in contemplation of a dispute both between employers and men, shewn by the threat to call out the men, and also between men and men, connected with the employment of the plaintiff'.43 Farwell LJ regretted this conclusion, because 'it inflicts a cruel hardship on the plaintiff, and it is no consolation to him that far greater hardships will doubtless be inflicted in the future on persons even more innocent than himself – persons who were not guilty even of failure to pay 10 shillings seven years ago'.44

An altogether different note was struck by Kennedy LJ who thought not only that the verdict of the jury was perverse, but that there had been a miscarriage of justice visited upon Wade. In the judge's view, it was 'plain that there was, when Wade went to see [the foreman] and made use of the words which the jury have found to constitute a threat, and upon which the plaintiff's action is based, a dispute between other workmen and the plaintiff, and that what Wade did was in furtherance of that existing dispute'. According to Kennedy LJ, the same evidence revealed that Wade's conduct was in contemplation of a dispute between the workers and the employer if the fine was unpaid. Thus, Wade 'obviously had in view' a dispute between the workmen, who had expressed their determination to cease their work at Readhead's if the plaintiff was allowed to continue working without paying the fine'.[45] Kennedy LJ also disputed the claim that the prime movers among the workmen were motivated by jealousy caused by Conway's promotion to the position of chargeman. But even if they had been so moved, that would not 'affect the reality of the existence of a trade dispute'. In the view of Kennedy LJ, 'there are many disputes, many serious disputes, in matters other than trade in which some at least of the originators or partisans are actuated by indirect or personal motives, but the disputes will none the less be real disputes on that account'.[46]

Renewing Battle in the House of Lords

Despite his apparent misuse of Bacon, Sir George Farwell threw down a heavily spiked gauntlet for the House of Lords, which clearly caused some discomfort. *Conway v Wade* was clearly seen to be a big case for the House, with a Bench of seven judges being assembled for the purpose. Although 1909 was the occasion of a number of other memorable decisions,[47] only one other case heard that year was decided by a Bench of this size.[48] In moving into the House of Lords, the case travelled into a new political realm, with no fewer than five of the seven judges who heard the case having been MPs at some point earlier in their careers, three sitting as Liberals (Lords Loreburn, Shaw of Dunfermline, and James of Hereford), and two as Conservatives from Irish constituencies (Lords Macnaghten and Atkinson); the only two without this kind of political baggage were Lords Collins and Gorrell. Of this seven who decided unanimously for the plaintiff, two (Lords James of Hereford and Macnaghten) sat in *Allen v Flood* where they were on the side of the defendant.[49] More importantly, two of the seven judges who took part in *Conway v Wade* (Lords Loreburn and James of Hereford) had also played an important part in the legislative business of the House of Lords while the Bill was being passed. They had crossed swords (very gently) in the Lords' proceedings and the stage was now set for a return match, albeit in a different venue playing to different rules. In the end, however, it was a damp squib, with neither pressing any advantage. Lord Loreburn beat a retreat, perhaps stung by 'some opinions expressed in the Court of Appeal with regard to [the] Act and the motives supposed to have actuated those who passed it'.[50]

The Lord Chancellor's Retreat

Lord Loreburn's position was nothing if not unusual.[51] Before his elevation as Lord Chancellor, he had been plain Sir Robert Reid, QC. A radical liberal, Reid was a good friend of the TUC (toasted as such at a TUC dinner to celebrate the passing of the 1906 Act),[52] and was greatly admired on the Labour benches in the House of Commons.[53] Not only had Loreburn been involved in drafting the Trade Disputes Bill,[54] he also moved the Second Reading debate in which he described it as 'just and honest', fully expecting it to be given a Second Reading by his peers 'willingly and cheerfully'.[55] Loreburn's parliamentary responsibility for the Bill extended beyond Second Reading to deal with difficult points raised in Committee, where he revealed a steely determination to reject any amendment that would have the effect of restricting its scope. An attempt by Lord Balfour of Burleigh to knock out what became section 3 of the Act was met with the retort from Loreburn that he always thought *Lumley v Gye* [56] to be 'bad law', as did 'a great number of [his] confreres and many occupants of the Bench'.[57] On clause 4 of the Bill, Lord Loreburn stood firm against amendments designed to dilute its terms, insisting that trade unions were to be treated like other unincorporated associations, such as the National Liberal Federation and the Primrose League, restoring trade unions 'to the position they occupied before 1871'.[58] In the same way, he refused to give way to proposals to narrow the definition of a trade dispute in clause 5, commenting that

> *Our view is not that this Bill should be restricted to workmen in cotton mills, for example, or in collieries. We think that if a strike is legitimate with one set of people a strike is equally legitimate with others, provided it complies with the law.*[59]

Such was the primitive nature of Britain's constitutional arrangements and the promiscuous conduct of Britain's political class that Lord Loreburn now had the curious task of interpreting and applying his own Bill in a judicial forum. Here we find that, between enactment and operation, a difference of emphasis is evident; what was presented in the legislative process as a Bill of liberation, was now being subjected to a judicial process of restraint by its erstwhile champion. Lord Loreburn's speech began by placing restraints on section 3, drawing a tortuous distinction between the situation where 'the inducement was accompanied by violence or threats (always remembering that a warning is one thing and a threat is another)', and where 'there was no violence and no threat, and yet the inducement involved a breach of contract'. Section 3 was designed only to deal with the latter case (about which there was said to be uncertainty after *Lumley v Gye*), but not the former, in relation to which 'there is no change'.[60] Lord Loreburn's other concern related to the scope of section 5, which he held not to apply where – as was deemed to be the case here – 'some meddler sought to use the trade dispute as a cloak beneath which to interfere with impunity in other people's work or business'. In that situation, 'a jury would be entirely justified in saying that what [the defendant] did was done in contemplation or furtherance, not of a trade dispute, but of his own designs, sectarian, political, or purely mischievous, as the case might be'.[61] According to Lord Loreburn, the defendant in this case

> *must be taken to have acted as a mischief maker in order to injure the plaintiff from unworthy motives, accompanied by threats that he would cause Messrs Readhead's men to come out, in a matter with which he had no concern; for it is admitted that, though district delegate of the union, he was acting without authority.*[62]

The Scale of the Retreat

Lord Loreburn was followed by Lord James of Hereford. However, the latter disappointed all expectations, and, as already suggested, the potential conflict with Lord Loreburn did not materialise. Indeed as we shall see, Lord James of Hereford took a position less unfavourable to the scope of the Act than had Lord Loreburn. One of the Bill's sternest critics delivered a dull speech, despite his evident anger about the 1906 Act, anger laid bare in private correspondence with the Duke of Devonshire. The latter referred to Lord James of Hereford as being 'furious with the Opposition leaders because they will not go to extreme lengths in opposing the Trade Disputes Bill'.[63] These concerns about the Bill had attracted the attention of the *Law Times*, which had remarked that in the course of the parliamentary proceedings on the Bill, Lord James of Hereford had been the only peer to have had 'the courage of his convictions'.[64] He earned this distinction by insisting on a division in Committee on clause 4, which in his view was 'an attack on the constitutional law'.[65] However, none of this hostility was to surface in *Conway v Wade*, deep rooted though it may have been. Lord James of Hereford stuck to the facts and did not hunt for legal scraps or use the occasion to rewrite the 1906 Act. So far as he was concerned, there were two questions of fact – the first was whether the acts complained of were the outcome of a trade dispute;[66] and the second whether Wade used threatening language to the employer 'with the intention of preventing the plaintiff retaining his employment'.[67] As to the first, there was no ground for disturbing the jury's finding that there was no trade dispute, a finding he would have shared had he been a member of the jury. As to the second, it was accepted that Wade had threatened the employer out of a spirit of hostility towards Conway, as a result of which 'a good cause of action was established'.

What is unclear from Lord James of Hereford's speech is whether the latter cause of action would have been permitted had there been a trade dispute. The implication of Lord Loreburn's speech (with which Lords MacNaghten and Gorrell concurred) is that the threats unprotected by section 3 would have been actionable, *even if there had been a trade dispute*. So much is clear from his remark that 'if there be threats or violence, [section 3] gives no protection, for then there is some other ground of action beside the ground that 'it induces some other person to break a contract', and so forth'.[68] Apart from Lord James of Hereford, this was a matter on which the other Law Lords who spoke in this case were also silent. The implication from both Lords Atkinson and Shaw of Dunfermline, however, is that there would be no liability and that the threat to call a strike would have been protected if on the facts a trade dispute had been found to exist. Lord Atkinson thought that the jury were justified in finding that Owen Wade had made a threat to the employer; and he continued by saying that he understood the Court of Appeal to be of the opinion that 'apart from the Trade Disputes Act 1906, the plaintiff would on these findings have been entitled to a verdict, notwithstanding that the defendant did not conspire with another, or with others, but merely acted alone'. This is an opinion with which Lord Atkinson concurred, suggesting strongly that Wade would have been protected if his action was in contemplation or furtherance of a trade dispute.[69] But on the facts, the Act did not apply, a view shared by Lord Shaw of Dunfermline. We are thus left with a remarkable irony. Lord Loreburn - the adviser to the trade unions, the architect of the Trade Disputes Bill, and the navigator of the Bill through the House of Lords - was responsible for gratuitously introducing a major limitation of the scope of the 1906 Act, a limitation proposed by none of the other – less radical – judges with whom he sat.

Reaction to and Impact of *Conway v Wade*

Sir George Farwell's rhetoric may thus have produced major concessions, with Lord Shaw of Dunfermline also obliged expressly to dissent from the opinion and language used by the Court of Appeal as to the object and intention of the Act.[70] But having done so, it was necessary to show that there was clear water on substantive issues between the two courts, demonstrated in Lord Shaw's case by a narrower construction of the phrase 'in contemplation or furtherance of a trade dispute'. Sir George Farwell – the devout common lawyer, the architect of *Taff Vale*, and arch-critic of the 1906 Act - was thus perhaps to ensure that there could continue to be room for manoeuvre for the courts in industrial disputes. The significance of this was not lost on the contemporary legal press, which had been outraged by the immunities of the 1906 Act. In welcoming the decision, the *Law Journal* noted that the Lords' interpretation of the 1906 Act 'gives juries considerable latitude'.[71] On the same day, the *Solicitor's Journal* expressed the hope that 'the decision will do something towards checking persecution of workmen who have small differences with the trade unions to which they belong; and towards stopping the use of the Trade Disputes Act 1906, as an entrenchment behind which such persecutions can be safely carried on'.[72] It was left to Sir Frederick Pollock in the *Law Quarterly Review* to intimate that it was too early to tell whether 'Farwell LJ's pessimistic view of the Act is at all modified by the declaration that it was not so bad as he thought it was'.[73]

Reaction of the Trade Unions

In contrast to the jubilation in the legal press about the House of Lords' decision, it is notable that it received only a muted response from the ranks of the trade union movement. At the Executive Council meeting on 30 July 1909 (three days after the decision), J N Bell 'gave a long and lengthy report of the decision', and he 'explained the nature of the judgment and the course to be taken for the future'. But the union was now pre-occupied with more pressing concerns caused by the decline in membership on the Thames, the Tees and the Clyde, with the General Secretary's third quarterly report for 1909 pointing out that

> *In the Engineering trade on the North East Coast, the number of unemployed men, both in August and September, stood at 20.3%. In the Shipbuilding trade the percentage of unemployed stood for September, on the Tyne and Blyth, 28.6%, or slightly less than in August. The Wear was 40.1% and the Tees and Hartlepools, 25.9%. In the latter two places there is a slight improvement, but in the Shipbuilding trade on the North East Coast there is still practically one man in three out of work.*[74]

These remarks were echoed by Owen Wade who reported in September 1909 that 'work during the quarter in the shipbuilding industry was only fair, in the ship-repairing very dull, and the prospect not very bright'.[75] But it is not only the NAUL that appeared to be mute in its response to Conway v Wade. The same is true of the TUC, there being no resolutions to condemn the decision, and – in contrast to Taff Vale - no campaign to secure its reversal. The only resolution at the TUC Annual Congress in 1910 on the Trade Disputes Act was from the Bleachers' and Dyers' union calling for an amendment to make it unlawful for employers during a strike or lock out to house strike-breakers in premises not certified for use as a dwelling.[76] And the only consideration of Conway v Wade at the TUC Annual Congress in 1910 was to report that all affiliates had made a financial contribution to the legal costs, as required by the Standing Orders.[77]

This apparently low key response is not, however, to be taken as indifference or inaction on the part of the TUC, which also had more pressing concerns following the *Osborne* judgment in December 1909. It was realised by David Shackleton in his Chairman's report to the Parliamentary Committee on 30 August 1909 (a month after the decision was announced) that 'the question of the composition of the juries trying these cases would have to be considered with a view to bringing about a reform of the jury system'.[78] So the problem lay not with the substantive law of the 1906 Act, but with the role of the juries in its administration, and this was to be the focus of the TUC's response to the decision, with a resolution on the jury system drafted by the Parliamentary Committee for presentation to Congress in 1910.[79] Moved by W J Davis of the Brassworkers, this claimed that the constitution of juries was 'unfair and partial', and called for a reorganisation of the system to ensure that all classes of the community were included on jury lists, and that jurors were adequately paid.[80] But although *Conway v Wade* appears to have been the catalyst for the TUC Parliamentary Committee's resolution, W J Davis had concerns about the legal system (and his own personal experiences) other than *Conway v Wade*, which he never mentioned in his conference speeches in 1910 or 1911 when the resolution was presented a second time. The resolution was carried on both occasions (as was a similar resolution in 1912),[81] a number of deputations were made to ministers on the question, and a departmental committee on jury law and practice was established by the Home Office in December 1911.[82] The main point to emerge from the reaction to the case, however, is this. Just as *Taff Vale* reinforced the realisation that fair laws required parliamentary representation (and the formation of the Labour Representation Committee), so *Conway v Wade* reinforced the realisation that fair laws passed by Parliament required a reform of the legal system if they were to operate as intended.

Limited Impact of the Decision

The TUC's wholly pragmatic response to *Conway v Wade* was soon to be justified by events which would have made it difficult persuasively to argue that it was any more than a mild irritation rather than a serious challenge to trade union freedom under the 1906 Act. In the wake of the latter's enactment, the number of working days lost as a result of strike action rose dramatically, from 2.3 million days in 1905. Although the figures varied from year to year, with only 2.1 million and 2.6 million days lost in 1907 and 1909 respectively, there were roughly 10 million days lost annually in 1908, 1910 and 1911, and a staggering 40.8 million days lost in 1912 alone. The last is a figure exceeded on only two subsequent occasions (1921 and 1926).[83] According to Pelling, the restoration of trade union freedoms 'initiated' this period of 'comparative industrial militancy',[84] though this may be to claim too much for the Act, which at best facilitated trade union action at a time of rising prices. By 1911, the government's concern was thus to contain rather than extend the scope of the Act. This was particularly true of section 2, with Winston Churchill (the Home Secretary who was also sympathetically receiving TUC deputations on the administration of justice) distributing a memorandum on 'Intimidation During Trade Disputes', making clear that picketing in numbers may take the pickets outside the protection of the Act, and also that it 'does not interfere in any way with the liberty of the workman, who may stop to speak to the pickets, or not, as he pleases'.[85]

The rising tide of militancy in fact produced a ferocious backlash from employers, with Chambers of Commerce and employers' associations demanding a revision of the 1906 Act. They had in mind the repeal of section 2 and the repeal or amendment of section 4. In October 1911, the TUC Parliamentary Committee circulated the members and officials of affiliates to draw their attention to this campaign, as well as to a memorial submitted to the Prime Minister by the Employers' Parliamentary Council which claimed that the trade union immunity has 'resulted in great injury to the trade and commerce of the country'.[86] Apart from the rising tide of industrial action since *Conway v Wade*, this campaign by employers provides further evidence that trade unions were not unduly incommoded by the House of Lords' decision which appeared to provide insufficient meat on which increasingly agitated employers could bite. But the campaign also reinforced the pragmatism and good judgment of the TUC's response to *Conway v Wade*. This was not the time to re-open the settlement of 1906, but the time to hold what you had. It was the good fortune of the trade union movement that the government was unconvinced by the employers' case for change, with G R Askwith (the Chief Industrial Commissioner) writing in a memorandum on 'Labour Unrest' circulated to Cabinet –

> *None of the many suggestions set forth, generally by uninformed persons, such as Compulsory Arbitration, Extension of Trade Boards, Copartnership, . . . Enforcement of Collective Bargaining, etc, nor any feasible course within the province of legislative enactment, could be . . . undertaken unless the method . . . was indicated on firm grounds or its utility proved in a manner which would convince the country that panic legislation had not been undertaken.*[87]

These views were supported by Sidney Buxton, President of the Board of Trade, who in a separate memorandum to his colleagues dated 13 April 1912 set himself against 'crude proposals' for prohibiting strikes, expressing concern that employers were looking to be able to 'attach union funds' and that powers of peaceful picketing might be abolished. So far as he was concerned, the wage rises secured by the wave of strikes were for the most part justified.[88]

The Legacy of *Conway v Wade*

In moving the Parliamentary Committee's resolution on the administration of justice at Congress in 1910, W J Davis made clear that the jury was not his only concern. He was troubled also by the attacks some judges made on trade unions, singling out Grantham J for particular mention.[89] It is, however, one of the other remarkable features of *Conway v Wade* that unlike the *Osborne* judgment in the same year,[90] it did not lead to a rash of legal actions against trade unions or their officials, despite the high incidence in the levels of industrial action in its immediate aftermath. Even more remarkable is that although a few High Court judges expressed undue hostility to the 1906 Act, they were quickly overturned by the Court of Appeal which showed no appetite to make use of the space provided by the House of Lords in *Conway v Wade*, providing even further vindication for the position adopted by the TUC. Quite why the courts should face in the opposite direction from Lord Loreburn is difficult to understand, though it is not to be overlooked that in restricting the scope of the 1906 Act, the Lords' decision in *Conway v Wade* nevertheless left the right to engage in lawful industrial action relatively undisturbed. Indeed, Lord Shaw of Dunfermline acknowledged that the term trade dispute had been given a 'very wide interpretation' by s 5(3), and Lord Loreburn made clear that secondary action was protected. This reinforces the view that although the House of Lords cut back the scope of the 1906 Act, there is a risk of exaggerating its impact in a flourish of hyperbole. This is not to deny, however, that *Conway v Wade* was to have a devastating impact, though, as has already been indicated, it was some time before the seeds planted in 1909 were to bear fruit.

From Conway v Wade . . .

The first of the reported cases decided after the House of Lords decision was brought by Robert Gaskell against the Lancashire and Cheshire Miners' Federation, as well as the General Secretary of the union and one of its officials.[91] Gaskell had been a member of the Constitutional Labour Union in St Helens when the defendant union announced that it wanted all miners at Bamfurlong Collieries to be members of the Federation. On 24 February 1911, union officials informed the employer that if they continued to employ Gaskell and two other men, the Executive Committee of the Federation had decided to call a strike. The employer continued to employ the three men, whereupon 14 days' strike notice was given by the union, following which the Bamfurlong three were first suspended and then dismissed. They now claimed an injunction and damages against the union in a case that raised a number of arguments making opportunistic use of the *Osborne* judgment. In the end, however, the Court of Appeal (with the same three members who had decided for Owen Wade) upheld a decision of the lower court that the conduct of the defendants was protected by the 1906 Act. Sir Herbert Cozens-Hardy gave short shrift to the suggestion that there was no trade dispute, before turning his attention to the question whether there were 'any threats used as distinct from information or warnings as to what might be the consequences in the temper of the men if non-union men continued to work'. The trial judge had held on the evidence that there were no threats, and it was not possible to interfere with his decision. For his part, the dreaded Farwell LJ agreed that the question had reduced itself to a question of fact.

Gaskell was decided in the Court of Appeal on 5 July 1912. The trade unions could be equally satisfied by the outcome of *Dallimore v Williams* [92] in the same court some four months later, a case that involved an application by an employer rather than an employee. Holmes Dallimore brought proceedings against a number of officials of the Amalgamated Musicians' Union who had induced a number of musicians not to play at a performance of his British Ex-Guards' Band as part of a union campaign demanding additional payments for Sunday working. The case was tried before a jury which found that the defendants had induced the plaintiff's employees to break their contracts, that there was no trade dispute, and that the acts of the defendants were done out of spite. These findings had been made following directions from Ridley J who had 'repeatedly expressed the view that a trade dispute meant a dispute between an employer and his men, or between the men'. This was said by the Master of the Rolls to be inconsistent with the definition of a trade dispute in the 1906 Act, who was also unimpressed by the finding of spite, even though there was 'abundant evidence' to support such a finding. Sir Herbert did not think 'it necessary for any person in order to get the protection of the Trade Disputes Act to say that the act done was entirely in furtherance of a trade dispute and that his mind was altogether free from malice'. *Conway v Wade* was expressly put to one side as a case decided 'on the facts as found by the jury', though it was conceded that there were some observations by the court 'which might some day require careful consideration'. Again the dreaded Farwell LJ concurred (joined on this occasion by Hamilton LJ), and a fresh trial ordered.[93]

. . . to Rookes v Barnard

The trade unions thus wrestled back the 1906 Act by successfully confining *Conway v Wade* to its facts. Paradoxically, a crucial role in this process was played by the Court of Appeal, as it played an equally crucial role following the commencement of hostilities between labour, capital and judiciary in the aftermath of the truce on industrial warfare imposed by the First World War. Fresh concerns about the scope of the Act were raised by the decision in *Valentine v Hyde*, another case with facts not dissimilar to those in *Conway v Wade*. In that case, Astbury J read *Conway v Wade* to restrict s 5 in two ways. First, that 'a dispute between workmen and workmen whether a man should be forced out of employment if he did not pay a fine to his own union was not a trade dispute within the meaning of the Act'.[94] Secondly, as not to cover 'the case of coercive interference in which the intervenor may have in his mind that if he does not get his own way he will take steps to bring a trade dispute into existence'.[95] However, this line of reasoning was questioned in the High Court in the following year, and brought to an end by the Court of Appeal in *White v Riley*,[96] though it was to cast a long shadow over trade dispute law, and became an important justification for a number of restraints developed in the course of the twentieth century. It was, however, some time before *Conway v Wade* was to make a significant re-appearance in the law reports, popping up in *Huntley v Thornton* where the plaintiff was awarded £500 against 11 defendants.[97]

Conway v Wade was resurrected most prominently, however, in *Rookes v Barnard* – in a case with not dissimilar facts - to justify the absence of immunity for the newly forged tort of intimidation. The case even had the complicating dimension that the three respondents were 'flagrantly violating a pledge not to strike, at least until constitutional means of resolving the dispute have been exhausted'.[98] In that case Douglas Rookes – a non-unionist - was dismissed from his employment following a threat by a number of union officers that there would be industrial action unless Rookes was dismissed. With no remedy against the employer (the dismissal was lawful) and no remedy against the union, Rookes sued three officials for damages, and was awarded £7,500 by a jury. The decision of the jury was reversed by the Court of Appeal on the ground that there was no actionable cause, and the Court of Appeal was in turn reversed by the House of Lords on the ground that the facts revealed an actionable intimidation for which there was no protection in either sections 1 or 3 of the Trade Disputes Act 1906. The speech of Lord Loreburn in *Conway v Wade* in fact makes the decision in Rookes all the easier to follow and understand, if not defend. For although it was acknowledged that Lord Loreburn's remarks on section 3 of the 1906 Act were obiter, they were nevertheless regarded as authoritative by the House of Lords in *Rookes v Barnard*. Lord Reid, in particular, relied on Lord Loreburn's views about section 3, commenting that 'there was no dissent from this by any other member of the

House, and, as Lord Loreburn was Lord Chancellor when the Act of 1906 was passed, he must have been well acquainted with its provisions'.[99] Lord Reid continued –

> *I would hold that what I have called the second meaning of [the first] part of section 3 is the right one – that it does not protect a person who induces a breach of contract by tortious means – both on the authority of Lord Loreburn and because it appears to me to be the better construction. The words 'on the ground only' are clearly intended to limit the scope of the section, and if the first meaning for which the respondents contend were right, there would be hardly any limit to its scope. It would give immunity in almost every case of inducing a breach of contract that seems likely to arise in connection with a strike or a threatened strike. Section 4 makes it quite clear that there is complete immunity for the trade union itself, and I cannot believe that the very guarded language of section 3 would have been used if it had been intended to give in addition almost complete immunity to all individuals acting in contemplation or furtherance of a trade dispute'.*[100]

Conclusion

So it is that a dispute about an unpaid 10 shilling fine came to occupy the attention of 13 judges and a jury in four courts between 1907 and 1909, and to contribute some 45 years later to one of the iconic labour law decisions of the 20th century. *Rookes v Barnard* was, of course, reversed by the Trade Disputes Act 1965 which made it clear that immunity applied to *threats* to break or induce a breach of a contract, as well as to *inducements* to breach a contract of employment. However, the legacy of *Conway v Wade* was to live on into the late 1970s, as the courts fastened upon the second and more prominent aspect of the decision. This was the aspect in which the House of Lords sought to restrain the definition of acts done 'in contemplation or furtherance of a trade dispute', in light of the provocation from Sir Herbert Cozens Hardy and Sir George Farwell respectively in the Court of Appeal. On at least three occasions in the 1970s, *Conway v Wade* was thus used narrowly to construe what was now TULRA 1974, s 29, in actions brought by employers to restrain industrial action, rather than by workers seeking relief for losses suffered because of the action of a trade union official.[101] In the *Star Sea Transport* case,[102] Lord Denning thought that *Conway v Wade* was authority for the need to put a limit on these statutory provisions, a point he developed at greater length in *Express Newspapers Ltd v McShane* where he said that

> *In construing the immunity the correct approach was shown 70 years ago by the House of Lords in* Conway v Wade. *The House then showed that the words of the statute are not to be construed widely so as to give unlimited immunity to law-breakers. They are to be construed with due limitations so as to keep the immunity within reasonable bounds. Otherwise the freedom of ordinary individuals to go about their business in peace would be intruded upon beyond all reason.*[103]

The use of *Conway v Wade* in this way was not brought to an end until the House of Lords intervened in *NWL Ltd v Woods*,[104] where three months after the former's 70th anniversary, Lord Diplock said that it was no longer to be regarded as authoritative, in view of changing parliamentary attitudes to trade disputes.[105] Apart from the fact that such a small issue could occupy so much time, the case nevertheless remains remarkable for other reasons, and several important questions remain unanswered. Not the least of these is the question of who supported the tenacious and determined Mr Conway? Presumably living in the same tight community as the trade unionists with whom he had fallen out, Conway would be an even more extraordinary man if he were able to pursue the course of conduct traced above unaided. Yet the only evidence to support collusion by the employer is the uncorroborated remark of J N Bell to the TUC Parliamentary Committee that the case represented 'an attempt of the employers to strike at the union'.[106] Against that is the fact that the employer's foreman was an important witness for Owen Wade, and was referred to in the legal proceedings as being a 'friendly witness'.[107] It is to be regretted that this dimension of the case will have to lay over until another day, with three requests to Hannay and Hannay in South Shields for information about the file having gone unacknowledged. On the other side, the evidence suggests that *Conway v Wade* is too easily dismissed as a case in which Owen Wade was simply pursuing a personal grudge rather than a trade dispute. The evidence from the union records suggests that he was acting with the full authority of his position to promote the legitimate interests of the union, and nothing more. It is revealing also that he had the backing of his union, which in turn had the backing of the TUC. So much then for Lord Diplock's claim that Owen Wade 'did not even have the support of the trade union of which he was only a subordinate official'.[108]

But Conway and Wade were not the only personalities of interest, with crucial parts in the drama being played by Sir George Farwell in the

Court of Appeal and Lord Loreburn in the House of Lords. The dispute between this latter pair was fascinating, especially as both were cut from the same cloth. One had been to Rugby, the other to Cheltenham College, and both had been to Balliol College, Oxford, with Reid graduating in 1868 and Farwell in 1869. Both were called to the Bar in 1871, and both became honorary fellows of Balliol College. But there the coincidences ended, though both played key roles in the history of the 1906 Act. By his judgment in *Taff Vale*, Sir George was a large part of the problem; while by his advice as a friend of the TUC from 1902 onwards,[109] and by his piloting of the 1906 Act through the choppy waters of the House of Lords, Lord Loreburn was a large part of the solution.[110] Following enactment, the two honorary fellows of Balliol College were to find themselves still on opposite sides. By a curious twist of fate, however, Sir George was to read the 1906 Act extravagantly and to decide for the defendant, while Lord Loreburn was to read it narrowly and to decide for the plaintiff. Yet by his performance in the Court of Appeal, it seems likely that Farwell LJ convinced a House of Lords already well disposed to the plaintiff to place some limits on the 1906 Act. To add to the drama, Lord Loreburn went further than anyone else in limiting the scope of the Act, and certainly much further than the circumstances required. But for all that, *Conway v Wade* was no *Taff Vale*. It seemed to have little immediate impact on the ability of trade unions to engage in industrial action, even if its presence was felt from time to time in a number of cases. *Conway v Wade* was, however, a step on the road to *Rookes v Barnard* and yet another extraordinary irony. For although the TUC wisely took *Conway v Wade* as a cue to reform the jury system, it was a reformed jury that held for the plaintiff in *Rookes v Barnard*.

Thanks to Dave Lyddon and John McIlroy, and to the staff of the National Working Class Movement Library, 51 The Crescent, Salford M5 4WX (www.wcml.org.uk)

Notes

1 The description of the 1906 Act as a 'Charter of Trade Unionism' is to be found in the TUC's popular centenary publication, TUC, *The History of the TUC 1868 – 1968* (1968), p 51.
2 [1909] AC 606.
3 [1898] AC 1.
4 *Ibid*, at p 177.
5 TUC Annual Report 1909, p 96, adopting verbatim the content of a letter from J N Bell, General Secretary of the National Amalgamated Union of Labour (NAUL) to the TUC Parliamentary Committee: TUC Parliamentary Committee, *Minutes*, 12/13 May 1908.
6 TUC Parliamentary Committee, *Minutes*, 16 June 1910.
7 *Rookes v Barnard* [1964] AC 1129.
8 Amy C Flagg, *Notes on the History of Shipbuilding in South Shields, 1746 to 1946* (1979).
9 See below.
10 H A Clegg, *General Union* (1954), p 15.
11 *Ibid*.
12 *Ibid*, pp 15 – 16.
13 NAUL, *Annual Report* 1907, p 3.
14 NAUL, *Third Quarterly Report* 1907, p 15.
15 NAUL, *Fourth Quarterly Report* 1907, p 16.
16 NAUL, *Annual Report* 1908, p 3.
17 NAUL, *Circular No 3*, 26 March 1908.
18 See for example, NAUL, *First Quarterly Report 1908*, p 15.
19 [1909] AC 506, at pp 509 (Lord Loreburn); and 521 (Lord Shaw of Dunfermline).
20 [1909] AC 506, at p 521.
21 *Ibid*, at pp 509 (Lord Loreburn) and 517 (Lord Atkinson).
22 [1908] 2 KB 844, at p 853.
23 NAUL, *Minutes of Executive Council Meetings and Circulars, Executive Council Meeting*, 12 October 1907.
24 NAUL, *Minutes of Executive Council Meetings and Circulars, Executive Council Meeting*, 1 November 1907.
25 [1908] 2 KB 844, at p 847.
26 NAUL, *Minutes of Executive Council Meetings and Circulars, Executive Council Meeting*, 15 November 1907.
27 NAUL, *Minutes of Executive Council Meetings and Circulars, Executive Council Meeting*, 20 November 1907.
28 NAUL, *Minutes of Executive Council Meetings and Circulars, Executive Council Meeting*, 8 May 1908.
29 TUC Parliamentary Committee, *Minutes*, 12/13 May 1908.
30 NAUL, *Minutes of Executive Council Meetings and Circulars, Executive Council Meeting*, 31 July 1908.
31 TUC Parliamentary Committee, *Minutes*, 4 September 1908.

32 TUC Annual Report 1908, p 182.
33 TUC Parliamentary Committee, *Minutes*, 18 May 1910. At its meeting on 28 July 1909, the TUC Parliamentary Committee noted the decision and took the initiative to request Bell to submit the costs of the union for re-imbursement. He had originally replied on 17 November 1909 to the effect that the costs were likely to exceed £1,000.
34 TUC Annual Report 1910, p 78.
35 [1908] 2 KB 844, at p 851.
36 *Amalgamated Society of Railway Servants v Osborne* [1909] 1 Ch 163, at p 196.
37 (1909) 25 *Law Quarterly Review* 3.
38 [1908] 2 KB 845, at p 853.
39 *Ibid*, at p 855.
40 *Ibid*, at p 854.
41 For Dicey's views on trade unions and the rule of law, see A V Dicey, 'The Combination Laws as Illustrating the Relation between Law and Opinion in England during the Nineteenth Century' (1909) 27 *Harvard Law Review* 511, esp p 531. On the 1906 Act, see A V Dicey, *Introduction to the Study of the Law of the Constitution* (8th ed, 1908), p 200.
42 [1908] 2 KB 844, at p 856.
43 *Ibid*, at p 857.
44 *Ibid*.
45 *Ibid*, at p 861.
46 *Ibid*, at p 862.
47 See *General Billposting Ltd v Atkinson* [1909] AC 118, *Addis v Gramophone Co Ltd* [1909] AC 488.
48 *The Schwan* [1909] AC 450.
49 Lord Macnaghten had also been in *Quinn v Leathem* [1901] AC 495.
50 [1909] AC 505, at p 510.
51 For an account of Loreburn, see R F V Heuston, *Lives of the Lord Chancellors*, 1885 – 1940 (1964).
52 TUC Annual Report 1907, p 64.
53 W Stewart, *J Keir Hardie – A Biography* (1921), p 222. According to Hardie (speaking of Loreburn), 'there is no man in politics with a cleaner record or a more democratic spirit'.
54 HL Debs, 4 December 1906, col 687.
55 *Ibid*, col 695.
56 (1853) 2 E&B 216.
57 HL Debs, 12 December 1906, col 295.
58 *Ibid*, col 299.
59 *Ibid*, col 306.
60 [1909] AC 506, pp 510 – 11.
61 *Ibid*, at p 512.
62 *Ibid*, at p 509.
63 Lord Askwith, *Lord James of Hereford* (1930), p 321 (Letter dated 13 November 1906).

64 (1906) 122 *Law Times* 147.
65 HL Debs, 12 December 1906, col 305.
66 [1909] AC 506, at p 514.
67 *Ibid*, at p 515.
68 *Ibid*, at p 511.
69 *Ibid*, at p 516.
70 *Ibid*, at p 520.
71 *The Law Journal*, 31 July 1909.
72 *Solicitors' Journal*, 31 July 1909.
73 (1910) 26 *Law Quarterly Review* 1. On Pollock, see N Duxbury, *Frederick Pollock and the English Juristic Tradition* (2004), pp 175 – 6 (on trade unions).
74 NAUL, *Third Quarterly Report 1909*, p 3.
75 *Ibid*.
76 TUC Annual Report 1910, p 159.
77 *Ibid*, pp 79 - 80, for a list of unions and the amount of the contribution. Only one union (telephone employees) failed to pay, and on being threatened with suspension from the TUC paid up before the end of the Annual Congress in 1910: *Ibid*, p 111.
78 TUC Parliamentary Committee, *Minutes*, 30 August 1909.
79 *Ibid*, 14 July 1910.
80 TUC Annual Report 1910, p 202.
81 See TUC Annual Report 1911, p 260; 1912, p 199.
82 See Cd 6817, 1913. Also HC Debs, 21 June 1918, col 674; Juries Act 1918; and Administration of Justice (Miscellaneous Provisions) Act 1933, s 6.
83 H Pelling, *A History of British Trade Unionism* (3rd ed, 1976), pp 293 – 6.
84 *Ibid*, p 133.
85 TNA, CAB 37/107/97. See D Lyddon and P Smith (this volume).
86 TUC Annual Report 1912, p 90. See D Lyddon and P Smith (this volume).
87 TNA, CAB 37/110/63.
88 TNA, CAB 37/111/66.
89 TUC Annual Report 1910, p 202.
90 *Amalgamated Society of Railway Servants v Osborne* [1910] AC 87.
91 *Gaskell v Lancashire and Cheshire Miners' Federation* (1912) 28 TLR 518.
92 (1912) 29 TLR 67.
93 Decided on the eve of the First World War, trade unions would have been further re-assured by the Court of Appeal's decision in this latter case that the action was protected, over-turning in the process yet another High Court decision based on 'opportune' and 'irrelevant' criticism of the 1906 Act, on this occasion by Darling J.
94 [1919] 2 Ch 129, at p 152.
95 *Ibid*, at p 153. See Bob Simpson and Roger Welch (this volume).
96 [1921] 1 Ch 1.
97 [1957] 1 WLR 321.

98 [1964] AC 1129, at p 1218 (Lord Devlin).
99 *Ibid*, at p 1173.
100 *Ibid*, at p 1174.
101 In addition to the two cases following, see *BBC v Hearn* [1977] ICR 685.
102 [1978] IRLR 507.
103 [1979] ICR 210, at p 218.
104 [1979] ICR 867, at p 878.
105 But compare *Express Newspapers Ltd v McShane* [1980] ICR 42, at p 55 (Lord Wilberforce)
106 TUC Parliamentary Committee, *Minutes*, 18 June 1908.
107 [1909] AC 506, at p 516 (Lord Atkinson).
108 *NWL Ltd v Woods*, above, at p 878.
109 Sir Robert Reid also advised the ASRS on its political fund rules which were subsequently ruled unlawful in the *Osborne* judgment, above. See J H Thomas, *My Story* (1937), p 213. Heuston, above, claims that it is for this 'previous connection' that Lord Loreburn did not sit in *Osborne* (p 163), the reversal of which he strongly supported. On Loreburn's support for the reversal of *Osborne*, see TNA, CAB 37/103/44; and TNA, CAB 37/104/57.
110 On the role of Sir Robert Reid, QC, see F Bealey and H Pelling, *Labour and Politics 1900 – 1906. A History of the Labour Representation Committee* (1958), p 80; and H Phelps – Brown, *The Origins of Trade Union Power* (1983), ch 2

Chapter Six

The Scottish Case: *Crofter Hand Woven Harris Tweed v Veitch*[1]

Douglas Brodie

Introduction

The case of Crofter is often associated with war-time, though in fact the litigation began in 1938. The underlying dispute related to the production of 'Harris Tweed' on the island of Lewis in Scotland. During the 1930s, collective bargaining had emerged on the island but its stability quickly came under threat from price-cutting. A number of manufacturers began to obtain cheaper supplies of yarn from the mainland and an obvious threat to collectively agreed terms and conditions was posed as a result. The TGWU tried to protect the collective interest by establishing a minimum selling price. Attempts to resolve the dispute were ultimately unsuccessful, and in January 1938 dockers in the port of Stornoway on Lewis were instructed by two officials of the TGWU to refuse to handle the imported yarn. The importers responded by seeking an interdict (the equivalent of an injunction) to stop the boycott. It was not maintained that there had been a breach of contract on the part of the dockers, but it was alleged that the officials had conspired to injure the importers' trade. The case was destined to go all the way to the House of Lords, and the importers attained the unusual distinction of losing at every level.

The Background to the Litigation

A proper appreciation of the background to the litigation involves some explanation of the historical intricacies of the Harris Tweed industry. The name 'Harris Tweed' originally applied only to tweed which had undergone all the processes of manufacture by hand in the Outer Hebrides. This trade practice received State endorsement in 1911 when a trade mark was granted by the Board of Trade. The trade mark became known as the stamp and applied to all tweed manufactured from island hand-spun yarn. Matters became more complicated when a number of manufacturers began to import yarn from the mainland. Their product was still sold as Harris Tweed, but was denied the protection of the trade mark. The motive for importing was the straightforward one of reducing manufacturing costs. All of this led to increasingly acrimonious relations between the two groups of manufacturers involved.

It appears that in the early 1930s conditions in the industry were flourishing. Against this backdrop of prosperity, in 1935, a collective agreement was concluded for the first time and dealt with wages and conditions of employment. The relevant trade union was the TGWU whose membership included not just workers in the industry on the island but also the dockers at the port of Stornoway. On the employers' side, the agreement was entered into by a local association of employers: the Harris Tweed Wages and Conditions Advisory Committee. At its inception, the Committee represented the employers in general but, by the time of the embargo, the importers had left and had formed in 1937 their own association (the Harris Tweed Yarn Purchasers' Association). Worker satisfaction with the conclusion of the agreement would have been tempered by the fact that it was fixed term and, more significantly, by the emergence of commercial rivalries.

The employers engaged in the importing of yarn were able to undercut and sell at lower prices. This practice posed obvious challenges to the level of terms and conditions of employment in the industry and, ultimately, to the stability and existence of the collective bargaining machinery. All of this prompted a meeting between the collective parties in July 1935. The TGWU emphasised the need to establish minimum selling prices. The union was also very clear as to how this might be brought about: action would be taken against the importers if they did not adhere to the minimum selling price. The TGWU formalised their position in a memorandum (dated 25 September 1935) which was circulated to all the employers involved (including the importers). It stated that trade union policy was to protect wages and conditions of employment from the effects of price cutting by, if necessary, placing an embargo on supplies: 'the only argument that price-cutters will ever understand and appreciate will be the joint power of the employers and this Union to put them out of business if they refuse loyally to abide by minimum selling prices.'[2] The memorandum further observed that 'It should be obvious to all concerned that the continued operations of the price-cutters will most assuredly bring about the ruination of both the market and the suppliers, as well as the means of existence of the workers.'[3]

A new collective agreement was entered into in 1936, and in 1937 the union proposed a revision in favour of the employees. A 10% rise in wages was sought. It was also proposed that it be a condition of employment that all employees be members of the union. The employers did not accept these demands and made counter proposals. Negotiations continued against a background of (or, at least, perceived) commercial difficulties for the employers and, in October 1937, the employers proposed wage reductions. The reason given was the impact of yarn imported from the mainland. It was said that imports had doubled since 1936 and that mills on the island were working at a loss. The union and the employers agreed that the latter would seek to arrive at an agreement with the importers. Should those negotiations be successful, it was anticipated that any need for a wage cut would be averted. The union agreed not to embark on industrial action whilst talks between the rival employers continued. In the event, in November 1937 the employers reported that no consensus had been found and that they intended to reduce the current rate of wages. It was clear that the industrial relations picture might begin to deteriorate. It was reported to the union that one of the large mill owners was threatening to leave the employers' association and start a price-cutting war against the importers. He backed down when faced with the threat of industrial action.

Negotiations between the two sets of employers continued and a meeting was held on Stornoway on 7 January 1938 presided over by the local Church of Scotland minister. He indicated to those present that industrial action was inevitable if consensus remained elusive. The consequences for the industry had been spelt out in blunt terms the day before (6 January 1938), in a letter to Mr Veitch (the Scottish Area Secretary of the TGWU) from Mr Skinner (the representative of the mill-owners). It was said that the matter of price 'seriously affects our ability to maintain present wage rates and indeed we must consider the wages question from an entirely different angle if we are to be faced with competition of mainland yarn on the present scale.' This prompted a rapid response from the union. TGWU members who were employed as dockers at Stornoway were instructed not to handle any consignment of yarn from mills on the mainland, with effect from 24 January 1938. The importers were warned of this by Veitch on 20 January. At the same time, the local shipping companies were presented with a list of importers whose orders the dockers would not deal with. It was alleged by the importers that the list had been prepared by the rival companies in pursuance of a conspiracy with the union, an allegation that was firmly denied.

In the Outer House[4]

At first instance the court had to consider arguments concerning both the common law and the trade dispute immunities. It was argued that the defenders were protected by s 4 of the 1906 Act. Given that they had been sued as individuals this argument was unlikely to succeed. It had already been held in England that an action would lie against a member or official of a trade union for a tort committed by him in acting on behalf of himself and the other members of the union.[5] The Scottish courts, albeit *obiter*, had also arrived at this view.[6] It was only to be expected that Lord Jamieson would hold that the defenders could not rely upon the section by way of defence. A much more mainstream argument was that the actions of the defenders were immune by virtue of sections 1 and 3 of the Act. This failed because it was found that the embargo had not been imposed in contemplation or furtherance of a trade dispute. Such a conclusion seems counter-intuitive. As we have seen, the negotiations in 1937 had revealed that the union and the manufacturers with whom it had a collective agreement had adopted diametrically opposed positions over pay. This could not have been more apparent. The proposal of the union was that a 10% increase should be made while the employers had proposed a reduction. It was also the case that the gap between the two sides had widened over the course of the year. Matters had become of sufficient concern for the union that the prospect of a boycott had been raised with the employers. It was 'common knowledge' that this might occur. The boycott was thus in 'contemplation' or 'furtherance' of a dispute within the meaning of section 5 of the 1906 Act.

In explaining why the finding that a trade dispute did not exist was made, it is necessary to return to *Conway v Wade*.[7] *Conway*, at this point in time, offered the primary judicial guidance on the meaning of 'dispute'. One general problem with the case was that the Lords had adopted a much more restrictive approach to the immunities than the Court of Appeal. A more specific and pertinent problem was that the meaning of the word 'dispute' was not properly explored. All that was said on the matter was that to gain the protection of the immunities 'a dispute must be a real thing, imminent or existing.' Within the context of a statutory framework that confers immunity for acts done in contemplation of a future dispute there can be no quarrel with a temporal qualification that stipulates that a dispute must be 'imminent or existing.' Beyond that, all that is said is that the dispute must be a 'real thing'. This is almost meaningless but it may reflect the judicial concern, very much evident in *Conway*, with disputes that are thought to be actuated by ulterior or improper motives. What would have been immensely helpful to lower courts (but was not forthcoming) would have been discussion of when, in the context of collective bargaining, matters moved from negotiation to dispute. It would not have been difficult to gain assistance from other areas of law. If we think of the traditional offer/acceptance analysis in the law of contract, we do not have difficulty in saying that there is a failure to agree when the offer and the acceptance do not match. Again, in the context of arbitration, the Court of Appeal has held (since *Crofter*) that a dispute arises in any situation where one party makes a request or demand of some sort which is refused by the other party.[8]

Where collective bargaining is concerned, by analogy, one might say that there is a dispute when a proposal is rejected by the other side. This was subsequently recognised by the Privy Council decision in *Beetham v Trinidad Cement*. It was held that a trade dispute exists wherever a "difference" exists.[9] Lord Denning, delivering the opinion of the Judicial Committee, stated that

> *a difference can exist long before the parties become locked in combat. It is not necessary that they should have come to blows. It is sufficient that they should be sparring for an opening. And it seems to their Lordships that the parties had reached that point here, even in regard to the claim for bargaining status. The union had applied for bargaining status. The company had ignored the request, just as it had ignored previous requests.'*[10]

On this basis, that is to say, applying the natural meaning of the words used, there was clearly a dispute in the *Crofter* case.[11] The difficulty with the *Conway* guidance is that the fundamental element of the statutory definition was not dissected. At root, *Conway* was more interested in adding qualifications to the scope of the immunity rather than expounding the core meaning. More particularly, the House of Lords insisted on a defendant acting from a proper motive, even though such a requirement would seem to be a gloss on the statute.[12]

Whatever view is taken of whether a trade dispute actually existed at the time of the embargo, one might have thought that a dispute was, at the very least, in contemplation.[13] The letter of 6 January 1938 warning of the likely consequences if agreement between the two sets of manufacturers could not be reached was surely material here. The contemporary judicial view is that a dispute is in contemplation when it is reasonably foreseeable that it might arise. It has also been said that an act will take place in contemplation of a trade dispute where it is done in expectation of and with a view to it.[14] Such approaches would seem to accord with the natural meaning of the language used and, on the application of either formulation, there was surely a dispute in contemplation in *Crofter*. It is interesting to explore the basis upon which Lord Jamieson held to the contrary. There were several strands to his reasoning. First, he appears to have taken the view that the stance of the union was out of line with the views of the membership. There was said to be a lack of any 'substantial demand' on the part of the members for an increase. Nor was the union assisted by the proper operation of the internal trade union machinery: 'The resolutions passed at meetings of members or delegates in October were mere endorsations of what the men were told their officials intended to put forward.'[15] In effect, the union was depicted as a third party intent on interfering in matters with which it was not concerned.

Such an analysis was by no means out of line with contemporary judicial thinking. Around about the same time an English court had taken the view, in *R v National Arbitration Tribunal, ex parte Bolton*, [16] that a difference between a trade union and an employer could not be a trade dispute. This was rebutted by Lord Wright when the case reached the House of Lords: 'It would be strangely out of date to hold...that a trade union cannot act on behalf of its members in a trade dispute, or that a difference between a trade union acting for its members and their employer cannot be a trade dispute.' [17] Somewhat surprisingly this did not kill off such arguments. In the later case of *R v National Arbitration Tribunal, ex parte Keable Press*, [18] it was argued that a trade dispute did not exist because the union was acting on a frolic of its own without reference to the wishes or the interests of its members. The argument was rejected on the facts, but it appears to have been accepted that, in principle, it might be successful, even though it would be difficult to make out. Very much in keeping with the opinion of Lord Wright, the Master of the Rolls (Greene) put forward the very sensible suggestion that the best evidence that a dispute exists is the fact that workers are prepared to strike

What better proof of the existence of a dispute in relation to the reinstatement of Howard one can have than the fact that the men come out on strike because he has not been reinstated I really do not know... Now, what does that mean? It means surely that the men are recognising and adopting as their own the action of the union taken on their behalf and in their name and are obeying the order of the union to back them up and support them in this dispute; and, even if the matter before the strike is to be regarded as a pure piece of intermeddling by the union without reference to the wishes and interests of the men, as soon as the men back up the union by supporting the union's demands for this reinstatement, in those circumstances I frankly cannot see how it can be said for a moment that no dispute existed.[19]

Apart from the foregoing, in holding that there was no trade dispute, Lord Jamieson made the rather remarkable suggestion that the union was not serious with regard to the accomplishment of its aims: 'The demand for a 10% increase was...originally put forward for the purpose of increasing membership of the union rather than with any intention of pressing it, and I doubt whether there had later been any real change of attitude.'[20] This ignores the fact that wage reductions were a distinct possibility. More significantly, the conduct of the dispute may have been viewed as irresponsible and unworthy of immunity. There is a further suggestion that the substance of the union's demands over pay were viewed as being unreasonable. It was noted that 'the wages being paid were largely in excess of those paid in spinning mills on the islands.'[21] In the eyes of Lord Jamieson it seems that the lack of reality involved in demanding significantly more than the current rates indicated that a dispute was unlikely to materialise. Even allowing for the limitations inherent in the guidance contained in *Conway*, the Lord Ordinary's reasoning on the applicability of the trade dispute formula is far from convincing. It also suggests through, for example, the appraisal of the reasonableness of the action, a desire to impose a regime of close control over the conduct of trade disputes. Nevertheless, the decision on the matter of trade dispute could not have been more crucial to the significance of the case: had it gone the other way, the law on conspiracy would have been irrelevant.

The Lord Ordinary did, of course, find that the economic delict (tort in England) of simple conspiracy was not made out. This is the element of the case that has rendered it seminal. In arriving at a decision on this point, a great deal of reliance was placed on *Sorrell v Smith*,[22] a case concerning the limits of lawful competition in the commercial context.

The House of Lords took the view that if the 'real purpose' of the conspiracy was to promote the interests of the conspirators no liability would arise. *Sorrell* provided a valuable rationalisation of the case law. It made clear that, where simple conspiracy was concerned, the behaviour of the participants could be justified and, moreover, justified by self-interest. There is nothing in the speeches to suggest that a trade union could not invoke this reasoning. This restatement of the law was heavily relied upon by the Lord Ordinary. He held that the immediate purpose of the defenders was to force producers to come to an agreement regarding the selling price of tweed and the exclusive use of island spun yarn. This was seen as promoting the interests of labour and, therefore, justifiable. *Sorrell* is the progeny of the two great economic tort cases of *Mogul Steamship v McGregor* [23] and *Allen v Flood* [24] (though the latter did not involve the element of combination). They share the same underlying rationale in that they assume that the courts should not seek to say what is unfair economic pressure. Instead, the economic torts should provide a remedy where independently unlawful acts have been committed in order to inflict economic harm. The policy justification for this was to be found in the Court of Appeal judgment of Fry LJ in *Mogul*: 'To draw a line between fair and unfair competition, between what is reasonable and unreasonable, passes the power of the courts'.[25] *Crofter* confirmed that that policy of absentionism was equally applicable in the context of trade disputes. As such, the decision is unsurprising; indeed, it was inevitable given the way in which the law of the economic torts had evolved.

Although *Crofter* is best known for its treatment of the law of conspiracy, the pursuers had also argued that liability should arise on the basis of unlawful interference with contractual relations and liberty to exercise the right to trade. Whilst these arguments were unsuccessful, they are worthy of note in that they anticipate the sort of arguments that were deployed with conspicuous success by employers in later years. The claim on the basis of unlawful interference in contractual relations is interesting because it was not alleged that the dockers had, in fact, broken their contracts of employment. It was however maintained that the delict of inducing breach of contract was not limited to direct persuasion, but extended to cases of indirect inducement of contract. It was claimed that the defenders had 'procured non delivery of goods which were consigned under contract to the petitioners.' The argument was somewhat under-developed and, for instance, it is not clear whether it was thought necessary for unlawful means to be present before the indirect form of the delict could be established. Certainly the Inner House took the view that unlawful means would be required: 'in any event, the case of *Lumley v Gye* is not an authority for the proposition that an act which is per se lawful becomes unlawful if it can be shown that, in the knowledge of the person doing it, it might directly or indirectly prevent a contract between third parties being carried out'.[26] The pursuers had also argued that the actions of the defenders amounted to a wilful interference in the pursuers' trade. This head of the pursuers' case was viewed as irrelevant given the absence of unlawful means. *Allen v Flood* [27] served to deny liability.

The Inner House[28]

Lord Jamieson had denied the existence of a conspiracy between the trade unionists and the mill-owners. The Inner House agreed with Lord Jamieson, while noting that 'it is proved, and I am prepared to hold, that there was some kind of understanding more or less defined between Mr Veitch and Mr Skinner that, if the union took action and imposed an embargo against the importers of yarn, the Union would in turn be assisted by the mill-owners to get 100% membership'.[29] Nevertheless the court was prepared, for the purposes of argument, to assume that such a combination did exist. This did not assist the pursuers in any way, which was only to be expected since the 1920s decision in *Reynolds v Shipping Federation* had, in a number of ways, anticipated *Crofter*.[30] In *Reynolds*, the aim of the conspiracy was to preserve the interests of the union by maintaining the closed shop, and thereby uphold a prop to collective bargaining. The court acknowledged that employers might also benefit from the existence of the closed shop: 'Here, the employers, instead of being forced against their wills into employing union men only, have recognised that advantages may arise from adopting such a course of action voluntarily, and have accordingly made an agreement with the trade union to that effect.' [31] The furtherance of such aims was seen as perfectly legitimate. The defenders' case may have been positively assisted by collective bargaining being seen as to the mutual benefit of employers and trade unions. It advanced 'the business interests of employers and employed alike'.[32] The element of mutual interest (between two collective powers whose interests will often conflict) did not render applicable the line of case law emanating from *Mogul*.

More generally, the Inner House did not find it difficult to uphold the finding of Lord Jamieson that the conspiracy was lawful. Differential treatment between Labour and Capital could not be justified. The wisdom of the policy of non-intervention advocated by *Mogul* was firmly endorsed: 'When judges are asked to draw an inference of an intention to injure from acts which, whether done singly or in combination, are in themselves not unlawful; I think they should proceed with great caution, and should decline to draw such an inference unless the consistence of the facts with an innocent intention is clearly and definitely excluded. Otherwise the doctrine of conspiracy may well become a doctrine dangerous to liberty.'[33] The legitimacy of the closed shop was also acknowledged: 'It seems plain that with 100% membership, a trade union is in a much stronger position for negotiation with the employers than would be the case if there were a number of non-union workers in the employment.'[34] The Inner House did not allow any disapproval of the language used to affect their judgment: 'But it is perhaps well to remember that in industrial, as in political, controversy, there is always a tendency – it might almost be said to be a tradition – to indulge in rhetorical extravagances and too great weight ought not to be attached, as justifying an inference of malice, to language which may indeed be immoderate and lacking in restraint, but may spring more from an excess of zeal than a corrupt intention'.[35]

The Inner House agreed that there was no trade dispute in existence. They also held that one was not in contemplation: 'while a question might have been envisaged as possibly or even probably arising at a future date, there was no imminence of such a question as to make it reasonable to say that there was a trade dispute 'in contemplation'.'[36] One might argue that this was not surprising since decisions of this sort are not readily interfered with by appellate courts. The question of whether or not a trade dispute exists is one of fact. As Lord Shaw of Dunfermline said in the *Conway* case 'whether the trade dispute was actual, impending, or probable is a question of fact in each case.'[37] Nevertheless, there is some evidence to suggest that the Inner House were quite content to go along with a restrictive approach to the application of the immunities. Lord Fleming's reasoning on this aspect of the case is of interest. He noted that

> *so far from being a dispute between the employers and workmen on these points there was a large measure of agreement upon them between Veitch and Skinner. The letter [of 6 January 1938] …cannot fairly be regarded in the nature of a demand by the employers for a reduction of wages but rather as an invitation to the trade union to impose an embargo.*[38]

It was certainly the case that a mutually agreeable solution to their differences was envisaged by both sides. But to say that there was no dispute is to ignore the fact that there were indeed very real differences. The significance of the letter of 6 January 1938 was surely that that solution was unlikely to be realised. The natural consequence of this was that relations between the two sides were likely to deteriorate and one could therefore at that point say that a dispute, if it did not yet exist, was at least in contemplation.

The House of Lords

By the time the case reached the House of Lords, the issues at stake were purely common law ones. There had been no cross-appeal to the Lords on the applicability of the immunities. The House of Lords were prepared to assume that there was a combination between the union and the employers. It must be emphasised that by this time the law on conspiracy had evolved in such a way that the prospects for the pursuers cannot have seemed favourable. It would have been very difficult to justify denying the respondents the benefit of the decision in *Mogul*. The courts accepted that non-intervention came at a price but that price was worth paying: 'It is true that the advantage or benefit may be at the cost of another's injury, but in a world of commercial and industrial ruthlessness, whose morality still shows some traces of the jungle, our Court of Law have wisely . . . refrained from prescribing counsels of perfection'.[39] Counsel for the appellants made highly extensive written submissions (running to over 100 pages) to the House of Lords. An attempt was made to distinguish the line of case law emanating from *Mogul* on the basis that, in effect, *Crofter* presented a situation that had not previously been addressed. It was argued that precedent revealed instances of combinations comprised of either commercial or trade union interest but it was said that *Crofter* was novel in that it was a hybrid and an unacceptable one at that: 'a self-interested alliance between big business and organised labour (whose interest are opposed) against small business has never yet been sanctioned by the courts. The petitioners regard it as an unholy alliance between two great powers to crush out of existence the small traders'.[40]

Thus the argument was a variant on the David and Goliath theme with the difference that David was being bullied by both Goliath and his brother. The submission was doomed to failure. The soundness or otherwise of the factual analysis was neither here nor there. The law of the economic torts has two touchstones of liability: illegality and conspiracy. Where conspiracy is concerned it makes no difference in law whether there are two conspirators or two hundred. Equally, it was hardly likely that the fact that the conspirators could be depicted as not being a homogeneous group would be material. Viscount Maugham noted that 'it is sufficient if all the various combining parties have their own legitimate trade or business interests to gain, even though those interests may be of differing kinds.'[41] It was also the case, as we have seen from the discussion of *Reynolds*, that the appellant's premise, that the underlying basis of the defence was novel, was unsound. On the common law, the House of Lords concluded that liability for the tort of simple conspiracy did not arise because

> *'the predominant object of the respondents in getting the embargo imposed was to benefit their trade-union members by preventing under-cutting and unregulated competition, and so helping to secure the economic stability of the island industry. The result they aimed at achieving was to create a better basis for collective bargaining, and thus directly to improve wage prospects. A combination with such an object is not unlawful, because the object is the legitimate promotion of the interests of the combiners.'*[42]

Crofter and Voluntarism

The period between the wars was said by Kahn-Freund to be one in which voluntarism extended to the courts.[43] He also claimed that the *Crofter* case showed '...the acceptance by the courts of the principle of non-intervention in industrial disputes.'[44] In a similar vein, Markesinis and Deakin have said that *Crofter* 'represents the high-water mark of judicial abstention in industrial disputes and of the courts' acceptance of the essential legitimacy of trade-union organisation.'[45] How valid are these claims? In arriving at any assessment, *Reynolds*, as well as *Crofter*, constitutes a crucial piece of evidence. Both cases clearly showed judicial understanding and recognition of trade union interests. In so doing, they reversed the inequity of divergence of approach so strongly evident in earlier cases. A comparison of the outcome in *Quinn v Leathem* [46] compared with that in *Mogul Steamship* provides the most graphic of illustrations. Looking beyond *Crofter* and *Reynolds* suggest that, on the whole, labour law cases between the wars showed a willingness to acknowledge trade union interests,[47] though there were prominent exceptions.

The evidence pointing to judicial acceptance of non-intervention is less clear-cut. For instance, one might doubt whether the courts would have refused to enforce a collective agreement. Three pre-war cases had appeared to assume that collective agreements were legally enforceable.[48] After the war, the decision in *Bradford Dyers' Association Ltd v National Union of Textile Workers* is relevant.[49] There the defendant unions had expressly agreed in submitting to a consent judgment that the collective agreement involved was binding and enforceable. Again

Kahn-Freund stated in 1943, after *Crofter* was decided, that conflicts as to rights were '...legal questions which - but for section 4 of the Trade Union Act, 1871- could be taken before a Court of Law.'[50] Is there any reason to assume that a court in the inter-war period would have viewed matters differently? Admittedly, an *obiter* statement by Lord Russell of Killowen in delivering the advice of the Privy Council in *Young v Canadian Northern Railway* is of relevance.[51] On one reading he seems to assume that a collective agreement could not be enforced by legal remedies. However, what reason in law would have existed to support such a stance? In the absence of Kahn-Freund's later writings, a court might well have held that an agreement was legally enforceable.

Any claim of judicial acceptance of a principle of non-intervention in trade disputes is difficult to assess. This is a result of the limited amount of case law during this period. The strength of the protection afforded by the trade dispute immunities was rarely tested during the period running from the end of World War One to the decision in *Crofter*. The 1919 case of *Valentine v Hyde* indicated that, were that to occur, problems might arise.[52] The dispute arose over the fact that the plaintiff refused to join the relevant trade union. It became clear that the employer would dismiss if the plaintiff maintained this position. It might have been thought obvious that this was a dispute between workmen and workmen connected with the employment of any person and accordingly a trade dispute within the meaning of the legislation. However, Astbury J insisted that 'some limitation must be placed on the expression 'connected with the employment or non-employment of any person' and went on to impose a requirement of directness and concluded that there was no trade dispute in existence. Moreover, even if a trade dispute had been in existence, immunity would still have been forfeited; apparently on the basis that the action was coercive. It must be said that coercion is integral to the taking of industrial action; to find against a trade union on this basis is, in effect, to condemn the validity of industrial action in general.

A similar dispute arose in *Hodges v Webb*,[53] but on this occasion a trade dispute was held to exist and doubt was cast over the reasoning in the case of *Valentine*. The stance taken over 'coercion' in *Valentine* was questioned, and Peterson J pointed out that there are 'few strikes or lock-outs in which either employers or workmen or both could not say that they were coerced.' More significantly, the reasoning in *Valentine* was struck down by the Court of Appeal in *White v Riley*: 'It is quite possible that the extension of this legislation, which was originally passed for the benefit of workmen in their disputes with their employers, to disputes between workmen and workmen, has produced results which many workmen in some trade unions did not anticipate, but it does not seem to me that there is any reason for not giving to the subsection its natural meaning.'[54] A further difficulty in assessing judicial attitudes to industrial action at this time is presented by the case of *National Sailors' & Firemen's Union v Reed*;[55] the decision has been much discussed and it can reasonably be argued that it provides strong evidence of judicial hostility to trade unions. It must also be borne in mind that the judge was, once again, Astbury J.

What does *Crofter* add to this debate? It must be said to be rather equivocal in this respect. The position is complicated by the fact that the union did not appeal the decision that the action was not immune to the Lords. Nevertheless, there is much that might be gleaned from the speeches at that level. Lord Wright's speech has probably attracted the most attention. This is not surprising. He displays genuine appreciation of the social significance of industrial action: 'The right of workmen to strike is an essential element in the principle of collective bargaining.'[56] He also acknowledges the implications of this position for the rights of employers. The employer's right to freedom to trade was not an unconditional one. Most pertinently 'where the rights of labour were concerned, the rights of the employer are conditioned by the right of the men to give or withhold their services.'[57] Armed by this analysis of the fundamental rights at issue, Lord Wright reviewed the case law. A decision in favour of the trade union was consistent with a line of authority going back to the judgment of Erle J in *R v Rowlands*.[58] There it was said that trade unions could combine for the purpose of obtaining a lawful benefit for themselves but not where the immediate purpose was to injure another. Lord Wright's purposive speech offers a strong recognition of the legitimacy of trade union interests. Adherence to that view would, in the context of trade disputes law, almost inevitably lead to judicial abstention. The difficulty is to assess just how representative of judicial thinking Lord Wright's speech was. Even where *Crofter* itself is concerned, as we have seen, the judgments in both the Outer and Inner House were much less encouraging. There is a real contradiction in the judgments when the treatment of the common law is compared to that of the statute. Where the former is concerned, the judges are anxious not to intervene. The wisdom or appropriateness of trade union action may be doubted but it is felt right that considerable leeway be given. The view being taken that if they do not resort to unlawful acts, they are entitled to further their interests in the manner which seems to them best, and most likely to be effecive. Matters changed when the statutory term 'trade dispute' was interpreted and applied. There was said to be no dispute, even though the parties disagreed; what more was required was left unsaid. In addition, a trade dispute was said not to be in contemplation even though it was accepted one would 'probably' arise. All this points to a restrictive approach, and one which would involve close judicial control over the legitimacy of trade disputes (the very antithesis of absentionism).

Conclusions

There are two strands to the decision in *Crofter*. In terms of the common law, *Crofter* consolidated the existing law and confirmed that simple conspiracy would have no role to play in trade disputes in the future. It should come as no surprise that a wide interpretation was given to the ambit of the decision in the later Court of Appeal decision in *Scala Ballroom v Ratcliffe*.[59] There the fact that the aims of the conspirators were not material did not matter: 'I am not prepared...to say that the interests which can lawfully be protected are confined to the material interests in the sense of interests which can be exchanged for cash. Lawful interests in my judgment may and I think do extend further than that...'.[60] The defendants were found to be justified in pursuing a policy of non-discrimination: 'the defendants in this case, who represent the members of the Musicians' Union, which includes amongst its members a great many coloured people, have a lawful interest to protect in looking after their members' interests and, taking the long view, in looking after their livelihood as well.'[61] Criticism of the stance taken over the common law by the court in *Crofter* is hard to find. However, with reference to *Crofter*, Wedderburn writes that 'Until 1979 it could be said that almost every major decision of the House of Lords...had not favoured or had failed to understand collective trade union interests since *Allen v Flood*. The one major exception, in war time, was *Crofter* (where the interests of the big union, coincided with those of the big employers).'[62] How important was the timing of the case, and the element of mutual interest, to the decision?

In truth, neither of those elements helps to explain the outcome in the case. The fact of the matter was that the law had moved firmly down a particular path; crystallised by the decision in *Sorrell*. It would have been impossible to have denied the defenders the benefit of this. It is worth noting that the opinion in the Outer House was delivered before the War had started, and throughout the case the courts were consistent in believing that the union was entitled to the benefit of *Mogul*. One might though speculate that Lord Wright's rhetoric (though not the substance of his judgment) was inspired, at least in part, by the challenge to civil liberties that war inevitably brings.

Crofter is obviously best known for its contribution to the law of simple conspiracy. As a result what it had to say about the statutory law of trade disputes has been lost sight of. Here, rather than vindicating trade union interests, the lower courts took a rather restrictive approach to the interpretation and application of the immunities. In my view *Conway* can be blamed for this to some extent. However, it would be wrong to make too much of this. The limited guidance handed down by *Conway* actually gave the court in *Crofter* a great deal of room for manoeuvre. *Crofter* is rightly celebrated for its consolidation of the common law in a manner consistent with trade union interests. Focussing on the endorsement of the right to strike by Lord Wright appeared to give a similar message so far as the immunities were concerned.

Nevertheless doubts remained as to whether an era of judicial respect for the immunities was being launched.

Notes

1 [1942] AC 435.

2 The proceedings in *Crofter* in the Outer and Inner House are not fully reported but the pleadings and the full Inner House judgments can be found in the *Session Papers*, along with the employer's written submissions to the House of Lords.

3 *Session Papers*, above, n 2.

4 Both the Outer and Inner House judgments are reported in part at *Crofter Hand Woven Harris Tweed v Veitch* 1940 SLT 210.

5 *Bussy v Amalgamated Society of Railway Servants* (1908) 24 TLR 437. See also *Vacher v London Society of Compositors* [1913] AC 107.

6 *Shinwell v National Sailors' and Firemen's Union* 1913 (2) SLT 83.

7 [1909] AC 506.

8 *Ellerine Bros v Klinger* [1982] 2 All ER 737. In addition it may be noted that it is not necessary that the recipient reply.

9 [1960] AC 132.

10 *Beetham*, above, at p 143.

11 And see *Health Computing Ltd v Meek* [1981] ICR 24, at p 32.

12 K.D.Ewing, 'The Golden Formula: Some Recent Developments' (1979) 8 *Industrial Law Journal* 133, at p 134.

13 A restrictive approach is also to be found in the earlier Scottish case of *Milligan v Ayr Harbour Trustees* 1915 SC 937 where Lord Salvesen had found that a dispute was not in contemplation because it was not imminent even though its occurrence was probable.

14 *Cory Lighterage v TGWU* [1973] 2 All ER 558, at p 565.

15 *Crofter*, above, n 4, at p 213.

16 [1941] 2 All ER 800, at p 814.

17 [1942] 2 All ER 425, at p 435.

18 [1943] 2 All ER 633.

19 *Keable Press*, above, n 18, 634.

20 *Crofter*, above, n 4, at p 213.

21 *Ibid*, at p 213.

22 [1925] AC 700.

23 [1892] AC 25.

24 [1898] AC 1.

25 (1889) 23 QBD 598, at pp 625-6.

26 *Crofter*, above, n 4, at p 224.

27 [1898] AC 1.

28 *Crofter*, above, n 4.

29 *Ibid*, at p 219.

30 [1924] 1 Ch 28.

31 *Reynolds*, above, at p 40.

32 *Ibid*, at p 39.

33 *Crofter*, above, n 4, at p 220.

34 *Session Papers*, above, n 2.

35 *Ibid.*
36 *Crofter*, above, n 4, at p 222.
37 [1909] AC 506, at p 522.
38 *Session Papers*, above, n 2.
39 *Crofter*, above, n 4, at p 219.
40 Employer's written submissions to the House of Lords which are contained in the *Session Papers*.
41 *Crofter*, above, n 1, at p 453.
42 *Ibid*, at p 447, per Viscount Simon.
43 'Labour Law' in M.Ginsberg (ed), *Law and Opinion in England in the 20th Century* (1959), pp 242-243.
44 Kahn-Freund, note 43, p 242.
45 B Markesinis and S Deakin, *Tort Law* (5th ed, 2003), p 526.
46 [1901] AC 495.
47 It should also be noted that in *Evans v National Union of Printing, Bookbinding, and Paper Workers* [1938] 4 All ER 51, at p 54 it was said that 'the great benefit of a trade union is that you can have collective bargaining between employers and employed'.
48 *Read v Friendly Society of Stonemasons* [1902] 2 KB 702, *Smithies v National Association of Operative Plasterers* [1909] 1 KB 310, *East London Bakers' Union and Goldstein, The Times*, 9 June1904 (K W Wedderburn, *Cases and Materials on Labour Law*, p 272).
49 *The Times*, 24 July1926 and discussed by Selwyn, 'Collective Agreements and the Law' (1969) 32 *Modern Law Review* 377.
50 0 Kahn-Freund, 'Collective Agreements under War Legislation' (1942-43) 5-6 MLR 112,138.
51 [1931] AC 83.
52 [1919] 2 Ch 129.
53 [1920] 2 Ch 70.
54 [1921] 1 Ch 1, 20.
55 [1926] Ch 536.
56 *Crofter*, above, n 1, at p 453.
57 *Ibid.*
58 (1851) 17 QB 671, at p 686.
59 [1958] 3 All ER 220 (O Kahn-Freund (1959) 22 MLR 69).
60 *Ibid*, at p 223.
61 *Ibid.*
62 Lord Wedderburn of Charlton, 'Industrial Relations and the Courts' (1980) 9 *Industrial Law Journal* 65, at p 70 (note 22).

Part 4

The 1906 Act: Parliament, Employers and Judges

Chapter Seven

The 1906 Act: The First Fifty Years – Industrial Relations, Picketing and the Employers' Challenge

Dave Lyddon and Paul Smith

THE passage of the Trade Disputes Act 1906 (TDA) was a defining moment in the historical development of trade unionism in the United Kingdom. Building upon the legislation of the 1870s and the arguments of the majority report of the Royal Commission on Labour 1891–94, the Act provided a robust legal framework for industrial action and trade union organisation. It gave immunity from tort liability for action 'in contemplation or furtherance of a trade dispute', including inducement of a breach of a contract of employment (a late amendment moved by Dilke, overriding the *Glamorgan* case[1] – see Saville, this volume). The Liberal government of 1906 promoted collective bargaining between trade unions (and their federations) and employers' associations. Although class-based, trade unions did not pose a class challenge and could be 'managed' if permitted to organise effectively. Together with the non-legally-binding nature of collective agreements in the United Kingdom the TDA ensured that the courts were excluded from collective bargaining. Collective *laissez-faire* was an apt term.[2]

Organised employers were not reconciled to the passage of the TDA but they lacked any direct political voice. Given the strength and clarity of the TDA's immunities for trade unions, the employers, often supported by chief constables and magistrates' benches, concentrated their criticism on s 2 of the Act, which made peaceful persuasion by pickets lawful, and on the problems of enforcement of s 7 of the Conspiracy and Protection of Property Act 1875 (CPPA), the main criminal law (until the use of the Public Order Act 1936, s 5) covering offences arising out of picketing. The scale and intensity of picketing until the mid-1930s was usually a reflection of unions' weakness, but in the 1950s employers' focus shifted markedly as the labour market tightened and trade union organisation developed in cohesion and extent. Picketing was then often superfluous and, where it occurred, was usually less intense. Increasingly, matters internal to the workplace, such as the closed shop and restrictive practices, came to dominate the employers' agenda. With the rising incidence of unofficial and unconstitutional (i.e. in breach of disputes procedure) strikes across a broad range of industries in the 1950s and 1960s, employers' organisations argued that unions' tort immunity be reduced. In this, they were joined by lawyers, the courts and the Conservative Party.

TDA: Resistance and Reception

The hostility of employers to any proposals to reform statute law and override the growing case law had been vividly displayed to the 1903 Royal Commission on Trade Disputes and Trade Combinations. Prominent witnesses included Frederick Millar,[3] secretary to the Employers' Parliamentary Council and the Labour Protection Association, who referred to the latter's campaign against intimidation (including 'the threat of future consequences') during picketing - described as 'labour union terrorism'. Picketing had of course been the cause of action in the *Taff Vale* case (see Lockwood, this volume). That railway company's managing director, Ammon Beasley, gave extensive evidence to the Royal Commission, which revealed a deep hostility to unions as coercive institutions that have 'done ... incalculable ... mischief to the individual working man'; collective bargaining had had a 'pernicious effect'. The Shipping Federation's statement presented its views on coercive picketing, trade unionism and any changes in the law in a typically robust manner. Sir Andrew Noble, chairman of Armstrong, Whitworth and official representative of the Engineering Employers' Federation (EEF), argued that for Parliament to override the House of Lords' decisions 'would be a direct inducement to revert to the previous unsatisfactory state of affairs, would stir up again hostile feelings between employers and employed'.[4]

Clegg, Fox and Thompson argue that court cases were not the main cause of the unions' difficulties before 1906. These lay rather in the recession of 1902-05, following as it did the employers' sustained assault on trade union organisation during the 1890s. This left them, especially the 'new' unions of labourers, in a debilitated state.[5] But the cumulative impact of the legal challenge to trade unions, strike action and picketing should not be underestimated: unions were cowed.[6] Given the declared opinions both of employers and the courts before the passing of the TDA, a sustained and possibly successful challenge to restrict its impact was to be expected but did not materialise. The courts stood largely aside.[7] One legal assault was indirect, being targeted at unions' political activities (the Osborne judgment);[8] another was a campaign by the Home Office and chief constables to supervise, restrain and, at times, disperse pickets.

Just before the Trade Disputes Bill had come to the House of Commons in March 1906, the Earl of Wemyss (formerly Lord Elcho) had led a deputation from the Employers' Parliamentary Council (formed in 1898 under his chairmanship) to the Home Secretary and the Attorney-General. The deputation laid 'more stress' on the question of picketing than on any other matter.[9] A last-ditch attempt in December 1906 to amend the Bill in the House of Lords by Wemyss, again speaking for the Employers' Parliamentary Council, which would limit pickets to three at each entrance of a works and prohibit picketing of workers' residences, also failed.[10] McIvor's assessment that employers' organisations before the First World War 'failed to develop an effective peak parliamentary pressure group' of equal efficacy and representativeness to the Trades Union Congress (TUC) Parliamentary Committee is apt.[11]

The liberating effect of the TDA upon unions was soon felt. During the Belfast dock strike, which started in July 1907, soldiers and police cordoned off the quays so that pickets could not contact those working. James Larkin, then a dockers' union organiser, had copies of the TDA printed and distributed. He approached the cordon, 'read the Act aloud ... and demanded the right to pass. The officers of the military and police ... were neither familiar with the provisions of the Act nor with their interpretation. After a brief and hurried consultation they allowed Larkin and a small party of his pickets to pass through the lines'.[12] He was later arrested for breaking a by-law that prohibited unauthorised meetings in the harbour,[13] but his claims for the TDA were a worrying sign for employers. In the long engineering strike in the north-east in 1908, a successful prosecution under the Conspiracy and Protection of Property Act 1875 (CPPA) of five workers in Newcastle for persistently following strike-breakers saw them claiming that they had tried 'to carry out the provisions of the Trade Disputes Act'.[14] More spectacularly, Cambrian Combine miners were accused of 'taking advantage' of the TDA in their protracted strike of 1910–11 which involved a number of 'riots'.[15]

Union membership grew steadily from 2.0 million in 1905 (11.9% density) to 2.6 million (14.6%) in 1910. It was only a question of time before unions, given workers' increased confidence with the upturn in the business cycle from 1911, would expand again in a series of organisation strikes to challenge employers' power to determine the pay-effort bargain. During the Great Unrest, 1911-14, union membership leapt to 4.1 million (23.0% density). The Board of Trade actively promoted collective bargaining, pressing employers to recognise unions as the appropriate representative bodies. Incremental steps were made, in many cases overthrowing long-held and cherished values, although such bargaining was of a minimal and modest nature, many groups of employers assuming that they could roll back any union advances in the next recession. In practice, the scale of the Great Unrest dwarfed the rise of New Unionism in 1888–90 and in many ways completed its work.

The 'Great Unrest'

'The great unrest ... burst out in a flood of strikes in the early summer of 1911'.[16] A national seamen's strike triggered a series of stoppages by transport workers' unions in Liverpool in June - with a co-ordinating role performed by the Liverpool strike committee of the National Transport Workers' Federation (NTWF) - which swept the port, ending in collective agreements.[17] Elsewhere, portworkers took their own separate action, with big strikes in Hull, Manchester, Cardiff and then London, overlapping with each other, lasting from June to August. Troops and police were mobilised. At the end of the seamen's strike in late July, employers, prominent among which was the Shipping Federation – an organisation for which strike-breaking was an 'important function'[18] – lobbied over claims of violence and intimidation and the failure of the police to take firm action. They were particularly concerned about the TDA's picketing provisions. The Home Secretary,

Winston Churchill, assured them that the Act did not sanction intimidation or threats of violence. But he promised to consider the advice given out to police. A Home Office circular, dated 11 August 1911, was speedily sent to chief constables.

Entitled 'Intimidation during Trade Disputes', the circular restated the CPPA, s 7, which made criminal offences of attempting to compel someone to abstain from work by, among other things, intimidating him 'or his wife or children'; 'persistently' following him; hiding his tools, clothes, or other property; watching or besetting workplaces or houses; and following 'with two or more other persons in a disorderly manner'. These were contrasted with the narrow ambit of the TDA, s 2: 'picketing *for the purpose of obtaining or communicating information, or of peacefully persuading any person to work or abstain from working*' (emphasis in original). Watching and besetting, criminal under s 7 of the CPPA, was allowed if it conformed to the above section of the TDA.

If the numbers of pickets were 'disproportionate ... as to exclude the idea of peaceful persuasion', then participants were liable to be charged with watching and besetting. It was 'desirable' for police to contact strike leaders and establish who were appointed as pickets: these 'should be provided with badges by the union, which the police should recognise and respect'. Such arrangements would enable police to judge whether the number of pickets was 'reasonable and justified'; at large works, with a big workforce, 'a numerous picket may be justified'. The police were reminded in the circular that workers had 'the fullest right, after due notice, to refuse to work' and could peacefully persuade others to do the same. If they stopped work without notice, this was 'a matter of civil justice, and does not concern the police' except in those circumstances covered by the CPPA ss 4 and 5, where breach of contract was a criminal offence.[19]

As this circular was being drafted, events erupted again in Liverpool. An unofficial strike by railway goods porters began on 5 August and three days later the NTWF committee called upon railway and other transport workers to strike in support. In response, the employers imposed a lockout throughout the port. The ethnic and sectarian divisions of Liverpool's working class, compounding those of occupation, industry and union, were set aside, however temporarily.[20] Troops and extra police were moved into Liverpool, and special constables enrolled. The strike committee issued permits for the movement of essential goods. A mass demonstration on 13 August (Bloody Sunday) was violently dispersed by the police. Although the strike ended messily, it was victorious.

Disputes elsewhere on the railways led to the railway unions starting their first national strike on 17 August, which involved the largest force of troops used in an industrial dispute to that point.[21] In Liverpool, the success of the various strikes was a setback for local companies, both large and small, and the city's Unionist political leaders, and they responded with a political campaign against the TDA. The city's magistrates, with Lord Derby, the Lord Mayor, as chair, had met daily throughout the strike in a special committee,[22] and frequently protested to the Home Secretary at intimidation, the ineffectiveness of the CPPA (the police had no power of arrest for CPPA, s 7 offences; they could charge people when evidence was forthcoming but this was 'often inaccessible after the event'),[23] and the need to repeal s 2 of the TDA. As ever, *The Times* was quick to add its support.[24] A report, by this committee, on intimidation claimed that the CPPA was ineffective as no witnesses could be found owing to the 'fear of bodily injury, and probably the greater fear of violence to the wife and home'. The TDA 'by authorising peaceful picketing, has introduced a form of terrorism unknown before it became law' and should be repealed. It was decided on 30 August to circulate this report to Justices of the Peace throughout the United Kingdom.[25]

The demand for repeal of the picketing law was supported by the chair of the Liverpool Steam Ship Owners' Association - a powerful voice of Imperial capital - who at its general meeting on 5 September had argued that 'such a thing as peaceful picketing is not, and cannot, be practised in the actual progress of a strike. ... [Pickets] are out to stop men from working ... the power behind the picket by which its orders will be enforced is the violence of the mob. ... We are entitled to the protection of the law against the illegitimate advantages derived from mob violence directed against willing workers'. The Liverpool justices met again on 20 September, when it was revealed that of the 100 replies from other magistrates' benches to its report on intimidation, 71 were in favour of making representations to Parliament for reform of the law.[26] Detailed proposals were drawn up, comprising limits on the number, identification, and authorisation of pickets, prohibition of picketing at any residence, and police power to arrest any person charged with an offence under the CPPA, s 7 or breach of any of the above proposed limitations.

This was part of a wider campaign, culminating in October 1911 when the Employers' Parliamentary Council, supported by 65 employers' bodies, made representations to the Prime Minister, Herbert Asquith, to protest against coercive picketing – 'a form of tyranny so gross and monstrous as to completely negative the rights of every law-abiding citizen who declines to subject himself to labour union domination' – and trade union immunity, which had relieved 'unions of responsibility for their actions during trade disputes, these bodies are thus specially privileged to do wrong to others'. For good measure, the memorial submitted that the formation of federations of unions 'into one gigantic body having as its object the organisation of strikes on a national scale is a conspiracy'.[27] Asquith declined to review the TDA, arguing that the existing law was adequate. Employers' opposition continued, with the Leeds Chamber of Commerce, for example, calling for a Royal Commission to investigate the Act.[28] The new Home Secretary, Reginald McKenna, responded with a circular in November asking watch committees for particulars of cases under the CPPA.

The replies contained a litany of complaints as to the limits of the law, especially given the support that strikers received from local communities. Despite heavy picketing in Rochdale, no prosecutions could be effected under the CPPA for lack of information. In Salford, although 70 police were mobilised, the sight of 100 pickets at various entrances 'was quite sufficient to make ... [non-strikers] turn back'; during a strike of women workers there the police were unable to get anyone to 'give evidence in support of a charge of intimidation'. A strike in Accrington had led to 20 being charged under the CPPA but most cases were dismissed or withdrawn because strike-breakers feared 'subsequent molestation'. In Walsall it was 'next to impossible' to obtain evidence to justify proceedings 'when large crowds, consisting mainly of the Hooligan class, assemble, attracted by picketing'. The chief constable of Leeds also complained of 'large crowds composed of sympathisers with the strikers, and other persons who collect round the premises affected by the strike' and that any action to disperse them was 'like setting a spark to gunpowder.' There was 'an impression among the public' that the TDA justified 'peaceful picketing in these numbers and in this manner'. His policy was 'to avoid accentuating the trade character of the disputes ... hence, the breaches of the law, wherever possible, have been treated as ordinary street offences'. Pickets also adjusted their behaviour to avoid falling foul of the law. During a long dispute in Merthyr Tydfil, there was a 'systematic practice' that non-strikers 'should not be approached by the same strikers on more than one occasion during 15 or 16 days', thus 'any record of proving persistent following with a view to cause workmen to abstain from work was nullified'.[29]

Sir Edward Troup, the permanent under-secretary at the Home Office, wrote to the Liverpool justices' committee on 7 November that 'it has generally been taken for granted that the Act [CPPA] contains no power to arrest for offences under section 7, and it is so stated in the General Orders of The Metropolitan Police. But the point has never been decided by any court, and as offences under sec 7 are in the nature of breaches of the peace, a policeman may have power … to arrest for offences committed in his sight.'[30] A further meeting of Liverpool magistrates, on 13 December 1911, repeated its previous demands but with a figure for picket numbers (three for each body of men, subject to a maximum of 12 at each entrance).[31] On 15 December the Home Secretary, McKenna, told a delegation of Liverpool, Birkenhead and Bootle magistrates that the existing law 'had not been utilised to the utmost'.[32]

Liverpool was exceptional in that determined and organised employers, if they so chose, were usually able to defeat (though not to destroy) unions and ignore attempts to arbitrate by the Board of Trade. In London the Dockers' Union was beaten in a second dispute in 1912. This was followed by the Dublin lockout, 1912-13, where the Dublin Employers' Federation, led by William Murphy, locked out members of the Irish Transport and General Workers' Union. The employers were able to call on the Royal Irish Constabulary, the Dublin municipal police, armed strike-breakers and the courts to counter the picketing (much of which was not violent).[33] The union was defeated and strikers forced back on the employers' terms. Murphy was 'received with cheers' at a meeting convened by the Employers' Parliamentary Council in February 1914, which called for an inquiry on the TDA. This request had already been made by the employer representatives on the Industrial Council.[34] Sir George, later Lord, Askwith, who chaired the Industrial Council inquiry, 1911–13, and was the government's Chief Industrial Commissioner 1911–19, was all too aware that 'Class feeling on the part of employers has been increased by suspicion and anger at … [the] supposed effects' of the TDA.[35]

The Liberal government refused to hold an inquiry, nor did it support parliamentary attempts to restrict the powers of pickets.[36] The Home Office's view was that policing methods, concentrating on public order, were generally sufficient. An internal memo in 1913 noted that it had not come across any instance where the TDA had 'enabled a successful defence to be set up to a charge of intimidation'. During the Great Unrest there was extensive use of the army, special constables and imported police in the biggest disputes. Morgan suggests that until the First World War 'the problem of dealing with industrial protest … was seen … basically as a concern for the police and police authorities rather than for central government'. This did not mean that central government did not have a view. Much could be done under the common law, as action against pickets in Chesterfield in 1912 showed: 'It might have been difficult to prove intimidation against individuals: to charge the ring leaders with unlawful assembly ... avoids this difficulty'.[37]

A major factor that diluted the employers' mobilisation against the TDA was the weakness of trade unions. There was no cohesive movement. Unions were constructed upon an 'immense variety of specific work contexts and distinctive group interests'[38] and remained confined to specific occupations, sectors and localities. The demarcation between craftsmen and labourers was wide and fiercely defended by the former's unions. The tensions between British and Irish workers were endemic. The gendered division of labour was entrenched; the marriage bar applied in many occupations and sectors in which women worked. Where such divisions coincided, workers' sectional horizons were compounded. The TUC had little authority over its constituents and many unions, especially those of labourers, were fragile organisations. Trade unions, imbued with a form of business unionism, displayed 'a militant, but sectional and defensive, economism' where powerful.[39] But the Great Unrest seemed for a time to presage a very different form of trade unionism, hence the employers' alarm.

Union organisation and collective bargaining made great strides during the First World War, aided by state support in return for union leaders' backing for the war. Its impact upon workers - inflation and dilution at home, conscription and death abroad - prompted many, especially those in manufacturing plants and crafts, to develop workplace union organisation to defend their pay and conditions. The Munitions of War Act 1915 made strikes or lockouts in munitions works a criminal offence, and by royal proclamation this could be extended to other sectors; compulsory arbitration was also introduced. The Act was of little use in major disputes, being amended in 1916 to abolish imprisonment for illegal strikes. When activists became exposed, there could be harsh punishment under the Defence of the Realm Acts but, in practice, apart from some notorious cases, this was mainly used as a threat.[40]

Significant strike activity continued, particularly during 1917 and 1918, and the fear of massive social unrest after the war led the government to set up the Whitley committee. Its reports of 1917-18 marked a significant step in the promotion of collective bargaining by the State, and its institutionalisation across swathes of the economy. Trade boards (later renamed wages councils), with union representation, filled many of the gaps. At the same time 'employers and employed were to be left to settle their own relations' and the government 'was warned, politely but clearly, to keep out'.[41] Acceptance of unions as representative institutions and collective bargaining as the necessary method of dealing with them 'co-existed ... with much genuine conflict in specific industries over union recognition, wages, working hours and the line defining the frontier of control at the workplace'.[42] The repeal of the Munitions of War Acts and the ending of wartime compulsory arbitration in 1919 restored the position of the TDA and free collective bargaining.

'Extreme industrial confrontation'

While the period 1910–26 has been rightly described as one of 'extreme industrial confrontation', the United Kingdom did not experience the 'fearful carnage between a para-military state police and industrial workers' evident in many European countries early in the 20th century, nor the 'habitual violence and loss of life that punctuated' labour struggles in the United States.[43] Instead, after the war, the enormous growth of the power of trade unionism, whose membership had more than tripled between 1911 and 1920, was defused by a sophisticated political strategy of containment, led by the Coalition government's Prime Minister, David Lloyd George.[44] Disputes that spilled over the confused line between economic and political action, a line that was still being defined and learned, were the exception and this was reinforced by the growing strength of the Labour Party. A High Court decision on the use of coercive tactics by union members was not taken up by other judges and was disapproved of by the Court of Appeal.[45] But unions were weakened by the end of the post-war boom in 1920; membership fell by one-third in two years, from 8.3 to 5.6 million. Government support for collective bargaining and trade boards declined and the Ministry of Labour's funds were cut.[46]

The character of major strikes changed after the war. The years 1919–26 witnessed 17 industry-wide stoppages as well as the General Strike. This was qualitatively different to any previous period. Even during the Great Unrest, only three of the 14 biggest disputes were major industry-wide strikes, the rest being at a district level. Days lost in industry-wide strikes and lockouts increased from one-quarter of the total in 1901–10 to one-half during 1911–14 and reached 80% in 1919–26.[47] This reflected not only the shift in bargaining levels and the successful union-amalgamation movement, but also the massive post-war economic readjustments allied to employers' attempts to roll back the 'frontier of control' in their favour. Serious attempts were made to broaden union solidarity through the Triple Alliance of coalminers, railway and transport workers, though this collapsed ignominiously in 1921. A few years later, what Clegg called 'the smell of class warfare' permeated the build-up from Red Friday, 31 July 1925, to the General Strike of May 1926.[48]

The Emergency Powers Act, passed within a fortnight of the start of the national miners' strike of 1920, provided for the declaration of 'states of emergency', and regulations under this Act in the 1921 and

1926 mining lockouts afforded the police potentially sweeping powers. The *Daily Herald* claimed that the police used the regulations during the 1921 lockout 'to initiate a reign of terror' in South Wales; the Home Office informed police that it was 'not desirable' to make arrangements with the strike leaders as to the number or badging of pickets (recommended in the 1911 circular), but instead to break up any picketing large enough to be 'likely to cause intimidation'. The Home Office was also concerned that not only were charges of riot notoriously difficult to prove but charges of intimidation were often either withdrawn by the police or the magistrates had difficulty in accepting police evidence.[49] The police continued with their independent criticisms of the TDA. The chief constable of Sheffield bemoaned in 1922 'so called "Peaceful Picketing" indulged in by gangs of aggrieved persons, accompanied by hooligans etc': 'pickets (if permitted at all) should be limited … to 4 or 6 persons at most; … processions … during such disputes should be punishable on the part of the ringleaders, by imprisonment'.[50] In 1925, the assistant chief constable of Liverpool suggested that pickets should wear badges because 'Communists and others take independent and unauthorised action before an actual strike starts in order to force the issue'; by picketing they effectively compelled a stoppage to take place.[51]

The fear of Communist intervention was taken up by the Shipping Federation in a deputation to the Home Secretary in October 1925. Its chairman presented a memorandum on 'Intimidatory Picketing'. He referred to a conversation with the Labour Home Secretary during the 1924 London dock strike, when the Metropolitan Police Commissioner, General Sir William Horwood, had stated 'I cannot do more … so long as the existing Act [TDA] is in force'. The Federation's attempts to move strike-breakers around the country came up particularly against third parties, often 'Communist agitators', being protected by the picketing laws. The Conservative Home Secretary, Sir William Joynson-Hicks, was not unsympathetic but 'the repeal of the Act would not remove the difficulties of intimidation'.[52] This meeting was followed by another Home Office circular, 30 December 1925, to chief constables restating the legal position on intimidation and molestation in relation to picketing. This document reproduced much of the original 1911 circular. What was missing was any reference to the badging of pickets, the document containing instead a reminder that the TDA conferred no right to hold meetings upon, or otherwise obstruct, the highway.[53]

During the General Strike, when around two million workers struck in support of the one million miners resisting wage cuts and a longer working week, the armed forces' role was to guard vulnerable points and to protect volunteer labour. The scale of deployment of special constables was also unusual, with numbers increasing from 98,000 to 226,000 during the nine days. The continuing seven-month-long miners' lockout constituted the first time in many years that the police had coped alone in a national strike – and this was to set the pattern for the future.[54] Nearly 1,400 arrests were made during the nine days of the General Strike, and a total overall from May to November of almost 8,000, of which about 40% were under the emergency regulations. For Ewing and Gearty the real purpose of these regulations in 1926 – to date the longest state of emergency – was to facilitate the breaking of the miners' action and a return to work. The police used increasing force as the lockout dragged on, and magistrates imposed exemplary sentences.[55] Figures from the small Warwickshire coalfield illustrate the extensive use of the CPPA. Of 68 offences dealt with by the end of July, 20 were under the emergency regulations and 45 under CPPA, s 7, for intimidation or watching and besetting.[56]

A further circular to chief constables, written by Sir Ernley Blackwell, legal under-secretary at the Home Office, was issued in October 1926 to counter attempts by miners' pickets to get 'safety men' to stop work. After stressing the need to have adequate police numbers available, the circular stated that the Home Secretary wished to draw attention to 'the special position' of safety men under the CPPA, s 5; if they 'wilfully and maliciously' broke their contracts, rather than lawfully terminated them by notice, they were liable to prosecution under that section. Further, as such an act was a crime 'within the meaning of section 3' of the CPPA, if two or more persons acted together to persuade the safety men to so break (rather than lawfully terminate) their contracts, the former would not be protected from criminal proceedings by the action being 'in contemplation or furtherance of a trade dispute'. Finally, even 'peaceful persuasion', allowed under the TDA, when 'applied to safety men for the purpose of inducing them to break their contracts of service contrary to [CPPA] section 5 ... would expose those [so] engaged ... to proceedings either under [CPPA] section 3 ..., or as inciters to the commission of the offence under section 5 of that Act'. This knowledge would 'strengthen the hands of the police' in dealing with the use of 'persuasion, which does not clearly amount to intimidation to induce safety men to cease work in breach of their contracts'. Where proceedings were seen as desirable, matters should be reported to the Director of Public Prosecutions as there might be 'certain technical questions' which required 'careful consideration'.[57] Police notices were posted in West Riding and Lancashire warning against the picketing of safety men but the union tactic at this late stage in the dispute was ineffective.[58]

The Trade Disputes and Trade Unions Act 1927

In the aftermath of the General Strike - its failure and the victimisation of union activists - union membership fell by 10%. Where it had still existed, workplace union organisation generally withered. It was a commonplace that many former shop stewards were active in the unemployed workers' movement. Perhaps because union organisation was weak, there was no onslaught on collective bargaining, dominated as it was by the employers' agenda. Union membership fell again in the financial crisis and world recession of the early 1930s, to 4.4 million in 1933.

In a judgment that was immediately criticised but was nevertheless important at the time in reinforcing the hostile climate, the General Strike had been denounced by Astbury J as outside the protection of s 5 of the TDA, which defined a trade dispute, and hence unlawful.[59] The Conservative government's response to the General Strike was to amend the TDA by the Trade Disputes and Trade Unions Act 1927 (TDTUA). The new Act had a symbolic purpose, setting the 'legislative seal upon the unions' defeat'.[60] Taking its cue from Astbury's judgment the Act made the instigation and organisation of general strikes liable to civil and criminal sanctions. During the Bill's preparation, the Ministry of Labour's advice was clearly conciliatory. Sir Arthur Steel-Maitland, the Minister, 'consistently viewed ... [the] task in the context of the future peaceful conduct of industrial relations. His influence is less apparent in the Bill than in the measures excluded from it'. The Home Secretary, Joynson-Hicks, insisted that acceptance of the employers' demands for repeal of the TDA, s 2, on peaceful picketing, would, in his words, 'be described as an attack on trade unionists and might lead to a combination of trade union voters of all shades of opinion against the Government'

The Act was the minimum agreed by a Cabinet committee, which heard evidence from Conservative groups and employers' associations, including the EEF and the National Confederation of Employers' Organisations (NCEO). A 'consistent theme' of the committee's work was 'to make the wording as vague as possible, on the principle that its deterrent effect would increase in proportion to the degree of confusion generated in the minds of trade unionists on questions of the legality of strikes and picketing'. On numbers picketing, the NCEO had suggested 'six, or anything you like' as long as there was a limit; the Master Printers wanted only one; while the EEF wished mass picketing to be illegal without defining 'mass'. The Cabinet committee decided at one point on a maximum of four at each entrance but changed its mind.

According to Anderson, any limit 'conflicted with the philosophy of making the legislation as vague as possible'. The committee considered the 1911 Home Office circular on picketing and its support for the wearing of badges but, despite initial support, this was rejected because, in its words, it 'would revive the popular misconception that a picket is a privileged person with rights and immunities different from those of the ordinary citizen'.[61]

Most of the TDA's provisions were left untouched. Strikes were declared 'illegal' if they had 'any object other than or in addition to the furtherance of a trade dispute *within the trade or industry in which the strikers are engaged*' (emphasis added) and were 'designed or calculated to coerce the Government either directly or by inflicting hardship upon the community', and it was a criminal offence to declare, instigate or incite illegal strikes (TDTUA, s 1). The right to picket was amended (s 3) so that attendance 'in such numbers or otherwise in such manner as to be calculated to intimidate any person in that house or place ['where a person resides or works ...'], or to obstruct the approach thereto or egress therefrom, or lead to a breach of the peace' was unlawful and was deemed to be watching and besetting within the meaning of the CPPA. The term 'to intimidate' now meant 'to cause in the mind of a person a reasonable apprehension of injury to him or to any member of his family or to any of his dependants or of violence or damage to any person or property, and the expression 'injury' includes injury to a person in respect of his business, occupation, employment or other source of income, and includes any actionable wrong'. The new meaning of 'to intimidate' was also construed as applying to s 7 of the CPPA. An official government handbook later admitted of the TDTUA that it made the law of picketing 'much more rigid and severe'.[62]

The Bill faced strong Labour opposition in the Commons and a massive national campaign organised by the TUC, which received little publicity: 'Never has so large a campaign received so little attention.'[63] The unions were compelled to rely on a future Labour parliamentary majority to effect change. The 1929 minority Labour government drafted a Bill to amend the TDTUA but, despite concessions, some Liberal MPs voted against and it collapsed early in 1931.[64] With the fall of the Labour government later that year - caused by the defection of the Prime Minister, Ramsay MacDonald, and some other senior figures to form a National government - repeal had to wait.

The TDTUA has been neglected because it was little used (apart from the change to the unions' political levy from contracting-out to contracting-in, and the ban on civil service unions affiliating to the TUC); Clegg, for example, argued that the 'visible impact' of the 1927

Act on unions was 'slight' and placed 'a relatively light curb' on their activities.[65] It was important nonetheless. Although much sympathetic industrial action was unaffected, a large grey area was open to challenge and this undoubtedly led some unions to be more cautious than they might have been otherwise, though there was little mood to generalise strikes beyond industrial boundaries.[66] No strike was declared illegal under the Act, but four Trotskyists were imprisoned in 1944 for furtherance of an illegal strike; eventually the convictions of the three remaining in prison were quashed on appeal.[67] The most used section concerning industrial action was that on picketing. That it was not employed more was a comment on the state of trade unionism at this time. From the beginning, though, there were cases.[68]

An internal Metropolitan Police memorandum noted in 1927 that after the passing of the TDTUA, the Home Office had not issued a circular clarifying the changes to the law on picketing. Eventually the Home Office agreed to changes being made in the 1932 revision of the police's General Orders. According to an official, this afforded 'a suitable opportunity for covering the whole ground ... *unobtrusively*' (emphasis added).[69] Later in 1933, a confidential memorandum was sent by the Metropolitan Police Commissioner to superintendents, pointing out that 'besetting' was unlikely to be observed by the police. Where it was alleged, 'arrangements should be made for observation in plain clothes when possible'.[70]

Clegg has argued that from 1927 trade union leaders wanted to avoid industrial action 'at almost any cost'.[71] A particular exception was the series of major disputes in the crisis-ridden cotton industry from 1929 to 1932. These culminated in 1932 when, first, the spinning and then the weaving firms ended their collective agreements. In weaving, especially, where the employers' 'more looms' campaign ran alongside wage cuts, there was 'a return to unregulated class warfare' on a scale not seen since the 19th century. A number of individual mill strikes led to an all-out strike in Burnley; strikes elsewhere in Lancashire were met with company-wide lockouts before a strike was called across the whole weaving sector (followed soon after by one in spinning).[72]Clegg's description of employers and unions 'moving from guerrilla warfare to a pitched battle'[73] gives some feel for the intensity of this crisis, normally overshadowed by the coal industry in accounts of the period. The CPPA, as amended by the TDTUA, was used in court cases during these strikes.[74] With the *Daily Telegraph* proclaiming 'Intimidation by Strike Pickets', and the Blackburn cotton employers' chairman condemning 'trade union terrorism, dictation and intimidation', the national secretary of the Cotton Spinners' and Manufacturers' Association asked the Home

Secretary to give a ruling on what constituted 'peaceful picketing' under the TDTUA. The Home Office reply was, as ever, that 'the Courts alone can decide in the light of the facts of each individual case'.[75]

Outside cotton, much of the industrial conflict in the period involving large-scale picketing was in the coal industry, where non-unionism and breakaway unions constituted serious threats to miners' solidarity. In South Wales there were 'many cases of mass picketing, with accompanying police violence', from the late 1920s to the mid-1930s. An incident at Taff Merthyr colliery at Trelewis in October 1935 led to the 'biggest mass trial of industrial workers ever held in Britain' in March 1936: fifty-five were convicted of serious riot.[76] During the Harworth miners' strike in 1936-37, against the breakaway Nottinghamshire miners' union, the new Public Order Act 1936 was used extensively, though there were a number of charges under the CPPA.[77]

As late as 1939, W H Thompson, then the leading practitioner in trade union law, could write: 'picketing in strikes is fraught with more risk than was the case before 1927, and it would be a bold man who would be dogmatic as to what exactly the legal rights of pickets now are'.[78] While the TDTUA had created a greater range of statutory offences arising from picketing, it had not given the police any greater statutory authority. This had been solved by the Public Order Act, which formalised existing ad hoc police practice and became the standard legal device against pickets.[79] Hence, prosecutions involving the TDTUA declined. In the period 1935–44 offences against the CPPA, s 7, as amended by the TDTUA, were as follows: of the 272 tried summarily during 1935–37, 219 were found guilty – 72 were dismissed, 76 were dismissed under their own recognisances with a probation order, 49 were fined and 12 imprisoned. Another 25 were tried summarily in 1938–39 but only five from 1940 to 1944; 16 were fined and one imprisoned during 1938–44. A few were tried on indictment (six in 1935, six in 1937 and one in 1940); of these only one (in 1943) was imprisoned.[80]

As unemployment fell, union membership picked up after the low point of 1933, reaching 6.3 million by 1939. There was no dramatic turning point, no strike wave. By 1939, employers' associations had come to accept trade unions as 'an integral and permanent part of the fabric of British society'. The associations' 'strategic commitment' was to 'moderate, constitutional and economistic modes of trade unionism' as a 'bulwark' against alternatives 'that challenged managerial prerogative ... and capitalist endeavour'.[81] Employers were thus more receptive to collective bargaining – though only up to a point. Clegg comments:

Most extensions of collective bargaining [in the late 1930s] came where unions were relatively weak. They lacked the strength to force the employers to the bargaining-table; and in most cases the employers did not have to be forced. They wanted to come, if they could have the assurance that their competitors would not be able to undercut them by evading the agreement.[82]

As far as possible, unions were denied any role at the workplace, where management retained wide discretion on recruitment and dismissal, or in work organisation. There was an important change in the character of strike activity: from the mid-1930s the pattern of unofficial and usually unconstitutional strikes, so characteristic of the 1950s and 1960s, became dominant.

By now the parameters of British trade unionism were formed: organised in a complex, overlapping set of bodies, centralised, focused on industry-wide collective bargaining, pay and conditions, committed to the Labour Party (and strongly anti-Communist), and opposed to industrial action for political ends. It was this framework into which new members flooded as a result of the novel conditions called into existence by the Second World War - full employment, political acceptance of trade unionism, and Order 1305, which extended relevant collective agreements to new factories and workers, imposed arbitration and banned industrial action. Despite record numbers of strikes, there was little large-scale industrial action, unlike during the First World War: in 109 cases 6,281 workers were prosecuted for striking under the Order, resulting in only three being directly imprisoned – at Betteshanger colliery in Kent in 1942 – and 4,146, including 225 women, fined.[83] An important innovation during the war was the role won by workplace representatives - shop stewards - in building union organisation *and* facilitating production. By 1946, despite enormous dislocation, union membership had grown to 8.8 million (43.0% density) and industry-wide collective bargaining had become widespread. Unlike after the First World War, there was no post-war slump.

Conclusion: Restoration of the TDA

The 1945 Labour government repealed the TDTUA in 1946, 'simply, brusquely, triumphantly':[84] 'The Trade Disputes and Trade Unions Act, 1927 ... is hereby repealed, and, subject to the transitional provisions ... every enactment and rule of law amended or otherwise affected by that Act shall ... have effect as if the Act of 1927 had not been passed.'[85] The Savoy Hotel strike in 1947 soon brought picketing into the public glare again. The Cabinet asked the Home Secretary whether there should be 'an authoritative statement made about the existing law in industrial disputes'. The current advice (the 1925 circular) was not considered appropriate and a much shorter draft was prepared. This did not draw attention to the CPPA, though referred to intimidation being illegal; it emphasised the police's duty to prevent obstruction of the highway. Eventually it was decided not to go public.[86] No one could guess that picketing, especially mass picketing, would cease to be a problem for public policy until the 1970s.

As Order 1305 remained in force until late 1951 (by agreement between the Labour government and the TUC), there was no full restoration of the TDA. During the Order's peacetime operation, the government refrained from prosecution of illegal unofficial strikers (and there were numerous opportunities given a number of important strikes) until the autumn of 1950, when ten gas fitters were sentenced to one month's imprisonment, pending appeal, at which the sentence was reduced to a fine. This was followed by a failed prosecution in an unofficial dock strike in February 1951. The industrial unrest that accompanied both cases prompted the Order's revocation.[87]

From 1951 until 1971, the TDA was again the major statute governing industrial action. British trade unionism was undergoing an important shift, not in its major parameters, but a hitherto rare depth was added in many areas of manufacturing, especially engineering, by workplace union organisation, co-ordinated by shop stewards. The 'temper' of labour had altered too - workers' expectations were growing. As the post-war boom gathered pace, workers' bargaining power increased, if unevenly, much to the discomfiture of those employers that had seen this as a wartime aberration. Once the power of dismissal was challenged, many employers had little else. Union leaders too were disorientated by workers' new-found power and confidence. Secondary industrial action, although always problematic given the sectional structure of British trade unionism, became an effective option in a growing number of workplaces and sectors. The scope of the TDA was now a practical weapon, whereas picketing became less important in winning disputes - less 'visible'. Coercion by employers, including the dismissal of activists

- as in the car industry until the early 1960s - remained viable if the costs could be met and justified.[88]

As discussed above, the TDTUA 1927 had called into question the legality of strikes with 'any object other than or in addition to the furtherance of a trade dispute within the trade or industry in which the strikers are engaged', though there are no cases that discussed the boundaries of trade or industry. Its repeal reinstated the lawfulness of all secondary industrial action. After the General Strike, D C Thomson Ltd, printers and publishers, had imposed a non-union shop in its works in Dundee, Glasgow and Manchester, but union membership had grown nevertheless and in 1952 the dismissal of suspected union members at Manchester was followed by a dispute and strike in Glasgow. NATSOPA declared an official dispute and organized solidarity action among newspaper distributors, with much success in London, Manchester, Liverpool and Birkenhead, according to an official Committee of Inquiry. Other unions did likewise at paper mills that supplied Thomson.[89]

The company initiated an innovative legal action against the TGWU general secretary, Arthur Deakin, claiming that he had indirectly induced a breach of its commercial contract of supply through unlawful means, inducement of breach of contract of employment. This was rebuffed on the facts by the Court of Appeal in 1952[90] (see Simpson, this volume) but the judgment's protection was narrow and 'unlocked the gate for any court that wished to intervene afresh'.[91] A subtle shift in public policy towards unions was apparent in the Court of Inquiry's report, which criticised the unions for organising solidarity action that breached their collective agreement with companies with which they had no dispute: 'How long collective bargaining could be expected to continue as an effective instrument for the furtherance of industrial relations if it came to be thought by either party that there was no sanctity behind their express agreements and they were at liberty to break them at will is not difficult to forecast.'[92]

The early post-war Labour and Conservative governments discussed whether to ban unofficial strikes and impose pre-strike ballots but both options were rejected.[93] The big strikes against redundancy in the car industry in 1956 gave the matter some urgency.[94] Discussions within the Ministry of Labour later that year on pre-strike ballots noted the 'violent conflicts within the political and industrial field' that might be generated'.[95] A memorandum argued that to legislate on this would show 'a complete lack of trust in the competence and responsibility of trade unions to manage their own affairs' as well as to 'give extremists the lead they may have been seeking'. All were reminded of Churchill's answer to the House of Commons in January 1954 of 'the established tradition in this country under which the trade union movement is left to manage its own affairs to the fullest possible extent without Government interference'.[96]

The first important political challenge to the TDA was *A Giant's Strength* in 1958, written by the Inns of Court Conservative and Unionist Society, which proposed, *inter alia*, the removal of union tort-immunity for secondary action, unofficial strikes and for all strikes unless preceded by a tribunal of inquiry. It noted, too, the ease with which protection given to trade unions in the *D C Thomson* case in relation to the use of unlawful means during a strike could be outflanked.[97] It was only a matter of time before both lawyers and employers exploited this lacuna in the TDA. A shift in judicial attitudes was apparent in *Rookes v Barnard*[98] and then, in a rash of cases (see Simpson, this volume), employers challenged the lawfulness of industrial action on the basis of the tort of loss by unlawful means, i.e. indirect interference and breach of commercial contract by inducement of a breach of a contract of employment.

Employers and their associations presented their views on the TDA to the Donovan Commission, 1965–68. There was no common position but the Confederation of British Industry, the new and comprehensive peak body of employers, declared that: 'The justification for the Act was the many difficulties which faced the trade union movement at the beginning of the century and which weighted the scales in favour of the employers. These difficulties have long since passed away and unions are no longer the weaker party.'[99] Before the publication of the Donovan Report in 1968 - which proposed the extension of unions' tort immunity to embrace inducement of breach of any contract[100] - the Conservative Party issued its new policy for changes in labour law, *Fair Deal at Work*.[101] By then three major forces had declared against the TDA and the liberties and role accorded to trade unions: many major employers and their associations, senior members of the judiciary, and the leadership of the Conservative Party. It was the shift inside the last that was the vital factor.

Thanks to Keith Ewing and Bill Wedderburn.

Notes

1 *Glamorgan Coal Co v South Wales Miners' Federation* [1905] AC 239.

2 O Kahn-Freund, 'Labour Law', in M Ginsberg (ed), *Law and Opinion in England in the 20th Century* (1959), p 224.

3 N Soldon, 'Laissez-faire as Dogma: The Liberty and Property Defence League, 1882-1914', in K Brown (ed), *Essays in Anti-Labour History: Responses to the Rise of Labour in Britain* (1974), pp 219-20, 224-6, 230-1.

4 Formed during the engineering lockout of 1897–98 'for the purpose of testing the whole question of picketing' and 'having for its primary object the suppression of the tyranny of labour unionism in connection with labour disputes and during strikes': Report of the Royal Commission on Trades Disputes and Trade Combinations (Chair: Lord Dunedin), Cd 2825, 1906. Evidence, Frederick Millar, 8 December 1904, Qq 3360, 3362 and 'Statement', p 202. Quotes from Millar, Q 3375, and 'Statement', p 202; Beasley, 13 July 1904, Q 1379; Shipping Federation, 12 January 1905, 'Statement', pp 301–3; Noble, 30 November 1904, 'Statement', p 162.

5 H A Clegg, A Fox and A F Thompson, *A History of British Trade Unions since 1889*, Vol. 1: 1889-1910 (1964), p 331 and ch 8; J Saville, 'Trade Unions and Free Labour: The Background to the Taff Vale Decision', in A Briggs and J Saville (eds), *Essays in Labour History* (1960).

6 A view held by the Board of Trade: R Davidson, 'The Board of Trade and Industrial Relations 1896-1914' (1973) 21 *Historical Journal* 571, at p 576. See also Clegg et al, vol 1, above, pp 326-7.

7 The scope of the Act was narrowed in *Conway v Wade* [1909] AC 506 (see Ewing, this volume), but the judges accepted the clear language of TDA 1906, s 4(1) in relation to union tort-immunity in *Vacher v London Society of Compositors* [1913] AC 107.

8 Amalgamated Society of Railway Servants v Osborne [1910] AC 87; see M J Klarman, 'The Judges versus the Unions: The Development of British Labor Law, 1867-1913' (1989) 75 Virginia Law Review 1487, at pp 1539-45.

9 *The Times*, 14 March 1906; Clegg et al, vol 1, above, p 173.

10 HL Debs, 12 December 1906, cols 276–82.

11 A J McIvor, *Organised Capital: Employers' Associations and Industrial Relations in Northern England, 1880–1939* (1996), p 77.

12 E Larkin, *James Larkin: Irish Labour Leader*, 1876–1947 (1989; first published 1965), p 30.

13 See *Larkin v Belfast Harbour Commissioners* [1908] 2 IR 214.

14 *Newcastle Daily Chronicle*, 12 May 1908, in The National Archives, London (TNA), HO 144/5491; The Times, 12 May 1908.

15 J Morgan, *Conflict and Order: The Police and Labour Disputes in England and Wales 1900–1939* (1987), p 158.

16 G D H Cole, *A Short History of the British Working-Class Movement 1789–1947* (1948), p 328. See also G Dangerfield, *The Strange Death of Liberal England* (1935), ch 4.

17 H R Hikins, '*The Liverpool General Transport Strike, 1911*' (1961) 113

Transactions of the Historical Society of Lancashire and Cheshire 169; E Taplin, *Near to Revolution: The Liverpool General Transport Strike of 1911* (1994).

18 L Powell, *The Shipping Federation: A History of the First Sixty Years, 1890–1950* (1950), p 11.

19 TNA, HO 158/15 (212,614). The CPPA, s 7 is still law in the Trade Union and Labour Relations (Consolidation) Act 1992 (TULR(C)A), s 241, with the offences now being arrestable; the CPPA, s 4, repealed in 1971, made it criminal for workers employed in supplying gas or water to the public to break their contract of service in circumstances where the public was likely to be deprived of its supply; s 5 was broader and concerned 'wilfully and maliciously' breaking a contract of service or hiring where it was known that it would 'endanger human life, or cause serious bodily injury, or ... expose valuable property ... to destruction or serious injury' – it is now contained in s 240 of TULR(C)A.

20 The role of the Mersey Quay and Railway Carters' Union - a union of Protestant carters - was vital: P Smith, 'A Proud Liverpool Union: The Liverpool and District Carters' and Motormen's Union, 1889-1946' (2003) 16 *Historical Studies in Industrial Relations 1*.

21 Morgan, above, pp 52–5, 171–5.

22 Liverpool Record Office, 347/MAG/1/1/9.

23 Morgan, above, p 151.

24 *The Times*, 22 August 1911 (editorial).

25 Justices of the Peace, City of Liverpool, '*Report of the Special Committee of the Justices about the Need of Legislation on the Subject of Intimidation*'. The report, dated 28 August, was adopted on 30 August 1911: TNA, HO 144/5491; Liverpool Record Office, 347/MAG/1/1/9.

26 For the Birmingham magistrates, 'the position is so different from that in Liverpool that the justices see no reason of acceding to their request': TUC Annual Report, 1912, p 93.

27 *Ibid*, pp 90-3. All quotations are from the memorial.

28 Morgan, above, p 179.

29 Letters to the Home Office from Chief Constable, Rochdale, 29 November 1911; Chairman of the Watch Committee, Salford, 1 December 1911; the Mayor, Accrington, 4 December 1911; Town Clerk, Walsall, 23 November 1911; Chief Constable, Leeds, 8 December 1911; and letter (forwarded to the Home Office) from Chief Constable, Merthyr Tydfil, to the Mayor and Chairman of the Watch Committee, Merthyr Tydfil: TNA, HO 144/5491.

30 TNA, HO 144/5491/212614/9, quoted in B. Weinberger, *Keeping the Peace - Policing Strikes in Britain, 1906–26* (1991), p 99, n 126.

31 City of Liverpool, '*Further Report of the Special Committee of the Justices on the Need for Legislation on the Subject of Picketing and Intimidation*' (dated 4 December 1911); the Liverpool head constable had suggested a maximum picket of 'three persons acting on behalf of any one interest or six persons in all', letter, 23 November 1911: TNA, HO 144/5491; Liverpool Record Office, 347/MAG/1/1/9.

32 TNA, HO 144/5491, Memo of the meeting.

33 P Yeates, *Lockout: Dublin 1913* (2001), pp 425-6.
34 *The Times*, 19 February 1914; The Industrial Council, Report on Enquiry into Industrial Agreements, Cd 6952, 1913, pp 17, 18–19, 22.
35 Lord Askwith, Industrial Problems and Disputes (1920), p 96.
36 Morgan, above, pp 183–4; TUC Annual Report, 1913, pp 149–50.
37 Morgan, above, pp 8, 177, 184.
38 R Hyman, *The Political Economy of Industrial Relations* (1989), p 27.
39 R Hyman, *Understanding European Trade Unionism: Between Market, Class and Society* (2001), p 68.
40 J Hinton, *The First Shop Stewards' Movement* (1973); K Knowles, *Strikes: A Study in Industrial Conflict* (1952), pp 117–18.
41 H Clay, *The Problem of Industrial Relations* (1929), p 152.
42 A Fox, *History and Heritage: The Social Origins of the British Industrial Relations System* (1985), p 278.
43 Morgan, above, pp 276, 280.
44 J Hinton, *Labour and Socialism: A History of the British Labour Movement 1867–1974* (1983), p 109.
45 *Valentine v Hyde* [1919] 2 Ch 129, where Astbury J, relying inter alia upon *Quinn v Leathem* [1901] AC 495, gave a restrictive view of TDA, s 5 immunity (at p 151) and excluded the protection of s 3 'by reason of the unlawful character of the means employed by them' (at p 154), i.e. 'moral intimidation, undue influence and coercive pressure' (at p 146). This fertile line of reasoning was not applied in *Hodges v Webb* [1920] 2 Ch 70 and was disapproved of in *White v Riley* [1921] 1 Ch 1 (CA).
46 C Howell, *Trade Unions and the State* (2005), p. 76.
47 H A Clegg, *A History of British Trade Unions since 1889, Vol 2: 1911-1933* (1985), p 26, Table 1, and p 550.
48 *Ibid*, p 558.
49 Morgan, above, pp 98, 190–7.
50 Correspondence between chief constables of Sheffield and Wakefield, 17 May 1922, in TNA, HO 144/5491.
51 Cited in Morgan, above, p 213.
52 Shipping Federation, 'Intimidatory Picketing: Deputation to Home Secretary', 13 October 1925, TNA, HO 144/5491.
53 TNA, HO 144/5491.
54 Morgan, above, pp 120, 130.
55 *Ibid*, p 211; K D Ewing and C A Gearty, *The Struggle for Civil Liberties: Political Freedom and the Rule of Law in Britain 1914–1945* (2000), ch 4.
56 Document from Warwickshire Constabulary, Chief Constable's Office, 1 August 1926, TNA, HO 144/1250 (Part 2).
57 TNA, HO 144/5491; for CPPA s 5, see n 19 above; the CPPA s 3, repealed in 1977 for England and Wales, concerned prosecution for criminal conspiracy in trade disputes where an act was criminal – though see TULR(C)A s 242.
58 J McIlroy and A Campbell, 'Fighting the Legions of Hell', p 94, and S Catterall, 'Police', p 254, both in J McIlroy, A Campbell and K Gildart

(eds), *Industrial Politics and the 1926 Mining Lockout: The Struggle for Dignity* (2004).

59 *National Sailors' and Firemen's Union v Reed* [1926] Ch 536, at pp 539-40. Astbury's judgment was criticised by A Goodhart, 'The Legality of the General Strike in England' (1926–27) 36 *Yale Law Journal* 464.

60 A Anderson, 'The Political Symbolism of the Labour Laws' (1971) 23 *Bulletin of the Society for the Study of Labour History* 13, at p 14.

61 A Anderson, 'The Labour Laws and the Cabinet Legislative Committee of 1926–27' (1971) 23 *Bulletin of the Society for the Study of Labour History* 37, quotes from pp 39, 43, 44, 48.

62 Ministry of Labour and National Service, Industrial Relations Handbook (1944), p 10.

63 TUC Annual Report, 1927, pp 248–59.

64 TUC Annual Report, 1931, pp 253–4.

65 Clegg, vol 2, above, pp 557–8.

66 For example, a TUC delegate reported that his union had been approached to strike 'to prevent blackleg goods being handled' but could not because of the TDTUA: TUC Annual Report, 1930, pp 376–7. Union leaders interviewed in 1931 were 'fearful' that the TDTUA 'might be invoked in almost any great strike': E Witte, 'British Trade Union Law since the Trade Disputes and Trade Unions Act of 1927' (1932) 26 *American Political Science Review* 345, at p 347.

67 Four members of the Revolutionary Communist Party were found guilty. Two were imprisoned for 12 months, one for six months and the other released, having served 13 days. The appeal was on the issue of 'furtherance': 'Trade Disputes and Trade Unions Bill, Notes for Second Reading' (approved for circulation, 6 December 1945), Appendix G: TNA, LAB 10/574; *R v Tearse and others* [1945] KB 1.

68 For example, cases in Chester: *Chester Chronicle*, 7 July, 20 October 1928; *The Times*, 18 December 1928, in TNA, LAB 2/1250/IR656/1928. In the October trial, concerning the same dispute as a dismissed case in July, a union district secretary was fined for watching and besetting and intimidating; as it was 'the first case of the kind brought under the new Act' (*Manchester Guardian*, 19 October 1928) he was allowed to appeal but lost.

69 'Memorandum re Section 3 of the Trade Disputes and Trade Unions Act, 1927', 10 April 1927, TNA, HO 45/19738.

70 Confidential memorandum, 13 June 1933, TNA, HO 45/19738.

71 Clegg, *A History of British Trade Unions since 1889*, Vol 3: 1934-1951 (1994), pp 421–2.

72 McIvor, above, pp 199–203.

73 Clegg, vol 2, above, p 522.

74 See *Daily Worker*, 19 September 1932, and *Cotton Factory Times*, 24 June, 23, 30 September, 14 October, 25 November, 9 December 1932. Also see, for example, *The Times*, 6, 13 August and 5 October 1932, when 13 pickets were charged with watching and besetting but found not guilty in Burnley Quarter Sessions as they only shouted for three minutes at non-strikers leaving a mill.

75 *Daily Telegraph*, 1 September 1932; Thomas Ashurst to Sir Herbert Samuel, 8 September 1932; reply by R R Scott, 12 September 1932: TNA, HO 144/21224.
76 Morgan, above, pp 219–24.
77 See, for example, TNA, HO 144/20729.
78 W H Thompson, 'Trade Unions and the Law Today', in G D H Cole, *British Trade Unionism To-day: A Survey* (1939), p 126.
79 Morgan, above, pp 225, 227–8.
80 'Trade Disputes and Trade Unions Bill, Notes for Second Reading' (approved for circulation, 6 December 1945), Appendix H, 'Intimidation', TNA, LAB 10/574.
81 McIvor, above, p 277.
82 Clegg, vol 3, above, pp 91–2.
83 'Trade Disputes and Trade Unions Bill, Notes for Second Reading' (approved for circulation, 6 December 1945), Appendix D, 'Prosecutions under Article 4', Order 1305, TNA, LAB 10/574.
84 C L Mowat, *Britain between the Wars 1918–1940* (1955), p 337.
85 Trade Disputes and Trade Unions Act 1946 s 1.
86 Cabinet Conclusions, 17 November 1947, and other documents in TNA, HO 45/25592.
87 N Fishman, '"A Vital Element in British Industrial Relations": A Reassessment of Order 1305, 1940–51' (1999) *8 Historical Studies in Industrial Relations* 43, at pp 57–71.
88 D Lyddon, 'The Car Industry, 1945–79: Shop Stewards and Workplace Unionism', in C Wrigley (ed), *A History of British Industrial Relations, 1939–1979* (1996), pp 189–95, 202.
89 Cmd 8607, 1952.
90 *D C Thomson & Co Ltd v Deakin* [1952] Ch 646.
91 Lord Wedderburn, *The Worker and the Law* (3rd ed, 1986), p 590.
92 Cmd 8607, above, para 149.
93 Lord Wedderburn, *Labour Law and Freedom* (1995), p 18.
94 Lyddon, above, pp 190–2.
95 Note by an official, 1 October 1956, TNA, LAB 10/1462.
96 'Note on Pre-Strike Ballots', 31 August 1956, TNA, LAB 10/1461.
97 Inns of Court Conservative and Unionist Society, *A Giant's Strength* (1958), pp 71–2.
98 *Rookes v Barnard* [1964] AC 1129.
99 Royal Commission on Trade Unions and Employers' Associations (RCTUEA), Selected Written Evidence (1968), p 176. 'Critics of trade unions always swear fidelity to the honourable unions of previous eras': Wedderburn, *The Worker and the Law*, above, p 36.
100 RCTUEA (Donovan), Report, Cmnd 3623, 1968, para 893.
101 Conservative Political Centre, *Fair Deal at Work: The Conservative Approach to Modern Industrial Relations* (1968).

Chapter Eight

The 1906 Act : the Second Fifty Years From *Thomson v Deakin* in 1952 to *P v NASUWT* in 2003

Bob Simpson

Introduction

The decision of the Court of Appeal in *D C Thomson & Co Ltd v Deakin* in 1952 marked the resumption of the legal framework for the right to strike created by the Trade Disputes Act 1906 after the repeal of wartime regulations in 1951. Like the *Crofter* decision of the House of Lords a decade earlier it was – and still is – a landmark decision in the judicial development of the common law 'economic torts', those civil liabilities against which the 1906 Act provided legal protection where action was taken 'in contemplation or furtherance of a trade dispute', the 'golden formula' which provides the key to the right to strike in British law.[1] These decisions point up an important feature of British experience of the law on industrial conflict. This is its dependence on the inter-relationship of two or more variables. In 1952 these were first the economic torts and second the golden formula defences in the 1906 Act.

The decisions of the House of Lords in the *Taff Vale* case and *Quinn v Leathem* in 1901 had shown that the legislation of the 1870s, in particular the Conspiracy and Protection of Property Act 1875, was insufficient to create an acceptable balance between capital and labour. While the 1870s reforms had restricted the scope for criminal liability to be imposed on those who threatened, organised or took part in industrial action, the courts had responded by extending the reach of the civil law of tort to provide employers with new causes of action through which to restrain the use or threat of industrial action by workers and trade unions. After 1906, the space for lawful exercise of the right to strike therefore depended on two issues. The first was whether the acts of union officials or others in calling on workers to strike or take other industrial action amounted to one of the 'economic torts' actionable by either employers of the workers concerned or some other party, typically a business customer or supplier of the employer, whose economic interests were or might be adversely affected by the industrial action. If that was established, the applicability of the 1906 Act became the second issue. While section 4 of the Act gave trade unions a complete defence against civil liability in the law of tort, actions against union officials – the general secretary for example – or other individuals who had committed one of the 'economic torts' were normally determined by a decision on whether or not the 1906 Act applied: was there a trade dispute as defined in section 5(3) of the Act in existence or 'in contemplation,' and if so, did one of the defences in section 1 or 3 of the Act apply so as to protect the 'organisers' of the industrial action from liability.

In *D C Thomson & Co v Deakin*, as in the *Crofter* case, the employers' case against union - organised industrial action failed on the first issue; no tort had been committed by the union officials. One of the most striking features of experience in the second half of the 20th century was a shift by the courts from a strict and narrow construction of the economic torts to an often unstated and more frequently unreasoned assumption that action by trade unions, their officials and other workers in threatening, calling for or organising industrial action was tortious. Legal disputes have increasingly focused on whether the 'golden formula' defences of the 1906 – and later 1974 or 1992 – Act were applicable, or, since 1984, on whether action called for by trade unions had the requisite support of a valid ballot. Thus, for example, in the latest case to reach the House of Lords where the right of a union to call on its members to take industrial action was in issue, *P v NASUWT*, there is no discussion of whether or not the action by the teachers' union NASUWT in calling on its members to refuse to teach an allegedly disruptive pupil (P) was actionable in tort; the union's case relied solely on the current version of the Trade Disputes Act defences and the validity of the ballot that it had held (see further below).

Against this background, experience of the Trade Disputes Act 1906, and its successors the Trade Union and Labour Relations Acts 1974 and 1976 and the Trade Union and Labour Relations (Consolidation) Act 1992 can be seen to have passed through a number of phases.

From *D C Thomson & Co Ltd v Deakin* to *Rookes v Barnard*

In *D C Thomson & Co Ltd v Deakin* the issue in dispute was a fundamental one: the right of a worker to belong to a trade union. D C Thomson were, in North American terminology, 'yellow dog' employers who required their workers to sign 'the document' – a written undertaking not to join a trade union while they were in Thomsons' employment. A dispute arose following the dismissal of a worker because he was a union member. The union action at issue in the case was taken by officers of the printing unions NATSOPA and NUPBPW, as well as the TGWU in relation to Bowaters, who supplied Thomson with paper. Bowaters were informed that workers employed by them might refuse to load supplies destined for Thomson and that lorry drivers might refuse to make any deliveries to Thomson. In laying down the requirements of the tort which Thomson alleged that the defendant union officials had committed, the Court of Appeal is generally regarded as having displayed a notable judicial reluctance to allow employers to easily invoke the economic torts as a tactic in industrial disputes. Each of the requirements of the alleged torts had to be clearly satisfied before liability would be established – and only then would union officials need to rely on the 1906 Act's defences. Thomson failed to establish that there was a *prima facie* case that the union officials had committed the tort alleged – procuring breaches of the contracts between Bowaters and Thomson – and so the action failed on that ground.

The adequacy of the 1906 Act as a guarantee for an acceptable 'right', or more accurately in legal terms 'freedom' to strike was not seriously called into question for the next twelve years. In a study of *Labour Legislation and Public Policy* from 1945 to 1990, two leading academic lawyers described the 1950s as 'the easy decade'.[2] That is certainly an appropriate characterisation of trade unions' experience of the law in industrial disputes as evidenced by reported cases. In 1955, a peculiarity of the drafting of the 1875 and 1906 Acts which excluded seamen from the scope of the protection against liability – civil or criminal – for conspiracy provided the shipping employer Cunard with grounds for a successful action against seaman, restraining them from conspiring to break or persuade others to break their contracts by going out on strike.[3] Two years later in *Huntley v Thornton*, an action brought by a union member who had refused to join in a strike complaining of subsequent action taken against him by some local officials, the judge held that there was no trade dispute and that even if there was the actions of some of the defendant officials were not in furtherance of a trade dispute so that they were not protected by the 1906 Act against liability to Huntley for conspiracy.[4] By contrast the next year in *Scala Ballroom (Wolverhampton) v Ratcliffe*[5] the Court of Appeal took a broad view of the interests which workers were entitled to pursue within the scope of the golden formula 'in contemplation or furtherance of a trade dispute' in holding that the Musicians' Union's boycott of a dancehall which operated a colour bar on the dance floor – only whites were allowed in to dance (not at the time of itself unlawful) – was not actionable as a civil 'conspiracy to injure', since the defendant union officials were pursuing what the law regarded as a legitimate interest. At the end of the 1950s, the legislative settlement half a century earlier seemed to be intact with the courts accepting that it required the law to provide a broad space within which exercise of the right to strike and the right to threaten strikes was legitimate.

From *Rookes v Barnard* to the Industrial Relations Act

The assumption that the courts had accepted that the policy of the 1906 Act was that the common law of tort should not be allowed to intervene in industrial disputes where action fell within the protection of the Act's 'golden formula' was shattered by the House of Lords' decision in *Rookes v Barnard* in 1964. Rookes, a draughtsman employed by BOAC, was dismissed – lawfully – after the defendant union officials had informed BOAC that draughtsmen employed by BOAC at Heathrow would come out on strike three days later unless Rookes, who had left the union because of disagreement over policies, was dismissed.[6] The decision of the House of Lords in *Rookes* is important for several reasons. For present purposes it is sufficient to say that if the Law Lords did not invent tort liability for intimidation, they resurrected it from some very old case law in a form that placed virtually all if not all strike threats at risk of legal restraint initiated by those against whom the strike was directed. Against this liability, the existence of which was not appreciated in 1906, the Trade Disputes Act provided no defence.

The significance of this decision in the history of the Trade Disputes Act cannot be overemphasised, as the commentaries of the two most distinguished labour lawyers of the time show.[7] 1964 also saw a change of government after the October General Election and the new Labour government sought to repair the damage through the Trade Disputes Act 1965 which was intended to do no more than restore the law to what it had generally been thought to be before the decision in *Rookes v Barnard.* It added a new section to the protections against civil liability for the economic torts in sections 1 and 3 of the 1906 Act, which provided that an act in contemplation or furtherance of a trade dispute would not be actionable in tort on the ground only that it consisted of a threat that a contract of employment would be broken or that the defendant would induce another person to break a contract of employment. The second limb covered union officials who organise strikes who are generally understood to be, in legal terms, inducing workers to break their contracts of employment; but for the second limb of section 1 of the 1965 Act they might have been denied the protection of section 3 of the 1906 Act on the ground that at some stage in a dispute they were *threatening* to induce workers to break contracts of employment (which the 1906 Act did not expressly protect), rather than *inducing* workers to break their contracts of employment (which section 3 of the 1906 Act did protect).

The Trade Disputes Act 1965 was presented as something of an interim measure, with the whole of the law, including the 1906 Act, under review by the Donovan Commission which deliberated from 1965 to 1968. The Donovan Report's comments on and recommendations for changes in this aspect of the law were, however, directed at what had become a moving target as judicial activism in the late 1960s called into question the integrity of the 1906 settlement. A full review of the case law of the 1965-69 period is beyond the remit of this chapter. It is sufficient to refer to three or four decisions to demonstrate the judicial willingness – in Scotland as well as England – to grant employers labour injunctions to restrain unions and workers from proceeding with industrial action which at first sight fell within the scope of the protection of the 1906 Act.

In *J T Stratford & Co Ltd v Lindley* [8] the defendants were officials of the Watermen's Union which had had previous requests for recognition by Bowker & King, a company like the plaintiff, Stratford & Co, controlled by Jack Stratford, refused. They instructed their members to place an embargo on barges hired out by the plaintiff and barges destined for the plaintiff's yard for repair. It was disputed whether this action amounted to a tort actionable by Stratford & Co, but if it was the defendants claimed the protection of the 1906 Act for their actions. This was denied by the House of Lords on two grounds; there was no trade dispute connected with 'terms of employment' within the definition – although recognition of a trade union can clearly be a term of workers' employment; and in any event there had been no recent request for recognition before the industrial action was initiated. In similar fashion, in 1966 in *Square Grip Reinforcement Co. Ltd v Macdonald* [9] the Outer House of the Court of Session in Scotland found that there was no trade dispute where, in pursuit of its claim for recognition, the TGWU called for action by workers employed by customers and suppliers of Square Grip. Moreover, the court held that section 3 of the 1906 Act could not apply in any event to action that amounted to an inducement of breach of a commercial contract between an employer and its customers or suppliers. Nor did it apply, the English Court of Appeal held in the same year to action amounting to inducing breach – or threatening to induce breach – of a labour only sub-contract between the main contractors on a building site, Higgs and Hill and the plaintiff company in *Emerald Construction v Lowthian*[10] There the defendant union officials' action was taken to put pressure on the main contractors to employ all labour working on site directly. The Court of Appeal decision in *Torquay Hotel Co Ltd v Cousins* in 1969 underlined the need to extend the protection for action which induced workers to break their contracts of employment to action which induced breach of *any* contract. In that case, the TGWU's action in informing oil companies – Esso and later Alternative Fuels – that drivers might be unwilling to deliver oil to the plaintiff's Imperial Hotel in Torquay was held to fall outside the protection of section 3 of the 1906 Act. No request for recognition by that hotel in Torquay had yet been made, although the union was actively seeking recognition at other hotels in the resort and this action was part of that campaign. The action was therefore, the Court of Appeal held, not taken 'in contemplation or furtherance of a trade dispute'.[11]

In summary the late 1960s saw a period of judicial activism which challenged the underlying basis of the 1906 Act even though Parliament had demonstrated its commitment to the integrity of that settlement by its response to the decision in *Rookes v Barnard* in the 1965 Act. The Donovan Report in 1968 had recommended further changes, one of which in particular - confining the key protection against liability for inducing breach of contracts of employment to action taken by *registered* trade unions – was highly controversial. In 1969 the Labour government's White Paper *In Place of Strife* moved the locus of debate over the law and industrial conflict into other areas with its controversial proposals for new government powers to require trade unions to hold ballots before strikes in certain circumstances and, independently of that proposal, to impose a 'conciliation pause' in special circumstances before otherwise lawful industrial action could be taken. The controversy which this aroused became a matter of historical interest only when the Labour government was defeated in the 1970 General Election by a Conservative party committed to a far more radical reform of collective labour law which involved the repeal of the Trade Disputes Acts.

The Industrial Relations Act 1971: A Brief 'Interregnum'

The Industrial Relations Act 1971 repealed the Trade Disputes Acts 1906 and 1965. In place of their statutory defences against tort liability for action taken 'in contemplation or furtherance of a trade dispute,' the 1971 Act introduced the North American influenced concept of 'unfair industrial practices', some of which were very similar to the judge made economic torts. The Act created a sort of specialist labour court, the National Industrial Relations Court (NIRC)), whose role included adjudicating on disputes in which it was alleged that unfair industrial practices had been committed. Among the unfair industrial practices created by the 1971 Act were inducing or threatening to induce a breach of contract and inducing breach of commercial contracts between employers who were party to industrial disputes and 'extraneous' parties.[12] However these activities were only 'unfair industrial practices' where the action taken was ' in contemplation or furtherance of an industrial dispute'. Unlike the 1906 Act which used the 'golden formula' to *protect* union officials and others against civil liability for organising industrial action, the 'new' formula in the 1971 Act only provided a boundary between the jurisdiction of the NIRC and the ordinary civil courts. Industrial action taken in contemplation or furtherance of an industrial dispute would almost invariably be at risk of infringing the section 96 unfair industrial practice (unless taken by a registered union). If it fell outside the 'new' formula, then it would be open to action in the ordinary civil courts where there was no longer any protection under the Trade Disputes Acts.

This state of affairs lasted for just under two and a half years, a time of extensive industrial conflict, much of which gave rise to litigation. At the time of its repeal in July 1974 the Industrial Relations Act 1971 had few supporters. As far as the restraints which it had imposed on the right to strike were concerned, they were seen to have generated undesirable and generally unproductive litigation at the expense of addressing the issues involved. The wisdom of the 1906 Act's approach in seeking to keep industrial disputes out of the courts by providing a broad space within which industrial action could be taken free from the threat of legal restraint, was reinforced by this experience.

The Trade Union and Labour Relations Acts 1974 and 1976: from 1974 to 1979

The Trade Union and Labour Relations Act 1974 (TULRA) is almost as important a milestone in the history of the right to strike and the law as the original Trade Disputes Act in 1906. Unlike the 1906 Act, TULRA had a remit which covered aspects of virtually the entire field of labour law.[13] Arguably its most important achievement, however, was the restoration of the Trade Disputes Act framework for the legality of industrial action in a form which was in Lord Scarman's words in 1979 'stronger and clearer' than the original legislation.[14] Section 14 of TULRA restored the complete immunity of trade unions from liability in tort.[15] Section 13 restored the golden formula immunities for individual defendants, including trade union officials, against liability in the economic torts in a form which, after the 1976 Amendment Act[16] took account of judge-made interpretation or extensions of these liabilities, in particular in the late 1960s, and signalled Parliament's intention that judicial outflanking of the trade dispute defences by modifying the tort liabilities so as to take them outside the protection of the golden formula defences should be discouraged.[17]

Other chapters in this book show that the experience of the 1906 Act at the hands of the judiciary was far from an even and consistent acceptance of the policies behind it. The judicial response to the more extensive provisions of the 1974 Act in the second half of the 1970s was similarly uneven, but perhaps most notable for a number of judicial pronouncements which scarcely disguised their hostility to the legislation. While some attempts to evade the 1974 Act's protections for the right to strike failed,[18] others succeeded in circumstances where it is strongly arguable that the legislative intention was that they should fail.[19] The integrity of the legislation was only restored after the change of government in 1979 made it likely that future legislation would seek to limit the statutory immunities in the 1974 Act against the judge-made and judicially developed torts. The trilogy of House of Lords decisions in 1979 and 1980 – *NWL Ltd v Woods*, *Express Newspapers Ltd v Macshane* and *Duport Steel Ltd v Sirs* [20] – nevertheless stands as a landmark, acknowledging the duty of the courts to decide issues on the construction of the legislation in accordance with the legislative purpose.

In those decisions, while there is some judicial sympathy for the policy behind the legislation of 1974-76 – and therefore for that which underpinned the 1906 Act – the freedom of the courts to develop the common law in a principled way is not called into question. One such development, which began in the 1970s and which ostensibly respects the legislative policy behind the 1906 and 1974-76 legislation, but which has created a still extant threat to its integrity, is the extension of the courts' power to grant remedies for losses caused by the application of 'economic duress' to the field of industrial disputes. While this threat did not become apparent until the 1980s, it is appropriate to note the development at this point since it is independent of the changes to the law made by the legislation of 1980-1993. Decisions of the House of Lords in 1982 and 1992 required the International Transport Workers Federation (ITF) to repay to shipowners sums which the shipowners had agreed to pay in settlement of particular disputes arising out of their use of 'flags of convenience', that is shipping registers in countries other than those of the beneficial owners. The ITF opposes the existence of such registers, but acknowledges that they are a fact of life. Where ships fly flags of convenience, ITF policy is therefore to persuade the owners - if necessary by threats of industrial action by members of affiliated unions which, for example prevents ships from leaving port – to agree to a standard form collective agreement on the terms of employment of the crew. This action, it has been held, may amount to actionable 'economic duress' to extort payments from the shipowners.[21] While the trade disputes provisions of the 1906 and 1974 Acts have never been expressly extended to provide protection for either trade unions or individuals against liability for this equitable wrong, the House of Lords accepted that remedies for economic duress should not be granted by the English courts in respect of action which was taken within the golden formula, 'in contemplation or furtherance of a trade dispute'. However, although the House of Lords was not unanimous in either case, this did not assist the ITF in the *Universe Tankships* decision in 1983 or the *Dimskal* case in 1992. This judge-made qualification to a judge-made liability does, however, illustrate the continuing influence of the 1906 Act's golden formula for protecting – or at least attempting to protect – the right to strike in English law.

It is, nevertheless, the legislative amendments to the 1974 Act's trade disputes provisions made over the period since 1979 which have given rise to justified calls for new legislation to restore at least some of the freedom to strike and take other industrial action which Parliament in 1906, 1965 and again in 1974-76 intended that trade unions, their members and workers generally should have.

From the Employment Act 1980 to the Trade Union Reform and Employment Rights Act 1993: Restricting the Golden Formula Immunities

While the Conservative government of the early 1970s attempted to rewrite the greater part of the entire body of collective labour law through the Industrial Relations Act 1971, the Conservative governments that were in power from 1979 to 1997 adopted a 'step by step' approach to restructuring the law. Most of the changes were made in six pieces of legislation: the Employment Acts 1980 and 1982, the Trade Union Act 1984, the Employment Acts 1988 and 1990, and the Trade Union Reform and Employment Rights Act 1993.[22] The intended effect was, amongst other things, to undermine the integrity of the 1906 settlement in its 'stronger and clearer' 1974-76 form. If the objective of the 1906 Act and its 1974-76 re-enactment can be said to have been to create a space within which it was recognised as legitimate and lawful for labour to use its collective strength in order to achieve some sort of balance of power with employers, the objective of the 1980-1993 legislation was to both reduce the size of that space and make access to it restricted and difficult. The relevant content of this legislation can be analysed in terms of four interrelated developments.

First, the legislation created a series of complex exceptions to the circumstances when the golden formula defences in the 1974 Act applied. The removal of these defences or 'immunities' from secondary action in two stages in 1980 and 1990 is the best known and most important of these. International labour standards which the United Kingdom claims to respect, recognise that in some circumstances it is legitimate for industrial action to be taken – and therefore for trade unions and others to call on workers to take industrial action – in support of other workers who are involved in disputes.[23] While it is true that these standards accept that limits can be imposed on the circumstances when secondary action is lawful, the complete exclusion from the trade dispute defences to civil liability in the economic torts in Britain since 1990 is a clear infringement of these standards.[24] Consistent with the logic of this position, the limited protection against liabilities which might otherwise be committed by pickets which is provided now by section 220 of the 1992 Act – the successor to section 2 of the 1906 Act and section 15 of the 1974 Act as amended in 1980 - does extend to immunity against liability for inducing workers to break their contracts of employment by not crossing picket lines to make deliveries or collect supplies, which could be described as secondary action where there is no dispute with the employers of these workers. But the restrictions imposed in 1980 on what since 1906 has always been a narrowly construed 'right to picket peacefully' in contemplation or furtherance of a trade dispute, means that this cannot really be described as an exception to the removal of the legal protection for the right to take secondary action.

The Employment Act 1982 also removed the golden formula defences from industrial action taken, or the threat of industrial action made, to put pressure on employers to enter into commercial dealings only with other businesses which recognised trade unions or which agreed that work done on any commercial contract with the employer would be done by union labour. These changes are perhaps the clearest demonstration of an objective underlying all the legislation of 1980 – 1993, which was to weaken and eventually completely undermine all the manifestations of collective regulation of labour relations.[25] They also highlight a policy that is evident from other changes made by this legislation; this is that the right of workers and their unions to take and organise industrial action should be confined to disputes over issues arising solely at the workplace of the workers concerned.

The second major change made by the legislation of 1980-1993 was the narrowing of the definition of a trade dispute in section 29 of the 1974 Act by amendments made by section 18 of the 1982 Act. The original definition of a trade dispute in section 5(3) of the 1906 Act had the merit of brevity and simplicity: 'any dispute between employers and workmen or workmen and workmen connected with the employment or non-employment or the terms of employment or the conditions of labour of any person'.[26] This was expanded in the 1974 Act in a number of respects, the main one of which was the setting out of a list of seven matters with one or more of which the dispute had to be connected, in place of the 1906 reference to 'employment or non-employment, terms of employment or conditions of labour'. The decision of the House of Lords in *NWL v Woods* in 1979 had underlined the importance and breadth of the words 'connected with' in this definition; the dispute was connected with the terms of employment of the crew of a ship flying a flag of convenience even though it was also part of the ITF's wider campaign to end the practice of ships flying flags of convenience. 'Any' connection with any of the listed subject matter was sufficient to qualify the dispute as a trade dispute. In 1982 this part of the definition was changed to the wording first used in the 1971 Act's definition of an industrial dispute, which since 1982 has required a dispute to 'relate wholly or mainly to' one or more of the listed items in order to qualify as a trade dispute.[27]

The significance of this change was soon made apparent in the *Mercury* case in 1984 where the Court of Appeal held that planned industrial action by post office engineers in a dispute over the introduction of Mercury, a private sector competitor to the then State owned British Telecommunications related *mainly* to the union's opposition to the 'liberalisation' of the telecommunications industry and planned privatisation of BT; there was therefore no trade dispute and the union could not rely on the golden formula defences against liability to Mercury, even though the planned action was also taken in pursuit of job guarantees for union members employed by BT.[28] It has to be acknowledged that since that case in 1984, trade unions have proved adept at preparing the ground for industrial action or the threat of industrial action in similar situations by ensuring that demands on employers related to issues falling within those listed in the trade dispute definition are sufficiently prominent to make clear that these are the issues to which the dispute *mainly* relates rather than union opposition to wider developments which may have created the situation in which the dispute arose.[29]

The other main amendments to the definition of a trade dispute concern the parties to a dispute. Not only did the 1982 Act exclude disputes between groups of workers from the definition. It narrowed the scope of the definition to disputes between workers and *their* employer, with workers defined to include former workers only where the termination of their employment was 'in connection with' or 'one of the circumstances giving rise to' the dispute. Apart from the undesirable complexity and lack of clarity thereby created, since it can be a matter of interpretation whether a dispute with workers who have been dismissed falls within the definition, this change reduces the ability of workers and their unions to take or threaten industrial action at a time when it might be effective to cause or influence an employer to change its intentions. In *University College London Hospital (UCLH) v UNISON* in 1999, the Court of Appeal upheld a decision that there was no trade dispute in existence or contemplation when UNISON threatened industrial action unless UCLH was prepared to guarantee that workers transferred to or newly employed in a hospital that was being built with private sector finance and would be managed by a private sector employer, would have terms and conditions at least as good as those established by collective bargaining for workers employed in the existing University College hospital. The reasoning behind this decision is open to serious question as a correct interpretation of the current trade dispute definition and golden formula.[30] Its restrictive interpretation of a restrictive law is indicative of how narrow the space for a lawful threat of industrial action has become and a reminder of how central the definition of a trade dispute is to the scope of the right to strike in Britain.

The third major change made to the 'trade disputes' provisions by the 1982 Act was the repeal of the complete immunity of trade unions from liability in tort which was originally contained in section 4 of the 1906 Act and re-enacted in section 14 of the 1974 Act. In one sense it might be thought that this was not a change of central importance; before 1982 where actions were brought against trade union officials, typically national officers such as, in major disputes, the general secretary, unions would normally stand behind their officers and meet the costs of proceedings in which the union was unsuccessful. The change was, however, of more than symbolic importance. Where a union rather than one or more of its officials was subjected to a labour injunction requiring the withdrawal of a call for industrial action, it became much more difficult if not impossible for the union to deny charges of non-compliance where its members continued their industrial action on the basis that it was not responsible for action taken by union members. The Employment Act 1982 not only repealed trade unions' tort immunity; it also set out a statutory code which specifies those persons for whose acts a trade union will be vicariously liable in circumstances where the golden formula immunities do not apply.[31] This extends the legal responsibility of trade unions to the acts of any member of a group of persons constituted in accordance with the union's rules, the purpose of which includes organising or co-ordinating industrial action, regardless of any provision in the union's rules about the authority such a group might or might not have to take action on the union's behalf. As in the period from *Taff Vale* in 1901 to the time the Trade Disputes Act 1906 came into force and again while the Industrial Relations Act 1971 was in force from 1972 -74, the extent of a union's 'vicarious liability' again became a central feature of the law of industrial conflict after 1982.[32]

Over the last 20 years, however, the main focus of English law on the right to strike has shifted away from the existence (or imminent existence) of a 'trade dispute' and the need for action to be taken 'in contemplation or furtherance' of that dispute, to the need for action by a trade union to have the support of a ballot. Originally enacted in 1984 – and then only as a pre-condition for the trade dispute protection against liability for inducing breach of contract – this part of the legislative framework for the law of industrial conflict has been regularly amended by subsequent legislation by both Conservative governments in 1988, 1990 and 1993 and Labour governments in 1999 and 2004. It has become progressively more convoluted and complex as well as more onerous for trade unions to comply with, not least because of the need to comply with complex requirements for 'notices' to employers of workers who are balloted and then called on to take action. It is the law on industrial action ballots which points up most clearly the change that has occurred from the time of the original Trade Disputes Act in 1906. That Act, the amending Act in 1965 and their re-enactment in a 'stronger and clearer' form in 1974-76 sought to create a space for legitimate exercise of the right to strike with which the law would not interfere. After the legislation of 1980-1993, the law now seeks to regulate the exercise of the right to strike, and does so in an increasingly restrictive way as recent experience shows.

Experience since Consolidation of the Law in 1992

The 1974-76 successors to the provisions of the Trade Disputes Act 1906, as amended by the '1980s' legislation, was consolidated – that is re-enacted without amendment – in the Trade Union and Labour Relations (Consolidation) Act 1992, which is where the modern law is found. It was almost immediately subject to further amendment in 1993, which perhaps most notably required all industrial action ballots to be fully postal and at the same time ended the 1980 scheme of state financial support for the costs incurred by trade unions in holding certain ballots, including ballots on industrial action. Unlike its predecessor in 1974, the Labour government elected in 1997 has not introduced any liberal reforms in the law of industrial conflict.[33] The changes made to the law on industrial action ballots in the Employment Relations Acts of 1999 and 2004 have rearranged the law somewhat; they have not made it more liberal, as the courts have recognised.[34]

The most recent experience in the courts of the modern equivalent of the Trade Disputes Act has been mixed. In 2000 and again in 2001 the Court of Appeal rejected arguments that threatened strikes were not in furtherance of a trade dispute because there were also wider political issues concerning the use of private sector businesses to provide public services involved.[35] These decisions confirmed the ability of unions to differentiate the political from the industrial side of their actions in order to meet the wording of the current trade dispute definition. The decision of the Court of Appeal in the *UCLH v UNISON* case, however, gives far more cause for concern over the adequacy of the current legal protection for the right to strike. As noted above, in that case threatened industrial action over the union's demand for guarantees on the terms of employment of workers who would be employed in a new hospital in the future were held to fall outside the protection of the golden formula on the ground that the dispute related to terms and conditions of employment with an unidentified future employer. In the light of increasing private sector involvement in the delivery of public services, this decision imposes severe limitations on the abilities of unions to look ahead and take timely action to protect their members' interests.

It might be said that as far as judicial interpretation of the 1906 Act's 'golden formula' is concerned, a century of experience ended on a positive note with the House of Lords' decision in *P v NASUWT* in 2003. Upholding the decisions of the lower courts, the Law Lords rejected an argument that the action of the schoolteachers' union in refusing to teach an allegedly disruptive pupil – for whom the school had, therefore, to arrange individual tuition by teachers specially brought in for this purpose – was not taken in contemplation or furtherance of a trade dispute. Giving the leading speech, Lord Hoffman provided useful reinforcement for the golden formula and the 1906 Act's structuring of the law in his dictum: 'a dispute about what workers are obliged to do or how the employer is obliged to remunerate them, at any level of generality or particularity, is about terms and conditions of employment' – and therefore a trade dispute within the current definition in section 244(1) of the 1992 Act.[36] At the same time, however, he endorsed one of the most discreditable decisions of the Court of Appeal in the late 1970s, *BBC v Hearn* where technicians threatened to refuse to transmit the Cup Final to South Africa because of the then South African government's apartheid policy. This, the Court of Appeal held, reversing the decision of Pain J, was not a trade dispute but, in Lord Denning's words 'coercive interference and nothing more'.[37] Coercive interference could be a perjorative description of most industrial action. The integrity of the Trade Disputes Act provisions in their modern form as the bedrock of the right to strike depends, as it always has done, on judicial acceptance of the constraints it seeks to impose on their freedom to develop and apply the common law in ways which restrict the right to strike and to threaten strikes. Lord Hoffman's recent endorsement of a decision which was clearly intended to get round these constraints does not inspire confidence in today's judges' respect for this legislative intention.

Evaluation

The history of the Trade Disputes Act 1906 and its successors over the period from the early 1950s to the early years of the 21st century is a catalogue of mixed experience. On the one hand, there are cases in which the courts' decisions acknowledge that the function of the legislation is to provide legal recognition of the right to strike by enabling workers and their representatives to make both a credible threat of industrial action and to take industrial action without being at risk of legal restraints or penalties. Even the latest decision of the House of Lords, *P v NASUWT* in 2003, can be seen to reflect this, although the clearest illustration of this feature of the case law remains the speech of Lord Scarman in *NWL v Woods* in 1979. Against this, however, must be set a significant number of reported cases in which judges at all levels have readily found that the golden formula defences did not apply in the cases before them. Of course in most cases, since the litigation on these issues is almost invariably concerned with 'labour injunction' applications for orders requiring the defendant unions and/or individuals to halt – or not to proceed with – calls for industrial action pending full trial of claims, which very rarely occurs, the judges have not been giving a final view on the application of the law to particular disputes. But the reality is that this distinction between the provisional view taken by the courts on proceedings for interim (formerly interlocutory) injunctions and the final view taken after full trial of the action is in practice but a technicality; whether labour injunctions are granted or refused, a full trial almost never occurs. The totality of the case law of the period since the House of Lords decision in *Rookes v Barnard* in 1964 is universally seen as having restricted the scope for lawful exercise of the right to take and threaten industrial action independently of – though since 1980 at least in line with – the narrowing of circumstances in which the modern version of the Trade Disputes Act 1906 can apply.

In summary it is possible to see vindication of the 1906 Act and its 'golden formula' as the bedrock of the right to strike in British law in the period since 1952 as qualified by three factors. The first is their vulnerability to idiosyncratic judicial construction. Judges who are unsympathetic to the Act, whether because of a dislike of industrial action and/or a concern to place a narrow construction on legislation which restricts the application of judge-made common law, have felt unconstrained in construing the legislation narrowly and expanding the common law in ways which evade the golden formula protections. While some of the judgments of Lord Denning MR in the 1960s and 1970s are perhaps the clearest illustrations of this feature, they are not alone. The decision of the Court of Appeal presided over by Lord Woolf in the *UCLH* case in 1999 has implications for the scope of the right to strike in English law which are just as serious as decisions of that Court when presided over by Lord Denning in the earlier period.

The second factor is related to, but distinct from, the first. It is the weakness inherent in the common law system which enables judicial creativity to outflank the intentions of Parliament. Just as the decisions of the House of Lords in *Taff Vale* and *Quinn v Leathem* in 1901 pointed up the weaknesses in the 1870s legislation, so too did the equally important landmark decision of the Law Lords in *Rookes v Barnard* in 1964 highlight the need for Parliament to be ready to respond – as it did in 1965 – to extend the golden formula protections to meet judicial extensions of the law. *Rookes v Barnard* has been followed by other less well-known developments in the law. The uncertain and largely uncharted waters of liability for 'economic duress' after the *Universe Tankships* decision over 20 years ago remain a constant threat to the golden formula's integrity even though the House of Lords accepted that this piece of judge-made law had to be subject to judge-made limitation in respect of action taken in contemplation or furtherance of a trade dispute. A similar threat to the integrity of domestic labour law could emerge from litigation in which employers argue that rights given to them under European Community law – competition law is the most obvious area – preclude reliance on the domestic labour law of member states.[38]

The third qualification to a positive assessment of the last half-century of the Trade Disputes Act is of course the law on industrial action ballots which has, since 1984 imposed a separate additional hurdle to the lawful exercise of the right to strike by trade unions and their officials. Suffice it to say that the intricate, often arcane and sometimes scarcely comprehensible detail of the law currently in sections 226A - 234A of the 1992 Act on ballots and notices to employers can and frequently does render the space for legitimate industrial conflict largely illusory. In short, while the second half century of experience of the 1906 Act and its successors has both positive and negative features, overall it points up the need for a new legislative settlement to give effect to the underlying objectives of the Trade Disputes Act 1906.

Notes

1 Bill Wedderburn's famous characterisation of this phrase in *The Worker and the Law* (1965), p 222: 'the bedrock of British workers' rights to organise and take effective industrial action'; see now 3rd ed,1986 at pp 520-1.

2 P Davies and M Freedland *Labour Legislation and Public Policy* (1993), chapter 3.

3 *Cunard S.S.Co Ltd v Stacey* [1955] 2 Lloyd's Rep 247.

4 *Huntley v Thornton* [1957] 1 WLR 321.

5 [1958] 1 WLR 1057.

6 The three defendants were officials of the Association of Engineering and Shipbuilding Draughtsmen (AESD) – now after subsequent amalgamations part of Amicus. Barnard was branch chairman, Fistal a shop steward at Heathrow and Silverthorne the divisional organiser, that is a full time officer employed by the union.

7 Otto Kahn-Freund, 'Rookes v Barnard – and After' (1964) 14 *Federation News* 30 and Bill Wedderburn, 'Intimidation and the Right to Strike' (1964) 27 *Modern Law Review* 257.

8 [1965] AC 269.

9 1966 SLT 232.

10 [1966] 1 WLR 691.

11 [1969] 2 Ch 106.

12 Industrial Relations Act 1971, ss 96 & 98.

13 That is not to say that it covered every aspect of labour law, but its re-enactment of key aspects of the trade union legislation of the 1870s in a modern form is often overlooked.

14 In *NWL Ltd v Woods* [1979] ICR 867, at p 886, where he referred also to the 1977 report of the Court of Inquiry into the Grunwick dispute, which he had chaired, which identified the policy of the 1974 Act as 'to exclude 'trade disputes'...from judicial review by the courts'.

15 This exception was qualified, as it had been in section 4 of the 1906 Act, so that unions could be liable in tort on claims for personal injuries or concerning property, where the claim did not arise out of acts done in contemplation or furtherance of a trade dispute: TULRA, s 14 (2).

16 The Labour government did not have a majority in the House of Commons when TULRA was passed in 1974. The process of restoring the 1906 Act's protections in a modern form was only completed by the Trade Union and Labour Relations (Amendment) Act 1976, passed when the government did have a majority in the House of Commons that could override amendments made to the legislation in the House of Lords in 1974.

17 TULRA also re-enacted, in section 15, in a slightly modified form the right to peaceful picketing from section 2 of the 1906 Act, and in section 17 it attempted to restrain the power of the courts to grant 'labour injunctions' to employers before hearing the defendants' case that the trade disputes protections applied.

18 *Camellia Tanker Ltd. v ITF* [1976] ICR 274; *Examite Ltd v Whittaker* [1977] IRLR 312; *Health Computing Ltd v Meek* [1981] ICR 24.

19 *BBC v Hearn* [1977] ICR 685; *Beaverbrook Newspapers Ltd v Keys* [1978] ICR 582; *Associated Newspapers Group Ltd v Wade* [1979] ICR 664; *Star Sea Transport Corporation v Slater* [1979] 1 Lloyds Rep 26.

20 *NWL Ltd v Woods* [1979] ICR 867; *Express Newspapers Ltd v Macshane* [1980] ICR 42; *Duport Steels Ltd v Sirs* [1980] ICR161.

21 *Universe Tankships of Monrovia Inc v ITF* [1982] ICR 262; *Dimskal Shipping Co v ITF* [1992] ICR.37.

22 The policies behind some of these changes were set out in a number of Green Papers: *Trade Union Immunities*, Cmnd 8128,1981; *Democracy in Trade Unions*, Cmnd 8778,1983; *Trade Unions and their Members*, Cm 95,1987; *Removing Barriers to Employment*, Cm 655,1989; *Unofficial Action and the Law*, Cm 821,1989; *Industrial Relations in the 1990s*, Cm 1602, 1991. A further Green Paper published in late 1996 gives some indication of how the logic of the 1980-1993 legislation might have been extended into new areas had the Conservative government remained in power: *Industrial Action and Trade Unions*, Cm 3470,1996.

23 See B Gernignon, et al, 'ILO Principles concerning the Right to Strike' (1998) 137 *International Labour Review* 441; and T Novitz, *International and European Protection of the Right to Strike* (2003), pp 288, 291-2.

24 See K Ewing, *Britain and the ILO* (Institute of Employment Rights, 2nd ed, 1994); P Germanotta, *Protecting Worker Solidarity Action: A Critique of International Labour Law* (Institute of Employment Rights, 2002).

25 See R Lewis and R Simpson, 'Disorganising Industrial Relations: An Analysis of sections 2-8 and 10-14 of the Employment Act 1982' (1982) 11 *Industrial Law Journal* 227.

26 See Jim Mortimer *The 1906 Trade Disputes Act* (Institute of Employment Rights, 2005) who rightly draws attention to the merit of the brevity and simplicity of the drafting of the 1906 Act.

27 The list of matters to one or more of which a dispute must now wholly or mainly relate in order for it to be a trade dispute is as follows:

(a) terms and conditions of employment, or the physical conditions in which any workers are required to work;

(b) engagement or non-engagement, or termination or suspension of employment or the duties of employment, of one or more workers:

(c) allocation of work or the duties of employment between workers or groups of workers;

(d) matters of discipline;

(e) a worker's membership or non-membership of a trade union;

(f) facilities for officials of trade unions; and

(g) machinery for negotiation or consultation, and other procedures, relating to any of the above matters, including the recognition by employers or employers' associations of the right of a trade union to represent workers in such negotiation or consultation or in the carrying out of such procedures.

28 *Mercury Communications Ltd v Scott-Garner* [1984] ICR 74.

29 *Associated British Ports v TGWU* [1989] IRLR 291, Millet J (the point was

not argued when the case went on appeal); *Wandsworth LBC v NASUWT* [1994] ICR 81; *Westminster CC v UNISON* [2001] ICR 1046.

30 *UCLH NHS Trust v UNISON* [1999] ICR 204. For an incisive critique see J. Hendy (2000) 29 *Industrial Law Journal* 53. UNISON unsuccessfully sought to take the case to the European Court of Human Rights on the basis that this decision made English law inconsistent with article 11 of the European Convention on Human Rights. See *UNISON v United Kingdom* [2002] IRLR 497.

31 This code, now contained in sections 20 and 21 of the Trade Union and Labour Relations (Consolidation) Act 1992, does not apply to actions brought against trade unions in tort in respect of activities not connected with trade disputes. In these cases the 'common law' principles laid down by the House of Lords in the case of *Heatons Transport v TGWU* [1972] ICR 308 apply.

32 See Bob Hepple 'Union Responsibility for Shop Stewards' (1972) 1 *Industrial Law Journal* 197.

33 The single possible exception is the enactment of a provision which makes the dismissal of employees who are taking part in industrial action which has been lawfully organised by a union, automatically unfair; see TULRCA 1992, s 238A, inserted by the Employment Relations Act 1999, s.16 & Sched 5 and amended by the Employment Relations Act 2004, ss.26-28.

34 See Robert Walker LJ in *London Underground Ltd v RMT* [2001] ICR 647, 661. While the pre-1999 obligation on unions to, in effect, inform employers of the names of workers to be balloted and called on to take industrial action (see *Blackpool and The Fylde College v NATHFE* [1994] ICR 648) was removed by the 1999 Act, it was replaced by what are arguably more onerous obligations on unions to provide employers with information about workers who are to be balloted and called on to take industrial action.

35 *UCLH NHS Trust v UNISON*, above; *Westminster City Council v UNISON*, above.

36 [2003] ICR 386, 393.

37 [1977] ICR 685, 693.

38 The issue arose in *Viking Line ABP v ITF* [2006] 1 Lloyds Rep 303, where the Court of Appeal referred a number of questions to the European Court of Justice. See chapter 11 below.

Chapter Nine

Judicial Mystification of the Law: Rookes v Barnard and the Return to Judicial Intervention

Roger Welch

Introduction

THE primary focus of this chapter is to analyse judgments and judicial statements concerning trade unions and industrial action from the middle of the nineteenth century to more recent times. This analysis reveals conceptual and philosophical links between past and present judicial perceptions of trade unionism. Taken together these judgments constitute what can be characterised as a process of legal or judicial mystification of industrial relations.

The essential method of this mystification is to apply common law concepts, doctrines and principles developed in entirely different contexts to the world of industrial relations and industrial conflict in order to impose legal liability. The imposition of these legal liabilities is implemented through language that distorts the nature of trade unionism and industrial action by depicting trade union behaviour in the worst possible light. Thus, the organisation of industrial action is recast as a conspiracy to engage in law-breaking, or to use illegal means to interfere with contracts or trade. Legislation designed to render industrial action lawful is declared to constitute privileges to engage in law-breaking. Where new common law liabilities are created to circumvent statutory protection given to unions and their members, industrial action can then be condemned as an excess of privilege.

The chapter will show how this process of legal mystification led to and provided the ideological justification for the *Taff Vale* decision in 1901.[1] Particular emphasis will be given to the decision of the House of Lords in the *Rookes v Barnard* case in 1964 and to cases decided in its immediate aftermath, as these judgments constituted a re-emergence of judicial intervention in industrial relation in the post World War II period. Moreover, these judgments sowed the seeds for the common law as it exists today and for the significant contraction in the scope of the trade union immunities that has taken place since 1980. The mystifications generated by these judgments are at the heart of common misconceptions that various forms of industrial action are illegal, and contribute to an ideological barrier to legal reforms that would both meet the requirements of international law and create rights to take effective industrial action.

Judicial Perceptions of Trade Unionism – Past and Present

At common law trade union organisation was and is regarded as constituting a restraint of trade. The legal basis for this was explained by Sir William Erle in his Memorandum to the Royal Commission on Trade Unions established in 1867. He stated:

> *As to combination, each person has a right to choose whether he will labour or not, and also to choose the terms on which he will consent to labour, if labour be his choice...They cannot create any mutual obligation having the legal effect of binding each other not to work or not to employ unless on terms allowed by the combination...A person can neither alienate for a time his freedom to dispose of his own labour or his own capital according to his own will, nor alienate such freedom generally and make himself a slave; it follows that he cannot transfer it to the governing body of a union.*[2]

Thus, trade unions do not provide collective representation for workers to seek to redress the imbalance of bargaining power that generally inherently operates in the favour of employers. Rather, the replacement of individual 'freedom' of contract with collectively determined terms and conditions of employment makes a worker a slave of his union.

Judges and Trade Unions

Judges perceive trade unions as, in the words of Lindley LJ in *J Lyons & Sons v Wilkins* [3], 'tyrants in their turn...engines of evil', or, as Lord Denning was to put it in *Express Newspapers Ltd v McShane*,[4] possessors of 'coercive power'. This is particularly the case where trade unions organise industrial action to further or defend the interests of their members. Thus in *Quinn v Leathem*, threatening to organise industrial action to prevent the use of non-union labour was defined a conspiracy to injure another's business. In the words of Lord Brampton the actions of the trade union defendants constituted:

> *a conspiracy formed by a number of unscrupulous enemies acting under an illegal compact, together and separately...Such a conspiracy is a powerful and dangerous engine...employed by the defendants for the perpetration of organised and ruinous oppression.*[5]

Anyone coming across these words out of context could reasonably assume they were describing a mafia-type organisation not a trade union.

The judicial perspective that the common law is the guarantor of individual freedom and trade unions are its enemies is further exemplified by Farwell LJ's judgment in *Conway v Wade*. Having made references to Magna Carta, the abolition of serfdom and the law as propounded by King Solomon, his view of the Trade Union Act 1871 is demonstrated by the following observation:

> *The freedom of the individual workman to make the best terms that he could for himself was, until 1871, curtailed by the application of the doctrine of public policy which treated combinations of workmen with the object of raising wages as conspiracies in restraint of trade, but the impediment was removed by the Legislature in that year.*

Similarly, Farwell LJ's view of the consequences of the Trade Disputes Act 1906 is encapsulated by his conclusion that:

> *It was possible for the Courts in former years to defend individual liber-*

ty against the aggression of kings and barons, because the defence rested on the law which they administered; it is not possible for the Courts to do so when the Legislature alters the laws as to destroy liberty, for they can only administer the law. The Legislature cannot make evil good, but it can make it not actionable.[6]

Trade Unions and Corporations Compared

It is instructive to compare these approaches to collective action organised by trade unions to analogous action by a trading association to protect its members from competition from rival traders. In a judgment that rejected contentions that the association was conspiring to injure the plaintiff, or acting in restraint of trade, Lord Halsbury stated:

> *It is impossible to suggest any malicious intention to injure rival traders, except in the sense that in proportion as one withdraws trade that other people might get, you, to that extent, injure a person's trade when you appropriate the trade to yourself. If such an injury, and the nature of its infliction, is examined and tested, upon principle, and can be truly asserted to be a malicious motive within the meaning of the law that prohibits malicious injury to other people, all competition must be malicious and consequently unlawful, a sufficient reductio ad absurdum to dispose of that head of suggested unlawfulness.*[7]

This judgment reflects a clear understanding of the realities of commercial competition and of the need for the law to accept those realities (and illustrates the *laissez-faire* attitude of the common law to acts, which under modern statute and European law, would be regarded as anti-competitive). However, neither Lord Halsbury and his judicial contemporaries nor judges today have shown a similar willingness to understand how the realities of industrial relations should lead to a similar approach being taken to trade union organisation and the use of industrial action.

The concept of unlawful means (or illegal means) has been and is at the root of judicial perceptions of industrial action and provides the basis for establishing legal liability. It is perhaps of some value to trace the origin of this concept. The earliest case in which it appears to have been used was in 1602 where it was held that it constituted illegal means to deprive a quarry proprietor of his trade by threatening his customers with mayhem.[8] The phrase was also used to describe firing cannon at inhabitants of Cameroon[9], and disturbing wild fowl by firing a gun.[10]

However, since the nineteenth century the concept of unlawful means has become common-place in case law concerning the use of industrial action. This has been so with respect to picketing, threats to organise industrial action and, of particular significance, the organisation of sympathetic industrial action. The semiotics of this terminology is clear. Acts that in most democratic countries constitute the exercising of legal, and in some cases constitutional, rights are according to the common law inherently acts of illegality. Even though typically this has led to the creation of tortious, rather than criminal, liability this vital legal distinction is often lost when it comes to the media reporting of industrial disputes and thus to popular understanding of the law.

The Judicial Mystification of Picketing

The example of picketing provides a particularly revealing insight into judicial attitudes past and present. In two 19th century cases arising from the same industrial dispute,[11] Erle J decided that there was a conspiracy to obstruct a manufacturer from carrying on his business, contrary to s.3 of the Combination Act 1825, and 'intimidation', 'molestation' and 'annoyance' of his workers by informing them by placards that their employer paid lower wages than other manufacturers in the locality. Following these decisions, the Combination of Workmen Act 1859 was intended to clarify that a worker could not commit a criminal offence if he sought peacefully (that is non-violently) to persuade another not to work. However, it remained an offence to intimidate others. Like unlawful means, intimidation is a flexible concept, and, in a case in 1867, Baron Bramwell provided an interpretation that continues to find reflection in judicial reasoning. He stated:

> *But even if abusive language and gestures were not used, if the pickets were so placed or so acted by watching the movements of the workplace and masters, or by black looks, or by any other annoyance...would be likely to have a deterring effect in the minds of ordinary persons, it would be 'molestation' and 'obstruction' against this statute.*[12]

Echoing this approach, in a case that arose out of the miners' strike of 1984-85, Scott J declared: 'a large number of sullen men lining the entrance to a colliery, offering no violence, saying nothing, but simply standing and glowering would be highly intimidating'.[13]

J Lyons & Sons v Wilkins

The judgment of Lindley LJ in *J Lyons & Sons v Wilkins*[14] is of particular importance as it demonstrates a judicial view of picketing that persists today – that picketing is often only lawful where it is reduced to a symbolic act. Moreover, Lindley LJ, like Baron Bramwell before him, combined the methods of legal mystification and restrictive interpretation to circumvent legalisation conferred by Parliament through statutory immunity from common law liability. Section 7 of the Conspiracy and Protection of Property Act 1875 legalised picketing to the extent that pickets were doing no more than attending at a place to communicate or obtain information. This is essentially the same as the basis of the immunity that has applied since the Trade Disputes Act 1906, but there was one fundamental difference. Whilst the 1875 immunity permitted picketing to communicate information it did not expressly cover picketing that went beyond acts of communication to include acts of persuasion. Lindley LJ exploited this loophole to find that seeking to persuade workers not to work was still a criminal offence in the form of watching and besetting.

In reaching this decision, Lindley LJ admitted that the line between persuading and giving information might be fine, but nevertheless he found that it existed and had been crossed. Lindley LJ's motivation for reaching this conclusion was clearly hostility to the liberalising legislation of the 1870s and a desire to prevent the use of picketing in circumstances where this was a necessary tactic to win an industrial dispute. He had already noted 'that the legislature, now, has legalised strikes', and had declared:

> *You cannot make a strike effective without doing more than is lawful.... The foundation of strikes is dictation. A strike is an attempt to dictate to the employer... Parliament has not yet conferred upon trade unions the power to coerce people and to prevent them from working for whomsoever they like upon any terms they like; and yet in the absence of such a power it is obvious that a strike may not be effective, and may not answer its purpose. Some strikes are perfectly effective by virtue of the mere strike, and other strikes are not effective unless the next step can be taken, and unless other people can be prevented from taking the place of the strikers.*[15]

The Legacy of J Lyons & Sons v Wilkins

It is interesting to note in passing that in *Quinn v Leathem*,[16] Lord Lindley (as he now was) took this circumvention of statutory immunity one stage further. Essentially he sounded the 'death knell' for the 1875 Act as a means for enabling a trade union lawfully to take industrial action by pointing out that, despite the above dictum that Parliament had legalised strikes, s 3 of the Act had no applications to civil actions. Given a context where industrial action through a series of judgments in the 1890s constituted tortious interference with contract and now tortious conspiracy to injure, the purpose behind the 1875 Act was effectively defeated. Whilst immunity from criminal liability was retained, the use of injunctions to restrain industrial action achieved the same result of preventing trade unions from organising lawful industrial action. With respect to picketing, however, the position resulting from *J Lyons & Sons v Wilkins* was not so very different to the one that exists today. Since the Trade Disputes Act 1906 it has admittedly been lawful for pickets both peacefully to communicate information and peacefully to persuade. But these rights are logistically impossible to exercise in practice, when other workers are permitted to simply drive through picket lines and refuse to stop to listen to the pickets' arguments. Any notion that it might be permissible for pickets to use peaceful means to stop vehicles for a limited period of time was rejected by the House of Lords in *Broome v DPP*.

In this case, Lord Reid effectively evokes and uses Lindley LJ's approach that picketing is only lawful within the strict letter of the law, even though this means that acts of picketing are rendered of little practical value where they are reduced to no more than a right to attend. Lord Reid explained the right to picket as:

> *the right to try to persuade anyone who chooses to stop and listen, at least in so far as this is done in a reasonable way with due consideration for the rights of others. A right to attend for the purpose of peaceful persuasion would be meaningless unless this were implied. But I see no ground for implying any right to require the person whom it is sought to persuade to submit to any kind of constraint or restriction of his personal freedom. One is familiar with the persons at the side of the road signalling to a driver requesting him to stop. It is for the driver to decide whether he will stop or not. That, in my view a picket is entitled to do.*[17]

This quote also illustrates a subsidiary dimension of legal mystification – the use by judges of inappropriate analogies, which both contribute to providing justification for a particular decision and disguise or ignore the industrial relations realities involved. In the mind of a judge a picket may have no greater status than that of a hitch-hiker. From a trade union perspective picketing has a rather more vital function than seeking a free lift, and, indeed, should be regarded as part of the rights to freedom of assembly and association guaranteed by Article 11 of the European Convention on Human Rights.

Privileges or Rights?

Another major feature of legal mystification, and one that is entirely facilitated by the method of providing statutory immunity from legal liability, is to recast what should be understood as the provision of rights in a negative form as privileges to break the law. This method was employed by Lord Brampton in *Quinn v Leathem*, and was both a reflection of the past and an indicator for the future in terms of facilitating and implementing judicial intervention. In *Quinn*, Lord Brampton declared:

> *the legislature in conferring upon trade unions such privileges as are contained in the Trade Union Acts 1871 and 1876...had not conferred upon any association or any member of it a licence to obstruct or interfere with the freedom of any person in carrying on his business, or bestowing his labour in the way he thinks fit.*[18]

Similarly, in *Conway v Wade*, Farwell LJ depicted the objective of the unions in overturning *Taff Vale* through the Trade Disputes Act 1906 as obtaining for themselves:

> *the unrestricted capacity for injuring other people by the use of that capacity which they had not, a privilege possessed by no other person or corporation in the realm...the general nature of the Act is in entire contradiction of those doctrines of personal freedom and equality before the law which have hitherto been its main aim and object.*[19]

Depiction of Right to Strike as 'Privilege'

The depiction of rights to strike as privileges to break the law was the ideological basis for attacks in the 1970s on the provisions in the Trade Union and Labour Relations Act (TULRA) 1974 which sought to implement the objectives of the Trade Disputes Act 1906 by drafting the immunities in as watertight a way as possible. These attacks were mounted by employers, politicians and the mass-media and were both encouraged by and reflected in judicial statements. Lord Denning was the judge who took the lead in adopting the approach pioneered by Lord Brampton and Farwell LJ. His hostility to the pro-union legislation of the 1970s was made quite explicit in judgment in the case of *BBC v Hearn*. He described the legislation in these terms.

I would only say that in three recent Acts, the Trade Union and Labour Relations Act 1974, the Employment Protection Act 1975, and the Trade Union and Labour Relations (Amendment) Act 1976, Parliament has conferred more freedom from restraint on trade unions than has ever been known to the law before. All legal restraints have been lifted so that they can now do as they will. Trade unions and their officers — and, indeed, groups of workmen, official or unofficial — are entitled to induce others to break their contracts — not only contracts of employment but other contracts as well — they are entitled to interfere and prevent the performance of contracts by others — all with impunity. Any such inducement or interference is not only not actionable at law. It is specifically declared to be "not unlawful." It is therefore proclaimed to be lawful.[20]

In *Express Newspapers Ltd v McShane*, Lord Denning effectively contradicted the last part of the above statement. He stated:

I would also draw attention to the fact that, when Parliament granted immunities to the leaders of trade unions, it did not give them any rights. *It did not give them a* right *to break the law or to do wrong by inducing people to break contracts. It only gave them immunity if they did… the words of the statute are not to be construed widely so as to give unlimited immunity to law-breakers. They are to be construed with due limitations so as to keep the immunity within reasonable bounds. Otherwise the freedom of ordinary individuals — to go about their business in peace would be intruded upon beyond all reason.*[21]

In *McShane*, Lord Denning had found sympathetic industrial action organised by the NUJ to be beyond the scope of the statutory immunities as in his view the action did not further the ability of the NUJ to win a dispute with owners of provincial newspapers. The Law Lords interpreted the phrase 'in furtherance of a trade dispute' as establishing a subjective rather than objective test and reversed the Court of Appeal decision. Thus (as is still the case today) providing a trade union believes a particular form of action will assist its cause, this aspect of the immunity is satisfied. However, the true sentiments of their Lordships are revealed by Lord Diplock's statement that:

…the consequences of applying the subjective test…have tended to stick in judicial gorges: so that great damage may be caused to innocent and

disinterested third parties in order to obtain for one of the parties to a trade dispute tactical advantages which in the court's own view are highly speculative and, if obtained, could be no more than minor.[22]

It is interesting to reflect on this judicial view of sympathetic, or, as it has now long been termed, secondary industrial action from the viewpoint of a quarter of a century later during which time such action has been substantially or entirely unlawful. The reality is that countless industrial disputes - some major such as the miners' strike, but the large majority minor in terms of their perceived newsworthiness - have been lost because unions have been hamstrung by an inability to organise lawful sympathetic action. This is despite the fact that it is clearly established that international law requires unions and their members to be accorded some rights to organise and take such action.

The Politics of Judicial Activism

It is acknowledged that an analysis reflecting an argument that judicial intervention into the arena of industrial conflict has occurred at specific points in history is open to the charge of conspiracy theory. However, if we look at the timings - in particular the 1890s, the 1960s and 1970s – it can be seen that these were periods where industrial militancy was an issue of concern to employers, governments, the State and the media and legislation was regarded by many as over-sympathetic to the unions in terms of shifting the balance of power too far in their favour. Thus, in the 1890s the National Free Labour Association was formed by William Collinson in response to the perceived threat of militancy associated with the 'new unionism'. Using the language of the judges he declared that it was: 'the right possessed by every man to pursue his Trade or Employment without dictation, molestation, or obstruction'.[23] The NFLA was to play a prominent role in organising 'blackleg' labour during the Taff Vale dispute. Following the decision in *J Lyons & Sons v Wilkins*, W J Shaxby produced a book called *The Case Against Picketing*. This was published by the Employers' Parliamentary Council, and its purpose was to provide advice on how to use the decision to act against pickets. In an editorial of 29 July 1898, *The Times* demanded: 'Unions should cease to be extra-legal in character...the time has come...for placing upon the unions a proper amount of corporate responsibility for illegal acts, which inflict injury upon employers or upon non-unionists'. The Law Lords were happy to oblige several years later by following this advice in the *Taff Vale* decision. This convergence between judicial decisions and a wider political assault on legislation designed to provide rights to strike was effectively to be repeated in the late 1970s (see below).

It is to be expected that where litigation against unions and their members is brought in such climates, many (if not all) judges will be predisposed to use their powers of judicial creativity to establish liability. As the above quotes have sought to substantiate, judicial thinking is underpinned by a philosophy that perceives what trade unionists would regard as no more than the taking of effective industrial action as an abuse of power generated by privileges that put unions above the law. By way of contrast, in the period between 1906 and World War II there was a process of judicial disengagement in industrial relations as part and parcel of a state strategy to use less coercive strategies to create a 'responsible' trade unionism free from industrial militancy. In the words of Winston Churchill:

> *It is not good for trade unions that they should be brought in contact with the courts, and it is not good for the courts...Where class issues are involved, it is impossible to pretend that the courts command the same degree of general confidence. On the contrary, they do not, and a very large number of our population has been led to the opinion that they are, unconsciously no doubt, biased.* [24]

This process was not, of course, a smooth and consistent one – particularly given the need from the perspective of employers and the State to defeat the General Strike of 1926. Nevertheless, by the beginning of the 1950s it would have been accurate to conclude that the judges, in line with the recognition of the realities of collective bargaining and trade unionism recognised by the majority of the Law Lords in *Crofter* [25], had collectively opted out of intervention in industrial disputes. In particular, as demonstrated by the decision in *D C Thomson & Co Ltd v Deakin* [26], there was a clear reluctance to create new liabilities in the law of tort that would circumvent the immunities contained in the 1906 Act.

Rookes v Barnard - The Re-emergence of Judicial Intervention

The industrial relations context which generated the decision of the Law Lords in *Rookes v Barnard* [27] is of significance, as had industrial action taken place it would have been both unconstitutional and unofficial and both these forms of industrial action were increasingly becoming focal points of concern on the part of State and employers in the early 1960s. Moreover, the object of the industrial action was to enforce the closed shop. This has always attracted some controversy as an industrial relations institution, as the collectivist philosophy underlying the closed shop conflicts with judicial perceptions of individual liberty. Indeed, aspects of *Rookes v Barnard* are reminiscent of the issues that led to the decision in *Quinn v Leathem*.

Nature of the Dispute – The Closed Shop

The dispute was caused by Rookes resigning from his union. The employer BOAC, in breach of a closed shop agreement with the union, failed to dismiss him. In response, two elected union representatives and a paid union official informed the company that industrial action would take place if Rookes was not dismissed. The company decided to dismiss Rookes, who then sued the union representatives and the official for damages. As will be elaborated below, it was not, and never has been, exactly clear what the House of Lords was deciding, but most commentators agree that, in deciding a threat to break a contract of employment constituted the tort of intimidation, the Law Lords were rendering potentially unlawful any industrial action which was preceded by a 'threat' to take that action, and were thus at a stroke undoing much of what the 1906 Act had sought to do; that being to provide protection to trade unionists from liability in tort for acts committed in the course of an industrial dispute.

The policy-based nature of the decision, and the fact that a number of judges had decided that the time was over-ripe for their re-entry into the arena of industrial relations, is clear from the judgments of all the Law Lords and from that of the trial judge, Sachs J, who stated in his summing up: 'You have to consider ... whether there was a deliberately engineered unofficial 'wild cat' strike, forced by these three, to use, at all costs, an illegal pressure, and whether on the other hand there was provocation which could reasonably be regarded as provocation for that line of conduct'.[28] Moreover, the language of the judge, and, as illustrated below, that of the Law Lords, was a resurrection of language which strongly echoed the sentiments and prejudices of the judges of the 19th and early 20th centuries, and ushered in a new era of judicial mystification of the nature of trade unionism and industrial action. This is perhaps symbolised by the extent of discussion by counsel as to the nature and scope of 'illegal means' and the invocation of ancient cases such as *Tarleton v M'Gawley*.[29]

The Approach of the House of Lords

The judgments of the Law Lords were characterised by ingenuity to ensure that the defendants were liable in tort but were not covered by the immunities provided by s 3 Trade Disputes Act 1906; and by a hostility to the aim of the defendants - the maintenance of a closed shop - which was thinly disguised by language and reasoning calculated to distort the nature of the defendants' actions. The determination to ensure that all the defendants were found to have committed tortious acts was perhaps epitomised by the fact that, whilst the essence of the liability was held to be a threat to break the contract of employment, one of the defendants, Mr Silverthorne, was an official of the union, the Association of Engineering & Shipbuilding Draughtsmen, and therefore had no contract with the employer, BOAC, which he could threaten to break. Nevertheless, the Law Lords were able to find that he was liable by disinterring the hoary tort of conspiracy which many had presumed dead and buried, at least with respect to industrial relations, after the House of Lords decision in *Crofter*.

However, the Law Lords were able to point out that s 1 of the 1906 Act covered simple conspiracy but not conspiracy to commit an unlawful act. The other defendants, as employees, had committed unlawful acts, to wit the threats to break their contracts of employment, and Silverthorne had engaged in a conspiracy with them to 'plot' this course of conduct. Therefore, once again, the language of conspiracy was used both to establish liability and distort the nature of the actions of trade unionists, who perceived themselves, and were perceived by other trade unionists, as engaged in the fairly run-of-the-mill activity of consultation between branch and union officials as to how best to carry out the wishes of the membership. In this case, the branch, of which Rookes had been a member, had resolved to strike if he was not dismissed, and it was the communication of this policy which was deemed to constitute the threat.

Rookes v Barnard, the House of Lords and Intimidation

Similar mystification, again with strong echoes of the past, can be identified in the method by which the Law Lords found that the tort of intimidation had been committed. The Court of Appeal had accepted that one of the major arguments against liability had been that intimidation, as a tort, should be confined to threats to commit acts of violence. Lord Reid revealed that his chief concern was to protect the interests of business, and used the established techniques of the process of legal mystification to achieve this objective. Thus, he proclaimed:

> *Threatening a breach of contract may be a much more coercive weapon than threatening a tort, particularly when the threat is directed against a company or corporation, and if there is no technical reason requiring a distinction between different kinds of threats, I can see no other*

grounds for making any such distinction...intimidation of any kind appears to me to be highly objectionable. The law was not slow to prevent it when violence and threats of violence were the most effective means. Now that subtler means are at least equally effective, I see no reason why the law should have to turn a blind eye to them.[30]

The Analogy with Violent Means

Therefore, according to this rather curious logic, trade unionists should be regarded as having engaged in unlawful activity for abandoning violence in favour of the 'more subtle means' of protecting their interests by threatening to withdraw their labour. And this conclusion is reached despite the fact that by both the standards of the law and, it is suggested, of the average person in society, the use of violence is regarded as constituting criminal behaviour whilst the withdrawal of labour, or threat thereof, is regarded at worst as a matter for the civil law, and at best as the exercising of a civil liberty, the very existence of which is regarded as essential in any society which wishes to regard itself, and be regarded, as democratic. Lord Hodson was quite explicit in his belief that industrial action would constitute an even greater evil than violent behaviour. He argued:

It would be strange if threats of violence were sufficient and the more powerful weapon of a threat to strike were not, always provided that the threat is unlawful. The injury and action is very often widespread as well as devastating, and a threat to strike would be expected to be certainly no less serious of violence.[31]

The economic consequences of strike action cannot be denied, but then neither can the consequences of a decision to close a business and thereby putting thousands out of work, perhaps permanently. Moreover, it must be remembered that, whilst labour lawyers today do put more emphasis on rights to strike as human rights than they did in the 1960s, it was the case that at the time of this decision Britain was a signatory of the European Social Charter of 1961 which, under Article 6(4) expressly provides for the right to strike, and had also ratified ILO Conventions 87 and 98. It was therefore surely fallacious to compare a threat to exercise a human right with a threat to inflict violence on another person. Lord Devlin's speech is interesting in that he did take up the argument that it appears, on the surface, rather bizarre to establish a legal position where a threat to strike is actionable but the taking of strike action without such a prior threat would not be. According to Lord Devlin this argument is without foundation because (again using the analogy of violent behaviour):

> *If A hits B without telling him why, he can hardly hope to achieve his object. Of course A might think it effective to hit B first and tell him why afterwards. But if then B injures C, it would not be because B had been hit but because he feared that he might be hit again. So if, in the present case, AESD went on strike without threatening, they would not achieve their object unless they made it plain why they were doing so. If they did that and BOAC then got rid of the appellant, his cause of action would be just the same as if AESD had threatened first, because the cause of the injury to the appellant would have been AESD's threat, express or implied, to continue on strike until the appellant was got rid of.*

The Reasoning of Lord Devlin

Lord Devlin's reasoning here, if applied generally to collective bargaining, would force a conclusion that striking is lawful providing you do not explain the reasons for the strike, either before its commencement or during the course of its duration, because once the reason is disclosed there is a threat to continue the action until the employer capitulates. Seeking to resolve an industrial dispute in this manner would clearly be ludicrous, and thus it is Lord Devlin's argument that lacks foundation. The real reason for Lord Devlin's decision, however, was a shared determination with the other Law Lords to compare industrial action unfavourably with acts of violence. In his view there was:

> *...nothing to differentiate a threat of a breach of contract from a threat of physical violence or any other illegal threat. The nature of the threat is immaterial ... All that matters to the plaintiff is that, metaphorically speaking, a club has been used. It does not matter to the plaintiff what the club is made of. Whether it is a physical club or an economic club, a tortious club or an otherwise illegal club.*[32]

Lord Devlin's conclusions on the nature of intimidation incorporate the ideological reason for his decision. He stated:

> *... I cannot doubt that the threat of a breach of contract can be a most intimidating thing. The present case provides as good an example of the force of such a threat as could be found. A great and powerful corpora-*

tion submits to it at once, for it was threatened with the infliction of incalculable loss and of grave inconvenience to the public which it serves. The threat is made by men who are flagrantly violating a pledge not to strike ... Granted that there is a tort of intimidation, I think it would be quite wrong to cripple the common law so that it cannot give relief in these circumstances. I think it would be old-fashioned and unrealistic for the law to refuse relief in such a case and to grant it where there is a strike of a fist or a threat to publish a nasty and untrue story.[33]

Lord Devlin's reasoning as to why s 3 of the 1906 Act did not provide the defendants with immunity is also worthy of examination both for its interpretation of history, and the delight in which the literal rule of statutory interpretation is invoked in order to ensure that, having taken great trouble to identify liability, the small problem of parliamentary intention should not be allowed to provide any sort of obstacle to its imposition. Lord Devlin reflected:

It is easy now to see that Parliament in 1906 might have felt that the only way of giving labour an equality of bargaining power with capital was to give it special immunities which the common law did not permit. Even now, when the sides have been redressed, it is easy to see that Parliament might think that a strike, whether reprehensible or not, ought not to be made a ground for litigation and industrial peace should be sought by other means.[34]

This dictum indicates that it was Lord Devlin's belief that legislation enacted in 1906 could well be out of date and thus no longer necessary. It provides an insight into general judicial attitudes, that trade unions are the Goliaths not the Davids of industrial relations, to be informed that the AESD had, at the very least, equality of bargaining power with that 'great and powerful corporation' BOAC. On the specific question of the immunities contained in s 3, and in response to the Court of Appeal, Lord Devlin polemicised:

But can your Lordships get that out of the words of the Act? . . . Section 3 could easily have read 'shall not be actionable on the ground only that it is a breach of contract or induces some other person' etc'; but it is not so written ... Or it may be that Parliament did not anticipate that a threat of breach of contract would be regarded as an intim-

idatory weapon. Whatever the reason, the immunity is not in the statute; the section clearly exempts the procurer or inducer and equally clearly does not exempt the breaker. It is not suggested that the House can remove the oddity by reading words into the Act that are not there.[35]

Rookes v Barnard – The Aftermath

The quotes from the judgments of the Law Lords stated above reveal a clear determination to find the defendants liable, and, in so doing, restrict the protection given to trade unions by the Trade Disputes Act 1906. As a decision imposing a new form of liability, *Rookes v Barnard* has been of little significance since 1965 when the Trade Disputes Act was amended to extend immunity both to a threat to break a contract and a threat to induce others to do so. However, the decision remains of utmost historic significance in that it heralded a return by the judges to intervention in industrial disputes and a return to the techniques of legal mystification as the method of intervention. The ideological consequences of portraying strike action to be at least as bad as inflicting violence are obvious, as is the resurrection of the language of conspiracy. The judgments indicated that the judicial abstention of the previous 50 years was the product, not of an altered attitude to trade unionism, but of a voluntary participation in the prevailing consensus of that period that judicial intervention could do more harm than good. Furthermore, the policy-based nature of the decision in that it was really concerned with showing judicial disapproval for particular types of industrial conflict - the closed shop, the unofficial strike, the unconstitutional strike - was revealed by the different interpretations of the decision given by both the Court of Appeal and the House of Lords in *J&T Stratford & Co Ltd v Lindley*[36], and by the different perceptions of the decision propounded in the House of Commons' debates on the Trade Disputes Bill 1965.

Repairing the Damage - The Trade Disputes Act 1965

One of the important aspects of legal mystification is the way in which judicial language converges with statements by politicians, and other influencers of public opinion such as journalists, and consequently percolates into the public consciousness. In the debates on the Trade Disputes Bill in 1965 both Ray Gunter, the Minister of Labour presenting the Bill, and Joseph Godber, the Opposition spokesman, agreed that the closed shop along with unofficial and unconstitutional strikes were problems that needed to be dealt with. The essential difference was that the Labour Government wanted the issues examined by the Donovan Commission, which was established the day before the Trade Disputes Bill was published, whereas the Conservatives wanted to keep aspects of the decision in *Rookes*. Godber argued:

> *the Bill safeguards anyone who induces others to strike in breach of contract. We all know cases where trade union authority has been set at nought by the activities of unofficial leaders...If such a Bill as this is to be brought forward, it should at least have been drafted to give immunity only to those acting specifically under the authority of the executive of the union concerned, thus hoping to strengthen the authority and the discipline of the union leaders.*[37]

In the context of the closed shop, however, Godber revealed a much sharper difference with the Government. He declared:

> *A closed shop achieved by voluntary means is one thing. One achieved by coercion or by threats is another; and for a large and powerful trade union movement to harry and hound a man and drive him from his employment is the negation of justice. Tyranny is no less evil if it is the tyranny of a trade union than if it were the tyranny of a despotic ruler*[38]

This view of the closed shop and supposed trade union power could just as easily have come from a politician or judge in the 19th century. The language used and the depiction of trade unionism as a form of tyranny clearly evokes, for example, the views of Sir William Erle, or Lord Lindley or Farwell LJ. It was also a view of the closed shop that was to inform Conservative thinking under both the Heath and Thatcher Governments, and provides the ideological basis of the (successful) assault on the closed shop that was to be mounted by the latter.

Another illuminating consequence of analysing judgments by focusing on what judges actually say, rather than on the overall decision, is the way this demonstrates that contrary to any notion of a pre-planned secret conspiracy to 'get the unions'; the judgments are in part a public conversation between judges as to whether, or the extent to which, they should use the common law to impose legal liability in a given context.

In the aftermath of the decision in *Rookes* the essential problem for the judges was that its logical consequence was that a threat to strike could be unlawful in circumstances where the organisation of it would not be. Essentially this could have forced trade unions to adopt a collective bargaining strategy that consisted of calling a strike and then informing the employers why (although as we see above in the view of Lord Devlin even this could constitute intimidation). It was this logic which was to cause concern even amongst the senior judiciary as soon as the decision was given. Moreover, initially, the judges themselves including most notably Lord Denning, given his anti-union decisions in the late 1960s and 1970s, displayed concern about re-entering the arena of industrial relations. Thus, in the immediate aftermath of *Rookes v Barnard*, Lord Denning in his judgments in the cases of *J&T Stratford & Co Ltd v Lindley* [39] and *Morgan v Fry* [40] spoke in terms of the need to recognise the right to strike.

From J&T Stratford & Co Ltd v Lindley to Torquay Hotel Co Ltd

The case of *J&T Stratford & Co Ltd v Lindley* is of a two-fold significance. It was the first judicial opportunity to review *Rookes v Barnard*, and it was also a case in which yet another tort not covered by the 1906 Act was developed. In *Stratford*, the House of Lords appeared to backtrack from a general position that a threat to strike is at least as serious as a threat of violence by restricting the decision to special circumstances such as enforcement of the closed shop or, as in *Stratford*, the use of sympathetic industrial action in circumstances that the judges regarded as illegitimate. It is with respect to the latter that the decision in *Stratford* [41] has been of longer term significance. This is because the Law Lords refined the elements of tortious liability for interference with commercial contracts to those established by the Court of Appeal in *D C Thomson & Co Ltd v Deakin*.[42] In so doing, they developed the tort which is at the heart of rendering unlawful the organisation of sympathetic industrial action for which today, other than in the context of lawful picketing, no immunity exists. The elements of this tort were further refined by the Court of Appeal in *Emerald Construction Co. Ltd v Lowthian* [43] and *Torquay Hotel Co Ltd v Cousins*.[44] The former case is of historical note in that it was the first case in which Lord Denning broke from earlier reluctance to intervene in industrial disputes. The latter case is of major significance because it foreshadowed the creativity that Lord Denning was to demonstrate in the 1970s and laid the basis for the law as it is today.[45]

The Court of Appeal decision in *Torquay Hotel* developed tortious liability in three major ways. First, along with other cases at this time, it firmly established that a party who brought about a breach of contract did not need to possess knowledge of the contract. It was sufficient that the defendant was recklessly indifferent to its existence, and was content to 'turn a blind eye to it'. Secondly, the defendant could incur liability even if an actual breach of contact was not procured, providing there was interference with its execution. Thirdly, Lord Denning effectively resurrected the consequences of *Quinn v Leathem*, albeit not by reference to the tort of conspiracy, by declaring it to be tortious to use unlawful means to interfere with the trade or business of another.[46] The decision in *Torquay* is also noteworthy because it provides another illustration of the use of analogies relating to contexts entirely divorced from the world of industrial relations in order to justify the imposition of liability to restrain industrial action. In seeking to justify his view that interference with contract was in and of itself a tortious act, Lord Denning likened the behaviour of the union to:

> *...an ill-disposed person', who, knowing of an actress's contract, 'had given her a potion to make her sick. She would not be guilty of a breach herself. But undoubtedly the person who administered the potion would have done wrong and be liable for the damage suffered by them.*[47]

Similarly, and using an analogy aptly characterised by Wedderburn as bizarre,[48] Winn LJ in seeking to broaden the meaning of the word 'inducement' argued:

> *...whilst granted...that a communication which went no further would, in general, not...amount to a threat or intimidation, I am unable to understand why it may not amount to an inducement...A man who writes to his mother-in-law telling her that the central heating in his house was broken down may thereby induce her to cancel an intended visit.*[49]

Thus are the worlds of whodunit mysteries and vaudeville (sexist) humour drawn upon to justify refinements in the elements of tortious liability in order to restrain trade union action.

Conclusion

Following the demise of the 'Social Contract', the late 1970s witnessed the return of judicial interventionism. Indeed historical parallels can be drawn between this period and the 1890s. Once again judicial concerns over the extent of trade union power converged with those of employers, politicians and the media. The Grunwick strike was the landmark event for this. During the dispute, in language reminiscent of the likes of Collinson and Shaxby, Conservative MPs spoke in terms of the 'coercive combinations of the trade unions'.[50] Sir Keith Joseph wrote in the Conservative Monthly News of 'mob rulers' and 'red fascism'.[51] Although Lord Denning was not called upon in his capacity as a judge to rule on the picketing that took place during the dispute, he nevertheless found it appropriate to make a political intervention. His sentiments were revealed at a public meeting when he proclaimed: 'The mobs are out. The police are being subjected to violence. Intimidation and violence are contrary to the law of the land. It should be condemned by every responsible citizen'.[52] It was also during this period that Lord Denning propagated the term 'secondary picketing' which he (prematurely) declared to be unlawful.[53]

The long term consequence of the process of legal mystification has been to inform public consciousness through statements by politicians and the media and even popular culture that various forms of industrial action are illegal, that is, contrary to the criminal law. This has been particularly the case with respect to sympathetic industrial action, unofficial action unsupported by a secret ballot and so-called secondary picketing.[54] The consequences of a prohibition of solidarity action and restrictions on picketing were shown most dramatically and tragically by the defeat of the miners in 1985. These prohibitions continue to be at the heart of the ongoing weakness of British trade unions when it comes to the organisation of industrial action that is both effective and lawful. The ongoing effects of legal mystification were demonstrated by the media coverage of the Gate Gourmet dispute, which took place in the summer of 2005. Once again the taking of solidarity action was castigated in the media for its illegal nature. In fact, it is the law itself that is at fault given the requirements of international law, as contained in ILO Conventions, that British law should provide for legal rights to organise and take sympathetic industrial action. Nevertheless, in the public mind it is the unions that must be controlled so that they are not able to break the law.

Therefore, it is suggested that unravelling the process of legal mystification is a useful element of any campaign to secure rights enabling trade unions to organise effective industrial action, as envisaged by the framers of the Trade Disputes Act. However, it is contended that such reform must be in the form of positive rights rather than a return to the method, last employed in 1974, of re-widening the scope of the statutory immunities.[55] No system of law, be it a system of rights or a system of immunities, can prevent judges from using their creativity to impose legal liability in circumstances which they regard to be appropriate. Be this the product of class instinct or legal philosophy (or both), judges have been, and are likely to remain, hostile to trade unionism. The historic problem with the immunities has been that, as the common law is left intact, judges are able to circumvent legislation by creating new liabilities and then depict that legislation as granting privileges to break the law rather than providing for democratic and human rights. In recognising the hugely progressive role played by the Trade Disputes Act historically, we must understand, albeit with the benefit of hindsight, that its method of creating rights through the provision of immunities has not proved to have served the trade union movement well

Notes

1 *Taff Vale Railway Company v Amalgamated Society of Railway Servants* [1901] AC 426.
2 Quoted in R Hedges and A Winterbottom, *The Legal History of Trade Unionism* (1930), p 52.
3 [1896] 1 Ch 811, p 823.
4 [1979] ICR 210, p 218.
5 [1901] AC 495, p 531.
6 *Conway v Wade* [1908] 2 KB 844, pp 854-856.
7 *Mogul Steamship Co v McGregor Gow and Co* [1892] AC 25, p 36.
8 *Garret v Taylor* (1620) 2 Roll Rep 162.
9 *Tarleton v M'Gauley* (1793) 1 Peake 270.
10 *Keeble v Hickeringill* (1707) 11 East 574.
11 *R v Duffield* (1851) Cox CC 404 and *R v Rowlands* (1851) Cox CC 436.
12 *R v Druitt* (1867) 10 Cox CC 592, pp 601 - 602.
13 *Thomas v NUM (South Wales Area)* [1985] ICR 886, p 906.
14 [1899] 1 Ch 269.
15 Above note 3, pp 822 - 823.
16 [1901] AC 495.
17 *Broome v DPP* [1974] AC 587, p 597.
18 Above note 5, p 531.
19 Above note 6, p 855.
20 [1977] ICR 685, pp 690 - 691.
21 [1979] ICR 210, p 218.
22 *Express Newspapers v McShane* [1980] ICR 42, p 57.
23 Quoted by J Saville, 'Trade Unions and Free Labour: The Background to the Taff Vale Decision' in A Briggs and J Saville (eds), *Essays in Labour History 1886 -1923* (1971), p 318.
24 Quoted in K Middlemass, *Politics in Industrial Society* (1979), p 158.
25 *Crofter Hand Woven Harris Tweed Co Ltd v Veitch* [1942] AC 435.
26 [1952] Ch 646.
27 [1964] AC 1129.
28 Quoted in *Rookes v Barnard* [1964] 1 All ER 367, p 368. Although Sachs J's comments were made in relation to the question as to whether exemplary damages should be granted, it is reasonable to view them as wide enough to cover the question as to whether or not a particular instance of industrial action should be regarded as lawful.
29 Above, note 9.
30 [1964] AC 1129, p 1169.
31 *Ibid*, p 1201.
32 *Ibid*, p 1209.
33 *Ibid*, pp 1218 - 1219.
34 *Ibid*, p 1219.
35 *Ibid*, pp 1219 - 1220.
36 [1964] 2 All ER 209 Court of Appeal; and [1965] AC 269 House of Lords.

37 HC Debs, 16 February 1965, col. 1035.
38 *Ibid*, col. 1037.
39 [1964] 2 All ER 209.
40 [1968] 2 QB 710.
41 In *J&T Stratford & Co Ltd v Lindley* [1965] AC 269 the House of Lords was able to impose liability by a restrictive interpretation that declared a recognition dispute to be an inter union dispute and thus not a lawful trade dispute with an employer
42 Above note 26.
43 [1966] 1 WLR 691.
44 [1969] 1 All ER 522.
45 It should, however, be noted that in 1969 Lord Denning was still keen to restrict liability to disputes which he regarded as unconstitutional or where he deemed a union to be acting unreasonably. He continued to believe it wrong to jeopardise the position of a trade union official who, after due notice, called a strike.
46 Above note 44, p 530.
47 Above, note 44, p 529.
48 Wedderburn, *The Worker And The Law* (3rd ed, 1986), p 588.
49 Above, note 44, pp 537 - 538.
50 See Ronald Bell, HC Debs, 30 June 1977, col. 578. Similar statements were made in the same debate by John Gorst, who was associated with the National Association for Freedom - Collinson's NFLA can be regarded as the direct predecessor of the NAFF.
51 Quoted in J Rogaly, *Grunwick* (1977), pp 77 - 78.
52 *Ibid*, p 128.
53 See *Associated Newspapers Group v Wade* [1979] ICR 669, p 695.
54 Indeed, even trade union activists may wrongly regard mass and secondary picketing to be inherently contrary to the criminal law – see R Welch, 'The Behavioural Impact on Trade Unionists of the Trade Union Legislation of the 1980s' (1993) 24 *Industrial Relations Journal* 236.
55 The policy documents of the Institute of Employment Rights typically argue for rights rather than immunities. For example, see K Ewing and J Hendy (eds), *A Charter of Workers' Rights* (2002), pp 89 - 98. For the author's arguments see R Welch, *The Right to Strike: a Trade Union View* (1991).

Part 5

Towards a Trade Union Freedom Act?

Chapter Ten

European Laws: Help or Hindrance?

Brian Bercusson

Introduction

THE history of the Trade Disputes Act 1906 over the past century epitomises the dilemma of an approach to protection of industrial action by workers and trade unions based on legislative immunities developed in the aftermath of the creation of common law liabilities. This century long pattern of development is oblivious to the UK having joined the European Community in 1973, and being a Member State of the European Union for the last third of this 100 years. When contrasted with European laws on industrial action, the UK law on industrial action, developed in isolation from European Community law, reveals at least three specific defects.

First, the UK law on industrial action is a national law developed in a context of employers and unions operating in a predominantly domestic market. This law is now faced with the challenges of globalisation, where the interests of workers are affected by the operations of multinational corporations in an international economy. Secondly, the reliance of the British labour law on industrial action on immunities has long been contrasted with a continental European tradition of assertion of the fundamental right of workers to take collective action, often protected by national constitutions of the EU Member States. Thirdly, unlike much else in British labour law, the law on industrial action has so far avoided coming into contact with EC law.[1]

These deficiencies are about to be challenged in two cases referred to the European Court of Justice (ECJ) at the end of 2005: the *Viking* case, referred by the English Court of Appeal;[2] and the *Laval* case, referred by the Swedish Labour Court.[3] The outcome may transform what has been the pattern of British legal regulation of industrial action during the past 100 years: to adapt it to the new exigencies of a globalised economic system, to bring it into line with a continental European tradition based on the fundamental right of workers to withdraw their labour, and to achieve this by invoking the power of EC law regulating a transnational economy to override the national system based on immunities.

The *Viking* and *Laval* Cases

Not surprisingly, it was an organisation of workers operating in the globalised market of international transport, the International Transport Workers' Federation (ITF), which has been in the forefront of current developments. These developments confront national laws protecting the economic power of workers taking collective industrial action with EC law protecting the economic power of employers exercising freedom of movement for goods and services. The campaign by the ITF against flags of convenience (FOC) involves ITF affiliates taking industrial action in support of other affiliated unions in dispute, often in other countries. The FOC campaign provides examples of industrial action which risk falling outside the immunities of British law. As such, it was the subject of some of the leading cases in the UK courts over the past 20 years.

Viking

The *Viking* case concerns industrial action by the Finnish Seamen's Union (FSU) in Helsinki against Viking Line Abp (Viking). Viking, a Finnish shipping company, owns and operates the ferry, *Rosella*, registered under the Finnish flag and with a predominantly Finnish crew covered by a collective agreement negotiated by the FSU. The *Rosella* operates between Helsinki in Finland, a member of the EU since 1995, and Tallinn in Estonia, which became a member of the EU in May 2004. During 2003, Viking decided to re-flag the *Rosella* to Estonia, which would allow the company to replace the predominantly Finnish crew with Estonian seafarers, and to negotiate cheaper terms and conditions of employment with an Estonian trade union. In late 2003, Viking began negotiating with the FSU about the possible re-flagging.

Negotiations between Viking and the FSU for a new collective agreement for the *Rosella* were unsuccessful and the FSU gave notice of industrial action beginning 2 December 2003. The right to strike is protected in Finnish law by Article 13 of the Finnish Constitution as a fundamental right in Finnish law. It is accepted that the FSU had a right to take strike action to protect its members' jobs and the terms and conditions of the crew.

The FSU, an ITF affiliate, requested that the ITF assist by informing its affiliates of the situation and by asking those affiliates to refrain from negotiating with Viking pursuant to the ITF flags of convenience policy. Under the FOC policy, affiliates have agreed that the wages and conditions of employment of seafarers should be negotiated with the affiliate in the country where the ship is ultimately beneficially owned. In this case, the *Rosella* would remain owned by Viking, a Finnish company, even if re-flagged to Estonia. According to the FOC policy, therefore, the FSU would keep the negotiation rights for the *Rosella* after the re-flagging. To support the FSU, on 6 November 2003, the ITF sent a letter to all affiliates in the terms requested. Further meetings took place and on 2 December 2003, a settlement agreement was reached. Viking claimed they were forced to capitulate because of the threat of strike action.

In August 2004, shortly after Estonia became an EU Member State, Viking commenced an application in the Commercial Court of England and Wales for an order to stop the ITF and the FSU from taking any action to prevent the re-flagging of the *Rosella*. Viking was able to start proceedings in England because the ITF has its headquarters in London. In June 2005, the English Commercial Court granted an order requiring the ITF and the FSU to refrain from taking any action to prevent the re-flagging, and further requiring the ITF to publish a notice withdrawing its letter to its affiliated trade unions. The judge considered that the actions of the ITF and the FSU were contrary to European law. The ITF and the FSU appealed against this decision to the Court of Appeal.

In a judgment given on 3 November 2005, the Court of Appeal decided that the case raised important and difficult questions of European law and referred a series of questions to the European Court of Justice (ECJ). It also set aside the order granted by the Commercial Court against the ITF and the FSU. Proceedings in London are on hold until the ECJ provides answers to the questions that the Court of Appeal has requested. Once the ECJ answers the questions referred to it, the case will be returned to the Court of Appeal for a final decision. However, the judgment of the ECJ will become part of European law and will apply throughout the EU.

Laval

Baltic Bygg AB, a fully owned Swedish subsidiary of Laval un Partneri Ltd. (Laval), a Latvian company, was awarded a public works contract in June 2004 by the City of Vaxholm in Sweden for construction works on a school. Negotiations on a collective agreement between the Swedish Building Workers' Union (Svenska Byggnadsarbetareförbundet ("Byggnads") and Laval began in June 2004, but Laval refused to sign a collective agreement on terms acceptable to Byggnads. Instead, Laval entered into a collective agreement with the Latvian Trade Union of Construction Workers. Byggnads gave notice of industrial action and industrial action was taken by Bygnadds and the Swedish Electricians' Union (Svenska Elektrikerförbundet) in late 2004, including a peaceful boycott of the building and construction work. The right to strike is protected as a fundamental right by the Swedish Constitution. Laval commenced proceedings before the Swedish Labour Court claiming, *inter alia*, violation of its freedom of movement under the EC Treaty. The industrial action continued and Baltic Bygg AB went bankrupt. The Swedish Labour Court referred questions to the ECJ.

Issues at Stake

Due to the ITF being based in London, Viking was able to initiate proceedings before the British High Court. As in the *Laval* case, the employer's claim was based on EU law: that the industrial action had violated the employer's freedom of establishment and to provide services, as provided in the EC Treaty, Articles 43 and 49. As the unions did in the Swedish Labour court in the *Laval* case with the Swedish Constitution, the FSU in the *Viking* case invoked the Finnish Constitution which protects the fundamental right to strike. At first instance in the English High Court in June 2005, the judge upheld the employer's complaint: EU law overrode any national law, even the national constitution of a Member State.

However, the EC Treaty provisions on free movement are not absolute. Free movement is limited by public policy considerations, both in the Treaty[4] and as developed by the European Court of Justice through its extensive case law. The reference to the ECJ by the English Court of Appeal in *Viking* highlights this issue of the limits to free movement: whether EC Treaty provisions on free movement may be limited by collective action which is lawful under national law. One specific issue raised is whether EU law includes a fundamental right to take collective action, including strike action, as declared in Article 28 of the EU Charter of Fundamental Rights.

The EU Charter and the European Court of Justice

The European Union's Charter of Fundamental Rights proclaimed at the summit held at Nice on 7 December 2000 attracted much attention, not least because it seemed likely that the Convention on the Future of Europe would propose that the Charter be incorporated into the Treaties. This has now come to pass: the EU Charter is Part II of the proposed Treaty establishing a Constitution for Europe.[5]

The EU Charter includes provisions which are at the heart of labour law and industrial relations in Europe.[6] The incorporation of the EU Charter into the primary constitutional law of the EU will have an impact not only on the EU's institutions, but perhaps even more, on the Member States, also bound by the Charter through the doctrine of supremacy of EU law. The inclusion of fundamental rights concerning employment and industrial relations in an EU Charter incorporated into the EU Constitution may well confer on them a constitutional status also within national legal orders. In some cases, the EU Charter's labour standards and industrial relations requirements may exceed those of some Member State laws. Again, the ECJ may adopt interpretations consistent with international labour standards, where again national labour laws may fall short. In sum, the EU Charter promises a renewal of labour law, both at European transnational level and within the Member States of the EU.

Incorporated in the EU Constitutional Treaty, the EU Charter would be part of a European constitution with potentially powerful legal effects, including direct effect and supremacy. Action at EU and national level would have to comply with the Treaty's fundamental rights. The European Court of Justice becomes a central player in the enforcement of the EU Charter. The Court will decide disputes where Member States are charged with failing to implement, or allegedly violating rights in the EU Charter. The Court has played this role in the past, relying on free movement of goods, services, capital and labour, guaranteed in the EC Treaty, to override national restrictions on free movement. The EU Charter provides a further means whereby the Court can promote European integration, this time in the social and labour field.

Litigation based on the EU Charter could become an important means of securing social and labour rights, and could influence the political agendas of both EU institutions and the Member States. For example, the European Court of Justice may be willing to recognise as protected by the EU Charter those fundamental trade union rights which all, or most, or even a critical number of, Member States insist should be protected. The Court may interpret the articles of the EU Charter on fundamental trade union rights consistently with other international labour standards and will be sensitive to where national laws have protected trade union rights. A litigation strategy could enable trade unions to use the rights guaranteed by the EU Charter to shape a system of industrial relations at EU level.[7]

The European Court of Justice's Response, or Lack of it, to the EU Charter

Since its proclamation on 7 December 2000, every Advocate General has cited the Charter in one or more Opinions, as has the Court of First Instance in a number of judgments.[8] However, the European Court of Justice remains extremely cautious in its response to the Charter as regards integration of the EU Charter into the Community legal order, preferring to rely on the existing range of international human rights instruments. The legal advice and policy orientations encouraging references to the Charter, to be found in the Opinions of all the Advocates General, were for long ignored or cautiously circumvented by the Court.

For example, an ECJ decision involving the EU Charter was the *Omega* case.[9] This concerned an alleged restriction on free movement of services and goods as a consequence of a German regulation banning a video game including play at killing people. The defence invoked the German constitutional principle of protection of human dignity as falling within the permissible public policy derogation to free movement. The ECJ concluded: (paragraph 41)

> *Community law does not preclude an economic activity consisting of the commercial exploitation of games simulating acts of homicide from being made subject to a national prohibition measure adopted on grounds of protecting public policy by reason of the fact that the activity is an affront to human dignity.*

In its reasoning, the Court recalled that fundamental rights form an integral part of the EU legal order and, in paragraph 34 of the judgment, specifically cited paragraphs 82 to 91 of the Opinion of Advocate General Stix-Hackl in the case. Paragraph 91 of the Advocate General's Opinion stated:

> *The Court of Justice therefore appears to base the concept of human dignity on a comparatively wide understanding, as expressed in Article 1 of the Charter of Fundamental Rights of the European Union. This Article reads as follows: 'Human dignity is inviolable. It must be respected and protected'.*

The Court itself would not directly cite the EU Charter. Rather, the first judicial reference to the EU Charter was made by the Court of First Instance (CFI) in a decision of 30 January 2002. In *max.mobil Telekommunikation Service GmbH v. Commission*, the CFI twice referred to provisions of the EU Charter, first Article 41(1) (Right to good administration), and then Article 47 (Right to an effective remedy and to a fair trial) in the following terms:

> *Such judicial review is also one of the general principles that are observed in a State governed by the rule of law and are common to the constitutional traditions of the Member States, as is confirmed by Article 47 of the Charter of Fundamental Rights, under which any person whose rights guaranteed by the law of the Union are violated has the right to an effective remedy before a tribunal.*[10]

Even as a mere political declaration, the EU Charter appeared to be accepted, by all the Advocates General and the CFI, but not yet the ECJ, as reflecting fundamental rights which are an integral part of the EU legal order.

The ECJ Finally Cites the Charter: 27 June 2006

The question was whether, and how long this could last. The answer arrived with the first citation of the EU Charter, five and a half years after its proclamation, by the European Court in *European Parliament v Council*, decided 27 June 2006.[11] Parliament sought the annulment of a sub-paragraph in a Council Directive on the right to family reunification. In doing so, the Court states:

> *The Parliament invokes, first, the right to respect for family life... This principle has been repeated in Article 7 of the Charter which, the Parliament observes, is relevant to interpretation of the ECHR [European Convention for the Protection of Human Rights and Fundamental Freedoms] in so far as it draws up a list of existing fundamental rights even though it does not have binding legal effect. The Parliament also cites Article 24 of the Charter.... The Parliament invokes, second, the principle of non-discrimination on grounds of age which, it submits... is expressly covered by Article 21(1) of the Charter.*[12]

In contrast, the Court refers to the Council's submission as adopting the following position:

Nor should the application be examined in light of the Charter given that the Charter does not constitute a source of Community law.[13]

As to the Court's own view of the precise legal effects of the Charter, the key text in the judgment is under the rubric 'Findings of the Court'[14] with regard to the issue 'The rules of law in whose light the Directive's legality may be reviewed'.[15] The Court states:

The Charter was solemnly proclaimed by the Parliament, the Council and the Commission in Nice on 7 December 2000. While the Charter is not a legally binding instrument, the Community legislature did, however, acknowledge its importance by stating, in the second recital in the preamble to the Directive, that the Directive observes the principles recognised not only by Article 8 of the ECHR but also in the Charter. Furthermore, the principal aim of the Charter, as is apparent from its preamble, is to reaffirm 'rights as they result, in particular, from the constitutional traditions and international obligations common to the Member States, the Treaty on European Union, the Community Treaties, the [ECHR], the Social Charters adopted by the Community and by the Council of Europe and the case-law of the Court... and of the European Court of Human Rights.[16]

In other words, while not legally binding itself, the Charter reaffirms rights which are legally binding due to their provenance from other sources which are recognised by EU law as legally binding sources.[17] The Court elides this subtle distinction (reaffirming other binding instruments v declaring rights) when, in another section under the rubric 'Findings of the Court', it uses the word 'recognises:

The Charter recognises, in Article 7, the same right to respect for private or family life. This provision must be read in conjunction with the obligation to have regard to the child's best interests, which are recognised in Article 24(2) of the Charter, and taking account of the need, expressed in Article 24(3), for a child to maintain on a regular basis a personal relationship with both his or her parents.[18]

The recognition was made easy for the Court, as noted by Advocate General Kokott in her Opinion of 8 September 2005:

In so far as it is relevant here, Article 7 of the Charter of Fundamental Rights of the European Union... is identical to Article 8 of the ECHR. Moreover, the first sentence of Article 52(3) of the Charter (Article II-112 of the Treaty establishing a Constitution for Europe) provides that its meaning and scope are to be the same.[19]

As interesting as her reference to the proposed Constitutional Treaty is the following statement of Advocate General Kokott:[20]

Article 21 of the Charter of Fundamental Rights of the European Union expressly prohibits certain forms of discrimination, including that based on age. While the Charter still does not produce binding legal effects comparable to primary law,(73) it does, as a material legal source, shed light on the fundamental rights which are protected by the Community legal order. (74)[21]

The EU Charter and the Member States

It is perhaps significant that the Court should have first cited the Charter in a legal action by one (supranational) EU institution, the Parliament, against another, the Council (representing the Member States). In this context, the statements of the Court concerning the Member States are important. The Court repeats the mantra that fundamental rights 'are also binding on Member States when they apply Community rules'.[22]

The tension between the law of the EU and that of the Member States is particularly evident in disputes over EU competences. The ECJ may rely on the Charter to support EU legislative initiatives based on the EU Charter against challenges from Member States or other EU institutions. The Charter may also be used by EU institutions challenging Member State failures to implement, or even violations of, rights in the EU Charter. In this way, as stated earlier, the ECJ plays a political role in overcoming political opposition to European integration, a role it has frequently fulfilled in the past, relying on fundamental freedoms (of movement of goods, services, capital and labour) guaranteed in the EC Treaty. The EU Charter now provides another legal basis on which the ECJ may choose to rely in overcoming challenges to European integration in the social and labour field.

The Pending Cases on Collective Industrial Action in the Single European Market

The EU Charter represents values which are integral to Social Europe. In the sphere of employment and industrial relations, these values include those reflected in the fundamental rights to collective bargaining and collective action embodied in Article 28 of the Charter. The pending litigation before the European Court confronts the Charter with freedom of movement in the Single European Market.

In *Viking* and *Laval*, employers are seeking to override national and international guarantees of the right to collective action, invoking their freedom of movement in EU law. The pending references to the ECJ pose the question of whether collective industrial action at EU level contravenes the Treaty provisions on free movement, or whether the ECJ will adapt the EU law on free movement to redress the balance of economic power on a European scale. The reference to the ECJ by the English Court of Appeal in *Viking* highlights this issue of the limits to free movement: whether EC Treaty provisions on free movement may be limited by collective action which is lawful under national law. One specific issue raised is the potential of Article 28 of the EU Charter, which provides for the fundamental right to take collective action, including strike action.

Three of the questions put by the English Court of Appeal to the European Court raise the issue of whether EU law includes a fundamental right to strike.23 The relationship between the EC Treaty's provisions on free movement and the fundamental right to take collective industrial action can be analysed using doctrines developed by the ECJ in analogous contexts. Two will be examined in more detail

1 Is there a direct conflict between free movement and collective action, in which one or the other prevails? [24]

2 How is the exercise of free movement to be balanced with a fundamental right to take collective action? [25]

The future of the UK law on industrial action, shaped over the past century by the immunities established in the Trade Disputes Act 1906, may be determined by the answer to these questions by the European Court of Justice.

1 Is there a direct conflict between free movement and collective action, in which one or the other prevails?

Does EU law recognise a fundamental right of workers and their organisations to take collective action and, if so, what is its relation to the economic freedoms in the Treaty? Recognition in EU law of the fundamental right of workers and their organisations to take collective action is supported by various sources.

a Article 136 EC: The Community and the Member States respect fundamental social rights

Article 136 of the EC Treaty begins:

> *The Community and the Member States, having in mind fundamental social rights such as those set out in the European Social Charter signed at Turin on 18 October 1961 and in the 1989 Community Charter of the Fundamental Social Rights of Workers....*

Article 6(4) of the European Social Charter of 1961 provides:

> *With a view to ensuring the effective exercise of the right to bargain collectively, the Contracting Parties... recognise: . . . the right of workers and employers to collective action in cases of conflicts of interest, including the right to strike, subject to obligations that might arise out of collective agreements previously entered into.*

Article 13 of the 1989 Community Charter provides:

> *The right to resort to collective action in the event of a conflict of interests shall include the right to strike, subject to the obligations arising under national regulations and collective agreements.*

b The EU Charter of Fundamental Rights of 2000 recognises the right to take collective action

The EU Charter of Fundamental Rights adopted at Nice on 7 December 2000 was published as a 'solemn proclamation' of the European Parliament, the Council of Ministers of the EU Member States and the Commission in the *Official Journal* of 18 December 2000.[26] The Charter has been invoked in EU legislation,[27] and cited repeatedly before the European Court of Justice and in judgments of the Court of First Instance. Article 28 of the Charter provides:[28]

> *Right of collective bargaining and action*[29]
> *Workers and employers, or their respective organisations, have, in accordance with Community law and national laws and practices,*

the right to negotiate and conclude collective agreements at the appropriate levels and, in cases of conflicts of interest, to take collective action to defend their interests, including strike action.

c Constitutions of the Member States protect the right to take collective action

Many EU Member State constitutions include guarantees of the right of workers and their organisations to take collective action. For example:

Germany: The Basic Law (Grundgesetz) states (Article 9(3)): "The right to form associations to safeguard and improve working and economic conditions is guaranteed to everyone and to all trades, occupations and professions. Agreements which seek to impair this shall be null and void; measures directed to this end shall be unlawful...". The courts have interpreted this provision to legitimise strikes.

Luxembourg: Article 11(5) of the Constitution provides that the law must guarantee trade union freedoms, implicitly also the right to strike, an interpretation formally confirmed by the Cour de Cassation (Supreme Court) in 1952 and in an "interpretative motion' passed by the Luxembourg Parliament Chamber of Deputies in 1956.

The Netherlands: In May 1980, the Netherlands government ratified the European Social Charter of the Council of Europe, which includes the right to engage in collective action. The High Court (Hoge Raad) on 30 May 1986 formally endorsed the right to strike as provided for in the Charter.

Portugal: The Constitution of the Republic of Portugal, Article 57 provides: '1. The right to strike shall be safeguarded. 2. Workers shall be entitled to decide what interests are to be protected by means of strikes. The sphere of such interests shall not be restricted by law'.

Spain: The 1978 Constitution, Article 28(2), affirms that 'the right of workers to strike in defence of their own interests is recognised. Article 37(2) also provides that the 'law recognises the right of workers and employers to adopt collective dispute measures.

Sweden: The Constitution (Regeringformen), Chapter 2, section 17, provides for the right to engage in industrial action as long as it does not conflict with obligations imposed by law or collective agreement.

The EU institutions have been careful to ensure that Community law does not impinge on these fundamental constitutional rights.

d General principles of EC law include protection for fundamental rights

Fundamental rights in the EU legal order have been developed by the ECJ as a result of the sensitivity of national constitutional courts to respect for fundamental rights protected by national legal orders. The need for general principles of EC law to include protection for fundamental rights is driven by the implications for national constitutional courts of the doctrine of supremacy of EU law when these courts are bound to protect national constitutional rights.[30]

e The Albany case

Of the questions referred by the English Court of Appeal to the ECJ in the *Viking* case, the first raised the analogy with the ECJ decision in *Albany*.[31] The *Albany* case was concerned with whether EU competition law is compatible with collective agreements fixing the price of labour (wages).[32] Advocate General Jacobs said the Treaty did not give clear guidance but concluded that, as the Treaty encourages collective bargaining and social dialogue, these are in principle lawful. Consequently, EU competition law cannot have been intended to apply to collective agreements.[33]

The European Court's judgment did not address issues of fundamental rights. But the Court cited the Maastricht Treaty's recognition of social dialogue agreements at EU level (Articles 138-139 EC) as grounds for holding collective agreements lawful regardless of Treaty provisions on competition law.[34] The question is whether the Court would come to the same conclusion as regards transnational collective action and the Treaty's provisions on free movement. As collective action is inextricably linked to collective bargaining and collective agreements, like collective agreements, therefore, it 'follows from an interpretation of the provisions of the Treaty as a whole which is both effective and consistent' that collective action also is not subject to the EC Treaty's provisions on freedom of movement.

Further, in his Opinion in *Albany*, Advocate General Jacobs was categorical as regards two specific rights:

> *The Community legal order protects the right to form and join trade unions and employers' associations which is at the heart of freedom of association. In my view, the right to take collective action in order to protect occupational interests in so far as it is indispensable for the*

enjoyment of freedom of association is also protected by Community law. [35]

This statement was made without explicit reference to EC competition law, relevant to the case before him, but with respect to Community law in general.

The importance of this categorical statement as to the protection by Community law of the right to take collective action is highlighted by the contrast drawn by Advocate General Jacobs with his view of the relative lack of protection of this right in Article 11 of the European Convention for the Protection of Human Rights (ECHR):

> *...nor does Article 11 necessarily imply a right to strike, since the interests of the members can be furthered by other means. [Schmidt and Dahlstrom v Sweden, 6 February 1976, Eur. Court HR Rep. Series A, 21 (1976) paragraph 36.]* [36]

f The right to strike in ILO Conventions

Finally, there is the right to collective action in international law according to ILO Conventions 87 and 98, ratified by all EU Member States. Although there is no express recognition of the right to strike in ILO Convention 87, it has been implied into Convention 87, Article 3, by the supervisory bodies. According to the ILO Committee of Experts:

> *'The right to strike is one of the essential means through which workers and their organisations may promote and defend their economic and social interests'. The jurisprudence of the supervisory bodies on the nature and scope of the right to strike is now extensive.*[37]

2 How is the exercise of free movement to be balanced with a fundamental right to take collective action?

EU law recognises a number of fundamental rights, and, where these conflict, a balance may be sought with the economic freedoms in the EC Treaty.

a The need to reconcile protection of fundamental rights in the Community with economic freedoms in the Treaty

In *Schmidberger*, an international transport undertaking brought an action against the Republic of Austria on the basis that its lorries were unable to use the Brenner motorway, the sole transit route for its vehicles between Germany and Italy, due to the failure on the part of the Austrian authorities to ban a demonstration which led to the closure of the motorway and consequent restriction of the free movement of goods.[38]

The Austrian Court referred the case to the European Court which began its judgment by stating 'at the outset that the free movement of goods is one of the fundamental principles of the Community'[39] However:

> *69 It is apparent... that the Austrian authorities were inspired by considerations linked to respect of the fundamental rights of the demonstrators to freedom of expression and freedom of assembly, which are enshrined in and guaranteed by the ECHR and the Austrian Constitution...*

> *74 Thus, since both the Community and its Member States are required to respect fundamental rights, the protection of those rights is a legitimate interest which, in principle, justifies a restriction of the obligations imposed by Community law, even under a fundamental freedom guaranteed by the Treaty such as the free movement of goods.*

The Court continued:

> *77 The case thus raises the question of the need to reconcile the requirements of the protection of fundamental rights in the Community with those arising from a fundamental freedom enshrined in the Treaty and, more particularly, the question of the respective scope of freedom of expression and freedom of assembly, guaranteed by Articles 10 and 11 of the ECHR, and of the free movement of goods, where the former are relied upon as justification for a restriction of the latter.*

b Economic freedoms may be restricted; also some fundamental rights

The Treaty explicitly allows for restrictions on economic freedoms enshrined in the Treaty.40 Some fundamental rights in the ECHR may also be subject to certain limitations, as the ECJ in Schmidberger explained:

> *79 Second, whilst the fundamental rights at issue in the main proceedings are expressly recognised by the ECHR and constitute the fundamental pillars of a democratic society, it nevertheless follows from the express wording of paragraph 2 of Articles 10 and 11 of the Convention that freedom of expression and freedom of assembly are also subject to certain limitations justified by objectives in the public interest, in so far as those derogations are in accordance with the law, motivated by one or more of the legitimate aims under those provisions and necessary in a democratic society, that is to say justified by a pressing social need and, in particular, proportionate to the legitimate aim pursued...*

> *80 Thus, unlike other fundamental rights enshrined in that Convention, such as the right to life or the prohibition of torture and inhuman or degrading treatment or punishment, which admit of no restriction, neither the freedom of expression nor the freedom of assembly guaranteed by the ECHR appears to be absolute but must be viewed in relation to its social purpose. Consequently, the exercise of those rights may be restricted, provided that the restrictions in fact correspond to objectives of general interest and do not, taking account of the aim of the restrictions, constitute disproportionate and unacceptable interference, impairing the very substance of the rights guaranteed....*

c The need for a balance to be struck and the wide discretion to be enjoyed by Member States

The potential conflict between fundamental rights and economic freedoms requires a judgment as to where the balance is to be struck. This is primarily for the Member States to establish. Again, the ECJ in *Schmidberger* explained:

> *81 In these circumstances, the interests involved must be weighed having regard to all the circumstances of the case in order to determine whether a fair balance was struck between those interests.*

82 The competent authorities enjoy a wide margin of discretion in that regard. Nevertheless, it is necessary to determine whether the restrictions placed upon intra-Community trade are proportionate in the light of the legitimate objective pursued, namely, in the present case, the protection of fundamental rights....

d Does the criterion of proportionality operate to limit national authorities establishing the balance between fundamental rights in the context of their national industrial relations systems, and, if so, how?

In the *Viking* and *Laval* cases, the objective of the national authorities in Finland and Sweden, reflected in their national laws, is to protect the fundamental right to strike enshrined in their constitutions. The public policy in these cases is the interest of society in a balanced system of industrial relations, an equilibrium established by Finnish and Swedish labour law as appropriate to Finnish and Swedish conditions and consecrated by their national constitutions' protection of the right to strike. The extent of the right to strike in national law is not absolute and unqualified. It is subject to the rules on industrial action laid down in national labour law. In specifying the rules, national authorities enjoy a 'wide margin of discretion'.

For example, the right to collective action as a fundamental constitutional right may be weighed against other constitutional rights. Where other constitutional rights (social, human) are involved, the balance may be found in legislative provision for a minimum level of services to be maintained. Employers may invoke other constitutional rights of an economic nature to contest the right to collective action where the collective action is aimed at the economic existence of the employer.

However, national courts are reluctant to apply a proportionality test in cases of such conflicts, as this involves interfering with the constitutionally protected autonomy of the social partners. Procedural limitations on the right to take collective action may be assessed against constitutional or international guarantees using the criterion of proportionality. Finally, it should be noted that invoking of the proportionality principle implies the existence of a fundamental right to take collective action, to be weighed against other rights.

Conclusion

The relationship between economic freedoms of movement and fundamental social rights to collective action may be determined by an interpretation of the relevant provisions of the Treaty and secondary legislation. This interpretation must be consistent with the evolving context of the EU from a purely economic Community establishing a common market to a European Union with a social policy aimed at protecting workers employed in the common market who are also citizens of the Union enjoying fundamental rights. This overriding interpretative principle may be designated as *ordre communautaire social.* [41]

From the beginning of the European Community, improvement of living and working conditions was stipulated as a social policy objective. EU and Member State regulation of social provisions 'shall have as their objectives the promotion of employment, improved living and working conditions, so as to make possible their harmonisation while the improvement is being maintained' (Article 136 EC). This may be achieved by adoption 'by means of directives, minimum requirements for gradual implementation' (Article 137(2)(b) EC).

Additionally, since the adoption of the new social policy provisions of the Treaty of Maastricht: 'Should management and labour so desire, the dialogue between them at Community level may lead to contractual relations, including agreements' (Article 139(1) EC) and 'Agreements concluded at Community level shall be implemented...' (Article 139(2) EC). Insofar as regulation of living and working conditions is left to social dialogue, the process of negotiation between the social partners, a crucial element in this process, is Treaty protected collective action.

The interpretative framework for the Treaty provisions on free movement comprises the accumulated body of EU social and labour law, the *acquis communautaire social*, including five principles of what may be called *ordre communautaire social*:

i a universal premise of international labour law based on the Constitution of the ILO to which all Member States belong: 'labour is not a commodity';[42]

ii the activities of the Community shall include 'a policy in the social sphere' (Article 3(1)(j) EC) and the Community and the Member States 'shall have as their objectives... improved living and working conditions' (Article 136 EC);

iii respect for fundamental rights of workers reflected in the Community Charter of the Fundamental Social Rights of Workers 1989, the European Social Charter signed at Turin on 19 October 1961 (both cited in Article 136 EC), and the EU

Charter of Fundamental Rights solemnly proclaimed by the European Parliament, the European Council and the Commission at Nice on 7 December 2000;

iv the distinctive characteristic of the European social model which attributes a central role to social dialogue at EU and national levels in the form of social partnership;[43]

v the common market principle of equal treatment of all workers without discrimination based on nationality.

In brief, the law on free movement in the EU is to be interpreted in the light of *ordre comunautaire social*: labour is not a commodity like others (goods, capital), free movement is subject to the objective of improved working conditions, respecting the fundamental rights of workers as human beings, acknowledging the central role of social dialogue and social partnership at EU and national levels, and adhering to the strict principle of equal treatment without regard to nationality.

It follows that collective industrial action is not subject to the EU law on free movement where the exercise of freedom of movement involving workers (not a commodity) has the intention and/or effect of undercutting working conditions, denies the exercise by workers and their organisations of fundamental rights, undermines the central role of social dialogue and social partnership, and/or promotes unequal treatment based on nationality of the workers. In other words, the four freedoms of transnational free movement (of goods, services, establishment and workers) are to be interpreted in light of a corollary fifth freedom: the freedom of workers and their organisations to take collective action to combat social dumping.[44]

The question is whether and how far the European Court will accept restrictions on transnational collective action, or will curb such action where there is a clash with free movement in the EU. Enforcement by the ECJ of a fundamental right to take collective action, as provided in the EU Charter, may provide the key to the future of the law on industrial action, shaped in different ways over past centuries in the Member States, including the United Kingdom.

Notes

1 One UK source estimates that 40% of UK employment law derives from EU requirements. See Better Regulation Taskforce, *Employment Regulation: Striking a Balance* (2002), cited in C Kilpatrick, 'Has New Labour Reconfigured Employment Legislation?' (2003) 32 *Industrial Law Journal* 135, at p 141.

2 Case C-438/05, *Viking Line Abp OU Viking Line Eesti v The International Transport Workers' Federation, The Finnish Seamen's Union.*

3 Case C-341/05, *Laval un Partneri Ltd v Svenska Byggnadsarbetareforbundet, Svenska Byggnadsarbetareforbundet, Avdelning 1, Svenska Elektrikerforbundet.*

4 Articles 30 (goods), 39(3) (workers), 46(1) (establishment), 55 (services), 58(1) (capital).

5 Treaty establishing a Constitution for Europe adopted by the Member States in the Intergovernmental Conference meeting in Brussels, 17-18 June 2004; OJ C 310/1 of 16 December 2004.

6 Freedom of association (Article 12), right of collective bargaining and collective action (Article 28), workers' right to information and consultation within the undertaking (Article 27), freedom to choose an occupation and right to engage in work (Article 15), prohibition of child labour and protection of young people at work (Article 32), fair and just working conditions (Article 31), protection of personal data (Article 8), non-discrimination (Article 21), equality between men and women (Article 23), protection in the event of unjustified dismissal (Article 30).

7 For this reason, it is important that trade unions should have direct access to the Court to intervene, or initiate complaints before the European Court to protect fundamental rights. For a note analysing the prospects for the ETUC's obtaining the status of a "privileged applicant" under the EC Treaty, Article 230. See B Bercusson, 'The ETUC and the European Court of Justice' (2000) 6 *Transfer: European Review of Labour and Research* 720. For a longer analysis, B Bercusson, 'Public Interest Litigation in Social Policy', in H-W Micklitz and N Reich (eds), *Public Interest Litigation before European Courts* (1996), p 261.

8 In the first 30 months of its existence, up to July 2003, there were 44 citations of the Charter before the European courts. For details of these 44 cases, see the Appendix, prepared by S Clauwaert and I Schömann, in B Bercusson (ed), *European Labour Law and the EU Charter of Fundamental Rights* (2006), p 633.

9 Case C-36/02, *Omega Spielhallen- und Automatenaufstellungs-GmbH v Oberbrgermeisterin der Bundesstadt Bonn*, decided 14 October 2004.

10 Case T-54/99, paras 48 and 57.

11 Case C-540/03.

12 *Ibid*, paras 31-32.

13 *Ibid*, para 34.

14 *Ibid*, para 35.

15 *Ibid*, para 30.

16 *Ibid*, para 38.

17 '[T]he constitutional traditions and international obligations common to the Member States, the Treaty on European Union, the Community Treaties, the [ECHR], the Social Charters adopted by the Community and by the Council of Europe and the case-law of the Court... and of the European Court of Human Rights'.

18 Case C-540/03, above, para 58.

19 *Ibid*, para 60.

20 *Ibid*, para 108.

21 Footnote 74 cites a number of Opinions of other Advocates General, including that of Advocate General Tizzano in Case C-173/99, *Broadcasting, Entertainment, Cinematographic and Theatre Union (BECTU) v Secretary of State for Trade and Industry* [2001] ECR I-4881, Opinion of Advocate-General, 8 February 2001, the second citation of the Charter before the ECJ some two months after its proclamation (see below, footnote 33), and other Opinions by Advocate General Kokott herself.

22 Case C-540/03, above, para 105. This leaves open the question of when it can be said that the Member State's law is implementing Community rules; see, for example, Case C-144/04, *Werner Mangold v Rudiger Helm*, decided 22 November 2005. The Court concludes: 'consequently, they are bound, as far as possible, to apply the rules in accordance with those requirements...'. This could be read two ways. First, Member States are obliged to apply Community rules in accordance with fundamental rights. If this is not possible, their application (indeed, the Community rule itself) is challengeable as violating fundamental rights. Alternatively, Member states are obliged to apply Community rules in accordance with fundamental rights only as far as possible. If this is not possible, their application (and the Community rule) is still valid. It would seem that the first interpretation is preferable, and supported by the Court's immediately preceding statement which appears to emphasise Member States' margin of appreciation, but again only 'in a manner consistent with the requirements flowing from the protection of fundamental rights': para 104.

23 *Question 7*: If collective action by a trade union or association of trade unions is a directly discriminatory restriction under Article 43 of the EC Treaty or Regulation 4055/86, can it, in principle, be justified on the basis of the public policy exception set out in Article 46 of the EC Treaty on the basis that *(a) the taking of collective action (including strike action) is a fundamental right protected by Community law*; and/or (b) the protection of workers? *Question 8*: Does the application of a policy of an association of trade unions which provides that vessels should be flagged in the registry of the country in which the beneficial ownership and control of the vessel is situated so that the trade unions in the country of beneficial ownership of a vessel have the right to conclude collective bargaining agreements in respect of that vessel, strike a fair balance between *the fundamental social right to take collective action* and the freedom to establish and provide services, and is it objectively justified, appropriate, proportionate and in conformity with the principle of mutual recog-

nition? *Question 9*: Where: - a parent company in Member State A owns a vessel flagged in Member State A and provides ferry services between Member State A and Member State B using that vessel; - the parent company wishes to re-flag the vessel to Member State B to apply terms and conditions of employment which are lower than in Member State A; -the parent company in Member State A wholly owns a subsidiary in Member State B and that subsidiary is subject to its direction and control; - it is intended that the subsidiary will operate the vessel once it has been re-flagged in Member State B with a crew recruited in Member State B covered by a collective bargaining agreement negotiated with an ITF affiliated trade union in Member State B; - the vessel will remain beneficially owned by the parent company and be bareboat chartered to the subsidiary; - the vessel will continue to provide ferry services between Member State A and Member State B on a daily basis; a trade union established in Member State A takes collective action so as to require the parent and/or subsidiary to enter into a collective bargaining agreement with it which will apply terms and conditions acceptable to the union in Member State A to the crew of the vessel even after re-flagging and which has the effect of making it pointless for the parent to re-flag the vessel to Member State B, does that collective action strike a fair balance between *the fundamental social right to take collective action* and the freedom to establish and provide services and is it objectively justified, appropriate, proportionate and in conformity with the principle of mutual recognition?

24 By analogy with Case C-67/96; with Joined Cases C-115/97, C-116/97 and C-117/97, *Albany International BV v Stichting Bedrijfspensioenfonds Textielindustrie* [1999] ECR I-5751.

25 By analogy with Case C-112/00, *Eugen Schmidberger, Internationale Transporte und Planzuge v Republic of Austria* [2003] ECR I-5659.

26 OJ C 364/1. The Preamble to the Charter states: 'This Charter reaffirms, with due regard for the powers and tasks of the Community and the Union and the principle of subsidiarity, the rights as they result, in particular, from the constitutional traditions and international obligations common to the Member States, the Treaty on European Union, the Community Treaties, the European Convention for the Protection of Human Rights and Fundamental Freedoms, the Social Charters adopted by the Community and by the Council of Europe and the case law of the Court of Justice of the European Communities and of the European Court of Human Rights'.

27 By early 2001 there were already 43 references to the EU Charter of December 2000 in EU legislation: J Kenner, *EU Employment Law: From Rome to Amsterdam and Beyond* (2003), p 512, note 11.

28 Part II of the proposed Treaty establishing a Constitution for Europe incorporates the EU Charter. Treaty establishing a Constitution for Europe adopted by the Member States in the Intergovernmental Conference meeting in Brussels 17-18 June 2004; OJ C 310/1 of 16 December 2004. Article 28 became Article II-88 of the Constitutional Treaty.

29 See a detailed commentary on Article 28 of the Charter initially drafted by Bruno Veneziani, University of Bari, Italy, based on detailed discussions in

the European Trade Union Institute's (ETUI) Research Group on Transnational Trade Union Rights, and finally edited in B Bercusson (ed), *European Labour Law and the EU Charter of Fundamental Rights* (2006), p 291.

30 P Craig and G de Búrca, *EU Law: Text, Cases and Materials* (3rd ed, 2003), ch 8. The argument that the EU legal order protects the fundamental right to take collective action, reflected in Article 28 of the EU Charter, is supported by an Opinion of 8 February 2001 of Advocate General Tizzano concerning a complaint that UK legislation denied certain workers a right to paid annual leave. While 'formally, [the EU Charter of Fundamental Rights of December 2000] is not in itself binding' (paragraph 27), he states unequivocally: (paragraph 28) 'I think therefore that, in proceedings concerned with the nature and scope of a fundamental right, the relevant statements of the Charter cannot be ignored; in particular, we cannot ignore its clear purpose of serving, where its provisions so allow, as a substantive point of reference for all those involved - Member States, institutions, natural and legal persons - in the Community context. Accordingly, I consider that the Charter provides us with the most reliable and definitive confirmation of the fact that the right to paid annual leave constitutes a fundamental right'. Case C-173/99, *BECTU*, above.

31 Question 1: 'Where a trade union or association of trade unions takes collective action against a private undertaking so as to require that undertaking to enter into a collective bargaining agreement with a trade union in a particular Member State which has the effect of making it pointless for that undertaking to re-flag a vessel in another Member State, does that action fall outside the scope of Article 43 of the EC Treaty and/or Regulation 4055/86 by virtue of the EC's social policy including, inter alia, Title XI of the EC Treaty and, in particular, by analogy with the Court's reasoning in Case C-67/96 *Albany* [1996] ECR I-5751, paras. 52-64'.

32 Case C-67/96, *Albany, ibid.*

33 However, he went on to posit a number of detailed conditions on which collective agreements were lawful.

34 Paras 59-60: 'Certain restrictions of competition are inherent in collective agreements between organisations representing employers and workers. However, the social policy objectives pursued by such agreements would be seriously undermined if management and labour were subject to Article [81(1)] of the Treaty when seeking jointly to adopt measures to improve conditions of work and employment. It therefore follows from an interpretation of the provisions of the Treaty as a whole which is both effective and consistent that agreements concluded in the context of collective negotiations between management and labour in pursuit of such objectives must, by virtue of their nature and purpose, be regarded as falling outside the scope of Article [81(1) EC]'.

35 *Albany*, above, paras 158-159. In support of this view the Advocate General argued: (paragraphs 138-139) '138 The Court's case-law gives more guidance on the general question whether Community law recognises [*inter alia*, 'the general right of a trade union or association to take collective action in

order to protect occupational interests']. The Court has consistently held that 'fundamental rights form an integral part of the general principles of law whose observation the Court ensures. For that purpose the Court draws inspiration from the constitutional traditions common to the Member States and from the guidelines supplied by international treaties for the protection of human rights on which the Member States have collaborated or of which they are signatories [Opinion 1/94, [1996] ECR I-1759, paragraph 33].' The European Convention has special significance in that respect. [Case C-260/89, ERT [1991] ECR I-2925, paragraph 41 of the judgment]. 139 In *Union Syndicale, Massa and Kortner* [Case 175/73 [1974] ECR 917, para 14 of the judgment] the Court stated: 'Under the general principles of labour law the freedom of trade union activity recognised under Article 24a of the Staff Regulations means not only that officials and servants have the right without hindrance to form associations of their own choosing, but also that these associations are free to do anything lawful to protect the interests of their members as employees. Thus, the Court arguably recognised, first, the individual right to form and join an association and, secondly, the collective right to take action. The fundamental nature of those two rights was confirmed in *Bosman* with respect to freedom of association in general [Case C-415/93, [1995] ECR I-4921, paras 79 and 80 of the judgment] and in *Maurissen* more specifically with regard to trade unions [Joined Cases C-193/87 and C-194/97, *Maurissen and European Public Service Union v Court of Auditors* [1990] ECR I-95, paras 11 to 16 and 21 of the judgment].'

36 *Ibid*, paras 143-145. The full quotation from the Advocate General's Opinion is as follows: 'Taking first the ECHR, the central relevant right guaranteed by the Convention (Article 11) is the individual right to form or to join a trade union... As regards the right of trade unions to take collective action, the European Court of Human Rights relied on the phrase 'for the protection of his interests' in Article 11(1) of the ECHR in holding that freedom of association included the rights that were 'indispensable for the effective enjoyment or 'necessarily inherent elements of trade union freedom. [*National Union of Belgian Police v Belgium*, 27 October 1975, Eur Court HR Rep, Series A, 19 (1975), paragraph 39.] Article 11 therefore also 'safeguards the freedom to protect the occupational interests of trade union members by trade union action, the conduct and development of which the Contracting States must both permit and make possible. [*National Union of Belgian Police v Belgium*, paragraph 40.] However, that apparently broad statement seems to cover only a core of specific activities... nor does Article 11 necessarily imply a right to strike, since the interests of the members can be furthered by other means. [*Schmidt and Dahlstrom v Sweden*, 6 February 1976, Eur Court HR Rep Series A, 21 (1976) paragraph 36.]'. This narrow view of Article 11 ECHR may need to be reconsidered in light of the European Court of Human Rights' subsequent decision in *Wilson v United Kingdom*, [2002] IRLR 128, decided 2 July 2002. The European Social Charter (ESC) is the sibling of the ECHR, adopted in 1961 by the Council of Europe, and dealing with social and eco-

nomic rights. Of particular importance is Article 6(4) which makes provision for the right to strike. The leading text on the European Social Charter describes Article 6(4) as a 'landmark in international labour law. It represents the first occasion on which the right to strike was expressly recognised by a treaty in force'. D Harris and J Darcy, *The European Social Charter* (2nd ed, 2001), p 104.

37 According to Gernigon et al, since 1952 the Freedom of Association Committee has recognised: 'the right to strike to be one of the principal means by which workers and their associations may legitimately promote and defend their economic and social interests'. They continue in the following terms: "Over the years, in line with this principle, the Committee on Freedom of Association has recognised that strike action is a right and not simply a social act...". B Gernigon, A Odero and H Guido, 'ILO Principles Concerning the Right to Strike' (1998) 137 *International Labour Review* 441, 443. There is also a fuller account in ILO, *Freedom of Association – Digest of Decisions and Principles of the Freedom of Association Committee of the Governing Body of the ILO* (4th ed, 1996).

38 Case C-112/00, *Schmidberger*, above, para 16.

39 *Ibid*, para 51.

40 'First, whilst the free movement of goods constitutes one of the fundamental principles in the scheme of the Treaty, it may, in certain circumstances, be subject to restrictions for the reasons laid down in Article 36 [now 30] of that Treaty or for overriding requirements relating to the public interest...'. *Ibid*, paragraph 78.

41 The ECJ recognised the implications of this transformation for the nature of the EU in a case concerning the exclusion of part-time workers from supplementary occupational pension schemes. As formulated by the national court posing the question for the ECJ, the claim for a retrospective application of the principle of equal pay would risk distortion of competition and have a detrimental economic impact on employers. Nonetheless the Court concluded: '...it must be concluded that the economic aim pursued by Article 119 of the Treaty, namely the elimination of distortions of competition between undertakings established in different Member States, is secondary to the social aim pursued by the same provision, which constitutes the expression of a fundamental human right'. (Case C-50/96, *Deutsche Telekom AG v Schroder* [2000] ECR I-743, paragraph 57). Economic provisions of the Treaty have come to be re-interpreted in light of changes in the scope of activities of the EU. "The Treaty competition rules are porous: the very scope of Article 81(1) is influenced by policy objectives located elsewhere in the framework of EC law and policy. It is worth recalling that both Articles 28 and 49 on the free movement of goods and services respectively offer similar insight into the way in which the Court interprets EC trade law in a manner that seeks to avoid trampling other regulatory objectives underfoot". S Weatherill, *Cases and Materials on EU Law* (6th ed, 2003), p 526. The ECJ's decision in *Albany* is a crucial illustration where the Court acknowledged that the EU Treaty provisions on competition policy must be conditioned by other Treaty provisions on social policy; specifi-

cally, collective action in the form of collective bargaining/social dialogue.

42 The Philadelphia Conference of 1944 adopted a Declaration defining the aims of the International Labour Organisation subsequently incorporated into the ILO Constitution which affirmed: 'labour is not a commodity'. The Preamble to the Community Charter of the Fundamental Social Rights of Workers of 1989 states: 'Whereas inspiration should be drawn from the Conventions of the International Labour Organisation...'.

43 See B Bercusson and N Bruun, *European Industrial Relations Dictionary* (2005), especially pp 4-11.

44 Though not tested, the implication is that this fifth freedom is capable of direct effect. At least vertical direct effect, so that if national law were to restrict collective action combating social dumping, such national law violates EC law. Indeed, a State failing to take action to prevent social dumping violates its Treaty obligations to respect this freedom (Case C-265/95, *Commission v France* [1997] ECR I-6959).

Chapter Eleven

British Trade Union Rights Today and the Trade Union Freedom Bill

John Hendy and Gregor Gall

Introduction

At its annual congress in September 2005, the TUC unanimously endorsed Composite 1 which, amongst other things, called for a Trade Union Freedom Bill.[1] Later that month, by a majority of 70% to 30%, the Labour Party conference passed a resolution calling for the freedom for workers to take solidarity action.[2] These were momentous decisions for the British labour movement, the significance of which had just been demonstrated by the Gate Gourmet dispute, where the effect of the current legal restrictions rendering unions virtually impotent to protect their members against aggressive employer tactics was starkly highlighted.

Gate Gourmet – A Very British Coup

At Gate Gourmet, on 10 August 2005, 667 low paid workers, mostly middle-aged Asian women, and mostly members of the TGWU, gathered in the works canteen to discuss the implications of the introduction by the company that day of 130 agency workers on lower rates of pay than themselves. Whilst their union representatives were talking to management, the workers in the canteen were instructed by megaphone to return to work within three minutes or be sacked. Those who failed to return to work (virtually all) were sacked. Those who turned up the next day were given the choice of signing new contracts on worsened terms or being unemployed. According to the *Daily Mirror*,[3] the introduction of the agency workers to provoke a dispute and hence justify dismissals was a pre-planned stratagem to reduce the size of the workforce, and the pay and conditions of those who remained, the subtext of which was to boost profitability.[4]

British Airways at Heathrow had, in 1997, hived off its in-flight food operation on a 10 year contract to Gate Gourmet (which had provided management services for the in-flight catering since 1982). Gate Gourmet is a trans-national corporation dedicated to in-flight catering with, in 2005 according to its website, 109 kitchens in 29 countries and employing 22,000 employees. In 2002, it had been taken over by the Texas Pacific Group. Gate Gourmet supplied all BA's onboard catering on flights from the UK. After the hive-off, BA remained Gate Gourmet's major UK customer.

The anger and shock of the Gate Gourmet workers at the employer's tactics quickly reverberated round their communities, home to many airport workers including many BA baggage handlers. BA baggage handlers and some check-in staff walked out in support for of the sacked Gate Gourmet workers for a day on 12 August, with the effect that BA flights ground to a halt and the airline lost, it is said, some £40 million in the process. The strike became the national news event of August 2005. Gate Gourmet was brought to the negotiating table under pressure from BA, in consequence of the pressure of the action by their baggage handlers and check-in staff. Ironically, according to the TGWU, it had been intervention by BA which had induced Gate Gourmet to seek to lower its costs by worsening terms and conditions and reducing the size of the workforce. Both the baggage handlers and the check-in staff were TGWU members.

The strike by the Gate Gourmet workers had the effect of preventing BA flights flying with catering for over a month. It remained a significant news story with much support for those who had lost their jobs and much dismay at the employer's tactics. But the relatively poor settlement which the TGWU was able to negotiate at Gate Gourmet reflected the former's inability, after the 24 hour walkout at BA, to exert sufficient industrial leverage on Gate Gourmet or BA to better the terms or get the bulk of the sacked workers reinstated. Of the 813 workers sacked, 272 were reinstated and 411 given the equivalent of their redundancy entitlement. For 130 there was neither employment nor compensation. In short, Gate Gourmet was able to shed 541 workers' jobs by paying the equivalent of redundancy to 411.[5] Despite the high-profile nature of the dispute, the political leverage this created, the damage to its business reputation, and pressure from BA (conscious of its own public image as well as suffering the diminished service provided by Gate Gourmet – as well, of course, as being nervous of further unofficial action by its own staff), Gate Gourmet, even as sole UK supplier to BA of in-flight catering was able to dig in its heels and ride out the storm. It claims that its services returned to normal by December 2005 in spite of much campaigning, lobbying, press work and protesting outside its Heathrow factory.

The stoppage in the Gate Gourmet canteen prior to the dismissal was of course – by reason of its immediacy - un-balloted and not preceded by the statutory notices required by ss.226, 226A, 231A, and 234A Trade Union and Labour Relations (Consolidation) Act 1992 (as amended) ('the Act'). Accordingly, the union, consequently deprived of statutory protection of s 219 for calling or supporting such industrial action, was obliged to repudiate it under s. 26, so as to protect against any residual damages claims.[6] A further consequence was that since the action was neither lawful nor official, the very limited right to claim unfair dismissal (ss 238 and 238A) for those dismissed for taking official lawful industrial action was not available to the Gate Gourmet workers.[7]

Yet further, s 233(3)(a) made it impossible for the union to restore legal protection by holding a ballot and serving notices because there appeared to have been a 'prior call' to participate in the industrial action without the support of a ballot and statutory notices. Repudiation of such a prior call by the union pursuant to s 21 provides no answer to this twist.[8]

So far as the BA check-in staff and baggage handlers were concerned, their action was likewise un-balloted and not preceded by the statutory notices. The union had to repudiate it for that reason in order to protect against the very real danger of a damages claim by BA (and perhaps others). As importantly, the action was also 'secondary' action. Whilst no doubt, had there been time,[9] these workers could have been balloted (and appropriate notices served), that would not have afforded the TGWU legal immunity since balloted or not, ss 224 and 244 make it unlawful in all circumstances for a union to organise or support industrial action of any kind against an employer which is not party to the primary dispute. Had the dispute occurred whilst Gate Gourmet was part of BA, these latter provisions would not, of course, have posed a problem. The case illustrates how the increasing practice of hiving off and contracting out (in both the public and private sectors) brings with it the unavoidable and insurmountable hurdle of the unlawfulness of secondary action, a point made forcefully by the International Labour Organisation in heavily criticising this (amongst many other) aspects of the UK's industrial action and trade union laws.[10]

The Gate Gourmet case shows, as many other disputes have over the last quarter century, the degree to which the anti-union laws of the Thatcher era remain in place to deny workers and their unions the ability to mobilise to create effective countervailing power against management prerogative. It perfectly illustrates the accuracy of Tony Blair's analysis in 1997 that the changes Labour intended to bring about 'would leave British law the most restrictive on trade unions in the western world.'[11] The Gate Gourmet case demonstrates clearly the consequences of the absence of the right to strike in the UK.

And yet, whilst other European countries, in particular, have much better records than the UK in their respect for the fundamental rights of workers and unions enshrined in international law, it is instructive to see how Gate Gourmet fared in Germany.

Gate Gourmet, Germany: History Repeats Itself

Two months after sacking its British workforce, Gate Gourmet engaged in a parallel dispute at Düsseldorf airport. The charter airline carrier, LTU, had sold its in-flight catering division operating out of Düsseldorf airport to Gate Gourmet in 2001 in the wake of a restructuring programme. The catering workers previously employed by LTU then saw their wages and working conditions worsen. This pressure increased after the 2002 takeover by Texas Pacific Group of Gate Gourmet. And after three years of increasing exploitation and speed-ups, aggravated by the company's refusal to consider the union's demand for a wage increase, the workforce voted to strike. From 7 October 2005, 80 of the Gate Gourmet's 120 workers at Düsseldorf struck and set up a permanent picket line.

In Germany, official and legal strikes are only permitted when a collective bargaining agreement has expired and not during the course of one. So, following a deadlock in collective bargaining negotiations, which began in August 2005, over the renewal of their collective bargaining agreement, the workforce balloted for industrial action. The workers' union, NGG – the food, beverages and catering workers' union, called for a wage increase of 4.5% to cover inflation plus compensation for the increasingly onerous working conditions. In response to the pay and conditions claim, Gate Gourmet demanded concessions in return: an increase in working hours from 38.5 to 40, working time flexibility, and a reduction in both holiday leave (from 30 days to 25 days) and shift premiums. When the union negotiating committee refused to enter into discussions on these issues - many of which are not subject to negotiations at company level but at sectoral level - Gate Gourmet invoked the threat of redundancies.

After seven weeks, Gate Gourmet remained intransigent - taking two weeks to respond to the state arbitration agency's offer for mediation, suggesting the possibility of ending the collective bargaining agreement through de-recognition of the union, and using, as in Britain, strike-breakers from a labour agency for production and delivery of the in-flight meals. By early on in the strike, the company had spent more money withstanding and breaking the strike than the cost involved in settling the union's claim. Indeed, Gate Gourmet had been prepared to withstand the wrath of (and possible legal action by) its customers by reason of the below standard service provided by strike-breakers to Gate Gourmet - and by Gate Gourmet to LTU. This suggested that Gate Gourmet approached the dispute with the intention of inflicting a heavy defeat on the concerned workers in order to erode their terms and conditions and collective strength, and increase profitability. The wider purpose behind the strike has been to serve a stark warning to Gate Gourmet's other 22,000 workers around the world of the response they face if they oppose their employer's demands for speed-ups. 'If well organised workers in Germany and the UK can be defeated, what chance for those in cheap labour and high unemployment countries?' was the message. The drive to increase profitability, of course, was the ultimate purpose.

Although the Düsseldorf workers remained united, with many being non-German and women workers, they were isolated with some 40 of their co-workers breaking the strike. Other NGG union branches sent solidarity messages, but their members kept working, and non-union workers in Gate Gourmet's Frankfurt operation 'scabbed', providing meals for use on flights out of Düsseldorf. On 6 December 2005 and under some pressure from the strike, Gate Gourmet met with the union and came to an agreement, whereby the company's demands to increase the working hours and to reduce holidays were accommodated in return for the union's pay demands. This would not have pleased the strikers but before they were able to vote on accepting the agreement or not,

Gate Gourmet's European manager renounced the agreement under instruction from Texas Pacific Group. Gate Gourmet returned to the bargaining table on 23 December 2005 but by 6 March 2006, no progress was made and the workers remained on strike. Finally a deal was struck on 7 April 2006. Hours have been increased to 40 per week, and the remaining aspects of the deal are not what the union wanted.

The parallels with the battle between the TGWU members at Heathrow and Gate Gourmet are obvious. The same scenarios of erosion of conditions, strike provocation, strike-breaking, union busting and further erosion of conditions have been played out under the direction of a trans-national corporation. But is that where the parallels end? Both strikes were unable to bring sufficient leverage to bear on the company so that the unions were forced into making compromises of one sort or another. Why was this?

Although union and non-union members broke the strike at both Heathrow and Düsseldorf, it is not this that defeated the unions. Rather, their impotence was the direct consequence of the limitations on the right to strike in both Britain and Germany. The limitations in Britain deny unions and workers the right to aggregate their resources as companies routinely do. In Germany there is no specific legislation on strikes and the right to take industrial action is based on the guarantee of freedom of association in the Basic Law. Thus the existing law on industrial action has evolved almost entirely on the basis of court judgments, and the Federal Labour Court has created several restrictions on the right to take industrial action. Thus for example, a strike must be conducted by a union, be in pusuit of an aim that can be regulated by collective agreement, and follow the 'ultima ratio' principle of being the last resort as a means of achieving the aim in a dispute. Solidarity and sympathy strikes are consequently extremely rare and ineffectual. This rarity and ineffectualness are closely linked.

The restrictions on industrial action have been the subject of adverse findings against both Germany[12] and the UK by the supervisory bodies of international labour laws (which have been ratified by both countries). The ILO supervisory bodies have ruled that sympathetic strikes should be lawful providing that the primary strike is lawful.[13] Even the European Court of Human Rights has held that industrial action against an employer by a union which had no members employed by the employer with the intention of forcing the employer to observe a collective agreement to which neither it nor its employees were a party amounted to the pursuit 'of legitimate interests consistent with Article 11 of the Convention'.[14]

In 1998, the Council of Europe's Committee of Ministers recommended that Germany change its restrictive legal provisions on industrial action because they do not conform to the Council's European Social Charter[15] by reason that all strikes not aimed at achieving a collective agreement are banned as are strikes not endorsed by a trade union. In 1997, the Committee of Ministers made a similar recommendation to the UK in respect, in particular, of the failure of UK to protect striking workers from dismissal.[16]

What is particularly notable is that in Germany there is the positive legal right to strike whereas in Britain there is none. The right to strike is, of course, subject to restrictions in every country in which it exists. The question, always, is 'Where the limits are drawn?' It must not be assumed that the mere existence of the right to strike is a panacea for workers and their trade unions. The cases of Germany and Gate Gourmet in Germany highlight this well. Thus, the nature and complexion of the right to strike are just as important as the bare right strike to strike itself. But, in the UK, the establishment in statute of a positive right to strike would be an essential first step towards the implementation of a real right to strike in practice.

Friction Dynamics – The Forgotten Dispute

In December 2002, an employment tribunal decision in Liverpool announced that 86 workers dismissed by their former employer Friction Dynamics Ltd, a car parts manufacturer, had won their claims for unfair dismissal. They were sacked for taking strike action to resist effective de-recognition of their union, the TGWU, as a precursor to imposing adverse changes to terms and conditions of employment. The strike had been called after a ballot in favour and after service of the appropriate statutory notices. The employment tribunal held that a letter by the employer to the workers on the second day of the strike amounted to a dismissal. The tribunal rejected the employer's claim that they were not dismissed until they received a formal dismissal letter the day after eight weeks from the start of the strike. Had the tribunal accepted that, the workers would have been barred from an unfair dismissal claim because s238 provided that unfair dismissal protection only extends for eight weeks (now amended to 12 weeks) from the commencement of the action.[17]

The tribunal victory was, however, next to worthless. Their jobs were lost and reinstatement orders inconceivable because the employer went into administration in August 2003.[18] Reinstatement orders are anyway not automatic - indeed, they are only ordered in 0.04% of cases.[19] Even where reinstatement is ordered, the employer may disregard the order, though enhanced compensation will follow. There is no provision for the contempt of court proceedings, daily fines, sequestration and the other remedies for disobeying a court order which are so familiar to trade unions. The employer's insolvency had the inevitable consequence that the workers could only recover their basic awards and that compensation came from the taxpayer, not from the employer.[20] The workers remained on strike and on picket duty for two and a half years before finally calling it a day.

The obvious and probably the only way by which the union could have protected the interests of its members at Friction Dynamics, or at Gate Gourmet, would have been to call for solidarity action by fellow trade unionists employed in situations where leverage could be exerted on the employer in dispute. If the law permitted, the TGWU could have called on its members in the vehicle factories not to handle Friction Dynamics parts or called on its lorry driver members not to deliver supplies to, or collect goods from, Friction Dynamics. The union could have called on its BA baggage handler members and perhaps its delivery driver members too in the Gate Gourmet dispute. If so, it seems overwhelmingly likely that a negotiated settlement to these disputes without such destruction of jobs, terms and conditions could have taken place.

Though the Friction Dynamics case is now little more than a tale of heroic defeat known to trade union activists, Gate Gourmet, for a brief period last summer and autumn, attracted wide public and political support for the Gate Gourmet workers and sympathy for the TGWU. This public concern gave a massive impetus to the call for a Trade Union Freedom Bill, which had been first mooted in early 2005.[21]

The timing for such a Bill has a very particular resonance, as this book shows, for 2006 is the centenary of the passing of the Trade Disputes Act 1906 which secured for unions greater legal freedom to take industrial action than they enjoy today. But it is not just the historical coincidence of a centenary that makes the proposal for a Trade Union Freedom Bill so apposite and salient. The tragedy suffered by the Gate Gourmet workers in 2005 starkly summed up in a very public manner the injustices that workers have experienced over the preceding 25 years as a result of the anti-union Conservative legislation enacted in pursuit of an ideological antipathy to effective trade unionism.[22]

The Trade Disputes Act 1906 and Collective Bargaining

The freedom granted to trade unions by the 1906 Act was of course, appreciated by unions and their members at the time. But few can have realised what an impact that legal freedom would have on the conditions of life of working people. The Act gave unions an unprecedented ability to force employers to conclude collective bargains. The Act was therefore one, perhaps the most important, of the factors[23] which led to the progressive extension of collective bargaining which, by 1975 benefited some 85% of the UK workforce. Collective agreements and their normative effects, in turn paved the way for the huge improvements in the conditions of work and of life for working people in the 20th century. The Trade Disputes Act 1906 was achieved by trade union pressure both in and outside Parliament and the securing of such an Act was the key demand which had led the unions to establish the Labour Party a few years earlier (as earlier chapters in this book demonstrate).[24]

The 1906 Act was drafted in such a way as to give legal protections against judge-made anti-union law rather than establishing fundamental positive trade union rights. This drafting anomaly has allowed the freedom to organise industrial action to be characterised in the UK as a *privilege* rather than a *right*.[25] Nonetheless, despite a series of judicial and legislative attacks and modifications, the formula established by the 1906 Act substantially secured trade union freedom to take action to protect workers for three quarters of a century. In the last 25 years however, that freedom has been dramatically curtailed. Indeed, in 1906, British trade unions had far greater freedom to organise industrial action than they do today, 100 years later. For example, under the 1906 Act, they were free to organise solidarity action and were subject to none of the technicalities of ballots and notices which nowadays provide the usual peg for anti-strike injunctions[26].

It is particularly ironic that in these 100 years, British trade union law should have achieved pre-eminence as the 'most restrictive in the Western World' and that unions should have less freedom in Britain than they did 100 years earlier because during those 100 years, the UK has ratified international treaties (largely drafted by British diplomats acting on the instructions of government)[27] requiring (amongst other union rights) the guarantee of the right to strike: see ILO Convention 87 of 1949, the Council of Europe's European Social Charter of 1961, the International Covenant on Economic, Social and Cultural Rights 1966 and the Charter of Fundamental Rights of the European Union of 2000. The supervisory bodies of those treaties have held that the UK's restrictions on the right to strike are incompatible with the UK's treaty obligations.[28]

The massive restrictions on trade union freedom implemented by the Conservative governments of the 1980s and 1990s were brought about by a succession of legislation so that their impact was gradual. And alongside the sharp rise in unemployment and the defeat of many of the strongest groups of organised workers, like the miners, in well planned and often lengthy conflicts, the cumulative effect of the 'most restrictive laws in the Western World' has been profound. It has signalled and helped the reinforcement of employers' power to act unilaterally in their search for increased efficiency and profitability.

Collective Bargaining Over the Last Quarter Century

In 1979, when Mrs Thatcher came to power, around 78% of workers (some 17.5 million) had minimum terms and conditions of work negotiated by a trade union on their behalf.[29] This level of collective bargaining was a significant, perhaps the most significant, pillar maintaining working class standards of living. It also provided a minimal level of industrial democracy in workplaces, curbing the right of employers and managers to act unilaterally. From this high level of coverage, by the autumn of 2005 only 35%, some 7.0 million workers (in an expanded labour market), had that protection.[30] The remainder were left to the diktat of management and labour market forces. Thus some 16 million workers are now without the benefit of coverage of collective bargaining, the coverage of collective bargaining having been slashed by over one half over those 25 years.

What makes this all the more dramatic is that the continuing fall in collective bargaining coverage has taken place despite the introduction of the statutory recognition machinery which came into effect in June 2000. Coverage fell continuously from 1975 to 1998, reaching a low in that year of 35.3%. In anticipation and then in consequence of the introduction of the statutory recognition procedures, collective bargaining coverage then rose slightly to 36.3% in 2000 (7.2 million workers).[31] Thereafter, the trend reversed: down to 35.7% in both 2001 and 2002; 36.0% in 2003;[32] before reaching the new low of 35.3% of workers covered in 2005. By 2005 then, fewer workers were covered by collective bargaining than in 1998 - prior to the introduction of the recognition machinery and even though the union membership density rate remained the same at 35.3%.[33]

The number of workers benefiting directly from the statutory recognition machinery has been small. Cases of recognition awards by the CAC (either through balloting or membership audits) or through CAC applications being used to solicit voluntary agreements have, since June 2000, numbered just 216, covering around 100,000 workers[34]. By contrast, the number of entirely, voluntary recognition deals has been just over two thousand, covering just over one million workers[35]. Of course, many of these agreements would have been far more difficult to gain without the presence of the statutory procedure. aA swathe of employers have been susceptible to the change in employment law, whereby both a political signal and a change in employment regulation was signified by Schedule 1 of the Employment Relations Act 1999. But the number of new voluntary recognition agreements owes as much, if not more, to the efforts of the unions under the project of 'union organising' as they do to the introduction of statutory recognition. Rather than the rise in voluntary recognition agreements mechanically following the change in law, which would have seen employers approaching unions, the unions' 'union organising' activities have been able to take advantage of a relatively more favourable legal climate to extract union recognition from employers. So the change in the recognition law was necessary without being sufficient to bring about the rise in the number of new recognition agreements gained.

Although the counter-factual position of 'how much worse would the situation be without the statutory procedure?' can rightly be posed to try to get a measure of its impact, what is also evident is that the aggregate input of previously uncovered workers now becoming covered by collective bargaining is not solely or even mainly due to new recognition agreements, whether the result of the statutory procedure or not. The expansion of employment in the public sector since 1998, where there is already union recognition and collective bargaining, has contributed around 0.7million workers to the aggregate total of workers covered by collective bargaining.[36] Finally, it should be noted that the highpoint of the influence of the statutory recognition procedure passed some time ago. In 1998, 128 new deals were signed. This rose consecutively to a high point of 685 new deals in 2001 (the first full year of the procedure's operation). But, by 2005, the number of new deals signed had fallen back to 131, the level prior to the enactment of the Employment Relations Act 1999.[37] This suggests that the influence, both direct and indirect, of the statutory union recognition procedure is not sufficient to restore previous levels of collective bargaining, particularly where employers' responses are militantly anti-union.

UK collective bargaining coverage is now the lowest in Western Europe and the dramatic loss of coverage over such a short time scale appears unparalleled anywhere in the world. Comparable figures for collective bargaining coverage in 2004 in other western European countries are: Austria: 98%; Belgium, Finland, France, Italy, and Sweden: around 90%; Netherlands and Spain: 80%; Denmark: 77%; Norway: 75%; Germany 70%; and Greece 65%.[38] Coverage in many of these countries has declined over recent years but only by a few percentage points.[39]

The scale of the loss of collective bargaining coverage in the UK is, of course, not to be explained solely by the restrictions on the legal freedom on the part of unions to take action on behalf of their members: that is but one factor and there are many others.[40] On the other hand, if collective bargaining levels in the UK are to be restored to anything approaching the levels in other major western European economies, collective agreements have to be made. In the absence of law or normative government policy requiring sectoral multi-employer collective bargaining, industrial action (or its threat) is an essential, indeed the primary, means of redressing the inherent imbalance of power in the employment relationship and bringing the employer to the negotiating table.[41] The statutory recognition procedure cannot do this job. Its central feature is that it fosters enterprise level agreements of the most limited kind and it has no real teeth to force collective bargaining to occur.[42] Indeed, it was designed to accommodate an existing voluntarist or 'collective *laissez faire*' industrial relations set-up in which the pendulum of influence had clearly already swung towards the employers.

The Trade Union Freedom Bill

Trade unionism provides the fundamental means by which workers seek to redress their fundamental imbalance of power at the workplace. In doing so, trade unionism requires a minimum of legal space free from legal restraint in which to act.[43] Instead, in neo-liberal Britain, it is hemmed in by an anti-union legal regime, 'the most restrictive in the western world'. Trade union freedom of action is so legally confined as to be verging on the non-existent. What is needed, therefore, is a 'Trades Disputes Act' for 2006. It should restore to trade unions the freedom to carry out their fundamental purpose, defined by s 1 of the 1992 Act as 'the regulation of relations between workers and employers', a purpose protected by the European Convention on Human Rights which requires that trade unions are free to protect the interests of their members. In the *Wilson v UK*[44] case, the European Court of Human Rights held that:

> *It is of the essence of the right to join a trade union for the protection of their interests [guaranteed by Art11 of the European Convention on Human Rights and Fundamental Freedoms] that employees should be free to instruct or permit the union to make representations to their employer or to take action in support of their interests on their behalf. If workers are prevented from so doing, their freedom to belong to a trade union, for the protection of their interest, becomes illusory.*

The right to strike is an essential element of trade union freedom and the UK has ratified that right in the international treaties. Thus, the ILO has always held that the right to strike is fundamental (as an incident of Convention 87), and the European Social Charter, Article 6(4), as well as the International Covenant on Economic, Social and Cultural Rights 1966, Article 8(i)(d), expressly guarantee the right to strike, as does the Charter of Fundamental Rights of the EU 2000.[45]

The TUC proposal falls far short of the legal freedoms established by the Trade Disputes Act 1906 or the rights required by the UK's ratified international obligations. This is perhaps inevitable since faced with the implacable hostility of the government and the opposition parties, the TUC have sought a formula which, though not inconsistent with the breadth of the Congress resolution, does not go beyond the scope of the Labour Party resolution. Its hope is thus to attract the support of substantial numbers of Labour MPs. An Early Day Motion put down in the House of Commons and supporting a Trade Union Freedom Bill had attracted 187 signatures by October 2006 (See Appendix 4). At the same time as broadening the appeal within the House, the TUC has been conscious of the need to avoid losing the enthusiasm of the activists in the movement whose organising is necessary to create the momentum to gain the achievement of any significant part of the Trade Union Freedom Bill. The task of persuasion of all parts of the labour movement remains to be undertaken. It is this balancing of political considerations which cause us to describe the proposed Bill as modest, moderate, and mild.[46]

Of course, there is also a job, outside the law, for unions to do. To avail themselves of the possibilities which may be opened up by such legal reform embodied by the Trade Union Freedom Bill, the unions need to increase not only the formal basis of union influence, that is union membership through recruitment and organising, but they also need to increase their mobilising capacity, and thus leverage, by generating strong and cohesive workplace unionism which is knitted together by extra-workplace structures. More resources need be devoted to recruiting and organising; the TGWU has committed to spending around 10% of its expenditure to this end every year. The latter will require assertive industrial and political union leadership. A confident and vibrant union movement is needed to allow the potential of greater freedom to be turned into the actuality of greater freedom from which will be achieved the beginnings of workplace democracy and commensurate improvements in wages and conditions of workers. The high tide of the 1960s and 1970s is probably the best benchmark of union organisation to which the union movement should aspire. That is perhaps why Bob Crow, RMT general secretary, has made a plea for the re-establishment of a national shop stewards' movement.[47]

Scope of the Proposed Trade Union Freedom Bill

1 Protection for Lawful Industrial Action

The right to take industrial action is a fundamental human right guaranteed by all the international treaties cited above.[48] It is guaranteed by many European Constitutions. Its importance in redressing the imbalance of power between the worker and the employer is obvious and much written about. As the Constitutional Court of South Africa stated recently:[49]

> *[The right to strike] is of both historical and contemporaneous significance. In the first place, it is of importance for the dignity of workers who in our constitutional order may not be treated as coerced employees. Secondly, it is through industrial action that workers are able to assert bargaining power in industrial relations. The right to strike is an important component of a successful collective bargaining system.*

This echoes what was said in the highest court in the UK over 60 years ago:[50]

> *Where the rights of labour are concerned, the rights of the employer are conditioned by the rights of the men to give or withhold their services. The right of workmen to strike is an essential element in the principle of collective bargaining.*

The problem is that in Britain almost every form of industrial action constitutes a fundamental breach of contract by the worker, so entitling the employer to dismiss, discipline or sue the worker.[51] This is an infringement of individual liberty and a negation of the right to strike. The failure of UK law to protect (or even recognise) the worker's right to take lawful industrial action was highlighted in the Friction Dynamics case.

Many European national laws protect the worker's right to strike by providing that where a worker is taking lawful industrial action such action should be deemed not to break but to suspend the contract of employment. This too, is a requirement of international law binding on the UK.[52] Again and again, the absence of positive protection of the right to strike in the UK has been the subject of condemnation by the supervisory bodies of the relevant international laws.

The proposed Bill, however, does not go so far as the international laws ratified by the UK. The Bill would protect those taking lawful industrial action against being sued, sacked or otherwise penalised by the employer.

In relation to sacking, where the employer had purported to dismiss or proposed to dismiss or claimed some other form of termination of employment (eg, the legal doctrine of frustration), the termination would be set aside and rendered ineffective and unlawful unless the employer could show that the reason for termination of the worker's employment was not, to any degree, the worker's participation or proposed participation in lawful industrial action.

In relation to the imposition of a detriment on the worker by the employer, the same principle would apply that the employer would have to show that the reason for it was not, to any degree, the worker's participation or proposed participation in lawful industrial action. However, this would not invalidate the withholding of remuneration and benefits limited to that which the employee would have received had he or she not taken industrial action. It would also not prevent the employer from protecting confidential information.

This structure would permit a declaration that a threatened or purported dismissal/termination was void, and/or the granting of an injunction to restrain dismissal or other form of termination on this ground. Injunctions to restrain terminations of employment are nowadays attainable in the courts and may prove more effective than the cumbersome procedure of employment tribunals, even on interim relief applications. These measures are essential to guarantee to individual workers the freedom to take lawful industrial action (if they are prepared to forgo the wages and benefits that industrial action entails). Additionally, the proposed Bill would strengthen unfair dismissal on union grounds so as to provide automatic reinstatement to workers sacked for having taken lawful industrial action.

The existence of twin remedies here is not novel; since the beginning of the unfair dismissal scheme in 1971, employees have been able to apply both to the courts to enforce contractual rights (such as to damages for wrongful dismissal or injunctions to restrain dismissals in breach of contract), as well as to the employment tribunals to enforce the statutory rights (to claim reinstatement and compensation for unfair dismissal). Where the same issue falls to be decided the usual practice is for the employment tribunal proceedings to be stayed until the High Court case has been determined.[53]

2 Agency Replacement and Lawful Industrial Action

The proposed Bill will strengthen the law against using agency staff to break strikes, as in the Gate Gourmet dispute. The ILO has made it clear that it is a violation of Convention 87 for national law to permit the use of such staff to break lawful strikes.[54]

Already UK law prevents agencies supplying strike breakers. Regulation 7 of the Conduct of Employment Agencies and Employment Businesses Regulations 2003 bars an agency introducing or supplying a work-seeker to a hirer to perform (a) duties normally performed by a worker who is taking part in lawful industrial action ('the first worker') or (b) the duties normally performed by any other worker employed by the hirer and who is assigned by the hirer to perform the duties normally performed by the first worker. This does not apply if the agency does not know and has no reasonable grounds for knowing that the first worker is taking industrial action.

The proposed Bill would merely extend those Regulations by imposing a correlative duty on a potential hirer of agency labour to disclose the fact of industrial action, and by making it unlawful for the hirer to hire a work-seeker for such a purpose. It is to be observed that this modest provision does not catch cases where, to break the industrial action, the employer in dispute takes labour, temporarily or permanently, from a source(s) other than an agency; or where the employer in dispute shifts production elsewhere.

3 Industrial Action Injunctions

Industrial action is often stopped by a court order on an urgent application by the employer heard long before a proper trial can be arranged with all the relevant documents and witnesses.[55] An application for such an 'interim injunction' is weighted against the union because the law says that the employer has to show only that, at the stage of the urgent hearing, there is a 'serious issue to be tried' later at the full trial: the employer does not have to prove that it is likely to win at the full trial.[56] The ILO and the Council of Europe have condemned the easy way in which such interim injunctions are granted against industrial action in the UK.[57]

The injustice of this situation can be partly addressed by providing that an interim injunction shall not be granted unless it can be shown that the employer is more likely to succeed than the union at trial. This is perhaps what was intended by s 221(2) of the Act but it has been effectively ignored by the courts. Media interests benefit from a better worded constraint on interim injunctions to restrain media publication in s 12(3) of the Human Rights Act 1998, which states that no such injunction is to be granted to restrain publication before trial 'unless the court is satisfied that the applicant is likely to establish [at full trial] that publication should not be allowed'.

Trade unions also lose interim injunctions against industrial action because of the law's requirement that the judge must 'weigh the balance of convenience to see where the least risk of injustice lies pending trial.[58] This balance is heavily weighted against the union which would (unlike its members at the heart of the dispute) appear to sustain little more than a lost opportunity if the interim injunction was granted and reversed at trial, as against the employer which can invariably show it would sustain significant damage to its business and customers if the interim injunction were not granted.

The proposed Bill does not address this fundamental problem of injunction law. But it would provide some measure of redress to limit the operation of the balance of convenience rule. Thus, the Bill would specify certain duties on employers in relation to industrial action ballots and that breach of such duties would disentitle the employer to an interim injunction to stop industrial action regardless of the balance of convenience.

The first duty would be to supply information reasonably requested by the union to establish its balloting constituency of members.[59] A second set of obligations would replicate the employer's duties to allow a fair ballot on recognition set out in paragraphs 26 and 27 of Schedule 1A of the Act (and restricted there to recognition ballots, so requiring adaptation and extension to apply to industrial action ballots).

4 Scope of the Right to Strike and Definition of a Trade Dispute

The scope of the right to strike in the UK is plainly too limited, as the supervisory bodies of the relevant international treaties have made plain - repeatedly. The bar on solidarity action discussed above is the classic instance. The need for the capacity for sympathy strikes 'because of the move towards the concentration of enterprises, the globalisation of the economy and the delocalisation of work centres' noted by the ILO[60] runs in tandem with its observation that in the UK the trend to hiving down operations to associated companies increases the need for workers to be able to take solidarity action.[61] Indeed, the trend to contracting out operations to non-associated companies and the diversification of employers caused by privatisation are equally compelling factors requiring a modernisation of the law here.

The bar on solidarity action has been strongly criticised as a breach of the UK's international treaty obligations. It is worth citing the decision of the ILO Committee of Experts in 1994 (subsequently endorsed by the Council of Europe's European Social Rights Committee):

The Committee has always considered that the right to strike is one of the essential means available to workers and their organisations for the promotion and protection of their economic and social interests …

The current version of the 'immunities' is to be found in the Trade Union and Labour Relations Act 1974. The scope of these protections has been narrowed in a number of respects since 1980. The Committee notes, for example, that section 15 of the 1974 Act has been amended so as to limit the right to picket to a worker's own place of work or, in the case of a trade union official, the place of work of the relevant membership, whilst section 17 of the 1980 Act removes protection from 'secondary action' in the sense of action directed against an employer who is not directly a party to the given dispute. In addition, the definition of 'trade dispute in section 29 of the 1974 Act has been narrowed so as to encompass only disputes between workers and their own employer, rather than disputes between 'employers and workers' or 'workers and workers' as was formerly the case.

Taken together, these changes appear to make it virtually impossible for workers and unions lawfully to engage in any form of boycott activity, or 'sympathetic' action against parties not directly involved in a given dispute. …it appears to the Committee that where a boycott relates directly to the social and economic interests of the workers involved in either or both of the original dispute and the secondary action, and where the original dispute and the secondary action are not unlawful in themselves, then that boycott should be regarded as a legitimate exercise of the right to strike This is clearly consistent with the approach the Committee has adopted in relation to 'sympathy strikes'.

The Committee considers that a general prohibition of sympathy strikes could lead to abuse and that workers should be able to take such action provided the initial strike they are supporting is itself lawful.

Other changes to the definition of 'trade dispute' in the 1974 Act also appear to impose excessive limitations upon the exercise of the right to strike: (i) the definition now requires that the subject-matter of a dispute must relate 'wholly or mainly' to one or more of the matters set out in the definition - formerly it was sufficient that there be a 'connection' between the dispute and the specified matters. This change appears to deny protection to disputes where unions and their members have "mixed" motives (for example, where they are pursuing both 'industrial' and 'political' or 'social' objectives). The Committee also considers that it would often be very difficult for unions to determine in advance whether any given course of conduct would, or would not, be regarded as having the necessary relation to the protected purposes; (ii) the fact that the definition now refers only to disputes between workers and 'their' employer could make it impossible for unions to take effective action in situations where the 'real' employer with whom they were in dispute was able to take refuge behind one or more subsidiary companies who were technically the 'employer' of the workers concerned, but who lacked the capacity to take decisions which are capable of satisfactorily resolving the dispute; and (iii) disputes relating to matters outside the United Kingdom can now be protected only where the persons whose actions in the United Kingdom are said to be in contemplation or furtherance of a trade dispute relating to matters occurring outside the United Kingdom are likely to be affected in respect of one or more of the protected matters by the outcome of the dispute. This means that there would be no protection for industrial action which was intended to protect or to improve the terms and conditions of employment of workers outside the United Kingdom, or to register disapproval of the social or racial policies of a government with whom the United Kingdom had trading or economic links. The Committee has consistently taken the view that strikes that are purely political in character do not fall within the scope of the principles of freedom of association. However, it also considers that trade unions ought to have the possibility of recourse to protest strikes, in particular where aimed at criticising a government's economic and social policies... The revised definition of 'trade dispute' appears to deny workers that right.

The Committee considers that the overall effect of legislative change in this area since 1980 is to withdraw protection from strikes and other forms of industrial action in circumstances where such action ought to be permissible in order to enable workers and their unions adequately to protect and to promote their economic and social interests, and to organise their activities... Accordingly, it would ask the Government to introduce amendments which enable workers to take industrial action against their 'real' employer and which accord adequate protection of the right to engage in other legitimate forms of industrial action such as protest strikes and sympathy strikes, as guaranteed by Articles 3, 8 and 10 of the Convention.

These views have been reiterated by the ILO subsequently right up until the present date.[62]

The proposed Bill does not go so far as to meet the UK's international obligations in this respect. It proposes that, subject to clear and stringent limitations, one group of workers should have the freedom to take industrial action in support of another group of workers involved in a trade dispute. The limitation is based upon confinement of permissible solidarity action to three situations where the union reasonably believes that the employer to be subject to solidarity action has a substantial connection to the employer in dispute. This would exclude situations where industrial action was extended to employers who had no connection with the employer in dispute or to workers who had no connection to the workers in dispute. This then is a long way short of the requirement of international law. Nevertheless, these changes would hopefully ease the restrictions on international industrial action, the importance of which is growing because of increasing globalisation and the significance of which was recently highlighted in the *Viking* case concerning flags of convenience.[63]

The three permissible situations proposed by the Bill are as follows. Firstly, where the employer in primary dispute and the employer subject to solidarity action are associated employers[64] (though this phrase should have a wider definition than that in s 297 of the Act). The second situation is where a second employer is covering the work of the strikers directly or indirectly and it is suggested that rather than extend the definition of solidarity action, such a situation is covered by making it a primary dispute – see below. The third situation is directed to the Gate Gourmet scenario where a particular customer (or it could be a supplier) dominates the employer's trade to such an extent that it can and does interfere (or the union believes it has interfered) in the employer's relations with its employees by insisting on a cut in terms or conditions or redundancies or other measures which the workforce is resisting. Putting it more legally, where a trade dispute exists about a proposal or decision of the employer, rejected by the workers, and the union reasonably believes that an intervention by one of the employer's principal suppliers or customers instigated the primary employer's proposal or decision, then action would be permissible against the identified instigator.

A further change to the definition of a trade dispute (s 244) is required by reason of the Court of Appeal's interpretation of the 1992 Act as barring industrial action to obtain guarantees for the future in a TUPE situation. The court held that, in effect the action was secondary to the dispute between the existing employees and their employer because it was intended to benefit future employees as well as existing ones and was intended to bind a future employer.[65]

A further change too, is necessary to complete the reversal of a Court of Appeal comment that appeared to make unions liable for failing to ballot members who might feel impelled upon to join the industrial action even though the union had no intention of calling on them to do so.[66]

Finally, s 127, Criminal Justice and Public Order Act 1994 requires repeal. Until 1993 it was lawful for a union organising prison officers to call on them to take industrial action so long as the union (like all others) complied with the statutory regime applicable to all unions. In 1994, the then government legislated in relation to prison officers (applicable both in the public and private sectors) to bar the calling of industrial action in all circumstances. The Labour leadership opposed the introduction of the section and has in the past promised to repeal it. But repeal is now made conditional on a contractually binding no-strike collective agreement which lays open any union to legal action for breach of contract if it calls for industrial action. The collective agreement presents precisely the same restraint as the statutory prohibition. Section 127 should be repealed without any such contractually imposed no-strike requirement. There is no apparent justification for singling out this class of employees for such discriminatory treatment, which, as the ILO held in 2005, is in breach of Convention 87.[67]

5 Industrial Action Ballots

The current industrial action balloting rules are so complex and onerous that compliance is almost impossible. Moreover, the intention and reality behind their complexity has been to undermine the ability of unions to mount effective industrial action by facilitating employer counter-preparation to render any attempts to do so ineffectual. Lawful industrial action cannot, thus, utilise the 'element of surprise' or even necessarily 'striking while the iron is hot'. Both the ILO and the European Social Charter supervisory bodies have held that the complexity of UK law on industrial action and, in particular, the law on balloting for industrial action, is not consistent with the respective international obligations.

The balloting rules require radical revision. In advance of that, the Bill makes a modest but highly significant change in preventing legal action for trivial, technical, accidental breaches of the balloting provisions. The key feature would be that the accidental breach could have no effect on the outcome of the ballot. This parallels electoral law which will not entertain a challenge to an election unless it can be shown that the alleged irregularity may have changed the result of the election. The effect of such a change to union industrial action ballots would be that the accidental omission of members who should have been balloted or the inclusion of persons who should not have been, will not render the ballot invalid so long as the number wrongly omitted or wrongly included could have had no effect on the result. The Bill would simply enlarge the existing provision excusing accidental failures (s 232B) and by making s 227 subject to reasonable practicability.

Ballots before industrial action are matters of internal trade union democracy and though such a legal requirement for such a ballot is consistent with international obligations, the entitlement of employers to intervene in such matters and to sue over an alleged balloting irregularity is a serious violation of the fundamental principle of trade union autonomy.[68] However, removal of that invasive privilege at this time is thought to be a stage too far and one not so necessary if the notice provisions are simplified as suggested below.[69] The Bill also proposes a change to deal with the bar on industrial action where there has been a 'prior call' – discussed above.

6 Industrial Action Notices

The statutory regime for pre-ballot and pre-industrial action notices to employers have caused a huge amount of litigation. A huge burden on unions to keep meticulous up-to-date records of their members' addresses, jobs, and workplaces has been the consequence. In a fast changing flexible workforce, in which changes of job, workplace and home address are often frequent and always worrying, the ordinary trade union member may be forgiven for forgetting to notify union head office of the change despite the imprecations of regular circulars and union journal notices. In fact, it has become virtually impossible to fulfil the obligation to provide by way of notice:

> *a list of the categories of employee to which the affected employees belong, and a list of the workplaces at which the affected employees work [and]'the total number of the affected employees, the number of*

the affected employees in each of the categories in the [first] list mentioned, and the number of the affected employees who work at each workplace in the [other] list mentioned, [together with] information as will enable the employer readily to deduce the total number of the affected employees,' the categories of employee to which the affected employees belong and the number of the affected employees in each of those categories, and the workplaces at which the affected employees work and the number of them who work at each of those workplaces. (Section 234A(3A – 3C))

In reality, these notices are of little practical value to an employer save as a potential ground for seeking an injunction.

The Bill would repeal the current requirements for giving the statutory notice (in similar extensive terms to those quoted above) that a ballot will be held and to supply to the employer a copy of the proposed ballot paper. There never was a legitimate reason for this notice requirement; whether and when to hold a ballot of union members is a matter of internal democracy. In any event, any reasonably competent employer would be aware that a ballot is to be held: the requirement to give the employer the result of the ballot would remain.

All the onerous formalities of the notice of industrial action should be replaced by an obligation on the union to give, where reasonably practicable in the circumstances reasonably believed by the trade union to exist immediately prior to the ballot, seven days notice[70] to the employer of the proposed commencement of industrial action. Such notice should specify the class or category of workers to be called on (using the union's categorisation), the nature of the action (ie, whether a strike or action short of a strike and whether continuous or discontinuous), and when it is to start or (if interrupted, re-start). The duty to provide the simplified strike notice would apply also to solidarity action.

Conclusion

The 'level playing field' that many hoped the Blair Labour governments would introduce into employment relations, has not transpired after nine years in office. Fundamental to the 'new' Labour project for the maintenance and extension of neo-liberalism has been the continued shackling of independent trade unionism.[71] The measures in the proposed Trade Union Freedom Bill would not restore the UK to compliance with its international obligations. Nor would they address key violations of trade union freedoms which are present in the current legislation – such as the prohibition in s 174 of the 1992 Act on unions expelling fascists from membership. But they would mark a significant stride in the right direction. These measures will disappoint many in the union movement as being insufficient to reverse the incursions of the Conservative legislation. These measures do, however, create a minimum legal space for unions to act to protect the interests of their members and restore some balance of power in industrial relations. So no matter the attested justice of the case for the immediate and complete repeal of all the Conservatives' anti-union legislation, the current weakness of trade unionism in Britain compels the adoption of a strategy which at least begins the process of rolling back those restrictions and does so in a way that can help start rebuilding the union capacity to be effective in expanding again the protections of collective bargaining. The primary means for doing this is judged to be that of working for this small but significant incremental change in a way that can build the widest and deepest possible alliance between different elements in the labour and trade union movement in order to create sufficient leverage to bring about a Trade Union Freedom Act. Only consequentially will the union movement then have the influence and power to both insist on the repeal of the anti-union legislation and on the introduction of trade union laws that meet all of Britain's ratified international obligations.

Notes

1 The resolution (Composite 1) called for the Bill to 'include: the abolition of restrictive balloting and industrial notice procedures; the right to strike and the right to automatic reinstatement for taking lawful industrial action; the freedom to take solidarity action for workers who are in dispute; and sectoral forums to establish minimum terms and conditions'.

2 The resolution urged the government 'to make amendments in the law needed to avoid a repetition of [the Gate Gourmet] case in the following areas: permitting lawful supportive action at least where there is a close connection between those involved, as permitted by ILO Conventions; simplifying balloting procedures; protecting strikers from dismissal; and barring the replacement of workers in dispute.' The resolution also sought urgent action in other key areas and 'in the longer term, conference calls on the government to ensure that UK employment law fully complies with the core international labour conventions to which the UK is a signatory'.

3 *Daily Mirror*, 12 August 2005.

4 It will be recalled that the tactic of provoking a strike after preparing a strikebreaking workforce was also employed in 1986 at News International at Wapping, London.

5 Figures from the Gate Gourmet website (www.gategourmet.com/797.asp), accessed 24 March 2006.

6 Though not much damage could in reality have been sustained in the 3 minutes of action whilst the workers were in breach of contract before their dismissal.

7 Furthermore, though space does not permit investigation of the issue, the union was constrained by an interim injunction in relation to picketing; though, interestingly, the judge held that picketing engaged Arts 10 and 11 of the European Convention on Human Rights: *Gate Gourmet Ltd v TGWU* [2005] IRLR 881.

8 See *Midland Mainline Ltd v RMT* (unreported, 14 January 2005, HC).

9 It would have taken some five to six weeks to fulfil the balloting and notice provisions before being able to take strike action and this may well have prevented the union from being able to strike 'while the iron was hot' (to use Lord Diplock's expression in NWL v Woods [1979] ICR 867, at p 879) and thus bargaining leverage may have been lessened or become non-existent.

10 See ILO, *Report of the Committee of Experts on the Application of Conventions and Recommendations*, 2000, pp 290-291 (in relation to the UK and Convention 87 – repeated about the UK in almost every succeeding year). The same approach was expressed by the European Social Rights in relation to the UK and Art.6(4) of the European Social Charter: e.g. Conclusions XVI-1, pp 688-9.

11 Tony Blair writing in the *Times*, 31 March 1997. The material passages for the labour lawyer read: 'Under our proposals... there would be nothing to prevent the employer dismissing people, and still no power to force their reinstatement. What there would be is merely the right to present a claim.

It was claimed ... That employers will not be able to dismiss people on strike. Untrue. That employees will get full employment rights from their first day. Wrong. Let me state the position clearly, so that no one is in any doubt. The essential elements of the trade union legislation of the 1980s will remain. There will be no return to secondary action, flying pickets, strikes without ballots, the closed shop and all the rest. The changes that we do propose would leave British law the most restrictive on trade unions in the western world'. The latter passage is not to be confused with the variant that Britain has the most lightly regulated labour market in Western Europe, a claim made, no doubt, with the *Times* article in mind, in the White Paper, *Fairness at Work*, Cmd 3968, 1998.

12 See e.g. European Social Rights Committee, Conclusions XVII – 1, pp 11-13; XVIII – 1, pp12-13 (findings of non-conformity with Art.6(4), European Social Charter).

13 ILO, *Digest of Decisions and Principles of the Freedom of Association Committee of the Governing Body* (4th ed., 1996), para 486.

14 *Gustafsson v Sweden* [1996] 22 EHRR 409 at p 439. Nor was Sweden under an obligation under Article 11 to protect the employer against the union action: p 438. See T Novitz, [2006] *Lloyds Maritime and Commercial Law Quarterly* 242.

15 Recommendation No. R ChS (98) 2

16 Recommendation No. R ChS (97) 3.

17 Save for certain circumstances which prolong the period.

18 Though the business continued under a new guise as Dynamex Friction (BBC News (news.bbc.co.uk/1/hi/wales/north_west/3975555.stm) and A Chamberlain 'The truth about friction' *The Lawyer*, 3 November 2003.

19 Employment Tribunal Service, *Annual Report and Accounts*, 2004-5.

20 Employment Rights Act 1996, s 182.

21 By the United Campaign for the Repeal of the Anti-Union Laws, to which are affiliated 23 national unions.

22 See e.g. Lord Wedderburn, *Employment Rights in Britain and Europe* (1991), ch 8; S Auerbach, *Legislating for Conflict* (1990); P Davies and M Freedland, *Labour Legislation and Public Policy* (1993), pp 425 ff; P Smith and G Morton 'The Conservative Government's Reform of Employment Law, 1979-97: 'Stepping Stones' and the 'New Right Agenda'' (2001) 12 *Historical Studies in Industrial Relations* 131; S Deakin and F Wilkinson, *The Law of the Labour Market* (2005), ch 4.

23 Other factors included, of course, the support of government for the establishment of collective bargaining, an orthodoxy which was constant across all governments for over 80 years from the Conciliation Act 1896 onwards.

24 See also J Mortimer, *The Trade Dispute Act 1906* (Institute of Employment Rights, 2004); J Saville, chapter 4, above, and G Revell, *The Story of the Taff Vale Railway Strike* (RMT, 2006).

25 A point made during as well as immediately after the debates on the Bill: see Saville, above,. On the significance of the distinction to British trade union law see Lord Wedderburn, above, ch 4, and his *Labour Law and*

Freedom (1995), ch 1.

26 See G Gall and S McKay 'Injunctions as a legal weapon in industrial disputes' (1996) 34 *British Journal of Industrial Relations* 567, and G Gall 'Injunctions as a legal weapon in industrial disputes, 1995-2005' (2006) 44 *British Journal of Industrial Relations* 327.

27 The UK was instrumental in the founding of the ILO and in setting up its structures, in drafting the key Conventions and, in respect of Conventions 87 and 98 was the first government to ratify both (on 27t June 1949 and 30 June 1950, respectively) see A Alcock, *History of the International Labour Organisation* (1972); M Stewart, Britain and the ILO: the Story of Fifty Years (1969).; K D Ewing, *Britain and the ILO* (Institute of Employment Rights, 2nd ed., 1994).

28 See T Novitz, *International and European Protection of the Right to Strike* (2003); K. D. Ewing, above.

29 S Milner, 'The coverage of Collective Pay-setting institutions in Britain, 1895-1990' (1995) 33 *British Journal of Industrial Relations* 69. This includes terms set by institutions to which trade unions were parties such as Wages Councils.

30 H Grainger *Trade Union Membership 2005* (DTI, 2006), p 12 and table 28, p 39. This conclusion from the Labour Force Survey is supported by the WERS survey: B Kersley, C Alpin, J Forth, A Bryson, H Bewley, G Dix and S Oxenbridge, *Inside the Workplace: First Findings from the 2004 Workplace Employment Relations Survey* (DTI, 2005), p 20, found that in 2004, 35% of employees had their pay set by collective bargaining and 57% by management alone. Plainly the inability of unions to collectively bargain for members is one of the principal reasons for the decline in trade union membership since 1979. In 2004, there were 7,559,062 trade union members: *Annual Report of the Certification Officer*, 2005. In 1979, there had been 13.2 million trade union members: *Annual Report of the Certification Officer*, 1980.

31 Note the dramatic rise in the number of recognition deals recorded in the TUC survey, *Focus on Recognition*, 2004, p 2, where the number of deals doubled in 1999 over 1998, doubled again in 2000 and more than doubled in 2001, after which the number began to drop.

32 In 2003, because a fluctuation in the size of the overall workforce, although the percentage rose slightly, the actual number of workers covered (even more) slightly declined, i.e., 7.3m in 2002 to 7.2m in 2003.

33 That is an important observation for it has become apparent that the introduction of the statutory recognition machinery slowed and perhaps halted the spate of de-recognition initiatives of employers in the late 1990s. The extent to which an easing of the restrictions on trade unions organising secondary industrial action might allow unions to prevent de-recognition and so maintain collective bargaining coverage must therefore be in grave doubt. On the other hand, such an easing of restrictions would allow unions to seek to extend collective bargaining coverage.

34 G Gall, 'Trade Union Recognition in Britain – An Emerging Crisis for Trade Unions?' (2007) 28 *Economic and Industrial Democracy*, 88.

35 *Ibid.*

36 National Statistics Online, available at www.statistics.gov.uk/cci/nugget.asp?id=407. Figure for 1998-2005.

37 G. Gall, 'Trade Union Recognition in Britain', 89 above. The TUC record in their *Focus on Recognition* (April 2006), 61 deals (voluntary and statutory) for the year to October 2005 down from 179 the previous year and 166 for the year to October 2003. By March 2005, the CAC had received 444 applications in the fifth year of operation of the statutory mechanism. Of these, 46 resulted in recognition without a ballot and 70 in recognition after a ballot (out of 110 – 'a significant failure rate' as P Smith and G Morton point out in 'Nine Years' New Labour: Neo-Liberalism and Workers' Rights', (2006) 44 *British Journal of Industrial Relations* 401). Consequently, the interpretation of the impact of the statutory union recognition put forward by J Blanden, S Machin and J van Reenen in 'Have Unions Turned the Corner? New Evidence on Recent Trends in Union Recognition in UK Firms' (2006) 44 *British Journal of Industrial Relations* 169 is somewhat erroneous. Indeed, the Workplace Employment Relations Survey (WERS4/WERS 2004) confirms this (see B Kersley, C Alpin, J Forth, A Bryson, H Bewley, G Dix, and S Oxenbridge, *Inside the Workplace: Findings from the 2004 Workplace Employment Relations Survey* (2006), pp 120-122.

38 European Industrial Relations Observatory, *Collective Bargaining and Extension Procedures*, May 2005, available at www.eiro.eurofound.eu.int.

39 European Industrial Relations Observatory, *Collective Bargaining and Extension Procedures*, December 2002, available at www.eiro.eurofound.eu.int.

40 In particular the never ending loss of jobs in the traditionally well organised sectors such as manufacturing where 1m jobs have been lost since 1997 (*Guardian*, 17 March 2005).

41 As Kahn-Freund wrote: 'the main object of labour law has always been, and I venture to say will always be, to be a countervailing force to counteract the inequality of bargaining power which is inherent and must be inherent in the employment relationship'. (*Labour and the Law* (2nd edn., 1977), p.6 and see K. Klare, 'Countervailing Workers' Power as a Regulatory Strategy' and R. Welch, 'Into the Twenty First Century – the Continuing Indispensability of Collective Bargaining as a Regulator of the Employment Relation", both in H Collins, P Davies, and R Rideout, *Legal Regulation of the Employment Relation* (2000).

42 P Smith and G Morton (2001) 29 *British Journal of Industrial Relations* 119; S Wood, S Moore and K Ewing, 'The Impact of the Trade Union Recognition Procedure under the Employment Relations Act 2000-2002', in H Gospel and S Wood (eds), *Representing Workers: Trade Union Recognition and Membership in Britain* (2003); S Moore, 'Union Mobilization and Employer Counter Mobilisation in the Statutory Recognition Process', in J Kelly and P Willman (eds), *Union Organisation and Activity* (2004).

43 K D.Ewing, 'The Function of Trade Unions' (2005) 34 *Industrial Law*

Journal 1.

44 [2002] IRLR 128.

45 Though the latter is said to be subject to national laws and practices – whatever that means. Other instruments are as unequivocal as the European Social Charter and the International Covenant, eg Art.9 (3) of the Copenhagen Declaration of the Conference on Security and Co-operation in Europe. The modern, democratic Constitution of the Republic of South Africa follows the example of many western European States and embeds the right to strike in it (indeed in the Bill of Rights within it).

46 A Parliamentary draftsperson has said that the use of the word 'Freedom' in the title of the proposed Bill is objectionable because it is a slogan. This perhaps overlooks the use of the word in the Freedom of Information Act or in the European Convention on Human Rights and Fundamental Freedoms. A more substantial objection might be that the Bill will not achieve trade union freedom and that accuracy might require that it be entitled the 'Trade Union Restricted Freedom Bill'.

47 This plea was made at the RMT conference, 'The Crisis of Working Class Representation', 21 January 2006, Friends' Meeting House, London. At a second RMT conference in November 2006 a decision was taken to establish a Steering Committee to assist in organising a national shop stewards conference in 2007.

48 See T. Novitz, above, and the references therein.

49 *NUMSA v Bader Pop (Pty) Ltd* 2003 (3) SA 513.

50 Lord Wright in *Crofter Hand Woven Tweed v Harris* [1942] AC 435 at p 463.

51 *British Telecommunications plc v Ticehurst* [1992] ICR 383; (save for the exceptional circumstances of a case like *Burgess v Stevedoring Services Ltd (Bermuda)* [2002] UKPC 39): *Miles v Wakefield MDC* [1987] ICR 368, per Lord Templeman; *Wiluszynski v Tower Hamlets LBC* [1989] IRLR 259; *NCB v Galley* [1958] 1 WLR 16.

52 Thus, the UN Committee on Economic, Social and Cultural Rights held in 1997 and reiterated in 2002, in its regular reviews of the UK: 'that failure to incorporate the right to strike into domestic law constitutes a breach of Article 8 of the Covenant. The Committee considers that the common law approach recognising only the freedom to strike, and the concept that strike action constitutes a fundamental breach of contract justifying dismissal, is not consistent with protection of the right to strike. The Committee does not find satisfactory the proposal to enable employees who go on strike to have a remedy before a tribunal for unfair dismissal. Employees participating in a lawful strike should not ipso facto be regarded as having committed a breach of an employment contract . . . The Committee recommends that the right to strike be established in legislation, and that strike action does not entail any more the loss of employment, and it expresses the view that the current notion of freedom to strike, which simply recognises the illegality of being submitted to an involuntary servitude, is insufficient to satisfy the requirements of Article 8 of the Covenant . . .'

53 See *Carter v Credit Change Ltd* [1979] IRLR 361 and *Jacobs v Norsalta*

Ltd [1977] ICR 189; *Cahm v Ward and Goldstone Ltd* [1979] ICR 574; and *Warnock v Scarborough Football Club* [1989] ICR 489. Cf. *Automatic Switching Ltd v Brunet* [1986] ICR 542.

54 The hiring of workers to break a strike in a sector which cannot be regarded as an essential sector in the strict sense of the term, and hence one in which strikes might be forbidden, constitutes a serious violation of freedom of association: ILO, *Digest of Decisions and Principles*, above, para 570.

55 See G Gall, 'Injunctions as a Legal Weapon in Industrial Disputes in Britain 1995-2005', above.

56 *American Cyanamid Ltd. v Ethicon Ltd.* [1975] AC 396 at p 407 and on the perennial problem of the labour injunction in trade union law see the seminal chapter by Lord Wedderburn, *Employment Rights in Britain and Europe* (1991), ch 7.

57 Thus, the Council of Europe's Social Rights Committee held, in relation to the UK, in 1992: 'It is open to an employer to seek an interlocutory injunction in cases where a strike may be unlawful and that such an injunction may be granted provided the employer can show that there is a case to answer, without the court deciding the issue on the merits. Thus, any removal of "immunities" provides for more situations where a strike may be halted, quickly, reducing the effectiveness of the right to strike in achieving collective agreement'. And the ILO Committee of Experts held in 1994, in relation to the UK: 'The common law renders virtually all forms of strikes or other industrial action unlawful as a matter of civil law. This means that workers and unions who engage in such action are liable to be sued for damages by employers (or other parties) who suffer loss as a consequence, and (more importantly in practical terms) may be restrained from committing unlawful acts by means of injunctions (issued on both an interlocutory and a permanent basis). It appears to the Committee that unrestricted access to such remedies would deny workers the right to take strikes or other industrial action in order to protect and to promote their economic and social interests'.

58 That is, whether the least risk of injustice lies in the grant of the injunction in the event that it turns out at trial that it should not have been granted; or in not granting the injunction in the event that it turns out at trial that it should have been granted.

59 The fact that this was a statutory duty would overcome any objection under the Data Protection Act 1998.

60 See ILO, *Freedom of Association and Collective Bargaining (the General Survey of the Committee of Experts)*, above, para 168.

61 See ILO, *Report of the Committee of Experts on the Application of Conventions and Recommendations*, 2000, pp 290-291 (in relation to the UK and Convention 87 – repeated about the UK in almost every succeeding year). The same approach was expressed by the European Social Rights in relation to the UK and Art 6(4) of the European Social Charter: e.g. Conclusions XVI-1, p 688-9.

62 See, for example, the Observation on the UK made by the ILO Committee of Experts in 2004, International Labour Conference, 75th Session, which

stresses that: 'workers should be able to participate in sympathy strikes, provided the initial strike they are supporting is lawful, and to take industrial action in relation to matters which affect them even though the direct employer may not be a party to the dispute, and requests the Government to continue to keep it informed in its future reports of developments in this respect'.

63 *Viking Line ABP v ITF* [2006] IRLR 58.

64 Thus, overcoming the artificiality established in *Dimbleby & Sons Ltd v NUJ* [1984] ICR 386.

65 *University College London Hospital NHS Trust v UNISON* [1999] ICR 204.

66 *RMT v Midland Mainline Ltd* [2001] IRLR 813 at 816. Section 227 was amended in 2004 to reverse this, but a parallel amendment is required of s 232A (b).

67 Since it did not offer – at the least – binding arbitration or mediation in place of the right to strike.

68 A privilege granted by ss 219(4) and 232A of the 1992 Act. ILO Convention 98, Art 2 bars interference by employers in the establishment, functioning and administration of unions.

69 It should be noted that s 62 gives the right to members to bring legal action to enforce the statutory balloting regime. The Institute of Employment Rights Group of Experts have proposed that that right should be replaced by a right to sue only on the rule-book and that every rule-book would, by statutory requirement, contain a simplified balloting code which could later replace the statutory regime.

70 Given the difficulties of the concept of 'reasonable practicability', some members of the group thought that 3 days was preferable.

71 See K D Ewing, 'The Function of Trade Unions', above; A Milburn and D Coats, 'Why trades unions need a clause 4 moment, *Financial Times*, 2 March 2006, illustrates perfectly the New Labour view of 'modern' trade unionism and its philosophical underpinnings described in P Smith and G Morton, (2006) 44 *British Journal of Industrial Relations* 401.

Chapter Twelve

The Economic Case for the Trade Union Freedom Bill.

Simon Deakin and Frank Wilkinson

Introduction

THE Trade Disputes Act 1906 created a space within which trade unions could organise free from the legal restraints which had been imposed upon them for much of the 19th century. The vital first step was taken in 1875, when the trade dispute 'immunities' were first set out in the Conspiracy and Protection of Property Act of that year. This gave unions freedom from the common law of criminal conspiracy in respect of actions taken 'in contemplation or furtherance of a trade dispute'. The 1906 Act essentially extended the trade dispute formula to cover the economic torts. Together, these laws had a major impact. Although membership stagnated and even fell in some years of the 'Great Depression' of the 1870s and 1880s, it doubled between 1905 and 1914, and doubled again by 1920. This was a critical period which saw the extension of union membership and collective bargaining into previously under-organised sectors, in particular transport and services. Unions recruited more consistently than before among women and those in lower paid occupations. Without the freedoms guaranteed by the Trade Disputes Act 1906, this would have been impossible.

The Economic Context

A defining feature of the economic context for developments in union memberships was a series of inflationary cycles which arose from the interaction of collective bargaining, increased employment taxation, and full employment policy. The process began as a consequence of the growing institutionalisation of collective bargaining in the early 20th century. As collective bargaining was put into place at the end of the 19th century and gradually extended downwards to increased numbers of workers in the course of the 20th century, earnings' differentials significantly narrowed. Between 1913/14 and 1978, the percentage pay differential separating higher professionals from the lower skilled occupations more than halved (see Table 1). However, the erosion of the pay gap was not a steady, continuous progress. The narrowing effect was mainly confined to periods of high inflation: 1913/14-24, 1935/6-55/6, and 1960-78. In periods when prices were growing more slowly, the process of equalisation was reversed: this was the case between 1922 and 1936 and 1956 and 1960. Since 1980, the process has been even more marked. Figure 1 reports the changing differential in the average of the median earnings of male employees for representative high and low paid occupations, drawn from the New Earnings Survey. Between 1979 and 1989 the gap between high and low paid occupations widened from 85% to 146%, and by 2000 it had widened further to 163%.

Table 1. Skill differentials 1913/14 to 1978: percentage of earnings of lower skilled manual worker (male workers)

	1913/14	1922/4	1935/6	1955/6	1960	1970	1978
Higher professionals	521	455	492	354	380	254	244
Higher skilled manual worker	168	141	151	143	149	125	128
Lower skilled manual worker	100	100	100	100	100	100	100

Source, G. Routh, *Occupation and Pay in Great Britain* (2nd Edition, Macmillan, 1980)

Figure 1 . Earnings differentials: earnings of high paid occupations as percentage of earning of low paid occupation.

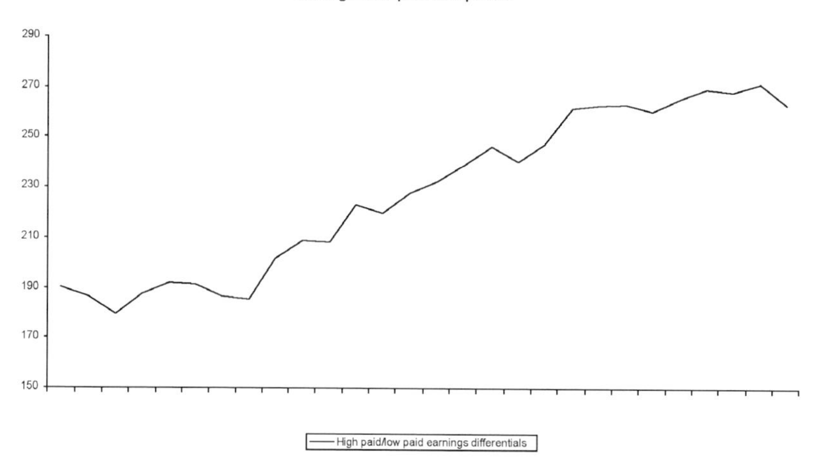

The narrowing of differentials during periods of inflation occurred in large part as a result of the widespread practice of making flat-rate wage settlements, which prevailed for much of the 20th century; the effect was that lower paid workers caught up, in real terms, with groups above them in the pay hierarchy.[1] By contrast, during recessions, differentials tended to widen because the least well paid, and the least well organised, suffered a disproportionate loss of bargaining power at times of low demand for labour, thanks to competition from the unemployed and the general increase in economic insecurity for these groups. This effect was particularly strong in the first few decades of the 20th century when competitive pressures in the disorganised trades were particularly intense, but was also marked after 1979.

A major external factor affecting the extent and duration of inflationary episodes was provided by shifts in the prices of imported goods relative to home-produced goods. Rising and falling import prices played a significant role in triggering each of the turning points in the long inflationary cycles of the 20th century (see Figure 2). Again, the system of wage determination was a major determinant in the process whereby import prices were transmitted into domestic inflation. Throughout the 20th century the intensity of wage demands and the degree of worker militancy were linked to shifts in the cost of living, so that when prices increased, so did wage claims.[2] Employers would respond to increased wage demands by increasing prices so as to maintain profitability. Under these circumstances, a fall in the price of imported goods, relative to those produced domestically, would exert a downward pressure on prices and so reduce the cost of living element in wage claims. When, on the other hand, import prices were rising relative to domestic prices, the downward pressure on both the cost of living and profits would be intensified, thereby building an upward pressure on wages and prices.

Figure 2. Trend in home costs and import prices 1875 to 2001 (nine year moving average).

Table 2 illustrates how the main constituents in the inflationary process operated in each of the main inflationary episodes of the 20th century. The importance of the external terms of trade is indicated by the increase in import prices relative to domestic costs in each inflationary upswing, and by the relative fall in import prices by comparison to home costs in the subsequent periods of decelerating prices. Table 2 also indicates that there was no clear relationship between the inflation cycle and growth in labour productivity, which was generally slower before the mid-point of the century than after, and particularly slow in the period up to and during the First World War.

The final three columns of Table 2 summarise the effects of changes in earnings and prices: earnings grew more slowly relative to prices in periods of accelerating inflation so that real take home pay increased more quickly during the deflationary part of the cycle. This is particularly the case for the period between 1895 and 1920, which followed a period from the early 1870s (the 'Great Depression') when falling import prices had exerted a strong downwards pressure on domestic prices relative to wages, and real take home pay had risen, as a result, by around 2% per annum. The period between 1933 and 1952 is an exception to the regular pattern since real wages grew even when price inflation was

Table 2. Average annual increases in prices, productivity and earnings in the inflationary episodes

Inflationary Episode	Home costs	Import prices	Labour productivity	Average earnings	Retail prices	Real take home pay
1895-1920	4.7	5.1	0	4.9	4.5	0.4
1920-1933	-3.9	-8.8	1.6	-3.1	-4.3	1.3
1933-1952	4.6	9.0	1.1	6.2	4.9	1.4
1952-1960	3.3	-1.0	2.3	5.8	2.8	2.2[a]
1960-1979	8.4	8.1	2.3	10.6	8.3	1.2[a]
1979-2005	4.6	2.0	1.8	6.7	4.8	2.2[a]

[a] including the direct tax effect.

Sources: C.H.Feinstein, National Income, Expenditure and Output of the United Kingdom, 1855 – 1965, Cambridge University Press, 1972; Office of National Statistic, Economic Trends Annual Supplement, HMSO, (various years); Office of National Statistics, Labour Market Trends, , HMSO, (various years)

accelerating; however, this can be explained by the effect of price controls and subsidies which were in operation during the Second World War.

Table 2 also illustrates the growing role of taxation. Until the Second World War, real take home pay consisted of money wages adjusted for retail prices. From 1940, income tax and, in the post-war period, rising national insurance contributions, increasingly eroded real take home pay, as the last three rows of the final column indicate. On average, these employment taxes reduced the annual increase in real take home pay by 0.7% between 1952 and 1960 and 0.9% between 1960 and 1979, whereas tax reductions added 0.4% to the average annual increase in real take home pay after 1979.

Trade Union Density and Activity

The ability of workers to maintain and enhance earnings levels can therefore be seen to have been dependent on a range of factors. Some of these would have been internal to the structure of particular unions or were influenced by labour history and culture, such as the degree of militancy or the capacity for self-organisation in a particular industry or occupation, but others were the consequence of wider economic factors: changes in price inflation, the incidence of taxation, and the extent of unemployment. As the bargaining environment changed, this affected the bargaining strength of workers, with further results for bargaining outcomes in terms of real take home pay, the extent of pay inequality, and price inflation. However, particular factors were more strongly linked than others.

Figure 3 suggests that there was a strong relationship between the inflationary cycle and changes in trade union membership and density (the proportion of the employed labour force in trade unions). Membership and density increased slowly between 1895 and 1905 but then increased rapidly to reach a peak of 8.2 million and 48% respectively by 1920. Membership then fell precipitously to a low of 4.2 million in 1933 when density stood at 23%, but then began to recover. By 1952, membership had risen to 9.3 million and density to 45%. During the 1950s growth in membership slowed and density was static, but it then rose again in the 1950s. From 9.5 million in 1960, membership reached 10.6 million in 1970 and 12.6 million in 1979, by which time density was 53%. After 1979 membership fell and by 2005 stood at 7.4 million, while density was only 3.2%.

Figure 3. Trade union membership and density 1895 to 2005

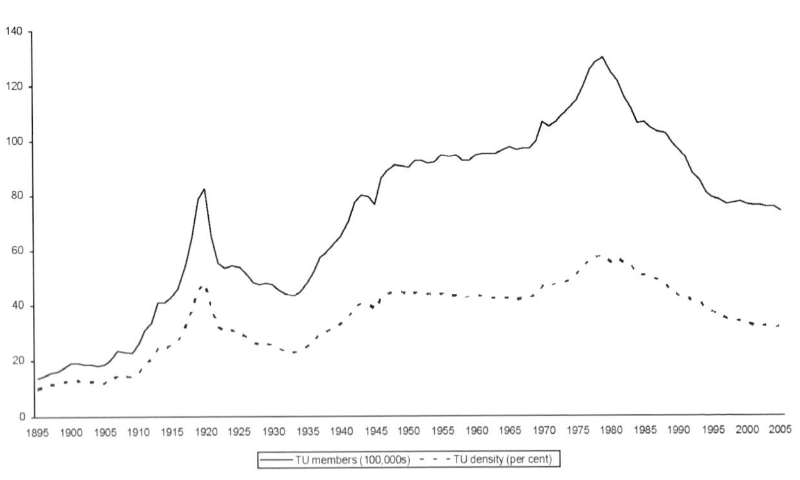

The pattern of strikes also closely reflects trends in inflation. This relationship is partly obscured between 1940 and 1960 by the large number of small strikes in the coal industry. The solid line in Figure 4 indicates the level of non-mining strikes, which reached high levels between 1910 and 1920, in the 1940s and again in the 1970s when inflation was high and rising.

Figure 4. No of strikes 1895 to 2005

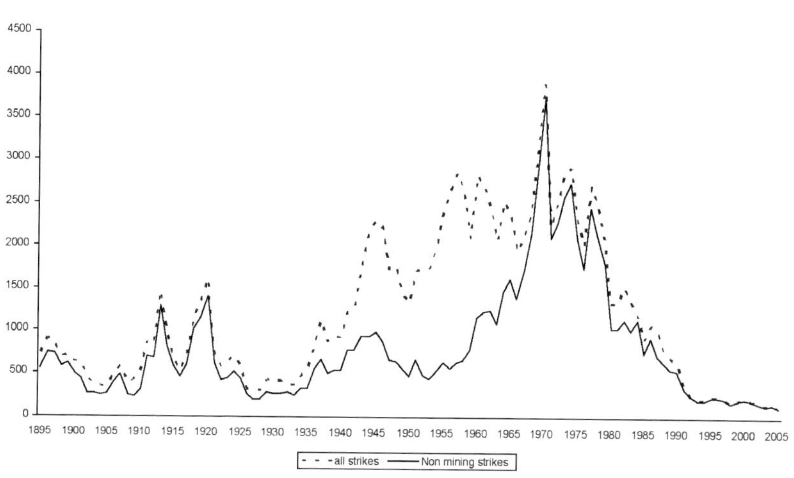

Thus inflationary upswings saw rising union membership and militancy in response to falling take-home pay, with the overall result tending towards greater equality in the earnings distribution. During these periods, increases in trade union membership were accompanied by the extension of trade unionism into less well-organised sectors and industries.

Figure 5 indicates the movement in annual percentage rates of unemployment. Between 1895 and 1920, unemployment was substantially lower than during most of the inter-war years (although, since unemployment figures before 1912 comes from the records of skilled craft unions whose members received unemployment compensation, the data for these periods are probably underestimates). Between the wars, unemployment remained high until 1940, but then fell rapidly away and remained below (for long periods, well below) 5% until 1976. Thus in two periods of low inflation, the 1920s and the period between 1980 and the present day, unemployment was high, but in another, for most of the 1950s, it was very low. The picture is repeated for the inflationary periods: between 1960 and 1979, when inflation was accelerating, unemployment was low by historical standards, but between 1895 and 1920 and 1933 to 1952 wages and prices began to rise when unemployment was also rising. There was therefore no simple relationship between unemployment and inflation.

Figure 5. Annual % unemployment 1895 to 2005

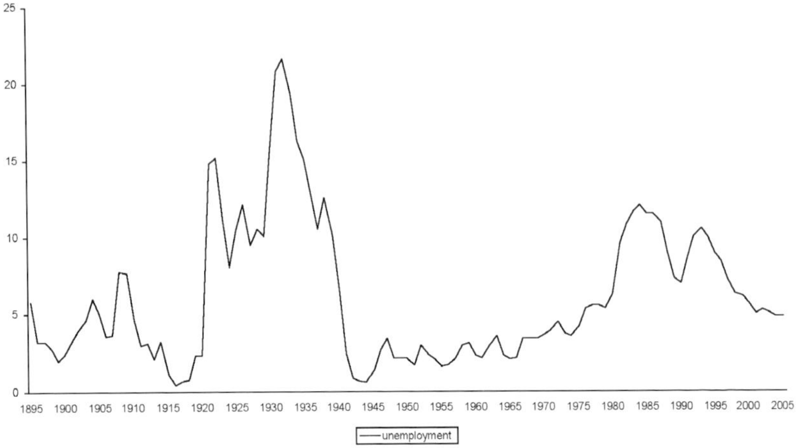

Table 3 sums up the trajectory, over the course of six inflationary episodes, of the factors making up respectively the bargaining environment, the bargaining strength of workers, and bargaining outcomes.

Table 3. Bargaining environment, bargaining strength and bargaining outcomes in inflationary episodes

Inflationary episode	Bargaining environment			
	Import prices relative to home costs	Productivity growth	Unemployment	Direct taxes on wages
1895 to 1920	Rising	Slow	Moderate then low	
1920 to 1933	Falling	Moderate	High	
1933 to 1952	Rising	Moderate	High then low	
1952 to 1960	Falling	Fast	Low	Rising
1960 to 1979	Rising	Fast	Low then Moderate	Rising
1979 to 2005	Falling	Moderate	High	Falling

From this it can be seen that the 1950s was a period when the economic environment was particularly favourable to orderly and stable collective bargaining: labour productivity was rising rapidly, import prices were falling and unemployment was low. Inflation was low, allowing real incomes to rise, but in contrast to other periods when low inflation saw a sharp decline in union membership (from the 1920s to the mid-1930s and the period from 1979 to 2000), union density was steady and membership was slowly increasing. This was reflected in rapidly rising real incomes. By contrast, in each of the periods of high inflation – 1895-1920, 1933-52 and in particular 1960-79 – the bargaining environment hardened, with the impact, in the last of these, of direct taxes on earnings, adding to the effect. The effect, in each case, was an increase in union membership and also in union militancy, measured in terms of the level of strike activity.

Thus across the twentieth century as a whole, the growth of collective bargaining and trade union membership has been a discontinuous process, with numerous, partial reversals. The policy preference for collective *laissez-faire* set the general context in which this process unfolded. From an early stage in its development, the British system was characterised by the absence of a general statutory floor to wages and conditions and by industry-specific bargaining which reflected the negotiating power of particular occupational groups. Under these circumstances,

Table 3. Bargaining environment, bargaining strength and bargaining outcomes in inflationary episodes

Bargaining strength			Outcomes		
Trade union Membership	Trade union density	Strikes (Non - mining)	Real take home pay	High pay / low pay	Price inflation
Rising rapidly	Rising rapidly	Rising rapidly	Falling then recovering	Narrowing	Rising
Falling rapidly	Falling rapidly	Falling rapidly	Rising moderately	Widening	Falling
Rising rapidly	Rising rapidly	Rising rapidly	Rising moderately	Narrowing	Rising
Rising rapidly	Stable	Falling	Rising	Widening	Falling
Rising rapidly	Rising	Rising rapidly	Rising rapidly then slowing down	Narrowing	Rising
Falling rapidly	Falling rapidly	Falling	Rising rapidly	Widening	Falling

shifts in real wages over time, brought about by price inflation and, latterly, by employment taxation, were reflected in sharp cyclical fluctuations in union membership and militancy. It is difficult to provide a general answer to the question of whether trade unions caused inflation or inflation caused trade unions, since the relationship between them was one of mutual reinforcement. What we can say is that because of the policy preference for leaving wage determination to the free play of collective forces, the industrial relations system was left highly vulnerable to the destabilizing shifts in the wider economic environment.

In this respect, the particular conjunctions of economic and institutional forces which operated at different points in the inflationary cycle proved to be decisive turning points. Just as the 1950s were a particularly benign period for collective bargaining, the 1960s and 1970s, for a combination of reasons, presented a completely different bargaining environment, one in which the fundamental tenets of the voluntary system would be tested to breaking point.[3] Instrumental in this was the attempts by successive governments to intervene in the process of wage determination to control inflation by means of incomes policies. These had significant inflationary effect as a consequence of their negative impact on real-take home pay. This is shown in Table 4 which gives the annual average increases in money earnings, real earnings and net real earnings. It also gives the price effect (the percentage reduction in the real value of money earnings resulting from the increase in retail prices), the tax effect (the percentage reduction/increase real earnings from an increase/reduction in direct taxes) and the combined price and tax effect. What Table 4 shows is how much stronger the price effect was in policy-on periods, especially in 1972-74 (Conservative Party incomes policy) and 1974-79 (Labour Party incomes policy). In the latter period price increases wiped out all but 1.3% of the increase in earnings. Table 4 also shows the importance of increasing direct taxes in reducing disposable income from employment in every period prior to 1974, especially from 1963 to 1969. Thirdly, Table 4 shows how, in the 1965-69 incomes policy-on periods all but a very small proportion of the real disposable value of money wage increases was removed by the combined price and tax effect, and in 1972-74 net real income fell as a consequence of rising prices and taxes. However, during 1974 – 79, reductions in direct tax compensated somewhat for the impact of rising prices. From 1979, as incomes policies disappeared as policy options, the erosive effect of prices on real wages advance declined and the tax effect became positive. Consequently, whilst in 1972 to 1979, on average, only 2.5% of the annual increase in money earnings was retained as an increase in net real income, in 1979 to 1997 this residual was 30.8%, and in 1997 to 2004 it was almost half. Table 4 goes far to explain why the 1970s was a turbulent period for industrial wages and why incomes policies, and especially Labour Party incomes policies, proved so unpopular to wage earners.

Table 4. Annual Percentage Increases in Earnings, and the Price and Tax Effects in Incomes Policy-On and Incomes Policy-Off Periods, 1960 to 2005.

	Money earnings	Price effect[1]	Real earnings	Tax effect[2]	Net real earnings	Tax and price effect[1]	Incomes Policy
1961-63	4.0	-82.5	0.7	+2.5	0.8	-80.0	On
1963-65	8.3	-50.6	4.1	-20.5	2.4	-71.1	Off
1965-69	6.3	-68.3	2.0	-24.4	0.4	-93.7	On
1969-72	12.0	-66.7	4.0	-6.7	3.2	-73.4	Off
1972-74	15.5	-82.6	2.7	-18.7	-0.2	-101.3	On
1974-79	15.7	-98.7	0.2	+3.2	0.7	-95.5	On
1979-97	7.8	-75.6	1.9	+6.4	2.4	-69.2	Off
1997-04	4.2	-59.5	1.7	+7.1	2.0	-52.4	Off
1960-04	8.5	-77.6	1.9	-1.2	1.8	-78.8	

[1] Difference between the increase in money and real income, as % of increase in money earnings. [2] Difference between the increase in real and net real income, as % of increase in money earnings. [3] Price effect plus tax effect.

Institutional Reform and Trade Union Freedom

Although it is not possible to find a consistent relationship between unemployment and inflation, there is no doubt that unemployment has its part to play in the inflationary process. However, this is by a dramatically different route to that proposed by the economics theories which advise government policies. The world wide recession and high levels of unemployment, triggered by the restrictive monetary policy response to inflation, causes primary product prices to collapse to the advantage of industrial producers. In Britain, high levels of unemployment coupled with labour market deregulation and social welfare reforms lowered the bargaining power of the least well paid reducing their relative earnings. The dampening of inflation therefore did not result directly from monetary adjustments but from the effects of the resulting economic depression and unemployment on the balance of power in labour and product markets. This, and reforms of the tax benefit system, provided for a regressive international and national reallocation of resources towards the well-organised core, easing the *burden* on distribution and reducing conflict there,[4] and allowing profits and the pay of high earners rise at the expense of the less well organised.

But the low levels of inflation have been secured at enormous human and material costs. Mass poverty has re-emerged in industrial countries and the world recession and the collapse of primary product prices has had a devastating impact on the economies and well-being in third world counties. Moreover, the policy tools used to secure these ends have adversely affected Britain's ability to maintain the rates of growth necessary to sustain the increase in real incomes underlying the decline in domestic inflation. The overvalued pound which serves to keep import prices down and high interest rates targeted at internal inflation has squeezed, and continues to squeeze, manufacturing and the other wealth creating sectors. As a result, the capabilities of generating the necessary resources to maintain living standards is threatened and the increase in the balance of payment deficit on current account means that in the long term it will be difficult to prevent sterling depreciating and the cost of imports rising.

The question arising from the history outlined in this chapter is: Is it possible to combine freedom for trade unions with low unemployment and stable prices? For the past thirty years or more, the conventional wisdom had been that this is impossible. Curbs on union power have been seen as the price that has to be paid to reducing inflation, and high levels of unemployment (even today they are high in historical terms) have been tolerated for the same reason. Is this inevitable? Our analysis suggests not. There have been periods in the past when high and rising levels of union membership were combined with price stability and full employment, the 1950s being the most recent. However, this period was the result of a rare, beneficent conjunction of internal and external forces. For most of the 20th century, the British economy was subject to periodic exogenous shocks, the result of shifts in the global terms of trade, and union strength rose and fell in line with the economic cycle. As a result, the effectiveness of collective bargaining, as a mechanism for reducing inequality and guaranteeing basic protection of living standards, was not constant.

What is needed is an enduring institutional settlement for trade unions, which puts beyond dispute their role in the economy. Conventional wisdom, once again, rejects this as either outmoded or utopian. After all, in age of globalization, what impact can labour law be expected to have? Here, we might bear in mind that the world of 1906 is not unlike our own: it was a time of insecurity of employment thanks to the growing use of outsourcing and sub-contracting, increased transnational mobility of both labour and capital and growing international trade in goods and services. Flexibility of labour was then termed 'casualisation', and globalisation, 'Imperialism'. None of this prevented the enactment of social legislation which reversed the rise of inequality, and which could do so again.

What is needed are effective mechanisms for controlling the impact of world price fluctuations on the domestic economy. This need is urgent for all the signs are that the demand for raw materials are again pressing on supply and oil and primary product prices are on an upward trajectory. This requires the development of institutions capable of resolving distributional conflicts underlying the inflationary process without resort to mass employment and widespread poverty.

Previous attempts to stabilise inflation in Britain by incomes policies, have failed for five broad reasons:

- Firstly, they were almost exclusively concerned with wage control.
- Secondly, wage controls were unevenly imposed and this undermined their effectiveness. The main weight of wage restrictions fell on certain groups, especially those in the public sector, with negative real wage consequences. The response was large wage claims that bought the incomes policies down.
- Thirdly, they were usually imposed as emergency packages including deflationary fiscal and monetary policies so that any benefits of wage restraint were dissipated in higher levels of unemployment and lower levels of productivity.[5]
- Fourthly, collective bargaining was fragmented. This means that in an inflationary spiral each bargaining group's wage increase is, in effect, every other bargaining groups price increase. Even if each separate group is successful in inflation proofing its pay in the short term, the longer term effect is an offsetting general increase in prices. On the other hand, if any group individually forgoes its wage increase in the interest of controlling inflation it will merely benefit all the groups at the expense of the real wages of its members. This can be avoided only if the wage bargaining is co-ordinated centrally. In this important respect the greater fragmentation of wage determination in the 1980s and 1990s has made inflation much more difficult to control.
- Fifthly, there were the destabilising effects of wide upward swings in world commodity prices such as happened in the 1970s. This

problem can only be solved by the creation of effective international institutions with responsibility for stabilising world prices.

The overcoming of the first four obstacles to internal price stability lies in the improvement of wage bargaining arrangements to ensure greater equality and a closer integration of inflation control with other economic and social objectives. These, in turn, require a greater involvement of labour organisations in the design and implementation of economic, labour market and social welfare policies. In this respect, the 'social corporatist' states of Northern Europe achieved a significant measure of success. These had higher growth rates than Britain in the 1950s and 1960s and were more effective in reducing inflation without high levels of unemployment in the 1970s and 1980s.[6] Their major advantages has been with their centralised collective bargaining systems.

Industry level negotiations between well organised employers and trade unions allows a greater understanding of the possible risks of spiralling inflation, including high levels of unemployment and lower levels of investment. The central bargainers are also better placed than the individual groups to gauge the risk of restrictive macro-economic policies and higher levels of unemployment as a response to higher wage inflation.[7] Centralise bargaining and the superior control it gives over inflation also forms the basis for a closer co-operation between unions, employers and government in industrial, labour market and social welfare policy. In the countries which achieved this degree of cohesion, high quality training and rapid retraining created a highly skilled and flexible labour force whilst high social welfare standards and full employment reduced labour market uncertainty and resistance for change. The resulting high rates of productivity made inflation more easy to contain and this in turn increased competitiveness and economic performance.

Such a programme requires freedom for trade unions. It is only then that they will be able to fully represent their members' interest giving them the confidence that they will not be called upon to bear the full costs of policy adjustments.

Notes

1 H A Turner, 'Inflation and Wage Differentials in Great Britain', in J T Dunlop, (ed), *The Theory of Wage Determination* (1957).
2 W W Daniel, *Wage Determination in Industry* (1976).
3 See P Davies and M Freedland, *Labour Legislation and Public Policy* (1993), contrasting 'the easy decade' of the 1950s (Ch 3), with 'the end of agreement' in the 1960s (Ch 6).
4 R Rowthorn, 'Conflict, Inflation and Money (1977) pp 215-240, *Cambridge Journal of Economics* Vol 1, No 3.
5 R Tarling and F Wilkinson, 'The Social Contract: Postwar Incomes Policies and their Inflationary Impact' (1977) pp 395 - 414 *Cambridge Journal of Economics* Vol 1, No 4.
6 R Rowthorn, 'Centralisation, Employment and Wage Dispersion, (1992) pp 506 – 523 *Economic Journal* Vol C11, No 3. R Rowthorn and A Glyn, *The Diversity of Unemployment Experience Since 1973* (1988.)
7 When bargaining is centralised, the argument goes, information about the consequences of wage increases is more complete at the centre and this means that the counter moves by capital and the state in the way of price increases and unemployment are more fully understood and responded to (N Bruno and J Sachs, *Economics of World-wide Stagflation* (1985); L Calmfors and J Driffill, 'Centralisation of Wage Bargaining' (1988) *Economic Policy* No 6.

Appendix 1

The Trades Dispute Bill 1906 (The Labour Bill)

First reading: 22 February 1906;
Second reading: 30 March 1906

[6 EDW. 7] Trades Unions and Trade Disputes

A Bill to Amend the Law relating to Trades Unions and Trade and other Disputes.

BE it enacted by the King's most Excellent Majesty, by and with the advice and consent of the Lords Spiritual and Temporal, and Commons, in this present Parliament assembled, and by the authority of the same, as follows:

1. It shall be lawful for any person or persons acting either on their own behalf or on behalf of a trade union or other association of individuals, registered or unregistered, in contemplation of or during the continuance of any trade dispute, to attend for any of the following purposes at or near a house or place where a person resides or works, or carries on his business, or happens to be

(1) for the purpose of peacefully obtaining or communicating information;

(2) for the purpose of peacefully persuading any person to work or abstain from working.

2. An agreement or combination by two or more persons to do or procure to be done any act in contemplation or furtherance of a trade dispute shall not be ground for an action, if such an act when committed

by one person would not be ground for an action.

3. An action shall not be brought against a trade union, or other association aforesaid, for the recovery of damage sustained by any person or persons by reason of the action of a member or members of such trade union or other association aforesaid.

4. This Act may be cited as the Trades Dispute Act, 1906.

[Bill 5]

Appendix 2

The Trade Disputes Bill 1906 (The Government Bill)

First reading: 28 March 1906;
Second reading: 25 April 1906

[6 EDW. 7] Trade Disputes

A Bill to Provide for the regulation of Trades Unions and Trade Disputes

BE it enacted by the King's most Excellent Majesty, by and with the advice and consent of the Lords Spiritual and Temporal, and Commons, in this present Parliament assembled, and by the authority of the same, as follows:

1. The following paragraph shall be added as a new paragraph after the first paragraph of section three of the Conspiracy and Protection of Property Act, 1875:

'An act done in pursuance of an agreement or combination by two or more persons shall, if done in contemplation or furtherance of a trade dispute, not be actionable unless the act, if done without any such agreement or combination, would be actionable as a tort.'

2. (1) It shall be lawful for one or more persons, acting on their own behalf or on behalf of a trade union in contemplation or furtherance of a trade dispute, to attend, peaceably and in a reasonable manner, at or near a house or place where a person resides or works or carries on business or happens to be, if they so attend merely for the purpose of obtaining or communicating information, or of persuading any person to work or abstain from working.

(2) Section seven of the Conspiracy and Protection of Property Act, 1875, is hereby repealed from 'attending at or near' to the end of the section.

3. An act done by a person in contemplation or furtherance of a trade dispute shall not be actionable as a tort on the ground only that it is an interference with the trade, business, or employment of some other person, or with the right of some other person to dispose of his capital or his labour as he wills.

4. (1) Where a committee of a trade union constituted as hereinafter mentioned has been appointed to conduct on behalf of the union a trade dispute, an action whereby it is sought to charge the funds of the union with damages in respect of any tortious act committed in contemplation or furtherance of the trade dispute, shall not lie, unless the act was committed by the committee, or by some person acting under their authority:

Provided that a person shall not be deemed to have acted under the authority of the committee if the act was an act or one of a class of acts expressly prohibited by a resolution of the committee, or the committee by resolution expressly repudiate the act as soon as it is brought to their knowledge.

(2) The committee may be a committee appointed either generally to conduct all trade disputes in which the union may be involved, or to conduct any trade disputes of a specified class or in a specified locality, or to conduct any particular trade dispute.

5. (1) This act may be cited as the Trade Disputes Act, 1906, and the Trade Union Acts, 1871 and 1876, and this Act may be cited together as the Trade Union Acts, 1871 to 1906.

(2) In this Act the expression 'trade union' has the same meaning as in the Trade Union Acts, 1871 and 1876.

[Bill 134]

Appendix 3

The Trade Disputes Act 1906

An Act to provide for the regulation of Trades Unions and Trade Disputes. 21st December 1906

Be it enacted by the King's most Excellent Majesty, by and with the advice and consent of the Lords Spiritual and Temporal, and Commons, in this present Parliament assembled, and by the authority of the same, as follows:

1. The following paragraph shall be added as a new paragraph after the first paragraph of section three of the Conspiracy and Protection of Property Act, 1875:

"An act done in pursuance of an agreement or combination by two or more persons shall, if done in contemplation or furtherance of a trade dispute, not be actionable unless the act, if done without any such agreement or combination, would be actionable."

2. (1) It shall be lawful for one or more persons, acting on their own behalf or on behalf of a trade union or of an individual employer or firm in contemplation or furtherance of a trade dispute, to attend at or near a house or place where a person resides or works or carries on business or happens to be, if they so attend merely for the purpose of peacefully persuading any person to work or abstain from working.

(2) Section seven of the Conspiracy and Protection of Property Act, 1875, is hereby repealed from "attending at or near" to the end of the section.

3. An act done by a person in contemplation or furtherance of a trade dispute shall not be actionable on the ground only that it induces some other person to break a contract of employment or that it is an interference with the trade, business, or employment of some other person, or with the right of some other person to dispose of his capital or his labour as he wills.

4. (1) An action against a trade union, whether of workmen for masters, or against any members or officials thereof on behalf of themselves and all other members of the trade union in respect of any tortious act alleged to have been committed by or on behalf of the trade union, shall not be entertained by any court.

(2) Nothing in this section shall affect the liability of the trustees of a trade union to be sued in the events provided for by the Trades Union Act, 1871, section nine, except in respect of any tortious act committed by or on behalf of the union in contemplation or in furtherence of a trade dispute.

5. (1) This Act may be cited as the Trade Disputes Act, 1906, and the Trade Union Acts, 1871 and 1876, and this Act may be cited together as the Trade Union Acts, 1871 to 1906.

(2) In this Act the expression "trade union" has the same meaning as in the Trade Union Acts, 1871 and 1876, and shall include any combination as therein defined, notwithstanding that such combination may be the branch of a trade union.

(3) In this Act and in the Conspiracy and Protection of Propert Act, 1875, the expression "trade dispute" means any dispute between employers and workmen, or between workmen and workmen, which is connected with the employment or non-employment, or the terms of the employment, or with the conditions of labour, of any person, and the expression "workmen" means all persons employed in trade or industry, whether or not in the employment of the employer with whom a trade dispute arises; and, in section three of the last-mentioned Act, the words "between employers and workmen" shall be repealed.

Appendix 4

Early Day Motion 1170 and signatures

CAMPAIGN FOR A TRADE UNION FREEDOM BILL
30.11.2005
Lloyd, Tony

THAT this House recognises that free and independent trade unions are a force for good in UK society and around the world, and are vital to democracy; welcomes the positive role modern unions play in providing protection for working people and winning fairness at work; notes the 1906 Trades Disputes Act granted unions the legal freedom to take industrial action; regrets that successive anti-union legislation has meant that trade union rights are now weaker than those introduced by the Trades Disputes Act; notes the overwhelming support at both the Trades Union Congress and Labour Party Conference for the Gate Gourmet workers and for improvements in union rights, including measures to simplify ballot procedures and to allow limited supportive action, following a ballot, in specific circumstances; further notes that these conferences called for legislation which conformed to International Labour Organisation Conventions ratified by the UK; and therefore welcomes the decision of the 2005 Trades Union Congress to campaign for a Trade Union Freedom Bill to mark the 100th anniversary of the 1906 Trades Disputes Act.

Signatures (187)

Abbott, Diane
Anderson, David
Anderson, Janet
Austin, Ian
Austin, John
Banks, Gordon
Barlow, Celia
Battle, John
Bayley, Hugh
Begg, Anne
Benton, Joe
Berry, Roger
Betts, Clive
Blackman-Woods, Roberta
Borrow, David S
Brown, Lyn
Brown, Nicholas
Buck, Karen
Burden, Richard
Burgon, Colin
Butler, Dawn
Campbell, Ronnie
Caton, Martin
Challen, Colin
Chaytor, David
Clapham, Michael
Clark, Katy
Clark, Paul
Clarke, Tom
Clelland, David
Cohen, Harry
Connarty, Michael
Cook, Frank
Cooper, Rosie
Corbyn, Jeremy
Cousins, Jim
Crausby, David
Creagh, Mary
Cruddas, Jon
Cryer, Ann
Cummings, John
Cunningham, Jim
Curtis-Thomas, Claire
Davidson, Ian
Dean, Janet
Devine, Jim
Dismore, Andrew
Dobbin, Jim
Dobson, Frank
Donohoe, Brian H
Doran, Frank
Dowd, Jim
Drew, David
Dunwoody, Gwyneth
Durkan, Mark
Eagle, Angela
Efford, Clive
Ellman, Louise
Engel, Natascha
Ennis, Jeff
Etherington, Bill
Farrelly, Paul
Flynn, Paul
Foster, Michael Jabez
Francis, Hywel
Galloway, George
George, Bruce
Gerrard, Neil
Gibson, Ian
Gilroy, Linda
Godsiff, Roger
Griffith, Nia
Hall, Patrick
Hamilton, David
Hancock, Mike
Harvey, Nick
Havard, Dai

Hemming, John	Henderson, Doug	Hendrick, Mark
Hepburn, Stephen	Heyes, David	Hillier, Meg
Hodgson, Sharon	Hoey, Kate	Hood, Jimmy
Hopkins, Kelvin	Howarth, George	Hoyle, Lindsay
Humble, Joan [R]	Iddon, Brian	Illsley, Eric
Jackson, Glenda	James, Sian C	Jenkins, Brian
Jones, Helen	Jones, Lynne	Jones, Martyn
Joyce, Eric	Kaufman, Gerald	Keen, Alan
Kemp, Fraser	Kilfoyle, Peter	Lazarowicz, Mark
Lepper, David	Lloyd, Tony	Llwyd, Elfyn
Love, Andrew	Mackinlay, Andrew	Malik, Shahid
Mallaber, Judy	Marris, Rob	Marsden, Gordon
Marshall, David	Marshall-Andrews, Robert	
McCafferty, Chris	McCarthy, Kerry	
McCarthy-Fry, Sarah	McDonnell, John	McGovern, Jim
McGrady, Eddie	McKechin, Ann	Meacher, Michael
Meale, Alan	Miller, Andrew	Mitchell, Austin
Moffat, Anne	Moffatt, Laura	Moon, Madeleine
Morgan, Julie	Mudie, George	Mullin, Chris
Murphy, Denis	Murphy, Paul	O'Hara, Edward
Olner, Bill	Osborne, Sandra	Owen, Albert
Pope, Greg	Prentice, Gordon	Price, Adam
Prosser, Gwyn	Purchase, Ken	Reed, Jamie
Riordan, Linda	Robertson, Angus	Robertson, John
Ruddock, Joan	Salmond, Alex	Salter, Martin
Sarwar, Mohammad	Seabeck, Alison	Sheridan, Jim
Short, Clare	Simpson, Alan	Simpson, David
Singh, Marsha	Skinner, Dennis	Smith, Geraldine
Smith, John P	Southworth, Helen	Stewart, Ian

Stoate, Howard
Strang, Gavin
Stringer, Graham
Tami, Mark
Taylor, Dari
Taylor, David
Taylor, Richard
Thornberry, Emily
Tipping, Paddy
Todd, Mark
Trickett, Jon
Turner, Desmond
Ussher, Kitty
Vaz, Keith
Vis, Rudi
Walley, Joan
Wareing, Robert N
Weir, Mike
Williams, Betty
Williams, Hywel
Willis, Phil
Wood, Mike
Wright, Anthony D
Wright, Iain
Wyatt, Derek

IER's latest publications

£6.50 for trade unions, £20 others
(unless otherwise stated)

Age Discrimination at Work
by Nicola Dandridge and Patrick Grattan

Federation News: the need for a Trade Union Freedom Bill edited by Carolyn Jones and Keith Ewing

The Information and Consultation Regulations: Wither Statutory Works Councils? by Roger Welch

Global rights in global companies: going for Gold at the UK Olympics by Keith Ewing

Labour Law Review 2006 by Jenny Eady and Betsan Criddle

Still Challenging Disability at Work by Lydia Seymour and Andrew Short.

Labour Migration and Employment Rights edited by Bernard Ryan (£12/£30)

Regulating Surveillance at Work by Hazel Oliver

The Impact of Contracting Out on Employment Relations in Public Services by Sanjiv Sachdev

Regulating Health and Safety at Work: An Agenda for Change by Phil James and Dave Walters (£12/£30)

COMPARATIVE NOTES 8: Canada's Take on Corporate Killing: the Westray Bill by Harry Glasbeek (£5/£10)

The 1906 Trade disputes act by Jim Mortimer (£5/£10)

Decoding some New Developments in Labour Standards Enforcement by Steve Gibbons

The Future of Company Law: fat cats, corporate governance and workers by Bill Wedderburn

Labour Law Review 2004 by Rebecca Tuck and Jennifer Eady (£5/£10)

Nine Proposals for the reform of the Law on Unfair Dismissal by Hugh Collins (£8/£30)

Pension Promises and Employment Rights by Bryn Davies, John Grieve Smith and Ivan Walker

Health and Safety: revitalised or reversed? by Phil James and David Walters

COMPARATIVE NOTES 7: Workers in Cuba: unions and labour relations by Debra Evenson (£5/£10)

Unfair Labour Practices: trade union recognition and employer resistance by Keith Ewing, Sian Moore and Stephen Wood

Labour Law Review 2003 by Rebecca Tuck and Jennifer Eady (£5/£10)

Acheiving Equality at Work edited by Aileen McColgan (£12/£30)

Implementing the Information and Consultation Directive in the UK: lessons from Germany by Glynis M Truter

Who is the employer? by Jill earnshaw, Jill Rubery and Fang Lee Cooke

A Charter of Workers' Rights (the summary) edited by Keith Ewing and John Hendy QC (£5/£10)

A Charter of Workers' Rights edited by Keith Ewing and John Hendy QC (£12/£30)

Labour Law Review 2002 by Rebecca Tuck and Jennifer Eady (£3/£10)

Protecting Worker Solidarity Action: a critique of international labour law by Paul Germanotta

The EU Charter of Fundamental Rights: waste of time or wasted opportunity? by Keith Ewing

Between a Rock and a Hard Place: the problems facing freelance creators in the UK media market place by Lionel Bently (£8/£30)

Whistleblowing and the Public Interest disclosure Act 1998 by Catherine Hobby (£8/£30)

Undermining Construction: the corrosive effects of false self-employment by Mark harvey (£8/£30)

COMPARATIVE NOTES 6: Labour's Labour Law: labour law reform in New Zealand under a labour government by Gordon Anderson (£5/£10)

Labour Law Review 2001 by Rebecca Tuck and Jennifer Eady (£3/£10)

Building on the National Minimum Wage by Bob Simpson

Employment Rights at Work: reviewing the Employment Relations Act 1999 edited by Keith Ewing (£12/£30)

International Trade Union Rights for the New Millenium by Keith Ewing and Tom Sibley (£8/£30)

Fairness at Work? the disciplinary & grievance provisions of the 1999 Employment Relations Act by Mike Clancy and Roger Seifert

Human Rights at Work edited by Keith Ewing (£12/£30)

Social Justice and Economic Efficiency published in association with the Cambridge Journal of Economics (£8/£30)

Challenging Disability Discrimination at Work by Mary Stacey and Andrew Short

COMPARATIVE NOTES 5: Resisting Union-busting Techniques:
lessons from Quebec by Laura Dubinsky (£5/£10)

Employment Rights: building on fairness at work (£5/£10)

Challenging Race Discrimination at Work by Karon Monaghan (£8/£30)

COMPARATIVE NOTES 4: Trade Union Rights in South Africa: the Labour Relations Act 1995 by Roger Welch (£5/£10)

Age Discrimination in Employment by Malcolm Sargeant

COMPARATIVE NOTES 3: Developing Recognition and Representation in the UK: how useful is the US model? by Brian Towers (£5/£10)

COMPARATIVE NOTES 2: Resolving employment Rights Disputes through Mediation: the New Zealand experience and ACAS arbitration by Susan Corby (£5/£10)

Fairness at Work and Trade Union Recognition: past comparisons and future problems by Lord McCarthy

Surveillance and Privacy at Work by Michael Ford

A Social Clause for Labour's Cause: global trade and labour standards - a challenge for the new millenium by David Chin

Roben's Revisited - the case for a review of occupational health and safety regulation by David Walters and Phil James

Low Pay and the minimum wage by Sanjiv Sachdev and Frank Wilkinson

In defence of trade unionism by Jim Mortimer (£5/£10)

COMPARATIVE NOTES 1: Tradition and Change in Australian Labour Law by Anthony Forsyth (£5/£10)

Every Worker shall have the Right to be Represented at Work by a Trade Union by John Hendy QC (£8/£30)